MW00331913

Democracy's XI

The Great Indian Cricket Story

Rajdeep Sardesai

✹ juggernaut

JUGGERNAUT BOOKS

KS House, 118 Shahpur Jat, New Delhi 110049, India

First published by Juggernaut Books 2017

Copyright © Rajdeep Sardesai 2017

10 9 8 7 6 5 4 3 2 1

All rights reserved. No part of this publication may be reproduced, transmitted, or stored in a retrieval system in any form or by any means without the written permission of the publisher.

The views and opinions expressed in this book are the author's own. The facts contained herein were reported to be true as on the date of publication by the author to the publishers of the book, and the publishers are not in any way liable for their accuracy or veracity.

ISBN 9789386228482

Typeset in Adobe Caslon Pro by R. Ajith Kumar, New Delhi

Printed at Manipal Technologies Limited, Manipal

To my parents, Dilip and Nandini Sardesai,
for whom cricket has been life and love

Contents

Acknowledgements

Contents

Introduction

The Great Indian Cricket Story

Unlike politics, cricket doesn't run in the blood: I am a living example of this truism. Right from childhood, I was desperate to follow in my father Dilip Sardesai's footsteps and play cricket at the highest level. I was provided the best equipment, first-rate coaching and top-class facilities. While I captained Mumbai schools and played first-class cricket at Oxford (which may be more a reflection on the quality of university cricket in England at the time), I never even came close to being an India cricketer. Once while playing for Combined British Universities against the Imran Khan–led Pakistan team in 1987, I was bowled by the magical leg-spinner Abdul Qadir for 2. On the way back to the pavilion, a Pakistani player said with a smirk, 'Arre, you come from India, and can't even play spin!' He was right: I didn't know how to pick a googly from a top-spinner. That day I decided to 'retire' to the less strenuous world of journalism, after a brief flirtation as a lawyer, my dreams of a professional career in the game shattered once and for all.

Often at a public gathering I am asked the question: why didn't you play cricket like your father? My answer is simple – a politician's son or daughter has a fair chance of getting elected and becoming a member of the Legislative Assembly or Parliament or even a prime minister, a business house may actively promote hereditary succession, but a Test cricketer's son cannot wear the India cap without being one of the eleven most talented players in the country. Even the children of film stars can aspire and succeed in joining their parents' profession even if they may not quite make it to the A-list. But a cricketer's child may not even be chosen in his school side, leave aside a Ranji Trophy or Test team, simply on the strength of a famous surname. There are no cricketing dynasties in India quite like our political or even film universe dynasties: nothing remotely like the Gandhi–Nehrus of the Congress and their regional party clones or the Kapoors of Hindi cinema. The closest we have to a 'House of Cricket' in India are the Amarnaths: the father, Lala, was the first Indian Test centurion, his sons Mohinder and Surinder played for the country, while a third, Rajinder, played first-class cricket.

In a sense, seventy years after Indian Independence, we could well argue that cricket is one of the few largely meritocratic activities in the country, a highly competitive game that mirrors the idealism of our founding fathers and the spirit of our republican Constitution that sought equal opportunity for all. The cosy family networks, the privileges of the elite, the patron–client relations have been thwarted at the gates of a cricket ground: there is a democratic fervour that makes cricket the ultimate authentic Indian dream that can have a transformative effect on the lives of players and society. This book is a journey to discover and relive that great Indian story – a story of dreams, sacrifice, opportunity, talent and success – through the prism of cricket and what I have chosen to call 'Democracy's XI', anecdotal mini-portraits of eleven cricketers who in their own unique way represent the universal and pluralistic appeal of the sport that cuts across class, caste, region and religion and has thrown up the real heroes of our time.

Where else but in Indian cricket will you have the son of a humble water pump manager in a public sector firm in Ranchi become an iconic captain and one of the wealthiest sportspersons in the world? Or the prodigious son of a scholarly professor-poet become the most revered Indian cricketer of all time and the first sportsperson to receive a Bharat Ratna? Or a gangly young man from the congested bylanes of Hyderabad defy the stereotype of the walled-city Muslim to achieve rapid superstardom by scoring centuries in each of his first three Tests? Or a young man whose family had never seen a Test match, whose father bought two buffaloes so the son could have a steady supply of milk at home, then go on to become a World Cup–winning captain and the greatest fast bowling all-rounder the country has seen?

It wasn't always like this. Cricket in pre-Independence India started off as a colonial leisure sport to be played in the elite clubs and gymkhanas of the presidency towns of British India. It was patronized by the princes and Parsee business elites of the Raj who saw cricket as a passport to social mobility and a chance to earn the goodwill of the ruling aristocracy. The merchants and maharajas who were the early patrons played and supported the sport as part of their loyalty to the Empire and to signal their own superior social status – is it any surprise that the early royals who played cricket were all batsmen, with bowling and fielding looked at as more menial tasks to be performed by 'lesser' men? Is it also any surprise that the first Indian team chosen to play England in 1932 had the Maharaja of Patiala as the captain and the Prince of Limbdi as his deputy? Palace intrigue and petty ambitions damaged the sport's growth in its infancy. It is purely fortuitous that the man who eventually led the Indian team for its first Test at Lord's was not a royal but the greatest Indian cricketer of his generation: C.K. Nayudu, a 'commoner', became captain only because the Patiala ruler dropped out before the tour began and the Prince of Limbdi (who was by all accounts a decent player) was injured on the eve of the Test.

Indian cricket in its early years wasn't just organized around feudal lines, it also had the odour of communal politics to contend with. The Quadrangular and Pentangular tournaments that were played in the maidans and gymkhanas of Mumbai in the early twentieth century reinforced religious identities: Hindus, Muslims, Parsees, Europeans and The Rest (including Sikhs and Christians) had separate teams. The tournaments reflected a deeply divided society that could not mount a unified challenge to the Raj. Communal cricket at a time of nationalistic zeal was an abomination but it suited the 'divide and rule' politics of our colonial rulers. Little wonder then that Mahatma Gandhi, who was inspiring a peaceful nationalist revolution across the country, was disdainful of cricket and its baneful impact on society. Dalits, whose cause Gandhi fought for so assiduously, were first denied the right to play, and later were kept on the margins. Historian Ramachandra Guha brilliantly captures the plight of the first Dalit cricketer of repute, Palwankar Baloo, in his book *A Corner of a Foreign Field*, telling us how he was forced to sit apart from his teammates during the tea interval and drink from a disposable clay vessel while the others sipped their chai from porcelain cups.

Despite tough laws, 'untouchability' is still a curse in parts of the country: there are still instances of Dalits being beaten, denied entry into temples or not allowed to take water from a well. But on the cricket field, no one has to endure the discrimination that a Baloo was subject to: we have had Dalit Test players, all too few one might suggest, but caste is no barrier any longer. Neither is religion an impediment: we have had great Indian cricketers shine from every community with the possible exception of a genuine Adivasi cricket hero, a gap which I believe will be filled too in the near future. It is even possible that if Gandhi were to see the sport today, he might actually like it. After all, the contemporary Indian cricket team is a microcosm of the India that Gandhi wanted to see – a genuine salad bowl society that has space for people across all social divides, offering hope in times of despondency.

I still recall how cricket lifted the gloom when, just weeks after the 26/11 terror attack in Mumbai, Sachin Tendulkar scored a brilliant 103 in the fourth innings in Chennai to take India to a famous victory. Or indeed when the Pathan brothers took India to a stirring win in a one-day international within a few years of the 2002 Gujarat riots having wreaked havoc in Muslim-dominated neighbourhoods of their home town, Vadodara. On the cricket field, there is no space for Hindu triumphalism or Muslim grievance, no question of Dalits being ostracized or a Kashmiri being alienated. Yes, cricket has been unable to bridge the India–Pakistan divide and matches between the two countries can sometimes descend into unhealthy competitive jingoism – an American cricket writer, Mike Marqusee, once described cricket matches between the two countries as 'war minus the shooting' – but I will never forget how a Chennai crowd once cheered a Pakistani team after they defeated India in a pulsating Test match in 1999 or how Pakistani spectators chanted medium-fast bowler Lakshmipathy Balaji's name in a game in Lahore in 2004. There is, truly, no line of control on the cricket field. A Parvez Rasool from Srinagar can wear the Indian cap with the same sense of unbridled joy as a Kuldeep Yadav from Kanpur or a Varun Aaron from Jharkhand. There is no space for vote banks or reservations in cricket: the only thing that counts in the final analysis is your ability to score runs or take wickets.

~

Cricket then is Indian democracy's alter ego, a metaphor for hope in a 'new' and better India. When institutions of public life falter, the citizen turns to the maidan to relive the innocence of his youth, and the idealism of the fledgling nation state born in 1947. As the ball soars skyward or the stumps are shattered, the flaws of nation-building seem inconsequential for a few seconds as we rejoice in the achievements of our homegrown heroes. There, on the field, as the eleven cricketers battle for India, Indian men and women see reflections of their own struggles to make their way in their country, their disillusionment eclipsed and their optimism rekindled. Nor is this mere Bollywood escapism. Instead 'Jana Gana Mana' was never better illustrated in flesh and blood than when it is sung by Team India, comprising as it does youths from every corner of the country. Accustomed to a daily diet of political degradation and economic drudgery, we can celebrate our cricketing success as there on the luminous green a dance of democracy plays out which is as satisfying as it is real.

How fitting too that in the seventieth year of Indian independence, this parallel universe of Indian democracy is no longer just about men. Women's cricket today is similarly hope-giving and a source of national reassurance. The remarkable run of the Indian women in reaching the World Cup cricket final in 2017 at Lord's was truly inspirational. Like the 1983 World Cup win, the march of the women in blue to a final which they were nail-bitingly close to winning is a potential gamechanger. Numbed by daily assaults on women in society, watching the buoyant confident athleticism of a Harmanpreet Kaur or the stroke play of a Mithali Raj makes our hearts skip a beat at the success of democracy in action on the pitch. In fact, Harmanpreet's innings of 171 not out against Australia in the 2017 World Cup semi-finals must rank as one of the greatest one-day innings ever. It certainly brought our entire newsroom to a grinding halt. The gender glass ceiling has been well and truly broken – yet another triumph for the sport. Jhulan Goswami, India's fast bowling spearhead and the highest wicket-taker in women's one-day cricket, tells me, 'When I was young, the boys didn't initially let me play with them, thinking I would get hurt. My parents said if I play cricket who will marry me! Now, no one will dare say that.'

Just as significantly, the sharp class divide that once threatened and even undermined Indian cricket in its early years has now almost entirely disappeared. Every year, the Indian Premier League (IPL) – the most lucrative cricket tournament in the world – makes stars out of talented young men from diverse backgrounds. Each year, there are feel-good stories of cricketers from poor families suddenly becoming crorepatis. In the 2017 IPL auction, for example, T. Natarajan, a young speedster from Tamil Nadu's Salem district, was offered a Rs 3 crore contract. His father is a daily-wage labourer while his mother runs a roadside chicken and snacks shop. When asked what he would do with the money, Natarajan grinned. 'I will build a house for my family and fund the higher studies of my two sisters and a brother.'

As cricket becomes part of a multimillion-dollar global entertainment industry, there are many Natarajan-like stories emerging today in Indian cricket, only re-emphasizing that if you have talent and determination then opportunities will come knocking and the sky is the limit. Umesh Yadav, the spearhead of the Indian pace attack, is a good example. His father was a loader in a coal mine in a hot and dusty village near Nagpur and Umesh dropped out of school after class twelve to try to join the army or police so that his family could escape from poverty. But the muscular young teenager's ability to bowl fast did not go unrecognized. Spotted first in a Vidarbha inter-district tournament, he was playing for India barely two years later. Today he drives the latest SUV and lives in a deluxe two-storey house. No member of his family will ever have to be a daily wage labourer again. 'If I didn't have my cricket, I might be directing traffic as a constable in Nagpur,' he says with a smile.

Cricket is not just a passion any longer, it can be a high-earning profession. To put the earnings of modern-day players in some context, Indian Test cricketers in the 1950s and 1960s were paid Rs 250 per Test match; a few 'professional' cricketers like Vinoo Mankad, Vijay Hazare and Dattu Phadkar were paid an 'extra' Rs 350 in the 1950s because they were considered 'indispensable' to the team. Today, Team India players earn Rs 15 lakh per Test match, apart from well-paid retainerships and hefty sponsor deals. Even domestic Ranji Trophy players receive a decent wage: in the 1950s and 1960s, first-class cricketers were paid just Rs 30 for a three-day game (including local travel and laundry), now they get paid Rs 25,000–30,000 per day. Till the early 1960s, even Test players travelled across the country for international games by train (an exception was made for the first time in 1961–62 when India won a home Test series against England and the 'reward' was an air ticket!) and often stayed in 'B' category hotels. Now, of course, the top cricketers live in five-star luxury and could probably afford private jets! 'We played cricket for the pride of wearing an India cap, money was not a consideration at all,' insists eighty-five-year-old Madhav Apte, one of the oldest living Indian Test cricketers, who made his Test debut in 1952.

The money-spinning IPL and the large and frenzied fan base has meant that India is now the capital of the global game. In September 2017, the media rights for the IPL were sold to Star India for five years for an eye-popping Rs 16,347 crores, more than the worth of all the other Twenty20 leagues put together. Till the 1990s, some of the world's best cricketers stayed away from playing in India, fearing disease and condemning our poverty; the likes of the English opening batsman Geoff Boycott, for example, were reluctant tourists to the subcontinent while the Australians toured India only once in the entire decade of the 1970s. Now the world itches to play in India, aware that this is the most profitable marketplace for the sport. The Indian economy has more than quadrupled in size since the turn of the millennium and is now one of the fastest growing economies in the world. From an India of scarce goods we have moved to consumerist nirvana, a country where multistorey malls and branded stores are a totem to a 'new' India of vaulting aspiration. Cricket has benefited hugely from the market expansion and the days when Indian cricketers had to struggle for an income are well and truly over.

But the real story of Indian cricket goes beyond the changing colour of money. In his wonderful Bradman Oration lecture in 2011, Rahul Dravid summed it up best: 'In India, cricket is a buzzing, humming, living entity going through a most remarkable time, like no other in our cricketing history. In this last decade, the Indian team represents, more than ever before, the country we come from – of people from vastly different cultures, who speak different languages, follow different religions, belong to different classes. I went around our dressing room to work out how many languages could be spoken in there and the number I have arrived at is 15, including Shona and Afrikaans.' (The team's support staff were from South Africa.)

So how did cricket succeed where so much else has failed and help to unify a diverse society? Nelson Mandela said evocatively during the historic 1995 Rugby World Cup in South Africa: 'Sport has the power to change the world. It has the power to inspire. It has the power to unite people in a way that little else does. It speaks to youth in a language they understand. Sport can create hope where once there was only despair. It is more powerful than government in breaking down racial barriers.' That World Cup, when a post-apartheid South Africa cheered the victory of the country's rugby team, until then a predominantly whites-only sport, unified a nation sharply divided by race.

Indian cricket has gone well beyond what a single World Cup rugby win achieved for South Africa in celebrating our oneness as a nation. So dominant is the role of cricket in the lives of millions of Indians that sociologist Ashis Nandy wryly remarked, 'Cricket is an Indian game accidentally discovered by the British.' Australian academic Richard Cashman in his well-researched book on Indian cricket, *Patrons, Players and the Crowd*, suggests that cricket succeeded in India because it appealed to traditional India notions of time and motion: there is a certain 'timeless' quality to the elongated drama of a five-day Test match, for example, that attracts a less modern society, one in which a blockbuster film must be three hours long! Cashman even argues that cricket was an acceptable game to Indians because it was 'non-violent' unlike a 'body contact' sport like football and fitted in with prevalent notions of 'purity' and 'pollution' in a caste-ridden society.

And yet, the cultural factors, while important, should not be exaggerated. There is something unique in the way Indians have embraced cricket much like the Brazilians celebrate 'o jogo bonito', or 'the beautiful game' of football: just sit at Eden Gardens in Kolkata to realize how a sport can enthuse a populace, almost magically transforming the humdrum of daily life in the big city into a dramatic adventure. Truth is, as cricket journalist Mihir Bose writes in *A History of Indian Cricket*: 'Nothing could be more English than cricket, and yet nothing could be more Indian than

the way the subcontinent has taken to the game.' Travel anywhere
in India and the sound and rhythms of cricket resonate from every
neighbourhood. I once sat spellbound watching a game of cricket
being played in a remote village on the foothills of the Himalayas
with the same enthusiasm as it would be played in a maidan in
Mumbai or a street corner in Kanyakumari. Tennis-ball cricket, in
particular, as played in mohallas and bylanes, defines an indomitable
Indian spirit – matches are sometimes played in pouring rain with
an intensity that is unmatched anywhere in the world. No surprise
then that some of our finest cricketers started their career in tennis-
ball tournaments.

How did cricket transform from an elite sport into a mass
spectator sport, from recreation for the privileged into an inclusive
national 'religion' where cricketers are our modern-day divinities?
In 1947, when India gained independence, cricket was already a
very popular sport, even though hockey prided itself as our 'national
game' because of our success at the Olympics. C. Rajagopalachari,
independent India's first Governor-General, was quoted as saying,
'The day might come when India would give up English, but not
cricket!' And yet, the game's early popularity was urban-centric with
Mumbai (then Bombay) and the more urbanized west coast of the
country dominating the sport, with Chennai (then Madras) offering
some competition even as Kolkata (then Calcutta) seemed to prefer
football. Seventy years later, cricket is the number one sport in every
part of the country with the possible exception of the northeast,
Kerala and Goa, where football still attracts the biggest crowds. And
while in the 1950s and 1960s the Indian cricket team lost or drew
more games than they won, today they are a world champion side.

There are, to my mind, four turning points in India's post-
Independence cricket history. The first is in the year 1971, when the
sport was liberated from Empire, cricket's equivalent of the freedom
at midnight moment of 1947. It was the year India scored overseas
victories in the West Indies and England for the first time, instilling
a self-belief in Indian cricket. For an adolescent nation that was

struggling to assert itself, the cricket wins of 1971 can be likened to the famous victory the same year in the battlefield over Pakistan that led to the formation of Bangladesh, to the Green Revolution that made India self-sufficient in foodgrain, the space programme that launched indigenous satellites, and the 1974 nuclear tests. Each of these landmark achievements gave Indian nationhood a boost and fulfilled a young country's yearning for self-reliance.

The second turning point is when India lifted the World Cup in 1983, an incredible win that stunned the cricket world, that sparked off huge interest in one-day cricket just when, almost serendipitously, colour television was also creeping into our lives. Until then, the crackle of ball-by-ball radio commentary was the sport's ubiquitous nationwide messenger; now television brought the cricketers into our homes in coloured splendour. Suddenly, our heroes appeared to be within touching distance. Radio was the primary medium for tracking Indian cricket till the mid 1970s – I was once hauled up in class as a schoolboy for listening to the commentary on my pocket transistor and exulting when the rival team's wicket fell. (My teacher who confiscated the radio was later spotted in the staff room ears glued to the same transistor!) The first Test cricket series to be telecast live in India was the 1974–75 India–West Indies ding-dong battle, and it was only in 1978, when India went to Pakistan for the first time after seventeen long years, that Indian cricket fans finally got to see an overseas series 'live' on our then black-and-white television sets.

The 1983 victory also lifted national morale at a difficult time: the early 1980s were a period of conflict and bloodshed that would culminate in the assassination of Prime Minister Indira Gandhi in 1984, arguably the most traumatic year in independent India's history and one that would firmly mark the end of an age of dreamy innocence. The assault on the Golden Temple, the horrific anti-Sikh riots and the Bhopal gas tragedy – 1984 was an unending year of pain. As always, in stressful times, cricket would provide solace to the soul.

The third defining moment is the opening up of the Indian markets in the 1990s in the aftermath of the path-breaking 1991 budget. Economic liberalization saw the unshackling of Indian entrepreneurship, allowing cricket to be a major beneficiary from the sudden spurt in the consumer goods market and an exponential rise in advertising revenues on cable and satellite television. Every match was now telecast live on private channels as the Supreme Court ruled in 1995 that airwaves were no longer a government monopoly. The financially successful 1996 World Cup played in the subcontinent was a sign that the balance of cricketing power was shifting from West to East. 'Live cricket on TV and an expanding marketplace, it was an unbeatable combination,' is how Harsha Bhogle, one of the most recognized TV cricket commentators in the country, puts it.

The fourth transformational moment, and arguably the most influential, came in 2008 when the IPL kicked off: a big-money sporting spectacle that suddenly gave cricket a glitzy Bollywood-like appeal. Growing up in the India of the 1970s, going to the circus was our ultimate night out. Under the big top, we watched acrobats perform in shimmering skirts, laughed as clowns hit each other, gasped as animals jumped through rings of fire and were dazzled by motorbike stunts. In twenty-first-century India, now the IPL is the biggest circus in town – only this is three hours of unscripted reality entertainment and the stars are top-class cricketers, with rich and famous franchise owners and scantily dressed cheerleaders in supporting roles. Six weeks of the IPL carnival every summer – where cricket becomes a television box office superhit – has dramatically altered the sport's ethos, bringing in new audiences and, importantly, taken the sport to every nook and corner of the country, riding on the power of a mighty multimedia and marketing machine. Regional IPLs in states like Tamil Nadu and Karnataka have become a force multiplier. With its unique 20-overs-a-side format, this is cricket that is fast and exciting, tailor-made for a younger, more aggressive India. With billionaire franchise team owners ready to spend crores to 'buy' even domestic players in the much-hyped player auctions, cricket has become a truly aspirational sport even for rural India. Almost every district in this country now has a turf wicket and a coaching academy.

The IPL's launch was perfectly timed with the Indian economy entering an age of rapid globalization, one where every major global brand now furiously competes for market share (the top two bidders for the IPL title sponsorship in 2017 were both Chinese mobile phone companies). Fortuitously, the IPL also started just a year after the young Indian team unexpectedly won the thrilling inaugural 2007 World Twenty20 tournament. Four years later, India lifted the 2011 World Cup on home soil. If 1983 was a bit of a fluke, twenty-eight years later, the victory at Mumbai's Wankhede stadium in front of the country's largest-ever television audience only confirmed India's status as a twenty-first-century cricketing superpower. Like in 1983, the 2011 win came at a troubling time for the country: political corruption had sparked off street protests, public anger and cynicism towards the 'neta' class was peaking even as growth was slowing and inflation was climbing. Cricket, as often has been the case in this country, provided a balm and a sense of renewed hope in the future. In mid 2017, when I was finishing this book, India was formally anointed the number one Test side and looks set to stay on top for a while.

~

It is in tracing this amazing rise of Indian cricket and how it links to strengthening our sense of nationhood that the story of our Democracy's XI is relevant. Each of the individuals whose life stories I have chosen to put the spotlight on is a reflection of how Indian cricket and society have evolved post-1947, of how cricket has discarded its colonial origins to become a mass sport, how cricket is a shining badge for multireligious pluralism, how the forces of market competition in an otherwise unequal society have created the democratic space for talent to flourish and for ambitions to be realized.

This is not a book about an all-time best Indian cricket eleven but a personal choice of eleven individuals who I believe in their own way shaped Indian cricket and made it the country's number one sport; it is, in a sense, a baton relay in which eleven people are participating and doing the best they can to ensure that the next generation is even better prepared for the challenges of the future. That my choice of eleven cricketers are all men could be held against me, but I have no doubt that one day a similar book will be written on the emerging women's cricket revolution.

My journey starts in the late 1950s with my late father who would probably never make it to any greatest-ever Indian team (as he would modestly tell you, 'I was good, but never great!'), but still remains the only Goa-born male cricketer to have played for the country (Shikha Pandey, an Indian women's team star, is also Goa-born). That he was born in the small town of Margao in 1940 and yet played for the country for over a decade in the 1960s and early 1970s makes him an oddity in the age in which he played the game. Cricket in that period was dominated by the major metro cities and even my father had to migrate from Portuguese-ruled Goa where he had limited exposure to the game all the way to Mumbai to realize his cricket dream. With financial constraints and inadequate infrastructure, the early years were a struggle for Dilip Sardesai. By contrast, today it is almost the norm for cricketers from the small towns to make it big in the sport, another reflection of how cricket has now transcended all geographical boundaries. Sardesai had one remarkable series against the West Indies in 1971, the year which, as mentioned earlier, gave Indian cricket a crucial self-belief to challenge the world, and where his high scores earned him the sobriquet 'the Renaissance man of Indian cricket'.

My father's captain for most of his Test career was Mansur Ali Khan Pataudi, also known as the Nawab of Pataudi. He was the rare prince amid a generation of middle-class cricketers who began to sparkle in the early years after Independence. But he wasn't a prince from a colonial era: he had earned his place in the team because of his talent and not his lineage. That he achieved success despite losing sight in one eye makes his achievements even more remarkable. He was a 'republican' prince, someone who welded a team from diverse backgrounds into a truly 'national' team for the first time. He provided Indian cricket a charismatic leadership at a crucial stage in its evolution; he was a prince by birth but Nehruvian by outlook, signalling the democratic impulses of a nation slowly shedding its feudal baggage.

The Pataudi era in the 1960s also sparked off a spinning revolution in Indian cricket, led by four unique spinners with vastly contrasting personalities. I was tempted to choose Bhagwat Subramanya Chandrasekhar in my eleven, arguably the greatest match-winning bowler of his generation. The story of Chandra, who despite a polio-afflicted arm could bamboozle the best batsmen in the world, is part of cricketing folklore. I have chosen Bishan Singh Bedi instead, who was perhaps post-Independence India's first cricket 'rebel'. He was as colourful as he was controversial, the Sardar of Spin who was both pious and pugilistic. In Bedi's combative persona, Indian cricket discovered a leader who was ready to push for player power for the first time. His bowling action was a sight to behold but it was his anti-establishment credentials in a period of political turbulence that make him an attractive choice for any team that views sport as redefining the status quo.

The age of the great Indian spinners coincided with the rise of the finest opening batsman India has produced. Sunil Gavaskar provided steel and substance to Indian cricket and, in no small measure, gave it self-respect. The stereotype of the timid Indian batsmen who were easily intimidated by fast bowling was defeated by a short man with a broad bat from Mumbai, appropriately named the Little Master. Blessed with unmatched concentration and near-perfect technique, Gavaskar took on the fastest bowlers in the world to give Indian cricket a new muscle. On the field, Gavaskar was the pride of the nation, shattering almost every record in Test cricket. Off it, he gave Indian cricket a hard, professional edge that had been missing for decades. His success through the 1970s – a decade when socialistic economics offered limited opportunities for upward mobility – gave the salaried urban middle class in particular a role model they could look up to.

If Gavaskar began his career with the spinners in their pomp, it would end with the exuberance of pace. Kapil Dev was once chosen as Wisden's Indian cricketer of the century, an honour that has as much to do with his all-round skills as it does with the sheer excitement he brought to the sport. Only Kapil Dev could have hit four 6s in an over to save a follow-on: he was truly sui generis. If Gavaskar redefined opening batting in the country, Kapil Dev broke several barriers: the first world-class fast bowler produced by India, the first serious talent from Haryana and, crucially, the first cricketer to wear his small-town rustic origins as a badge of pride. He played cricket with an energy that was infectious and made him a national folk hero – the cheery smile with which he lifted the World Cup in 1983 is imprinted in national memory. It was the most stunning victory, one that changed Indian cricket forever, making it a sport that was ready to step into the age of colour television and commercial success.

Mohammed Azharuddin is perhaps the most controversial choice in my team: that his name is indelibly associated with the match-fixing scandal that stained Indian cricket might lead observers to wonder why he has been picked. And yet, to measure Azhar's contribution to the sport only through the prism of still unproven charges of match-fixing is unfair to one of the most successful and durable batsmen-captains India has produced. He is also a symbol of Indian cricket's multireligious character. In the winter of 1992–93 in the aftermath of the bloody post-Ayodhya rioting, I was despairing of the future. Reporting on the Mumbai riots and blasts, I felt distraught. In that moment of despondency, Azhar's leadership and batsmanship gave me and millions of others a sense of hope: a proud Indian Muslim leading the country at a time when communal conflict threatened to rupture Hindu–Muslim relations.

No cricketer though has given the Indian cricket fan greater hope and joy than Sachin Tendulkar, the country's first sporting Bharat Ratna. As a Mumbaikar who played cricket with Tendulkar's brother, I had a privileged ringside view of his spectacular rise from the maidan to the pinnacle of the sport. I still remember the surge of pride one felt when Sir Don Bradman, the ultimate batting divinity, likened Tendulkar's batting style to his. For millions of Indians, Tendulkar was, and always will be, the 'God of Cricket', someone who is hero-worshipped for his achievements. That he made his Test debut at an age when most children are struggling with their algebra, marks him as a prodigy. That he was still playing international cricket when stepping into his forties is proof that he was near-indestructible. For close to a quarter of a century, there was a permanence of identifying Indian cricket with the genius of Tendulkar.

If Tendulkar was the first superstar-millionaire of Indian cricket in the age of global satellite television, his contemporary Sourav Ganguly is a folk hero of a different kind. In a way, Ganguly is to Bengal what Tendulkar is to India: a regional 'Big Boss' who came to represent the hopes and aspirations of a corner of a country which was crazy about the sport but had never produced a major homegrown star. His role as captain in a difficult period for Indian cricket can't be underestimated: he restored pride in the sport when the scar of match-fixing had led to disillusionment. His combative machismo helped break another stereotype: no longer would a Bengali middle-class gent be seen as a soft and dreamy coffee house intellectual. Ganguly was a tough cricketer ready to walk the talk.

If Ganguly was fire, Rahul Dravid was Indian cricket's ice-man. No Indian cricketer has carried himself with greater dignity and composure in whatever he did on and off the field than Dravid, a steely character. That he played much of his cricket in the shadow of Tendulkar means that we may never quite appreciate the magnitude of some of his statistical achievements (he has faced more balls than any other batsman in Test cricket, featured in more century partnerships, taken more catches, to name just three). Dravid, in a sense, is a throwback to an earlier era of the sport when cricket wasn't about sledging or showmanship but a hard sport played with the spirit of gentlemanliness. His career is proof that nice guys can finish first and that there is still space for integrity and values amid the cut-throat competition of contemporary sport.

If Dravid provides a comforting link with Indian cricket's genteel past, Mahendra Singh Dhoni has truly revolutionized its present. Dhoni is the iconic symbol of Indian cricket's march to the summit of the sport. He, after all, was Test captain when India became the number one side in the world and again when we lifted the World Cup on home soil in 2011. No cricketer would seem to have absorbed the pressure of leading India with greater calmness and maturity than Dhoni, one reason perhaps why he has succeeded so often in crunch situations. And yet, Dhoni's impact cannot be measured by runs made, catches taken or matches won: he is the cricketer who best represents how Indian cricket has been truly 'democratized' and become an engine for merit-driven social mobility. The first Ranchi-born cricketer to play for the country, his rise from ticket collector at Kharagpur railway station to lifting the World Cup less than a decade later, while becoming one of the wealthiest sportspersons in the world along the way, is the ultimate cricketing fairy tale. If there is a 'small-town' cricket revolution in India that has driven Indian cricket forward, then Dhoni is its poster boy.

Indeed, the 'power shift' in Indian cricket from the elite metropolitan clubs and gymkhanas to the 'aam aadmi' maidans of small-town India is almost complete. While children from wealthier urban homes have other sporting options – ranging from tennis to football – in Tier II and Tier III cities of India, cricket is a manic fixation. Small-town India has the hunger and facilities to see cricket as its ticket to breaking the class window – the majority of the players in Team India now come from outside the big cities. If the OBC (other backward caste) 'Mandal' revolution has changed Indian politics forever, then the 'Dhoni effect' has had a similar impact on cricket.

Leading the charge into a new century is Virat Kohli, the idol of the millennial generation. The torch of Indian batting has moved smoothly from Gavaskar to Tendulkar to Kohli now. And yet, like all great cricketers, he is distinctive in style, on and off the field, a batsman who can play all formats of the game with equal ease and with an unbridled aggression that mirrors the attitude of a new India. This is an India which oozes a certain self-confidence, bordering on 'me-first' arrogance, one which rewards excellence and isn't going to be meek and submissive when confronted with any 'foreign' challenge. Kohli is also a product of a hyper-globalized age where cricket is now 'cricketainment', a high-stakes sport that is umbilically tied to the global consumer marketplace. Indian cricketers from an earlier era who had to scrounge around for a proper bat must gaze enviously at the multi-crore bat contracts and brand endorsements of a Kohli. He is the prototype of the modern-day sportsperson: rich and successful, but also remarkably fit and focused. Indeed, money is a small part of the big picture: watch a Kohli fitness video on Instagram and you realize the enormous hard work and desire to succeed that has gone into the making of a champion.

In a sense, it is this burning passion for the game that unites this Democracy's XI. ('Junoon' or obsession is a word I have heard often from our cricket heroes.) Indian cricketers for almost the first fifty years after Independence may have faced many more hardships but they were ultimately the products of the age in which they lived – a pre-liberalization India didn't offer the bountiful opportunities that today's generation can revel in. And yet, who is to say that those cricketers played the sport with any less commitment than today's young men do? Or, conversely, that the lure of easy money has turned the heads of our twenty-first-century cricketers; if anything, the skill sets of today's gen-next Indian players have taken the sport to another level and made India arguably the best team in the world.

Where once the sport was played almost for fun, it has now acquired an edge of ruthless competitiveness that might also mirror the evolution of our political democracy. Electoral battles in this country are now fought with a cut-and-thrust intensity that might have taken away from the festive air that once accompanied an election contest. The stakes are higher and so is the pressure on the participants. The Board of Control for Cricket in India (BCCI), the supervisory body for the game, has promoted the sport well and given it financial muscle, but the board has also been trapped in the politics of a cosy club, allegations of conflict of interest, greed and corruption soiling the image of the game. If crony capitalism is a breeding ground for political corruption, then the BCCI czars have flourished through an opaque decision-making system managed by politically well-connected interest groups. The Supreme Court perhaps overreached itself in appointing in January 2017 a committee of administrators to run cricket, but the board's steadfast refusal to reform itself is largely responsible for its predicament.

Star players too have got ensnared in a commercial merry-go-round, encircled by marketing agents and big-ticket sponsors. The match-fixing and spot-fixing controversies exposed how some of our cricketing heroes had feet of clay, seduced by the lure of easy money. The unseemly removal of Anil Kumble as India coach in June 2017 because captain Kohli wanted him out is another sign of the times. Where once the Indian captain's appointment was hostage to the cricket board's internal power equations, now the players call the shots, their supreme authority directly linked to their market value and heightened public expectations. As Gautam Gambhir, man of the match when India won the 2011 World Cup, puts it, 'I do think that your father's generation would have enjoyed the sport more than our lot. I think they were romantics of the game while we are, at times, result-oriented robots.'

But while comparing cricketers from different generations makes for ideal barroom chatter, it may not be entirely fair to those who have had the distinction of representing their country through the ages. Today's cricketers are undoubtedly fitter and more prepared than those who played cricket for India before them, a 'team of top-class athletes' is how Gavaskar describes the modern generation. The professional edge and constant exposure to best practices in the sport place a premium on excellence like never before, best reflected in the rising fielding standards. From an era where the game was played at a languid pace, this is now a sport that symbolizes the energies and aspirations of a nation on the move.

And yet, who is to say that the batsmen of the pre-helmet era and uncovered pitches were not more gutsy or technically better equipped than the well-protected players of today? Or that the bowlers weren't as crafty? Truth is, there are no shortcuts when you want to be one of the eleven cricketers privileged to represent your country at any given time. Each cricketer who is part of this Democracy's XI has been blessed with talent, shepherded along by a kind family member, taught by an unselfish coach, adored by feverish fans and honoured by a grateful country.

~

Of course, no cricket team is complete without a twelfth man, and my eleven too has one. Eknath Solkar was my first cricket hero. As a six-year-old in 1971, I would go to the Cricket Club of India (CCI) and sit in the children's stand and watch him in action. He was arguably one of the most stylish cricketers of his time and certainly the best fielder of his era (no one has fielded with greater courage and athleticism at forward short leg). Once described as the poor man's Gary Sobers for his left-handed all-round skills, he carried himself with an easy swagger and joie de vivre that I guess appealed to my boyhood dreams. I remember crying inconsolably when he got out cheaply once and beaming just as easily when he offered me a Coca Cola bottle after a game.

But Solkar was more than just any other Indian cricketer: he is one of the sport's first subaltern heroes, another truly uplifting story of how cricket can transform lives. His father was the groundsman at the PJ Hindu Gymkhana, one of the many picturesque grounds that dot the Marine Drive landscape in Mumbai. His raw talent was spotted at the nets by the legendary Indian cricketer Vinoo Mankad, and was given support and encouragement by several club members, including my father, and the Mafatlal Group where he was employed. In 1971 in the West Indies, he and my father struck many memorable partnerships together, perhaps the duo benefiting from the comfort of having played for the same club side. In one Test, when Solkar kept playing and missing, a West Indian bowler let out a few expletives. Solkar, supremely self-confident, hit back with his own abusive words. When the West Indian captain Sobers complained, my father intervened: 'Look, Gary, Ekki [Solkar's pet name] doesn't know what you are saying and you won't understand what he is. So tell your bowler to mind his business and we will mind ours!'

Solkar died at the relatively young age of fifty-seven but his success on the cricket field ensured that his family was pulled out of poverty in one generation. The Solkar story though that stays with me is how he played a Ranji Trophy final in 1969 even as his father was on his deathbed. His father died in the middle of the game, he tearfully went and performed the last rites and then came back to guide Mumbai to a match-winning first innings lead. 'My father would have wanted me to play cricket and when I was batting, his spirit was always with me,' he later told a teammate.

It's the story which could be told just as easily by a Tendulkar when he returned to play in the 1999 World Cup after his father's death and then went on to score a magical century. Or by a Virat Kohli who as a teenager lost his father while he was batting overnight for Delhi, and yet, undaunted by personal tragedy, went out to bat the next day, scored a fighting 90 runs before lighting his father's funeral pyre. These valorous stories are part of the romance of Indian cricket and continue to inspire and motivate millions of Indians to dare to dream. This book is a story of those wondrous dreams and transcendental talents that will, hopefully, continue to illuminate our lives and this great game.

1

Dilip Sardesai

Renaissance Man from Goa

It was a mournful grey monsoon morning in Mumbai. My father lay dying in the ICU of the Bombay Hospital. He had been on dialysis for more than two years after a renal failure and the regular hospital visits had begun to weigh him down. Each time he struggled to walk from his hospital bed to the bathroom, I could see he was in great agony.

His threshold to bear pain was high: he had, after all, never even winced when being struck by a hard five-and-a-half-ounce cricket ball. His body had been badly bruised and his fingers often fractured but he had the resilient spirit of a boxer in the ring. He loved a scrap and had built a reputation for batting fearlessly against the fastest bowlers of his generation. That is why he was pushed up the order to open the batting as a twenty-two-year-old in the West Indies in 1962 when no one else was willing to take up the challenge. That is why he would never take a step back in an era where three to four bouncers an over was the norm. But now I sensed he was ready to give up the fight. 'Look after everyone in the family,' he told me quietly and then gazed out of the window.

Outside the hospital stretched the Cross Maidan, one of the many cricket grounds spread across South Mumbai. The maidan was an integral part of my father's life, it was where he had played and practised for hours after first arriving in the city from Goa to improve his game. His dreams of playing cricket for India were nurtured in these maidans of Mumbai where he had scored many centuries. Even after retirement he would spend hours here talking and watching cricket. As he looked longingly from his ICU cubicle at the palm trees swaying in the monsoon breeze, the memories of a life well spent must have come flooding back. The batsman was ready to call time, looking down on this maidan of his youth as if bidding farewell to that green expanse of hope and optimism.

I knew he loved nothing more than sitting in a tent at the Cross Maidan in his shorts and a loose T-shirt, sipping chai and watching the next generation of Mumbai cricketers emerge from the shadows. It was his home away from home where the sound of ball on bat would provide comfort from any physical distress he was feeling as his body weakened.

In one corner of the hospital room was a small television showing an India–Ireland match. My father's eyes moved from maidan to match with unfailing regularity. Suddenly, almost unmindful of the pain he was in, he got up excitedly and let out an expletive. Rahul Dravid, a cricketer he greatly admired, had just been dismissed trying to fend off a short ball. 'How could he get out like that?' muttered my father. 'I can understand other batsmen getting out like that but not Rahul. He is technically perfect!' For the next few minutes, he took up an imaginary batting position and demonstrated how a bouncer should be played – eye on the ball, head swaying away at the last moment.

This is the last, most cherished memory I have of my father. Exactly a week later, on 2 July 2007, Dilip Sardesai passed away. He had played his final innings. Till the very end he remained an obsessive cricket romantic, someone for whom playing with a straight bat was part of the journey of life, a journey that had begun in a most unlikely corner of Indian cricket.

~

The stadium was swaying to the rhythm of drumbeats. You could have been in Rio, Sao Paulo, Barcelona, Madrid, Manchester or Munich – any of the great homes of football. But this was Fatorda stadium in Margao, a sleepy Goan town that awakens only to the sights and sounds of the beautiful game. FC Goa was playing Delhi Dynamos in the inaugural Indian Soccer League in 2014, the glitzy equivalent of cricket's billion-dollar baby, the IPL. Raucous Goans, around 25,000 of them, had crammed into every corner of the stadium.

Sitting next to me was the Goa deputy chief minister Francis D'Souza who would leap with delight every time a player from the home side lashed out at goal. I had been introduced to the minister as 'Rajdeep Sardesai, TV personality and son of Dilip Sardesai'. He responded with, 'Ah, you are son of Dilip baab, he is our very own pride of Goa. Great man, but you know this is a land of football, not cricket. Here, we kick the ball first, then we learn how to hit it!'

Goa is India's smallest state by area, and the fourth smallest in terms of population. To the outside world, it is defined in rather exotic terms as the country's tourist capital with its sandy beaches, warm waters, bars and shacks, alcohol and drugs. The lure of 'good times' draws lakhs of domestic and foreign visitors to its tranquil shores. But most Goans feel their state is the prisoner of an image trap. After all, the so-called swinging, free-living bohemian paradise (now increasingly a builders' nirvana, a concrete playground of holidaymakers from across India and the world) is in reality a dignified conservative society defined by the spirit of 'communidade', the Portuguese term for a tightly knit village community. It is a pious land, where wayside shrines and folk deities mark the spirit of devotion that exists in every Goan home, whether it is Christian or Hindu. The Portuguese withdrew from Goa in 1961 after more than 400 years of colonization but Goan society still revolves around village panchayats. The state's idyllic natural beauty is matched by a sense of serene communal harmony with church spires and village temples happily coexisting in an atmosphere of 'susegad' (derived from 'sossegado', the Portuguese word for 'quiet').

The long years of Portuguese rule influenced Goa in several aspects, including its sporting interests. For the large Catholic community in particular – which in 1947 constituted well over 30 per cent of Goa's population – football was an expression of identity, with local churches supporting village football teams. It was as if the sport connected Goans with the wider Portuguese colonial diaspora from Rio to Lisbon. Amidst the swaying palm trees and lush green rice fields, the football ground was a space for young Goans to conjure dreams of following in the footsteps of idols from other lands – Pele, Maradona, or in recent times, Ronaldo or Messi. Into this football-crazy world stepped Dilip Sardesai, who remains India's only Goa-born male cricketer till date, even though nearly 300 have represented the country in Tests.

~

Amidst the stirrings of the Quit India Movement in other parts of the country, in 1940 Goa was still under the firm rule of the Portuguese. Margao, its trade and commercial heartland, was relatively tiny with a population of just around 50,000.

The Sardesais were a typical middle-class Gowd Saraswat Brahmin family. The Saraswats are a small fish-eating Brahmin community along the west coast of India who trace their origins to the Saraswati river in the Himalayas. Legend has it that when the river dried up, there was a large-scale migration of the Saraswats to different parts of the country, including the Konkan coastline across Maharashtra, Goa and Karnataka. 'We even fought in Shivaji's army and were awarded a large tract of land,' my father's elder brother Anand tells me when I meet him to trace the family history.

Whether they were Shivaji's warriors or not, the sense is that the Sardesais had very little left of any land, wealth or privilege in the 1940s. My grandfather Narayan was an insurance agent while his mother Saraswati was raising a large family and like many women of that generation spending a substantial part of her life going in and out of maternity homes. The extended Sardesai joint family included several cousins and uncles and they all lived together. 'We could have put up two cricket teams of just the Sardesai men in the house,' says Anand.

The family wasn't wealthy but there was always enough food on the table, especially fish, which in Goa is a staple diet. Dilip Sardesai was the fifth child in a family of six, the youngest of the men in the house and possibly the most pampered. He would often visit his elder sister's home in the neighbouring village of Kurpe, climb palm trees, pluck mangoes and jackfruit and swim in the river. His brother Anand was a freedom fighter, part of the guerrilla-like groups taking on the Portuguese in their battle to liberate Goa. 'I would be in and out of jail but made sure that Dilip, who was much younger than me, would be kept away from any trouble,' he says.

Like in many middle-class Brahmin families, education was seen as the ultimate weapon of survival and upward mobility. Dilip was sent to the local New Era School in Margao where studying Portuguese was mandatory and English was the medium of instruction after class four. While football was the main sport, there were a handful of boys – mostly from the Saraswat community – who also played cricket. They included my father's cousins, one of whom, Sopan, would go on to represent Bombay University.

On the way to school was the Margao market where Narayan 'Master' would sit with his sowing machine outside a nimbu pani shop. The tailor loved cricket and would become Dilip's first window to the game, showing him paper clippings of Indian Test cricketers and telling him stories of Vijay Merchant and Vijay Hazare, the champion batsmen of the era. 'Narayan Master introduced me to the game and gave me my first bat,' my father told me. Many years later, when he was playing a Test match in Mumbai, he invited Narayan to watch the game and see the big city. It was his way of repaying an old debt.

And yet the fact is that Dilip, like many of his generation, had no formal cricket coaching as a schoolboy, no visual imagery of the sport on television to emulate, no proper cricket kit. There was no cricket ground in Margao at the time but it did have a large empty field behind the railway tracks where kids would play. The area didn't even have a turf wicket for cricket practice, but an old mat which served as a pitch. 'I liked the idea of holding the bat in hand and hitting the ball hard. The faster the bigger boys bowled, the harder I hit them,' was how my father explained his initiation into the sport.

The first time his family realized that young Dilip might have a special skill was when a Reserve Bank of India team from Mumbai came to Margao to play a local game in 1955. 'Dilip scored a hundred in that game as a fifteen-year-old. That evening, the opposition captain came and told me that we should send him to Mumbai if we wanted him to become a better player,' Anand tells me. Dilip was finishing school that year, and going to Mumbai for college and cricket seemed a natural progression.

By a happy coincidence, my grandfather was already planning a move to the city for the economic security of his large family. Migrating for work is part of the Goan way of life – thousands of Goans travel to Mumbai and other cities even now to seek employment and fortune. It was a little more difficult to make the move in Portuguese-ruled Goa because of the complex web of work permits and identity cards that were required. But my grandfather was determined, and in 1956, Dilip along with his parents and elder brothers left his beloved Goa for Mumbai. This was his chance to finally play in the big league.

Years later, my father would tell me how much he missed the joys of childhood in Goa, the fish and the mangoes, the palm trees and the paddy fields. But in 1956, another dream was driving him. It was the great Indian dream, one that many others from different parts of the country would share in the future. Over the years, cricket and cinema have drawn many Indians to the big cities in search of their golden rainbow. (It was around this period that the likes of Dharmendra, for example, made their way into the Hindi film industry from rural north India.) My father was chasing his own personal ambition: 'Yes, I wanted to play for India, but most of all, I just wanted to play cricket, I was in love with the game.'

~

Dilip reached the bright lights of Mumbai in early 1956 like any young man with a wish in the heart and a prayer on the lips. This was the year when Johnny Walker joyfully sang the ultimate Mumbai anthem along Marine Drive in the Hindi film *C.I.D.*, 'Ae dil hai mushkil jeena yahan, zara hatke, zara bachke, yeh hai Bambai meri jaan!' Five years later, the teenager from Goa who had never seen or played on a proper cricket ground as a schoolboy would be representing the country. Even though this was the Nehruvian India of five-year state planning, little planning had gone into the incredible rise of a young man from the colonial outpost of Goa to the centrestage of Indian cricket – only hard work, dedication, lots of talent, and yes, a bit of luck. Years later, I would ask my father to explain the secret of his almost instant success. 'I guess I was hungry,' he said, pointing to his by then expanded midriff. 'I just wanted it very badly.'

It wasn't easy, though. The structure of Indian cricket in the 1950s, like many other aspects of society, still had to pander to its feudal origins. The maharajas were slowly exiting – a few like the houses of Baroda and Mewar continued to patronize the sport and even 'employed' star players like Vijay Hazare, Vinoo Mankad, Salim Durani and Chandu Borde – but the new post-Independence cricket order was struggling to find its feet. Madhav Apte, who played for India in 1952, recalls how almost every player would be on the edge, never sure whether they would play the next game. 'We had selectors like one Mr Dutta Ray who had never played cricket but who became a selector because he had clout as a cricket board official,' says Apte. He even claims that in the early 1950s, there were whispers of fringe players 'buying' their way into the team for Rs 5000 if they had the right 'connections'. 'We had a lot of one-Test wonders in those days, players who played in one game, got their India cap and then mysteriously disappeared,' points out Apte, who was dropped from the Indian team despite averaging almost 50 runs per innings in the seven Tests he played for India.

In the universe of elite clubs, princely patrons and well-entrenched local networks, Dilip didn't have a godfather or benefactor. As a Goan Maharashtrian whose mother tongue was Konkani (later the official language of Goa), he struggled initially to adjust to a new environment. 'When I came to Mumbai, I knew no one except my cousin Sopan who was a good cricketer and had already begun to play for Bombay University. I am a purely self-made product,' he would later tell me with great pride.

The Sardesais settled down in Marina Mansion, a building in South Mumbai's crowded Chowpatty area overlooking the beach and the Arabian Sea. It is also in close proximity to the scenic Marine Drive, the city's majestic sea-facing boulevard where Mumbaikars living in cramped homes can breathe freedom and openness by just walking along the waterfront. It is here that many migrants to the city live out their urban fantasies. Superstar Amitabh Bachchan once famously admitted to having slept on a Marine Drive bench when he first came to the city.

The teenage Dilip's imaginings revolved around the cricket fields of the gymkhanas dotting Marine Drive – the Hindu, Parsee and Islam Gymkhanas had been cricket's battlegrounds in the early twentieth century when the sport was organized along communal lines. 'Every morning and evening I would go for a walk on the seafront, buy chana for 5 paise and watch cricket. I felt like I was in heaven!' he said.

The Chowpatty area was, and still is, a predominantly Gujarati neighbourhood, known for its excellent ice cream parlours and vegetarian food. The Gujaratis had been among the early converts to cricket, the leisurely pace of the game suiting a community not known for participation in strenuous physical activity. If Mahatma Gandhi was the Gujarati from Kathiawar who galvanized a nation to freedom, Vijay Merchant, who belonged to a prominent textile family of Mumbai, was arguably the first great Indian batsman and a role model for an entire generation of the city's cricketers.

Merchant had retired by the time Dilip arrived in Mumbai and it was another Vijay (Manjrekar) who had taken over the mantle of leading Mumbai's batting legacy. During this period Test players would regularly turn up on the maidans to play in Mumbai's highly competitive club cricket tournaments. When Dilip first saw Manjrekar bat, he was in a trance. 'In Margao I had only heard of these cricketers, so when I actually saw Manjrekar bat I was so excited I didn't sleep that night and was just practising my defensive stroke with a bat in hand. I could never imagine that one day I would be sharing a dressing room with him,' said Dilip.

Dilip first enrolled in Bhavan's College, a stone's throw from his home, and scored a century in his debut college game. A year later, he moved to Wilson College, a bigger, more prestigious institution in the same Chowpatty area. It had a rich history and counted then finance minister Morarji Desai amongst its alumni. It was also where Dilip got his first big break.

Dilip would go to the sea-facing college grounds every evening to play cricket and carrom, his other great sporting interest. One day the cricket team was short of one player and my father volunteered to fill the spot. He took two catches and scored 25 not out, enough to impress coach M.S. Naik. If a tailor on a Margao street had initiated the young boy into the sport, an elderly coach in Mumbai would help him graduate to the next level. Naik spent hours with his ward, perfecting his skill and technique. 'He was my first guru. I lost my father within a year of coming to Mumbai and Naik sir became a father figure to me,' recalled my father.

If he wasn't doing so at college, Dilip would practise on the terrace of his building. In the monsoon months, he would get other boys in the area to throw him a wet tennis ball to improve his reflexes. 'We would bowl and Dilip would bat till late in the night under the lights on the terrace,' recalls Mayuresh, a neighbour from those days. The terrace training taught my father a useful lesson imbibed by the batsmen of that generation: keep hitting the ball along the ground to avoid getting out. 'It was on the terrace that I perfected the art of batting straight because if I hit the ball in the air; then I had to go down four floors to get the ball and then climb up again!' my father pointed out. The wet tennis ball practice would also become part of the informal coaching manual of many an Indian batsman in the future.

The rigorous training began to pay off. In his two years at Wilson, Dilip piled up the runs and slowly began to get noticed. In 1958, he played for the college team against a strong Hindu Gymkhana side that included several Mumbai Ranji Trophy players. It was led by Vinoo Mankad, who like Merchant was an iconic figure in Indian cricket at the time, and arguably the greatest spinning all-rounder the country has produced. Mankad was a rarity in the age in which he played the game, a 'professional' cricketer in a world of amateurs. He would spend his summers playing in the Lancashire League in England. He was also the first Indian cricketer to advertise for Brylcreem, a popular British brand of hairstyling products at the time (he was paid a one-time fee of 300 pounds for the advertisement in 1952). When Sardesai scored 90 not out in a total team score of 120, it was enough to make Mankad believe he had seen a special talent. That evening, Mankad came to the dressing room and told Dilip, 'Beta, I am making you a member of the Gymkhana; from now on, you will play for us. Don't worry about the fees, I will take care of it!' Vinoobhai, as my father called him, would become an inspiration for life.

From Wilson, Dilip moved to Siddharth College, then a stand-out institution in Mumbai for cricket. 'My fees were waived and V.B. Prabhudesai, our cricket-crazy manager at college, had a simple rule for us – win matches for the college and I will ensure you graduate!' he recollected. The high scores in college cricket meant he was ready to take the next step. In 1958, he was picked for the Bombay University team for the first time. Over the next three years, he would dominate university cricket as part of a powerful Mumbai side, scoring centuries and double centuries almost at will.

Mumbai was becoming a dominant force in Indian cricket with the emerging Maharashtrian middle class as the engine of its success. The Samyukta Maharashtra Andolan, which was demanding a separate Marathi-speaking state to be carved out from the old bilingual Marathi- and Gujarati-speaking Mumbai state, was now peaking, and cricket became a badge of identity for the Maharashtrian community. Players like Manjrekar, Ajit Wadekar, Ramakant Desai and Bapu Nadkarni were part of this cricket mini-revolution stirring awake in Mumbai's maidans and Marathi-speaking middle-class colonies in areas like Dadar and Shivaji Park. Through the late 1950s and the 1960s, Mumbai would be to cricket what Bengal was to football – a nursery of the sport. In these two decades, 20 of the 73 cricketers to make their India debuts were from Mumbai. Between the golden period from 1958 to 1973, the Mumbai team never lost the Ranji Trophy. When India won a Test series in 1971 in England for the first time, the team had six Mumbai players, my father among them. University cricket provided the platform for the rise of Mumbai as a powerhouse of the sport. 'It was probably more difficult at the time to play for Mumbai than it was for India; the competition was fierce, but it was also great fun,' recalled my father. 'We were all very young, and would criss-cross the country by train, mostly in second class, playing cards and singing songs.'

Cricket wasn't just fun; it also provided employment. After his father's sudden death in 1958, Dilip needed a job. Back then, public sector banks and the Tatas were among the few companies employing sportsmen to play for their office teams. The Associated Cement Company (ACC), part of the Tata group, had former Test cricketer Madhav Mantri as the chief talent scout and general manager. (He

was also the uncle of the legendary Sunil Gavaskar.) Mantri had
seen the young Dilip bat in a match between Hindu Gymkhana and
his club Dadar Union and it was a clear case of love at first sight!
'The very first day I saw him play I knew he would play for India,
there was no doubt in my mind,' he tells me. Mantri, who would
become another father figure, offered Dilip a job in ACC for Rs
1200 per month in the purchases department. 'I didn't really have
to do anything much. I would clock in to work at 9 a.m., and by 2
p.m. leave for the ground!' my father recalled.

The biggest break would come soon after as Dilip was picked
for the trials of the Combined Universities team to play the visiting
Pakistanis in the winter of 1960. 'I went to the trials and there were
dozens of boys who seemed much bigger than me. I wasn't sure I
would get a chance,' my father told me.

He needn't have worried. The chief selector at the time was
Lala Amarnath, another larger-than-life figure in post-1947 Indian
cricket. The first Indian to score a Test century on his debut in 1933,
Lala's cricketing career is a celebrated and controversial one – he had
been sent back home from the Indian cricket team's tour of England
in 1936 after fighting with the Maharaja of Vizianagaram. But he
was an astute talent-spotter, someone who believed in meritocracy
and calling a spade a shovel. He saw Dilip play a perfect defensive
shot in the trials and called him aside. 'Look, son, I am going to pick
you in the team, but I don't know about these other selectors, some
of who don't know the ABC of technique. Thoda ek do ball hawa
mein maaro [Hit one or two balls in the air]; they will be happy. The
rest you leave to me.' A few lofted shots later, Dilip found himself in
the Combined Universities team to play Pakistan.

He didn't miss this opportunity. He scored 87 in that game, got
picked for the Board President's XI where he scored a century, and
was then made twelfth man for the Test match that followed. Less
than a year later, in December 1961, he lined up to make his Test
debut against England at the age of twenty-one, shaking hands
with Jawaharlal Nehru at the Feroz Shah Kotla stadium in Delhi.

He hadn't even played for the Mumbai state team but was now representing his country. He was introduced to Nehru as a 'young man who hails from Goa'. The prime minister looked at him and smiled. 'Ah, Goa! Don't worry, the Indian army will soon liberate your state.' On 17 December, 30,000 Indian ground troops marched into Goa. Two days later, it was freed of Portuguese rule. While Goa celebrated freedom, Dilip Sardesai rejoiced too; he had just become the 103rd player to wear the India cap. 'The first day I got the cap, I went to sleep wearing it, I was so excited!' he told me. From the paddy fields of Margao to the cricket stadiums of India, it had been a remarkably swift journey.

~

Life as a Test cricketer in the 1950s and 1960s wasn't easy. When Dilip first played for India, he would earn Rs 250 per Test match; once in 1956, when a five-day match finished in four days, Rs 50 was deducted from the fee! (When Sardesai retired in 1973, the Test fee had been raised to the princely sum of Rs 2500.) The players didn't even get a separate laundry allowance – possibly one reason they were loath to dive on the field. For a four-month tour to the West Indies or England, they were paid a lump sum of Rs 1500 with 7 pounds per week given as 'smoke money'! On the West Indies tour of 1952–53, Apte says the players had to stay three to a room, often in mid-level hotels. The Indian team on that tour took ten days to reach the West Indies, first travelling by air to London and then taking a 'banana' boat from Southampton to Port of Spain. 'Those days bananas used to be sent by boat from the West Indies to England so we had fruit for good company!' says Apte with a laugh.

Apte came from a wealthy Mumbai business family but the majority of the players were amateurs with day jobs in public sector banks or private companies whose management supported cricket. The players didn't do any endorsements or get lucrative bat contracts. (One of Dilip's contemporaries, wicketkeeper Farokh Engineer advertised for Brylcreem in the 1960s, like Mankad had in the 1950s, but he was an exception.) In fact, the first formal contract Dilip signed with a bat manufacturer was in 1965, the year he scored his first Test century, with no money on offer but a guarantee of three new bats a year. (By contrast, Mahendra Singh Dhoni earns Rs 6 crore per annum to put a sticker on his bat while Virat Kohli now has a Rs 100 crore–plus eight-year bat contract with MRF.)

When he went on tour for the first time to the West Indies in 1962, Sardesai carried just a single bat with him – today's players will have dozens on hand. When facing the dangerous West Indian pace attack, they didn't have helmets, chest guards or even proper gloves and thigh pads. 'When I was hit by a ball on the thigh for the first time on that tour, the foam of the thigh pad I had carried from India almost came apart,' recalls Salim Durani, who was also on that team.

To try and reduce the pain of ball striking body, the players would wrap towels around their thighs. Chandu Borde, who was also on that West Indies tour, remembers spending every evening after a game rubbing on Amrutanjan, a traditional Indian balm. 'There was no front foot rule so the West Indian fast bowlers would bowl to us from 18 yards and every second ball was a bouncer. It was scary!' he tells me. Years later when my father watched the younger players bat with helmets and yet get struck on the temple, he would turn to me and smile. 'I didn't wear a helmet but was never hit on the head even when the bowlers bowled four bouncers an over. Maybe there was nothing in my head to hit!'

The reality of the physical dangers of the sport hit home on that 1962 West Indies tour, which was a classic David versus Goliath battle. The mighty West Indians were led by Frank Worrell and had on their team champion batsmen like Gary Sobers, Rohan Kanhai and Conrad Hunte as well as terrifying fast bowlers in Wes Hall and Charlie Griffith. Aged twenty-two, Dilip and most of his team members had not experienced such fiery pace. India was demolished 5-0 in the series but one agonizing day in Bridgetown, Barbados,

changed many lives forever. A bouncer delivered (rather 'chucked')
by Griffith hit the Indian skipper Nari Contractor on the head. As
he collapsed in a heap, there was shock and fear. The unconscious
and bleeding captain was rushed to the hospital. 'I would be lying if
I said that I wasn't scared. We were all frightened, and just holding
the bat was an effort for the next few days,' said my father. Contractor
survived, barely, after an emergency operation, and several teammates
donated blood, but the doughty batsman never played for the country
again (more on the Contractor saga in Chapter 2).

Dilip was chosen for the West Indies tour as a reserve middle-
order batsman – a young man on tour to learn and gain experience.
The injury to Contractor changed all that. Ironically, just two days
before the ill-fated Barbados match, Contractor had taken my father
aside for a walk on the beach. 'Look, dikra [son], no one in this team
wants to open the batting with me and face the West Indian fast
bowlers; they are all scared. You have a good technique and plenty
of courage; why don't you open?' Dilip had never opened the batting
but now saw an opportunity to make a place for himself in the Indian
team. He consulted Polly Umrigar, who was his captain in the ACC
office team and highly respected for his cricket acumen, and the other
senior batsman in the side Manjrekar, his batting role model. They
advised him to grab the chance. 'The best thing about Dilip was that
he was always unafraid and ready to fight on the field,' says Borde.

In the Bridgetown Test just days after Contractor was hit, Dilip
opened the batting for India for the first time. He batted bravely and
skilfully to score 31 and 60 in the two innings; the latter score the
slowest Test 50 by an Indian batsman at the time. From a middle-
order batsman with a reputation for playing spin bowling well, he
was now a technically correct opening batsman. 'Had I remained a
middle-order batsman, I would have scored many more runs since
I was a natural strokeplayer,' my father said wistfully. 'But in those
days, you didn't have a choice; you did what you were told.'

Over the next decade, Dilip would play thirty times for India,
averaging almost 40 runs an innings, his scores including an unbeaten

double century in Mumbai against New Zealand in 1965 that was then described by K.N. Prabhu, the pre-eminent cricket chronicler of the 1960s, as 'one of the finest Test innings played by an Indian batsman'. But in the latter half of the 1960s, injury, poor form and selectorial whims meant he could never quite achieve the promised heights.

'In the 1960s, you were on trial in almost every match. Today, if a player fails, he always gets another chance. Then, if you failed even once, the door was shut on you,' said my father regretfully. He remembered how a selector once came to the dressing room and told him, 'You get out cheaply in this match and you are out of the next game.' With only half a dozen Test matches played on average in one year (there was no one-day cricket at the time), players could end up spending extended periods on the sidelines.

The uncertainties of a cricket career mean the stability of family life is hostage to the sport's invariable ups and downs. My mother Nandini met my father as a sixteen-year-old fangirl in 1960. 'I was in love with cricket and cricketers and was constantly looking for their autographs [the 1960s' version of the selfie!] when I met your father in a restaurant,' she says. A romance blossomed over long-distance letters. 'At first, my parents, especially my mother, wasn't thrilled. Cricketers weren't considered a prize catch like they are today. Plus, I was still in my teens.' Her father was in the Indian Police Service, her mother came from a family of distinguished civil servants. My father's family were from small-town Margao. 'I guess there was a clash of social classes but that made me even more determined to follow my heart,' says my mother, who retired as head of the sociology department at Mumbai's St Xavier's College.

Early married life was tough. Let my mother tell the story. 'When we got married, we didn't have a house, a car, even a fridge, nothing that you take almost for granted today. We finally moved into a rented one bedroom, hall and kitchen home [one BHK as they call it today] in the central Mumbai area of Worli. Since we didn't have a car, Dilip would go to office in a BEST bus with his cricket kit bag. Even when he scored a double century for India in a 1965 Test match, he came home after hitching a ride with a friend in a taxi. We got a second-hand car in 1967, and then with the Rs 30,000 gift given by the chief minister of Goa, Dayanand Bandodkar, we bought our first house in upscale South Mumbai in a distress sale in 1968. It was gradual upward mobility where nothing came easy.'

Just put my mother's story in context – a leading Test cricketer in the 1960s didn't own a car or a house for much of his career, travelled to office by bus (a taxi was a luxury for rare occasions), and had no financial security. These days, even before a player represents his country, a lucrative IPL contract can make him a crorepati several times over. But Dilip had no regrets. 'I never grudged any modern player their riches. If you play a sport well, you should be paid well. I guess we didn't think about the money then because we just didn't realize our professional worth,' he told me.

By the end of the 1960s, life was finally getting easier for the Sardesais off the field. They now had their own house, a car (the good old Fiat) and two children (my sister, my father's favourite child as I teased her, was born a few years after me). But on the field, Dilip wasn't sure if he was wanted in Indian cricket any longer. He had been dropped for New Zealand's visit in 1969 as the chairman of selectors Vijay Merchant opted for 'younger' players. 'It was crazy. I was twenty-nine, at the peak of my batting form, and yet I was considered too old. Yes, I had put on weight but to drop me only because Mr Merchant wanted to experiment with younger players was something I found hard to accept,' was my father's response.

Dilip was outspoken and didn't hide his anger, even confronting Merchant, whom he had admired as a teenager: 'I told him in front of several people that if he didn't like my face he should say so but stop making cock-and-bull excuses to leave me out of the team.'

As the 1970s dawned, Dilip wondered if he would ever play for India again. 'I was just looking for one final chance to prove myself. I wanted to show my family, fans and, yes, Mr Merchant that I still had some cricket left in me,' he told me later. Making a comeback is never easy in Indian cricket, and was even tougher in an age where players were seemingly beholden to the cricket board and its all-powerful officials. But destiny was about to provide the most glorious twist in Dilip's career – the player who had been almost written off by most pundits would now be at the heart of a turning point in the history of Indian cricket.

~

1971 is the year of Indira Gandhi, her 'garibi hatao' slogan and the socialist rhetoric that propelled her to power with a huge majority. It is the year of Sam Manekshaw, the Field Marshal who led the war for liberating Bangladesh. It is the year of Rajesh Khanna, Bollywood's original 'phenomenon' who delivered a string of mega hits at the box office. It is also the year of Ajit Wadekar and the Indian cricket team which conquered new frontiers by winning a series in the West Indies and England for the first time.

If India discovered a new star in Sunil Gavaskar during the West Indies tour, the series also heralded the re-emergence of Dilip as the pivot in the Indian batting line-up. There was no cricket on television but the ball-by-ball radio commentary would transform an entire generation into cricket addicts. 'While we slept at home, Gavaskar and Sardesai in the West Indies would be batting and scoring runs all night over the radio!' recalls Harsha Bhogle, one of the faces of India's cricket television revolution, who was then a schoolboy. Gavaskar scored a world record 774 runs in his debut series while Dilip scored 642, including a double century and two centuries. Years later, at the annual Sardesai Memorial Lecture, Gavaskar would generously remark, 'It was Dilip who showed us the way to play the West Indian fast bowling, we only followed him!'

The irony is that Dilip almost didn't make that tour. He was the last member of the sixteen-player squad to be picked. The selection controversies had begun with the captain's choice. Mansur Ali Khan Pataudi, or Tiger, had been the Indian captain since 1962, pitched into the top job at the age of twenty-one because of the injury to Contractor. He had led Indian cricket with skill and fortitude for a decade when Merchant decided it was time for a change. Dramatically, he chose the Mumbai 'commoner' Wadekar to replace the 'prince', more evidence perhaps that Indian society was finally shaking off its class divide (see Chapter 2 for more). Wadekar had been Dilip's batting mate since their college days. Explains Wadekar: 'It was my first tour as captain and I wanted at least a few players around me who I could totally trust. So when I was allowed to choose one player, I plumped for Dilip right away.' Merchant wasn't thrilled but allowed the captain to have his way.

This was the chance Dilip had been waiting for. From the moment he landed in the West Indies, he felt his moment of redemption had come. 'I remember on the flight to the West Indies we stopped off in New York to watch a boxing match between Muhammad Ali and Joe Frazier. Frazier stunned Ali and I had images of the match playing in my head. If Frazier could beat Ali, I could take on the West Indies!' recalled my father. There was another reason he felt at home in the Caribbean islands. 'They reminded me of my home in Goa, the beaches, the sea, the palm trees – it was like being back in Margao!'

Dilip was picked for the first Test in Kingston, Jamaica only because another rising star Gundappa Viswanath was injured. He knew this was his final chance. When he went in to bat, India was 75 for 5 and most pundits dismissed the team as a 'club side'. 'Look, I had seen the great West Indies fast bowlers of 1962, compared to them this side was popatwadi [a Mumbai maidan word for "useless"]. I told my partner Eknath Solkar to bat as if we were playing at Hindu Gymkhana on Marine Drive,' he said. Dilip and Eknath stitched together a record partnership; the former going on to score 212, the first double century by an Indian batsman on foreign soil.

That innings would see the best of his batting art – rock-solid technique, no fear of fast bowling, quicksilver use of feet against spin, and a sharp cricket brain. For example, just before the West

Indies were to take the second new ball, my father told Solkar to deliberately keep getting beaten at least one ball in every over to the spinners and say 'well bowled' loudly so that captain Sobers would delay taking the new ball. 'Sobers was the greatest cricketer I ever played with but he wasn't such a good captain. He actually thought his spinners had us in trouble when all we were doing was pretending to struggle,' was my father's version.

Cricket lends itself easily to hyperbole and nostalgia can sometimes add many layers to a story of cricketing greatness. But the 212 in the West Indies is etched in the memory of Indian cricket fans like V.V.S. Laxman's magical 287 years later at Eden Gardens – an innings whose significance clearly stretched beyond the boundary. 'Dilip's innings in Kingston changed Indian cricket forever,' says his captain Wadekar. 'It gave us the self-belief and confidence that we could face the West Indies.'

Just how much it has stayed in the public consciousness was brought home to me many years later at Bhubaneswar airport. A Central Industrial Security Force security head came up to me and offered to escort me to a VIP lounge. I presumed he had seen me on television and asked him whether he liked the news. 'Sir, I don't watch much television news but I think you are Dilip Sardesai's son. Dilip Sardesai, Kingston 1971, 212, no?' If someone could remember a Test match score almost fifty years later only through radio commentary then it had to be a very special innings. My father too didn't forget it: when he applied for a phone number, 212 were the first three digits!

The batting feats didn't stop with the double century in Jamaica. In the next Test, Dilip scored a match-winning century as India defeated the West Indies for the first time. By the time the third Test in Barbados began, he was in 'the zone', as sportspersons call it. At Bridgetown airport, he was asked by a customs official whether he had anything to declare. He said, 'Nothing to declare except runs. I have scored runs in the first two games, I will score more now!' Sure enough, he scored 150 in the third Test after the team was down and out at 70 for 6. For the West Indies cricket fans, he was now affectionately called 'Sardee maan'. By the end of the tour 'Sardee maan' had been overtaken by 'Little Master' as young Gavaskar piled on the runs. Not that Dilip had any regrets at the rise of a new star who almost overshadowed his achievements. With typical humility, he would often say, 'Sunny is an all-time great, the rest of us were only good!'

The West Indies triumph was only the appetizer. A few months later, the Indian team travelled to England and defeated the English on their home turf. This time it wasn't Sardesai but another comeback man, leg-spinner B.S. Chandrasekhar, who did the trick with a mesmerizing spell in the final Test at the Oval. My father scored 54 and 40 in that game, two innings that had a crucial impact on the result. 'I shall never forget the scene when we won. An English friend offered to take me to the main members' lounge at the Oval. There was deathly silence; the English in their jackets and ties couldn't believe that the Indians whom they had taught the game had now defeated them,' my father remembered. The next day a headline in the sports pages of a British newspaper said it all: 'The mighty Empire falls to brave Indians!'

I remember the victorious day well. I was only six years old but it was Ganesh Chaturthi visarjan day in Mumbai, the biggest festival in the city when Ganesh idols are immersed in the sea. We had gone to Chowpatty to our Marina Mansion home, now occupied by my father's elder brother, for Ganesh puja. Amidst the puja chanting, everyone was listening to the radio commentary. When the winning stroke was hit, the entire neighbourhood came on to the streets to burst crackers and I was lifted on the shoulders of my uncle as we immersed the idol of the Elephant God in the sea. I felt like the most important six-year-old in Mumbai that evening.

When the players returned a few days later, they got the biggest welcome ever received by an Indian team. Indira Gandhi, not one to miss out on a photo-op to be part of the jubilant national mood, hosted a tea for the players in Delhi. Then a special flight took them to Mumbai. The road from Mumbai airport to the CCI was a sea of people – a special motorcade in open-top Buicks had been organized and the players got a first taste of the kind of adulation that would soon become the norm every time India won a major series. 'We were always recognized as Test players; after 1971 we were not just heroes but superheroes,' recalls Wadekar. Cricketers soon had their faces on ice cream sticks and soft drink bottle caps, an early sign of the future commercial value of the sport.

At the CCI, a special function was held to honour the players. In his speech, Merchant, the man who had almost finished my father's career, was effusive in his praise. 'Dilip Sardesai should be seen as the Renaissance man of Indian cricket.' My father could only smile contentedly. He had proved his point. He had taken sweet revenge in the best possible way for any cricketer – with the bat.

~

Dilip retired after the 1972–73 season, barely a year after the glories of 1971. He was only thirty-three years old, relatively young in cricketing terms. He had hoped to retire in a blaze of glory after his last series against the visiting English side but it wasn't to be. 'I guess the mind was willing but the body wasn't,' he would later tell me. Perhaps having shown the world what he was capable of, there was little motivation to continue. To put it in context, Sachin Tendulkar retired at the age of forty, and most modern-day players go into their late thirties before calling it a day. But today's cricketers are also far fitter and have much greater monetary incentive to stay on in the sport. Dilip had no such drive left. 'If there was the kind of money in the sport then that there is now, I would have kept playing but in the 1970s, you couldn't make a professional career out of the game so I decided to focus on building a life after cricket,' he said.

But the afterlife didn't quite go according to the script. Having worked in ACC and the Vissanji group of industries, my father decided to try and set up his own business in commodity trading using the 'contacts' he had built over the years. It was a big mistake.

He made poor business decisions, chose the wrong people as business partners, eventually found himself heavily in debt and even faced a foreign exchange violation case from which he was later discharged. 'I guess I trusted people easily but didn't realize that business isn't like a cricket match where you play according to the rules,' he lamented. His health deteriorated and after he suffered from renal failure in 2004 he had to undergo dialysis over a prolonged period.

And yet his passion for cricket was undimmed. Early in the morning you would find him at the CCI with his scrambled-eggs-and-toast breakfast, talking cricket with fellow club members. On weekends, he would be scouring Mumbai's maidans, watching local matches and scouting for young talent. He had an eye for the right stroke like a music maestro has for the perfect note. As a selector, he once took a night train to Ahmedabad to attend a meeting because he was told that a player he was fond of would be dropped by the other selectors. 'Over my dead body,' he said with characteristic firmness.

He could be blunt with his criticism but when he saw a talented youngster, he would express his delight with childlike enthusiasm. I recall him calling me up excitedly when he first saw teenage Rohit Sharma bat. 'Lovely strokeplayer, now only if he can tighten his technique, he will play for India one day,' he told me. Technique was almost an obsession for him, which is why he couldn't quite understand the evolving format of the game which placed a premium on hitting the ball into the air. 'I only hit one six in my Test career because I was taught that if you keep the ball along the ground then no one can get you out, and the longer you bat the more runs you will score,' he said.

He also coached the Mumbai under-22 team one summer in the mid-1980s. I was part of the training camp but my father was dismissive of my ability. 'You just don't have it in you to make it,' he said with typical candour and no thought of dynastic succession. Sanjay Manjrekar, then a budding young cricketer, was also one of his trainees. For hours, Dilip shared his technical insights with Manjrekar, convinced he was the next champion batsman to emerge from Mumbai. Maybe it was his way of passing on the baton; after all, Sanjay's father Vijay had guided him all those years ago when he was finding his feet in the game.

Mumbai cricket was blessed with this relay race in the art of batsmanship, from Merchant to Gavaskar to Tendulkar with the likes of Dilip playing their bit roles. He considered playing for Mumbai almost as important as donning the India cap. 'When I played for Mumbai, we never lost,' he would tell anyone who cared to listen. Indeed, in thirteen years of domestic cricket, he was never once on the losing side, which is some kind of a record. His attitude to Mumbai cricket was typified by a word that has become part of the city's cricketing folklore, 'khadoos'. Literally translated, it means a stubborn determination to succeed. In cricketing terms, it means a refusal to give up, to bat for long hours, to win at all costs.

The wins were always achieved with an infectious smile. This was a generation of quasi-amateur cricketers who never had computers or video replays to guide them, didn't really bother about statistics, and in Dilip's case at least didn't fuss too much over diet or fitness. What they had though was a lot of fun, and yes, plenty of food and drink (like the stereotypical Goan lazing in a shack, Sardesai loved his beer). My father shared a delightful story that reflects the approach of the cricketers of the 1960s to food and fitness. A five-day Test match in those days would have a rest day. During a match in Delhi in the mid 1960s, my father and another foodie cricketer Hanumant Singh decided to test their appetite on the off day. They ventured to Moti Mahal in Old Delhi for a tandoori chicken competition. I'm not sure who won the battle to devour the maximum chicken legs but the fact is that both star batsmen struggled with a stomach upset the next morning and couldn't take the field. Can you imagine any of today's super-fit, 'zero carb' diet cricketers ever attempting such food fiestas in the middle of a game?

This relatively casual approach to fitness also showed up in fielding, an area of the game that got little attention in Indian cricket at the time. Never a great athlete and prone to putting on weight, Dilip self-confessedly wasn't a great fielder. Once, in a Test match in Adelaide in 1967, he was chasing a ball and the batsmen were threatening to run 5 runs when my father deliberately kicked the ball over the boundary so that only four could be counted. It was a typically street-smart way of playing the game but as Bishan Singh Bedi, another contemporary who wasn't too fussy about fielding, recalls, Dilip 'had all of us on the ground rolling in laughter'.

It was this ability to enjoy the game without expecting any instant gratification and a down-to-earth humility that perhaps sets the cricketers of that generation apart. I don't think my father ever wore a branded watch; he preferred his Kolhapuri chappals and bush shirt to any fancy clothes, and enjoyed crab, clams and prawn curry rice at his favourite Anant Ashram restaurant in a pokey little central Mumbai lane to any five-star meal. He was happiest cracking jokes in a cricket dressing room and once blushed at a school function when he was introduced as a 'legend'. 'I just consider myself lucky that I played for India and maybe had more fun off the field than on it,' he told the audience.

To draw a parallel, Hindi cinema in the 1950s and 1960s was also an age of innocence, of romancing in the hills and singing in the rains, of the idealism of a Raj Kapoor, the mischief of a Dev Anand and Shammi Kapoor and the intensity of a Dilip Kumar. Cricket was a little bit of it all and Dilip in his own way was a product of quieter, gentler times. When he passed away in 2007, sociologist Shiv Visvanathan paid him one of the best tributes. In an article titled 'Sardesai was India before Hell Broke Loose', he writes: 'Sardesai represented a certain naivete which Hrishikesh Mukherjee's films portrayed – of an India of PSUs and Ambassador cars. Remember at that time the colour was white, cricketers were not the men in blue. There was a starched sense of morality to Sardesai. His was a nationalism of a beautiful kind, one that you could trust and respect.'

I don't think my father would be swayed by such wonderful accolades. He was content with having earned the chance to play a sport which gave him an identity he could scarcely have imagined as a young boy in Margao. As a newspaper headline put it succinctly the day after he died: 'Dilip Sardesai: Goan spirit, Mumbai heart, India's soul.'

2

Mansur Ali Khan Pataudi

Nawab of the Republic

Two paper boats bobbed in a clear, still pool in the heart of Lutyens'
Delhi. A crowd of venerable citizens – jurists, ministers, bureaucrats
and editors – crowded around it cheering their floating progress
like a horde of eighteen-year-olds. In the power-soaked cocoon of
Delhi's most exclusive diplomatic enclave, grown men and women
had reverted to hooting-cheering adolescents.

This faux Oxford and Cambridge boat race had come alive under
the hot Indian summer sky at a venue surrounded by security guards
and liveried domestic staff. This was the residence of the British
high commissioner and the top diplomat was hosting the annual
Oxford–Cambridge Society dinner in the mid 1990s; the Raj may
have been long gone but the Oxbridge badge was still a ticket into
charmed circles.

As the grandees cheered and applauded, a hush suddenly descended
over the gathering. 'Look, Tiger is here,' an awestruck guest pointed
out. In the raucous party of seemingly adolescent VVIPs, the Nawab
of Pataudi Mansur Ali Khan and his begum Sharmila Tagore had
walked in with a regal air. Order was restored as the host rushed
to greet the prized couple and everyone forgot about the race in the

swimming pool. Tiger retreated quietly into a corner with his drink and a few friends; Sharmila chatted obligingly to fans, and the party resumed, this time with a little more dignity. Tiger was in the room and the jungle needed to come to order.

Tiger had retired from Test cricket in 1975. If the aura was still intact two decades after his retirement, it is a testimony to his legacy in the game. 'He was a hundred years ahead of anyone else in Indian cricket,' former India captain Bishan Singh Bedi tells me. 'When he walked on the field, he oozed class and leadership,' another spinning great Erapalli Prasanna remarks. 'When you think of Indian cricket in the 1960s, you only think of Tiger,' is how cricketing genius Gundappa Viswanath describes his contribution.

Yajurvindra Singh, a former Indian cricketer who idolized Tiger, recounts how even after retirement when Tiger travelled by train, everyone in his compartment wanted to catch a glimpse of Nawab saab. Unmindful of the attention, the star would sit with his whiskey glass and hum a ghazal. 'When we stopped at a station, Tiger's personal attendant took his tiffin to the station kitchen to get the food warmed up. The stationmaster ensured that the train waited at the platform till the former India captain's food was heated. Such was his appeal,' remembers Singh.

Tiger, the son of the eighth Nawab of Pataudi, Iftikhar Ali Khan, and the Begum of Bhopal, was born with a silver spoon. Pataudi was a tiny principality on the Delhi–Haryana border while Bhopal was an infinitely larger and wealthier princely state.

The year was 1941, and Mahatma Gandhi was about to sound the bugle of the Quit India Movement. But the young Tiger was far removed from the bustle and excitement of the freedom struggle. In his autobiography *Tiger's Tale* written in 1967, Tiger says, 'I grew up in the state of Pataudi in what might loosely be described as a palace. Our home contained some 150 rooms and also boasted extensive grounds, stables and garages. The family must have employed well over a hundred servants at the time, seven or eight of whom were my own personal attendants.'

Cricket was an intrinsic part of Tiger's younger years. The Indian princes had a rather chequered relationship with the sport, and it was the Maharaja of Patiala Bhupinder Singh who was the original patron of cricket in the country. As mentioned in the Introduction, he was even chosen (some would say 'imposed') as captain of the Indian team on its first Test tour to England in 1932 before dropping out at the last minute on health grounds. More controversial was the Maharaja of Vizianagaram, or 'Vizzy', who was named captain of the Indian team for the 1936 tour of England despite his limited cricket ability. There were allegations that he had 'bought' his way to the captaincy. The 1936 tour was the scene of the first big conflict in Indian cricket, with the team's star player Lala Amarnath, as mentioned earlier, being sent home by Vizzy on 'disciplinary' grounds.

The house of Pataudi, though, could claim a more distinguished cricket lineage – the only other princely family with similar pedigree were the Nawanagars of Saurashtra which had produced the first two cricket wizards from the east, Ranjitsinhji and Duleepsinhji. Like Ranji and Duleep, Iftikhar Pataudi played for England and was good enough to score a century on debut for England in 1932. He also captained India in 1946, the first and only cricketer to play for both countries. He was not just a fine cricketer but also a man of principle. Refusing to concur with the controversial 'Bodyline' tactics of the English captain Douglas Jardine on the 1932–33 tour of Australia, where the English fast bowlers relentlessly targeted the Australians, he was dropped from the team. He would later remark caustically, 'I am told Jardine has good points. In the three months on tour, I am yet to see them.'

Iftikhar, however, had limited influence on his son's cricket. 'I can't really remember watching him bat but he was probably more technically correct than I was,' Tiger would later tell me. He did recall one incident that stuck in his mind. 'I was eight or nine years old and fielding in a match at cover with my father at extra cover. The ball skied in my direction and I was getting ready to take a catch. Suddenly I saw two large hands pop up over my head. My father took the catch and turned to me, and simply said, "Sorry, my son, I can't trust you at your age."'

On 5 January 1952, Tiger was celebrating his eleventh birthday with his three sisters when his mother entered the room with a terse message: 'Your father is dead.' Iftikhar had died from a heart attack during a polo match, while in the saddle. He was just forty-one. 'Tiger never celebrated his birthday after that,' Sharmila Tagore tells me. Ironically, many years later, his family persuaded him to celebrate his seventieth birthday. It would turn out to be his last. 'The servants later told me that we should never have celebrated, it brought only bad luck,' says Sharmila.

Tragedy would somehow always lurk uneasily around the corner throughout Tiger's life on and off the field. Each time, though, he would stick it out till sunshine burst through the gloom – a reflection of the man's courage and determination to never allow personal misfortune to deflect him from pursuing his dream of following in his father's footsteps and playing cricket for India. But there was one big difference – his father had been raised as a child of the Raj and had cut his cricketing flannels playing for England; the son would become a nawab of republican independent India.

~

Tiger spent his formative cricketing years almost entirely in England. While Indian cricket in the 1950s was slowly beginning to find its feet with the rise of the urban middle class in the maidans of Mumbai, the young Tiger was being educated in the sheltered world of Winchester College. His royal roots were his calling card.

When his father completed his Winchester application form, to the column 'Other aptitudes?', the simple answer he gave was 'My son'. And yet it was soon apparent that Pataudi junior was a special, precocious talent. By 1957, when he was sixteen, he had broken all the school batting records and made a county debut for Sussex. 'He was a school prodigy,' says Abbas Ali Baig, the former Indian Test cricketer who played with Tiger at Oxford. 'Even though he was coached in England, his batting wasn't typically English. He didn't have the classical defensive technique, loved to hit the lofted shot, and had wonderful hand–eye coordination. Above all else, he was quite simply a breathtaking fielder.'

The final remark is significant. The early princes who played cricket, including the great Ranji, were outstanding batsmen but were not known for their fielding skills. In the Brahminical worldview, fielding was seen as a lower-caste occupation. Indian cricket's heroes in the 1940s and 1950s, from Vijay Merchant to Vijay Hazare, were all great defensive batsmen who could bat for long hours but Tiger would redefine the skill set by being an aggressive batsman who fielded in the outfield like a 'tiger on the prowl'. 'I guess I was just a good athlete,' he told me once in an interview. 'I loved any and every sport, be it cricket, hockey, racquets, billiards. All I needed was a moving ball to hit.'

In 1959, Tiger was awarded the title of 'The Most Promising Young Cricketer of the Year'. A year later, he followed the family tradition by going to Balliol College at Oxford. His academic subjects were meant to be languages, including Arabic and French, but his real interest was the cricket pitch. Like his father, he scored a century in his very first year in the all-important game against Cambridge. This was a period when Oxbridge cricket still showcased some of the best talent in the game.

When I went to Oxford in 1986 the universities had ceased to be a nursery for cricket. When someone tells me now, 'Wow, you are an Oxford Blue, that's something to cherish,' my honest answer is, 'The Oxford University I went to isn't the same place for cricket that it was in the Tiger era. It's easier to play for Oxford now than it is for Bombay University.' He and Baig were in fact the last two Indians to play Test cricket after going to Oxford. Imran Khan would be the last Pakistani to do so in the early 1970s.

By 1961, Tiger was captain of the Oxford cricket team and its star batsman. He scored centuries against the major county sides and was on the verge of breaking his father's record for the most runs in a season. Like Pataudi senior, he seemed destined for greatness. But fate would change Tiger's life yet another time. On 1 July 1961, after a long day in the field against Sussex in the sleepy coastal town of Brighton, Tiger decided to hitch a ride in a Morris 1000 being driven by wicketkeeper Robin Walters. The rest of the Oxford players got into a minivan. Barely had Tiger sat in the front seat when a big car pulled into their path and hit them straight on.

Baig, who was in the minivan, recalls, 'We saw Tiger get out of the car holding his right eye, which was bleeding slightly. It didn't seem like a major accident and when we took him to hospital we thought he would soon be discharged.' But it wasn't so simple. A splinter from the windscreen had entered his eye and surgery would be required. The pupil of the eye was stitched up, leaving him practically without vision in his right eye. 'I guess the initial feeling was that Tiger would struggle to play cricket again, especially because in the first few months he could barely locate the line of the ball since he would see two of everything,' says Baig.

This is how Tiger himself described the trauma of losing an eye. 'As any boxer who has had one eye closed by the blows of the opponent will tell you, it causes a loss of judgement and distances. For example, when trying to light a cigarette, I found I was missing the end of it by a quarter of an inch. I would pour water from a jug straight onto the table instead of the glass,' he wrote in *Tiger's Tale*.

But with the help of family and friends, Tiger worked hard at overcoming his disability. He spent hours at the net, driven by his sheer passion for the game, changing his stance and even adjusting his style to meet the ball. In a quite heroic feat, less than six months after the accident, in December 1961, Tiger made his debut for India against England in Delhi, and two Tests later scored his first Test century in Chennai. As an example of triumph over adversity, this must rank as one of the greatest sporting achievements of all time – a cricketer who had lost vision in one eye making the necessary adjustments to overcome his disability within a few months.

Tiger was typically modest about it when he wrote: 'Since my accident to my right eye at the age of twenty-one I have had to compromise with my ambition to become a truly great batsman. I have concentrated instead on trying to make myself a useful one, and a better fielder than my father was.'

I remember asking my father, the Test cricketer Dilip Sardesai and a contemporary of Tiger, just how good he was as a cricketer. Pataudi, after all, ended his Test career with an average in the mid-30s, hardly a marker of greatness. 'Never forget he played with one eye and still scored runs, just think how good he would have been with both eyes,' was my father's straightforward response. That he was touched by genius is underscored by a story my father tells me of what many consider Tiger's finest innings – a battling 75 at Melbourne in 1967. 'It was a green wicket against a good pace attack. He had injured his leg and we were 25 for 5. Tiger didn't even have his own bat so he just picked up a bat that was lying around in the dressing room and with one leg and one eye hit the Australian bowlers all over the stadium!' said my father with infectious enthusiasm.

I ask Sharmila whether her husband spoke often of the accident. 'No, that was a taboo subject, he just did not like to talk about it. Nor was there any trace of self-pity. I just think the accident made him even stronger in his commitment to cricket,' she answers. We can, of course, have an endless debate on 'what if' Tiger Pataudi had not met with an accident. But life has a strange way of compensating for misfortune in the unlikeliest of circumstances. Tiger overcame a calamity and lived to tell the tale, and his roller-coaster journey was about to see another twist. Cricket was about to deal Tiger a bouncer that would change his life and Indian cricket forever.

~

In the history books, India's 1962 tour of the West Indies will go down as an unmitigated disaster. Facing arguably the best team in the world, the young Indian side – nearly half of the sixteen-member squad were in their early twenties – was pummelled into the ground by the West Indians led by the cricketing knight Sir Frank Worrell. The lead bowlers were the fearsome pace duo of Wes Hall and Charlie Griffith.

The Indian team was battered 5-0 in the series. 'It was not even David vs Goliath, it was bakras [sheep] versus wolves,' my father would later tell me. Like him, Tiger was also playing his first overseas series for India. Tiger was the vice captain of the team and was expected to be a faithful understudy to Nari Contractor, then well established as the undisputed leader and a dogged opening batsman.

Contractor belonged to the small Parsee community, which had contributed immensely to Indian cricket in its early years, providing the sport with talent, financial muscle and a generosity of spirit. The 1962 side, in fact, had four Parsees in the team – Contractor, Farokh Engineer, Rusi Surti and Polly Umrigar – a remarkable achievement considering the Parsee population was just 1.3 lakh in the 1960s. This has never been replicated – no Parsee has represented India since Engineer's last Test in 1975. The large Parsee presence, my father would always point out, 'ensured we were never short of humour over a long four-month tour'.

But on 16 March 1962 in the match against Barbados, there was no time for Parsee jokes. As mentioned in the previous chapter, that was the day Contractor was hit on the head with a sickening bouncer from Griffith, then the fastest in the world.

Contractor remembers the dark day well. 'It was the period just before lunch when it is never easy to concentrate. I faced ten balls from Griffith. From the other end, the non-striker Rusi Surti shouted, "Skipper, be careful, this man is chucking the ball." I told him to tell the umpire instead of disturbing me. Just before Griffith bowled the eleventh ball, the area behind the bowler's arm went black because someone in the pavilion opened a window in a dark room. In those days, we didn't have a proper sightscreen to help us in sighting the ball better. To be honest, I just didn't see that eleventh ball which hit me on the head.' Contractor sank to the ground.

'It was frightening, we heard a thud-like noise, almost like someone has been knocked out in a boxing match,' says Erapalli Prasanna who was, like Tiger, then just a twenty-one-year-old playing his first series. As players from both sides rushed to help him, Contractor got up slowly, cursing himself for losing sight of the ball. But on reaching the dressing room, it was clear that the damage was grave; he was bleeding from the ears and nose. He was rushed to hospital and subjected to an emergency operation as several players from the same blood group volunteered to give blood. Among them was twelfth man Chandu Borde, the first to rush to Contractor. 'My hands were shaking when I first lifted Nari. We didn't have any team doctor with us or any medical support like you have today. We just took Nari to the nearest hospital which didn't even have a proper neurosurgeon. But time was running out, so the one surgeon at the hospital, a Dr Ford, went ahead and did the best he could and saved Nari's life,' remembers Borde.

'There was an eerie silence in the dressing room,' recalls Prasanna. 'Some of us were in tears, others too dazed to even say anything. Tiger, who was lined up to bat, sat in a corner quietly. He seemed more composed than the rest of us, and if he was fearful, he didn't show it.'

Contractor survived but would never play for the country again. It was left to Ghulam Ahmed, the team manager, to convey the news to Tiger. 'It is obvious that Nari cannot play on this tour, so it is now for you to lead the side.'

At twenty-one years and seventy-seven days old, Tiger became India's youngest ever captain. Fate had robbed him of an eye; now captaincy had been thrust on him in the midst of another catastrophe. The Tiger era had begun, and it would redefine Indian cricket.

~

Captaining India is arguably the secondmost important and difficult job in the country after that of the resident of 7 Lok Kalyan Marg. But the position of the India captain, much coveted like the prime ministership, can also be a crown of thorns. In the 1930s, the unwritten rule was that only royalty was 'fit' enough to captain India. When India first toured England in 1932, the captain who replaced the original skipper the Maharaja of Patiala was the Maharaja of Porbandar, whose cricketing skills were limited. He scored just two runs on the tour, less than the number of Rolls-Royces in his garage! Fortunately, at the last moment, wiser counsel prevailed and the team's finest player at the time C.K. Nayudu eventually had the distinction of leading India in its first Test at Lord's. In 1936, the Maharaja of Vizianagaram 'plotted' his way to captaincy. In 1946, Vijay Merchant, easily the best batsman in the country, was bypassed and Pataudi senior made the captain – a prince yet again preferred to a commoner.

In the 1950s, high intrigue marked the choice of captain. Lala Amarnath and Vijay Hazare rotated the post between them in the early 1950s. 'A captain was decided purely by the politics of the board and the whims of the selectors. If Hazare was the choice of the West Zone and South Zone, Amarnath was the appointee of the North Zone and East Zone,' says Madhav Apte, who played for India in 1952–53. Apte remembers how Amarnath was captaining the Indian team against Pakistan when the news was 'leaked' that Hazare would be the captain for the next tour to the West Indies. 'At an official dinner at the end of the fourth Test against Pakistan, Amarnath let the selectors and the board know what he thought of them with some choice abuse in Punjabi!' says Apte with a laugh. Ironically, Amarnath himself was the chief selector in 1958–59 when the visiting West Indians were confronted inexplicably with four different Indian captains over five Tests. 'It was like a lottery,' says Borde, who made his debut in the series.

The fourth Test in Chennai was the most bizarre. Polly Umrigar was appointed the captain and even garlanded at a civic reception on the evening before the game only to resign a few hours later. 'I was in the adjoining room and through the keyhole I saw Umrigar crying in front of the selectors and board officials because they would not give him the team of his choice. Even the garland given to him at the reception was taken away,' recalls Borde. At midnight, the despairing officials went to the room of the team's seniormost player, Vinoo Mankad, and pleaded with him to become captain. Mankad went for the toss the next morning only to develop a rash while fielding. He was substituted by G.S. Ramchand, who then got hit on the head while batting, with Hemu Adhikari stepping in as a replacement. 'Not only did we have four captains in series, we had four captains in one game – a world record,' says Borde with a laugh. The best of India's cricketers had been defeated by the machinations of cricket board politics, the kind that would make electoral politics appear as the stuff of kindergarten.

Which is why the young nawab was battling fate and history when he took over the top job. 'Captaincy was the making of Tiger,' the late Raj Singh Dungarpur, a great friend of Tiger's, once told me. But it wasn't easy. As a twenty-one-year-old, he had to first earn the respect of the seniors in the side. While players like Manjrekar and Umrigar were helpful, it wasn't a smooth ride. The fact that Tiger's personality was that of a slightly aloof introvert didn't help. 'In his first few years as captain, Tiger was a little tentative; it took him a little while to find his feet and establish his leadership credentials,' Baig tells me.

The 1964 home series against Australia was a turning point. He hadn't scored runs leading up to the Tests, and there were whispers about the captain's sacking. Tiger ended the speculation in emphatic fashion, scoring a century in the first Test and then leading India to a stunning victory in the second Test in Mumbai. 'That win over Australia was the most satisfying and possibly a decisive moment. I had proved to the team and to myself that I could lead,' said Tiger about the moment.

Through his career, Tiger would captain India in 40 of the 46 matches he played for the country. It was almost as if being captain was his prerogative. Of these, India won only 9 while registering 19 losses, hardly a record to be proud of. But statistics don't tell the true story of what Tiger's leadership meant for Indian cricket.

It was during the 1960s that the romantic illusions spun by the fight for independence were beginning to wear thin. The battle for linguistic states in several parts of the country were pitting communities against each other, the middle castes were leading agrarian revolts, and the urban youth was being drawn towards Naxalism. Nehru's prime ministership had weakened after the China debacle and his death in 1964 would leave a political vacuum. Cricket, too, mirrored this sense of upheaval and conflict, and was in search of a calming influence. Tiger would provide the glue to hold Indian cricket together. 'Make no mistake, it was Tiger who made us feel that we were playing for India as a team. Not Maharashtrians or Tamilians or Hyderabadis, not Hindus, Muslims, Sikhs, but Indians first and last,' says Bedi, who made his Test debut in 1966–67 under his captaincy.

The parallels with India's first prime minister are uncanny. Tiger was a Nehruvian democrat in outlook, striving to bring a measure of meritocracy to a feudal cricketing society. Tiger and Jawaharlal were both charismatic anglicized aristocrats who grew up in the sheltered umbrella of colonial privilege and were tutored in the best liberal traditions of Oxbridge. Yet their elite upbringing did not prevent them from discovering and celebrating their Indian roots – if the fiery passion of the freedom movement saw Nehru give up his cosseted lifestyle, then the excitement of cricketing achievement led Tiger to clasp the democratic spirit of the times. Merit and equality became the signature tune of Tiger's captaincy as Indian cricket underwent a gradual transformation.

A new generation of mainly middle-class Indian cricketers now had a leader they could trust and respect. Prasanna, whose bowling blossomed under Tiger's leadership, says that the players respected their captain because he fought for their interests. He recalls how Tiger was once incensed that the board hadn't paid the players their match fees on time. 'We were paid only Rs 250 a Test match at the time. Tiger didn't need the money so when Mr Chinnaswamy [then board treasurer] came to distribute the cheques, Tiger turned around and told him, "Please give my money to the cobbler who mends our shoes, he needs it more." He said it without raising his voice but the message was loud and clear,' remembers Prasanna.

On the field, too, Tiger was a man of few words. 'You wouldn't hear him shout and scream ever on the field, but he knew what he wanted from his players and expected us to deliver,' says Bedi. Both Bedi and Prasanna were key figures along with S. Venkataraghavan and Chandrasekhar, making up the spin quartet that would bring great success to India in the 1970s. 'The seeds of that revolution were sown by Tiger. He was a captain who always wanted to win and realized quickly that spin was the way to win matches,' says Prasanna.

This even meant jettisoning the idea of having a proven fast bowler in the team. In 1967, India opened the bowling with Budhi Kunderan, originally in the side as a wicketkeeper. The spin attack was boosted by sharp close-in fielding, another Tiger contribution. 'I remember he insisted on picking Eknath Solkar in the team only because he wanted young cricketers who would field well,' Bedi points out.

Ironically, Tiger was devoured by the revolution he sparked. In 1970, he was stripped of his captaincy by the casting vote of the chairman of selectors Vijay Merchant, and, as mentioned earlier, replaced by a middle-class 'commoner' from Mumbai's Shivaji Park, Ajit Wadekar. Many saw this as Merchant's 'revenge' for being bypassed as captain by Iftikhar Pataudi on the 1946 tour of England. Maybe it was part of the inevitable change every cricket team must endure – Tiger, after all, had been captain for almost a decade then. Merchant's gamble paid off. As we've seen earlier, in 1971, India scored breakthrough overseas wins over West Indies and England under Wadekar's leadership. 'The captain may have been Wadekar but this was Tiger's team. He had given us the self-belief to win. I feel sad that he isn't given enough credit for 1971,' says Bedi.

Tiger would make one last comeback as captain in 1974–75

against the West Indies. Raj Singh Dungarpur, then in the selection committee, had pushed Tiger to come out of near-retirement to lead the side. 'We needed inspiration to play a strong side, which only Tiger could provide,' Dungarpur, himself from the Rajasthan royal family, would later tell me. Maybe Dungarpur, like a section of the Indian cricket establishment, was still influenced by the Tiger cult and the unshaken belief that the nawab had a Midas touch.

With slowing reflexes, Tiger's batting had fallen away and he was struggling with his eyesight. But his courage was never in doubt even when pitted against the searing pace of the West Indians. 'He could have easily refused to play,' said Dungarpur, 'but Tiger was too proud an individual to back out from a fight.' He could still summon the odd stroke of inventive leadership, as he proved while enabling India to come back from a 2-0 deficit to level the series, before losing the last game in Mumbai to Clive Lloyd's imperious batting. The third Test in Kolkata is a case in point. On the last day, West Indies needed a hundred-odd runs to win the game with 8 wickets in hand. 'Tiger knocked at my door around 11 p.m. the night before and told me, "Look, the wicket is turning. Don't worry about the runs. I want you and Chandra to get me the wickets,"' recalls Prasanna. The next morning, the West Indians attacked Chandrasekhar and hit him for a few boundaries. Tiger was unfazed, persisting with his match-winning bowler and eventually winning the game. 'Only Tiger could have pulled that win off,' believes Prasanna to this day.

That was Tiger's last major contribution on the cricket field. He was, in a sense, ending his career like he had begun it – attempting to put Indian cricket on the world map. Cricket writer Suresh Menon puts it well: 'Tiger led the Self-Respect Movement in Indian cricket that gave the players dignity, confidence and the ability to look the world in the eye.' It's a legacy that would endure beyond the boundary.

The Tiger story cannot be complete without referring to his most durable partner in life, Sharmila Tagore. On screen, Sharmila forged a hit pairing with stars like Rajesh Khanna and Dharmendra. But it was her real-life marriage to Tiger that is the stuff of Bollywood dreams. I meet the actor at her home in the upscale south Delhi colony Vasant Vihar. She recalls: 'I met Tiger in December 1963 in Kolkata. We had gone to a party at the invitation of [Test cricketer M.L.] Jaisimha because we were all fans of his. We used to listen to the radio commentary and were always on the hunt for players' autographs. And there was Tiger in a corner wearing a Sussex sweater. I wouldn't say it was a case of love at first sight, but I did find him different. He was gracious and soft-spoken, and we agreed to keep in touch. And we did!'

Sharmila came from the high-class bhadralok family of the country's poet laureate Rabindranath Tagore. She played her first movie role at the age of thirteen in the Satyajit Ray classic *Apur Sansar* and then achieved instant stardom in Hindi cinema with *Kashmir Ki Kali* in 1964. The courtship lasted a few years before they married in 1968. Says Sharmila, 'I guess we just enjoyed each other's company. We would go out for a drive, or for a movie or dinner, nothing extravagant. And yes, we didn't have to worry about any TV cameras chasing us like they do today.'

And yet, while today it is not unusual to have a cricket–cinema celebrity match-up, in the 1960s, the Tiger–Sharmila love affair was unique. Two top stars in their respective fields – one a Muslim, the other a Hindu – with scarcely a hint of tension or competitiveness. They were temperamentally very different too; he was more laid-back and easy-going, she more assertive and belligerent. The secret of their marital success, Sharmila says, was the space they gave each other to pursue their dreams. 'Tiger would sometimes drop in on a film set, and I would sneak away and go and watch him play. We enjoyed each other's success and not once did he tell me to stop doing films after marriage.' In fact, some of Sharmila's biggest hits, including epic films like *Aradhana* and *Mausam*, would come post-marriage.

A liberal and progressive education shaped their worldview. Sharmila recalls how early in their relationship *Filmfare* magazine carried a cover photo of the actor in a bikini that sparked a furore. 'He was playing for Sussex and I was shooting for *An Evening in Paris* in Europe. I was very agitated when he sent me a telegram that read, *Relax! You could only be looking very nice!* His words were enough to calm me down.'

The relationship affected Tiger's cricket – nearly – only once. The Indian team was set to go to Australia and New Zealand for a five-month tour in 1967–68. 'Tiger didn't want to be away from me for that long and said he was pulling out of the tour. I then had board officials and the team manager come to my house to ask me to persuade Tiger to change his mind, which I did!' says Sharmila with a laugh.

That Tiger's contemporary Jaisimha played Cupid in the relationship is perhaps appropriate. Pat and Jai, as the duo was called, were Indian cricket's Jodi Number One in the 1960s, at least as far as female following went. They were, in the words of Jaisimha's wife Jayanthi, 'soulmates who had a unique chemistry, almost as if this was a bond from a previous birth'. At a time when most Indian players came from solid middle-class backgrounds, Pat and Jai were symbols of a more affluent social class (Jaisimha's father ran a successful construction company in Hyderabad). Both had similar tastes; they liked whiskey, cigarettes and, yes, the attention of women. 'Jai was the extrovert, Tiger much quieter and more self-contained, but they were both real charmers,' Jayanthi reminisces.

It was Jaisimha who convinced Tiger to move from Delhi to Hyderabad to play in the Ranji Trophy for the erstwhile Nizam state in the mid 1960s. The more relaxed pace of life in Hyderabad suited Tiger; when he was not playing cricket, he could pursue his other great passion, shikaar, or simply get away to be with his sister who lived in the city. Tiger, in fact, was happy to play under Jaisimha's leadership for Hyderabad even though he was India captain at the time. Baig, who was part of a Hyderabad side that once had half a dozen Test players, says that the Deccan sojourn made Tiger 'one of the boys' and not the shy, aloof nawab he had first encountered in Oxford. 'We would mostly travel by second class in trains for domestic matches and Tiger could be great fun. He would sometimes bring his tabla or harmonium, would sing "Mera lal dupatta malmal ka", or even do the famous "hiran" dance, a bit like an item number of today.' Jayanthi says, 'I taught Tiger to eat with his hands. At home, he wasn't Nawab saab, he was always Pat.'

This transition from feudal prince to honorary Hyderabadi reflects how Tiger could adjust to a universe that had little in common with his early years in Winchester or Oxford. If Allahabad and UP's dusty lanes were where Jawaharlal Nehru broke the shackles of his Oxbridge elitism, it was in the long train journeys across the Deccan that perhaps Tiger discovered the 'real' India. Or more accurately his friends and peers discovered an individual who was a perfect blend of the East and the West, someone who once at a graduation lecture at Winchester spoke in English, Urdu and Latin. He could go pheasant shooting in England and have a drink with his Oxford mates in a pub, but he could also play the tabla and join sarod maestro Amjad Ali Khan in a jugalbandi at home. 'I remember we had gone to a sarod recital in Bhopal once when it began to rain. We all rushed indoors and Tiger and Amjad just entertained us through the night with their music. It was a real jam session,' says Sharmila.

Saif Ali Khan, his actor son, recalls how schoolmates in boarding school in England were enamoured with the idea that his father was a real-life prince. 'When he first dropped me off in school, my father was driving a vintage Rolls-Royce so everyone was very excited. But the next time he came visiting, he drove in a Morris Minor with a leaking radiator. It just didn't matter to him what car he drove, he had a kind of quiet confidence that went beyond the superficial,' says Saif.

And while he was blessed with typically understated British

humour, he could just as easily switch personas to a more desi-style prankster. Viswanath relates a story of how Tiger once gave him the biggest fright of his life. 'We had been invited by Tiger to his estate in Bhopal on the rest day of a match. Suddenly we heard gun shots and a band of dacoits entered our room. They told us that they had shot Prasanna dead and we were next. I was tied to a tree and was in tears when suddenly Tiger appeared on the scene laughing. The "dacoits" were his staff and the whole episode had been stage-managed!' On another occasion, he invited team wicketkeeper Farokh Engineer to 'come and see me at my large white marbled home in Kolkata in the evening'. An unaware Engineer reached and kept knocking at the historic Victoria Memorial gate! 'I guess I got him that day,' said Tiger with a laugh.

But what was no laughing matter for Tiger was the prospect of a long flight. He was terrified of air travel. 'I remember Jai and Pat would tank up with alcohol before taking off. He would much rather take a train,' Jayanthi tells me. Clearly the man who was a Tiger on the cricket field was a nervous pussycat in the air!

~

In 1969, Prime Minister Indira Gandhi announced the abolition of royal titles and privy purses (annual payments made by the government to princely families), and Parliament formally passed the law two years later. The Nawab of Pataudi was now Mansur Ali Khan. He had lost his captaincy in 1970, now even his princely title and privileges were gone. In 1971, Pataudi contested the elections as a candidate of the Vishal Haryana Party from Gurgaon and lost his deposit as Indira Gandhi's 'garibi hatao' wave swept the country. 'Tiger was angry with the way in which the privy purses issue was handled by the government; he saw it as a betrayal of the promises made in 1947. But it was Amma [his mother] who goaded him into contesting the election,' says Sharmila.

Tiger would stand for election once more. In 1991, he was the

Congress candidate from Bhopal on the advice of his 'good friend' Rajiv Gandhi. He would lose again. Admits Sharmila, 'I guess he wasn't cut out for politics. He told me, "How do I lie and make false promises to the voter that I know I cannot keep?"' For a man known to play by the rules on the cricket field – Tiger had the reputation of walking when out without waiting for an umpire's decision – the wheeling and dealing of politics did not suit his character.

As India and Indian cricket began to rapidly transform, Tiger perhaps found himself out of sync with the new aggressive, commerce-driven mindset of cricket as big business. 'He may have been a nawab but he was never money-minded or into shopping or clothes. His few indulgences were colourful cashmere socks and having his suits tailored at Savile Row. And, yes, he liked spending a little extra to fly British Airways because the British accent of the pilot seemed to soothe him,' says daughter Soha Ali Khan, now an actor in the Hindi film industry.

Nor was he someone who enjoyed loud and large social gatherings, the kind which the national capital seems to thrive upon. 'He was probably most content just being at home by himself and reading a book on history,' Soha tells me. Tiger was a voracious reader. He would devour the morning newspapers and a range of books from Umberto Eco to Salman Rushdie to Romila Thapar. He was also a very good cook. 'You would often find him in the kitchen sharing his favourite tandoori or Afghani recipes with his staff, and he would rustle up scrambled eggs for breakfast in a jiffy when he stayed with me once in Mumbai,' says Soha.

The cricketer who had been thrust into stardom with his exploits on the field was a quiet, retiring man off it. The later part of his life reflected this search for solitude – a game of bridge with friends, summers in Central London with his wife, going on shikaar, a drink at the Bombay Gymkhana bar, watching his favourite British comedy serials, listening to Urdu poetry and ghazals or catching up on old war films like *The Guns of Navarone*. Tiger slowly drifted out of public life. Occasionally, he would do expert commentary for a cricket game. He was even the editor of Kolkata-based sports magazine *Sportsworld* for a while in the 1980s.

Mudar Patherya, who worked in the magazine as a cricket writer at the time, recalls how mesmerized the youthful editorial team was to have Tiger as their editor. He also says the cricketer wore his fame very lightly. 'He never gave us an inkling of how good a player he had been except once when we were at the Dalhousie Institute Club in Kolkata playing a friendly game. One of us asked him to stand in the covers and the ball went in his direction. Tiger was a few beers down but our forty-seven-year-old rifled the ball in from his wrist and the chair we were using as a stump literally exploded with the force of his throw. While we were awestruck, Tiger quickly went back to his drinks with the hint of a smile,' remembers Patherya.

The understated approach was quintessential Tiger – a prince who was born in luxury but who embraced the spirit of egalitarianism as one of cricket's life lessons. He would happily bring a case of Heineken beer from Delhi by train for his *Sportsworld* staff and then insist on taking back a huge leg of mutton cased in ice to feast on in Delhi. 'You get better mutton in Kolkata,' he would tell his junior colleagues. And whenever he stayed at the Oberoi Grand in Kolkata, he would always inquire of the waiters how they were and how many years away from retirement they were so he could perhaps have the benefit of their service at his home! He may have been 'Nawab saab' at home but he was acutely aware that the walls between the princely elite and the aam aadmi were slowly but surely breaking.

His aristocratic streak meant he could just switch off from the world around him, preferring to rest like a tiger in his private lair. One of his few close friends was Lokesh Sharma, a Delhi-based businessman with interests in sports and media. 'It is wrong to say that Tiger was lazy and didn't want to work hard after retirement. He may not have been cut out for a nine-to-five job but he was very disciplined. We once had to leave for a cricket match shoot at 6 a.m. in Ludhiana, and Tiger was in the hotel lobby by 5.45 a.m. It's just that while he was always aware of the big picture, he didn't want to be part of the picture himself,' Sharma tells me.

His temperament was ill-suited to the cut and thrust of cricket board politics. 'Tiger encouraged us to form a players' association; he was always there to support our causes but you could not expect someone like him to bow and scrape before board officials, which is what you have to do to succeed,' says Bedi. Tiger was invited to the IPL governing council in 2008 as the new Twenty20 format sought to gain respectability. But two years later, he took the board to court because they hadn't paid him his dues for attending the council meetings. 'It was messy and avoidable,' admits Sharmila.

Tiger landed himself in a bigger mess in 2005 when he was arrested under the Wildlife Protection Act for allegedly hunting a blackbuck in Haryana's Jhajjar town. He evaded arrest for almost a fortnight before surrendering in court. I tried to contact him in this period for an interview but to no avail. When we met later, he sounded contrite: 'I knew you were trying to get me to react but what could I have said on television. I may have made a mistake but you don't want me to be held guilty in a TV studio, do you?' For a few weeks at least, Tiger felt like a hunted man.

As he did in the aftermath of the Gujarat 2002 riots. 'I don't know what's happening in the country; how can people kill in the name of religion,' he rang up and told me once with an unusual trace of anger. He was the quintessential Nehruvian secularist, someone who wore his religious identity rather lightly. He was a believer who always carried his taveez with him, but had little time for elaborate public rituals. His family had splintered during Partition (the former Pakistan Cricket Board chief Shahryar Khan is a first cousin) and he saw religious conflict as a blot on his idea of a pluralistic India.

And yet, through the good times and the bad, he never lost his dignity or his dry sense of humour. When his daughter Soha was applying for an Australian visa, one of the columns asked the question: 'Any criminal record?' 'He told me, "Just write to them that it isn't necessary to fill the column because Australia is, after all, an island of convicts." Then he just chuckled to himself,' recalls Soha. The sharp wit was almost second nature. When Patherya asked him once when he thought he would be able to play again after losing an eye, he replied straight-faced, 'When I saw the English bowling!'

It was this ability to never allow life's vicissitudes to change his inner self that defined Tiger's character. A lesser man would perhaps have been weighed down by the repeated close encounters with grief and misfortune – losing a doting father on your eleventh birthday, an eye when at twenty-one, and nawab status at thirty. But he never became bitter or cynical; he just accepted the hand that was dealt to him with grace. Maybe the true sportsman in him realized that sometimes winning and losing didn't matter; it was how you played the game that really counted. On his deathbed, as he battled a lung affliction, his last words to his wife Sharmila were not excessively emotional: 'Can I have some mince pies from Jaipur?' he asked quietly with a flicker of a smile.

As historian Mukul Kesavan wrote when Tiger passed away in 2011: 'He remained untouched by the squabbles and sleaze that attended cricket's transformation into big business in India. As a consequence, death finds him happily embalmed in fond radio memories; still tigerish in the covers, still a prince amongst men.'

~

On a steaming hot summer morning in May 2016, I travelled to Pataudi, a small town in Haryana with a population of just over 25,000 people. Pataudi is around 25 kilometres from Gurugram, just off NH-8 (the Delhi–Jaipur highway) in the foothills of the Aravali range. The small principality had been bequeathed to Faiz Talab Khan, the first Nawab of Pataudi, as a reward for helping the British East India Company in the second Anglo-Maratha war in 1804.

The town I am visiting, though, has little connect with the past. Neighbouring Gurugram is now a totem of India Inc 2.0, with reportedly more multinational corporation investment per square kilometre than any other piece of real estate in the country. The entire stretch from Gurugram right up to the town of Manesar is dotted with plush business offices and industrial complexes. As the car veers into Pataudi town, the landscape begins to take on a more mofussil look, although the Haryana government has assured that Pataudi too will soon be part of this rapidly expanding industrial corridor.

It isn't difficult to find the Pataudi Palace, the most recognizable construction in the town. The white colonial structure, built in the style of the grand old imperial buildings of Delhi (the architect Robert Tor Russell also designed the capital's iconic Connaught Place area), lies in the middle of 22 acres of farmland and gardens. Cotton, wheat and vegetables grow in the dry fields while peacocks playfully strut around the gardens. Once a Neemrana Hotels property, Pataudi's son Saif – he and wife Kareena are amongst Hindi cinema's most glamorous couples – has taken back the palace since 2014 for their personal use. Furious renovation work is going on in the main building.

Sharmila Tagore has very kindly offered me a glimpse into the world of Pataudi. My guide Ghyasuddin, who has been working for the family for over twenty years, takes me through the dozens of rooms in the palace and the adjoining houses, Qamar Manzil and Nafees Manzil. With high ceilings, large beds, beautiful chandeliers, book-lined shelves (ranging from translations of the Quran to volumes on the First World War) and numerous black-and-white family photographs, the Pataudi Palace is like a little jewel of colonial India hidden away in modern-day Haryana. The archival photos are mainly of the father–son sporting duo, playing polo, billiards, squash, tennis, and of course, cricket. While the father is mostly featured in line-ups with a team of Englishmen, the son proudly wears his India cap and blazer.

'Sarkar bahut achhe the [My boss was a good man], sir,' Ghyasuddin reminisces. 'Hamesha hamara khyal rakhte the [He always took care of us].' To his friends, he was Pat or Tiger, but here in Pataudi, he is always Sarkar, or even His Highness, conscious of his duties as the nawab. 'I think he rather liked being called His Highness at official functions,' recalls Soha wistfully.

In the gardens just opposite the palace, there is a small mosque. Next to it, in one corner, father and son lie buried next to each other with simple Quranic inscriptions on the tombstone. It is not extravagant, just a gentle reminder of how one princely family took forward the torch of Indian cricket in the years just after Independence.

I leave the palace and head to the local market. At a cold drink store, I set up an adda with the villagers and ask them about the Pataudis and their cricketing legacy. Most of the villagers don't seem too enthused. In this Ahir-dominated pocket of Haryana, the conversation instead veers to the contentious issue of Jat reservations and the sale price of land. 'If the government gives reservations to Jats, what will happen to us?' asks one villager. 'We must get a better price for our farmland once industry comes here,' says another. In 2016, cricket history doesn't matter as much as more urgent issues like jobs and real estate.

And then a young man in a flaming red T-shirt and wavy hair tells me how proud he is of the Pataudis. 'Haan sir, maine ek baar dekha hai Saif aur Kareena ko. Woh toh hamare Nawab saab hai! [I have once seen Saif and Kareena, he is our nawab!]' I wonder how Indian cricket's most glittering star of the 1960s would feel about being known as the 'father of Saif'. He would probably have a quiet chuckle.

3

Bishan Singh Bedi

Sardar of Spin

It was a crisp winter afternoon in the national capital, ideal conditions for cricket. India Gate loomed in the backdrop of the National Stadium, where a small crowd watched just one player in a bright pink turban. He approached the crease with his signature smooth, slow lolloping run, his body thickened at the waist, grey flecks in his beard, the gimlet stare in the eyes fixed on his target. The sardar had aged but his spirit appeared undimmed, along with his ability to spin a cricket ball.

The first ball was a full toss that the batsman hit for four. The bowler simply grinned through his facial hair, like someone who had just finished a large glass of lassi, clapped and exclaimed, 'Good shot!' The next ball was again tossed up; it seemed to hang in the air for an eternity. Thinking it was another easy full toss, the batsman stepped out to drive, only to find the ball dip and curve away from him like a hissing cobra that had suddenly changed direction. The batsman was stumped by yards. The bowler's smile widened and the twinkling eyes brought to mind a child who had just solved a complicated maths sum.

That match was a friendly game between journalists and Members
of Parliament (MPs) in 1994, my first such encounter. Now most
journalists don't make very good cricketers; neither do most MPs.
This is why the annual match in Delhi is usually a close affair. The
first of these matches was played in the 1950s, a tradition begun by
Jawaharlal Nehru, who was not known for his cricketing prowess
but as someone who gladly embraced its rituals. In the 1990s,
Madhavrao Scindia, Congress MP from the erstwhile Gwalior royal
family, carried forward the torch of princely patronage. Scindia was
an absolute cricket fanatic – the standing joke was that he would
rather watch a cricket match than attend a cabinet meeting.

During this particular encounter in 1994, Scindia was determined
to win the game and had lined up a few 'extra' players – including
local cricketers – to boost the ranks of the MPs and ensure victory.
'We don't have eleven players today so we need reinforcements,' he
told us as an excuse. You don't argue with MPs, at least not maharajas
in love with the game. The journalists' side was a motley crew of
pen-pushers, with one exception – we had lured the former India
captain Bishan Singh Bedi, then a forty-eight-year-old, into our
team. He had, after all, turned cricket columnist after retirement.
'He is a quasi-journalist,' we claimed in our defence. With Bedi
doing the star turn, the journalists edged the game.

After the match, high tea was served in the clubhouse. While
the journalists were busy cultivating the politicians, a disappointed
Scindia approached Bedi with a request. 'Look, Bishan, next time
you have to play for us and help us win.' As he sipped tea, Bedi
responded with a smile, 'Anything for you, Mr Scindia, but I'm
not sure I want to be on the same side as many of your colleagues.
They might infect me with their corruption.' The MPs within
earshot weren't amused. Bedi, though, didn't seem too perturbed.
His spinning fingers had bowled us to a win, now his sharp
retort had scored another point. Bedi had only lived up to his
reputation: the rebel without a pause, the Sardar of Spin who was

both wizard and warrior, charming and combative till the end of his playing days.

~

Despite the Maharaja of Patiala's early patronage of Indian cricket, Sikhs did not have a rich tradition in the sport. Hockey was the national game and a formidable array of Sikh players from Balbir Singh to Udham Singh drove the success of the hockey team in the Olympics from the 1930s through to the 1950s. In the cantonment towns and villages of Punjab, hockey players were the stars and cricket was never considered the main sport.

The frenetic speed and energy of a hockey match seemed to fit well with the martial tradition of the Sikhs. The first Sikh sporting superstar was the 'Flying Sikh' Milkha Singh, who just missed out on an Olympic medal in the 400 metre event of the 1960 Rome Olympics. In the first two decades after Independence, only three Sikhs played cricket for India: Bedi and the brothers Kripal Singh and Milkha Singh (not to be confused with the sprinter), both of whom represented Tamil Nadu. Punjab was a distant outpost on the country's cricket map and the scars of Partition had left the land bloody and divided; Lahore was the region's cricket capital and most of the best Punjabi cricketers had moved to Pakistan after 1947. Bedi, in a sense, was fighting both history and geography when he first turned to cricket in the late 1950s.

~

Amritsar, on the border with Pakistan, is a city of trade and spirituality. Its crowded bazaars are festooned with colourful textiles, leather goods, carpets and jewellery. It is also home to the Golden Temple, the holiest Sikh shrine whose serenity contrasts with the maddening traffic of the city's crowded bylanes. Bedi is a bit like the

city he was born in: fiery on the outside, but calm within. His father
Sardar Gian Singh Bedi was president of the local district Congress
committee, a Gandhian and a social worker who was highly respected
in the area. 'He was my role model always, a man of dignity and
peace,' Bedi tells me.

Gian Singh loved sport and particularly enjoyed tennis. The
young Bedi took to tennis initially but then had to choose between
tennis and cricket after he was told that a tennis injury would affect
his bowling arm. The family lived in a large house with a courtyard
and plenty of space to play. Bedi was the youngest sibling with four
elder sisters. 'I had a very happy childhood. My sisters doted on me
while my parents taught me discipline and independence. My mother
made it clear, for example, that I would have to wash my own clothes,
something which I did when I later toured with the Indian team,'
Bedi reminisces.

A school friend from St Francis School in Amritsar remembers
Bedi as a 'quiet, shy boy', hardly the larger-than-life, rumbustious
figure of his later years. I ask Bedi about his school memories and he
doesn't begin with cricket. 'We had this lovely history teacher called
Uma Behl and she used to come to class smelling of Godrej talcum
powder. I liked the smell so much that I made sure that I never missed
her class. Even today I use only Godrej talcum powder,' he says.

Like many young cricketers of the 1950s and 1960s, radio
commentary had a big influence on Bedi's decision to play cricket.
It is remarkable how just the sound of the radio without any visual
images of their heroes was enough to inspire an entire generation
to take to the game. It was almost as if the crackle of the airwaves
after a wicket or a boundary conjured up a million dreams. 'I was
twelve years old when I listened to the radio commentary as Subhash
Gupte took nine wickets against the West Indies in 1958. Somehow
I was mesmerized by the leg-spin of Gupte and wanted to emulate
him one day,' he says.

It didn't take him long. At the age of fifteen in 1962 he made his
Ranji Trophy debut for Northern Punjab since there was no unified

Punjab team at the time. Four years after that he played his first Test against the West Indies. The meteoric rise was fashioned by hours of hard work and an obsession with bowling. 'I would bowl for six to eight hours in a day till the sun went down. The more I bowled, the stronger my fingers and arm became,' he tells me.

I look at Bedi's fingers today; they are still strong and broad, almost as if they were created to spin a cricket ball. But why in the land of the tough and hardy Jat Sikhs did a young man choose the relatively less muscular option of spin bowling? 'I initially started playing cricket to lose weight! The first time I held a ball, I did try and bowl fast. But then Gurbachan Singh who was a coach at the Amritsar Gymkhana had one look at my figure and told me to opt for spin bowling instead since it required less athleticism!' he says and laughs.

That proved to be a wise decision. When Bedi enrolled at Khalsa College, the team didn't have a left-arm spinner; he more than ably filled the vacuum. One wonders how a relatively uncoached cricketer with no visible role models went on to develop the most perfect spin-bowling action in the sport. And then you think, how did Kishore da or Rafi saab master music or M.F. Husain learn to paint? Were they tutored, was their craft honed by years of rehearsal, or is there something more ethereal about great artistes that defies conventional wisdom? 'I guess it's a gift of God, guru ki kripa,' says Bedi, a devout Sikh.

This belief that talent is divine appears to be a running theme in the rise of many of India's early cricketing heroes. They didn't have facilities but they had passion, or 'junoon' as Bedi calls it, for the sport. Bedi's early guru was coach Gyan Prakash in Amritsar. 'I didn't learn how to bowl from him but he taught me how to use my mind, how to develop cricket sense. No computer taught me how to bowl, I learnt to use the eight inches between my two ears,' says Bedi with familiar chutzpah.

Spin bowling is ultimately the art of deception, of using the mind to outfox the opponent. Muhammad Ali used his twinkle toes to float like a butterfly in the boxing ring before stinging his opponents like a bee. Bishan Singh Bedi used his mind to deceive batsmen and the craft in his fingers to defeat them. He intimidated his rivals through cricket's most non-violent art form: spin bowling.

~

From 1966, when Bedi first represented India, to the tail end of his career in the late 1970s, India underwent a glorious spin revolution that would change Indian cricket forever. Brahma, the creator God in the Trimurti of Hinduism, has four faces looking in four different directions. But even he would have found it difficult to recreate the magic of India's spin quartet which dominated the sport for a decade and more. And mirroring the country's unique notion of unity in diversity, the four Indian spinners were distinctive individuals with sharply contrasting personalities but united in their purpose of taking wickets for India. It was like having four magicians perform in one show, each with a unique bag of tricks, each luring an unsuspecting batsman to his doom with their mastery over flight and turn.

Erapalli Prasanna, who made his debut in 1962, was the oldest of the four. He was a true-blue Kannadiga born in Shimoga, another remote corner in cricket's metro-centric geography at the time. As an off-spinner, he was almost a right-arm version of Bedi, shorter and stockier but with the same instinct to play mind games with batsmen through his control over the spinning ball. 'We were like Siamese twins I guess,' he says with a chuckle. 'We would share secrets and plot how to get a batsman out. It was almost as if we could read each other's minds.' Prasanna was a qualified engineer, even giving up the sport for five years after his first Test series because his father wanted him to complete his engineering degree first. 'In those days, it was a case of studies first, then cricket. My father, who was a government servant, allowed me to go on my first cricket tour in 1962 only because the Maharaja of Mysore intervened and promised him I would complete my degree on my return,' he recalls.

Prasanna's off-spinning rival was Chennai's Srinivas Venkataraghavan, another engineering graduate. Venkat fitted in with the stereotype of the stoic, unsmiling Tamil Brahmin and was a strict disciplinarian. I once met him at the Madras Cricket Club where he admonished a group of teenagers at the adjoining table for speaking too loudly. 'He was the professor, the intellectual amongst us bon vivants. We would be having a drink and he would be reading a book,' says Bedi. Venkat was more than just a spinner, though; unlike the others, he was a decent batsman and a fine close-in fielder who would later even go on to become an international umpire.

The final maestro making up this incredible foursome was also the most enigmatic and fascinating. Bhagwat Chandrasekhar, another Kannadiga, was a truly heroic figure. An attack of polio at a very young age had withered his right arm but that did not stop him from becoming, arguably, the greatest match-winning bowler in Indian cricket history. He was unconventional in every sense; he would take a long run-up for a spinner and bowl leg-spinning deliveries with a pace and variety that foxed the best players. The sight of Chandrasekhar with the ball, marking his run-up, was enough for an entire stadium in Mumbai or Kolkata to shout in unison, 'Boowwlled'. The sound would echo with a frenzy that would leave overseas batsmen shaken even before they played a ball.

When Chandrasekhar wasn't playing cricket, he liked to be far away from the action, quietly listening to a song by Mukesh or Saigal. 'If you wanted to find Chandra before a Test match in Mumbai, he would be in Mukesh's house for a private music concert,' recalls Bedi. Even now, Chandrasekhar prefers to be a recluse, refusing to carry a mobile – or at least choosing not to share the number! – and spending a lot of his time with his son in the US.

I ask Syed Kirmani, arguably the finest Indian wicketkeeper who played a fair bit with the four spinners, to compare them. 'Champions, all of them,' he says. 'Chandra was a genius and keeping to him was the biggest challenge. He could bowl leg-spin, googlies and top-spinners with almost the same action. And his faster one had the speed of a fast bowler. I remember he bowled a bouncer to Viv Richards once that went past the great batsman's nose. Viv turned around and asked me, "Is this guy bowling spin or is he Jeff Thomson [the fastest bowler in the world in the 1970s]!"'

Continues Kirmani, 'Prasanna was a wily fox who would defeat you in the air. His loop was such as if he was holding the ball on a string like a puppet-master. Venkat was not in the same league, he was flatter with his deliveries but very exact and determined. And Bedi was simply poetry in action. He could bowl six different deliveries in an over, including an armer, with the most effortless style. When you watched him bowl, you felt as if you were in a museum in the presence of a great artist.'

Why did India become the land of spinners while neighbouring Pakistan produced fast bowlers? The conventional explanation is the differing physical attributes of the two South Asian neighbours. The tall and muscular Pakistanis were seen to possess the physique to bowl fast while the less well-built Indians were more adept at bowling spin. I offer a slight variation to the theory. In India, cricket was an elite and urban middle-class sport till Kapil Dev's team won the 1983 World Cup and opened up the sport to a new generation. The Indian team was mostly full of players belonging to the Brahminical upper castes who perhaps considered fast bowling hard labour, especially in hot weather with unforgiving pitches. It is no surprise that three of the four spinning greats were urban Brahmins and mostly vegetarian with the Jat Sikh Bedi the only exception. The image of the Brahmin as more learned and less physical fits in with the idea of spin bowling as an art form where mind scores over muscle. When I suggest this to Prasanna, he laughs. 'We were vegetarian in our food habits, but strictly non-vegetarian when we were gobbling up opposing batsmen!'

Between them, the spin quartet picked up an astonishing 853 Test wickets. By contrast, the great West Indian fast bowling equivalent of Andy Roberts, Joel Garner, Michael Holding and Colin Croft put together had 835 wickets. Of the 98 Test matches in which one or more of the spinners played together, India won 23, lost 36 and drew 39 games. If those aren't striking figures, let's put them in context – India won only 7 out of 76 Tests till the arrival of the spinners. 'I think they changed the way we played the game. Until the spinners came, our main aim was not to lose the match. Now we could think of actually trying to win games,' explains former India captain Ajit Wadekar.

Wadekar should know. He was the captain of the team that scored a hat-trick of victories over the West Indies and England between 1970 and 1973, wins that catapulted Indian cricket on to the world stage. The finest performance was probably at the Oval in London in 1971 when India defeated England on its home turf for the first time. This is how my late father Dilip Sardesai remembers the game. 'The wicket was turning when Wadekar brought Chandra on to bowl. Chandra and I had gone to the horse races on the rest day of the match. A horse called Mildred won a race. When John Edrich came to bat, I told Chandra: "Isko Mildred daal [bowl him a Mildred]." He bowled the most vicious googly and shattered the stumps. After that, Chandra was unplayable and the English batsmen were psychologically destroyed. When we won the game the next day, it seemed as if every Indian living in England was at the Oval. One of them offered us free food and drink for life in his restaurant and named dishes after us!'

On that August day at the Oval in 1971, Indian cricket had tasted real freedom. Just months later, India would go to war with Pakistan and liberate Bangladesh in a decisive military triumph that renewed the country's self-confidence, earlier dented by the defeat in the 1962 Sino-Indian war. Chandrasekhar picked up 6 wickets, Venkat 2 and Bedi 1. The mantra of non-violence as defined by spin had won the day for the Indians yet again.

The match-winning performances would continue for at least another seven years till the fingers and arms began to tire. The great Indian spin quartet was conquered on the first tour to Pakistan in 1978. The host team's batting, led by Zaheer Abbas and Javed Miandad, was in prime form on flat batting tracks and the ageing

Indian bowling attack just couldn't match up. The spinners would be quickly pushed into retirement. 'It happened a little suddenly and was unfortunate but we had a bloody good ride along the way,' Prasanna reflects on the endgame.

England would be the venue of Bedi's final series in 1979. He was only thirty-three when he played his last Test, a relatively young age for a spinner. But no one had bowled more overs through the 1970s than the sardar from Amritsar. No one had taken more wickets for India when he retired: 266 wickets in 67 Tests. Only two left-arm spinners, Derek Underwood of England and Daniel Vettori of New Zealand, have taken more Test wickets. But no one has brought more joy to the cricket purist; when Bedi came in to bowl in his resplendent blue or pink patka, you couldn't help but be transfixed by his action, smooth and rich as the milk in his hometown. The English off-spinner Jim Laker once said that his idea of heaven was 'sunshine at Lord's, Ray Lindwall, the Australian fast bowler, bowling from one end, Bedi from the other'.

His critics say Bedi bowled like a millionaire, often giving away too many runs in his search for wickets. This is statistically untrue; Bedi is second best to the West Indian Lance Gibbs in terms of bowling maiden overs per Test match. Bedi explains his approach of clapping after being hit for six. 'You bowl to get a batsman out. If a Test batsman hits a few fours or sixes but I get him out for 30, isn't it better than bowling defensively and allowing him to just bat on and on and score a hundred?' The attacking instinct played a bit part in Bedi's prominent role in India's first-ever overseas wins in Australia, West Indies, England and New Zealand.

Sir Don Bradman suggests that Bedi is among the greatest left-arm spinners of all time. In a fitting tribute, Bradman writes, 'Bedi was a real study for the connoisseur. His ideal well-balanced run-up always brought him into the perfect delivery position. The ball was held well in the tips of long, almost delicate fingers which never seemed to get tired, but always retained great flexibility and control. There were regular but very subtle changes of pace – variations in flight, and always coupled with genuine spin. The end product was a delight to watch and I do not hesitate to rank Bedi among the finest bowlers of his type we have seen.'

No Indian cricketer had received higher praise from cricket's ultimate icon. But Bedi's true impact on Indian cricket lies not just in his contribution to the art of left-arm spin bowling but in the way he redefined the idea of leadership in Indian sport by putting player power above personal success.

~

The BCCI was set up in 1928. As its title suggests, its aim was to 'control' Indian cricket. Even though its duties included the selection of the 'national' team, it was run for a long time like a private club. The officials had the image of modern-day zamindars, typifying the feudal sports culture of the early post-Independence years. The cricketers, by contrast, were daily wage labourers, surviving on sheer talent and passion. 'We wore the India cap with pride but we got no economic benefit,' recalls Nari Contractor, India captain in the early 1960s. Contractor points out that when he made his Test debut in 1955, the players travelled across the country only by train and got no allowances apart from the Rs 250 they were paid per Test. (They got a Rs 50 bonus when they defeated England in a series in 1961–62!)

'Even if we wanted to eat a snack after a match, we had to pay from our own pockets. Once we weren't paid our match fee on time and complained to the board official who said the board didn't have the money to pay us right away. Finally, at the last minute, as we were boarding the Frontier Mail from Delhi to Mumbai with no money in our wallets a local board administrator came running to the station with a sackful of notes and distributed the money to us even while counting every last anna,' says Contractor.

My late father has a story that exemplifies the mai-baap relationship between the board and the players of the period. 'We were playing

a Test match in Chennai in the 1960s when the power in the hotel
went off. The board officials accompanying us were quickly taken
to a nearby hotel so they could sleep in AC comfort but we had to
sweat it out in the heat and literally had to plead to be shifted out.
And mind you, we had a Test match the next day.'

It was this unequal world that Bishan Bedi was determined to set
right. His tryst with official apathy began when he was a teenager.
Punjab cricket was controlled at the time by Hansraj Mohla,
one of the many cricket officials who couldn't hold a bat or ball.
'The man had an insurance business and no idea of the game. If you
gave him a suit piece as a bribe, he would select you! It was crazy,'
recalls Bedi.

In 1966 when Bedi played his first Test, he was paid Rs 700 for the
game. By 1971, when India won the England and West Indies series,
the match fee had risen to Rs 2000. 'We were being called world
champions, huge crowds greeted us at the airport but in monetary
terms, we got sweet f***,' says Bedi. The first whiff of change came
only in 1975–76 when there was a quantum jump in the match fees –
from Rs 7500 to Rs 16,000 by the end of the decade. Bedi was now
captain of the side and along with the team's other star player Sunil
Gavaskar had pushed the board for higher player salaries.

Bedi's rise to captaincy was not without controversy. In the
aftermath of India's disastrous tour of England in 1974, the board was
looking for a scapegoat and they found one in Bedi. He was accused
of not following captain Wadekar's instructions while bowling, of
appearing on a television programme without permission and refusing
to sign the board's financial contract. 'We were only being given
2 pounds a day as allowance. The government marginally increased
our foreign exchange quota and we were offered an additional
50 pence as daily allowance but the board was willing to make the
payment for only part of the tour. I refused to accept and was punished
for it,' says Bedi unapologetically.

The board's disciplinary committee decided to suspend Bedi for
the first Test against the West Indies in 1974–75 in Bengaluru. This

led to street protests. 'No Bedi, no Test' was graffitied across walls in the city, the matter was raised in Parliament, and a group of Sikh students even gheraoed the Delhi cricket board premises. Eventually a government official who was a cricket fan stepped in and forced the board president to the negotiating table. It had no choice but to allow Bedi to play the next game.

The incident highlights just how skewed the player–official relationship was even in the 1970s. If the socialist Indian state was mai-baap in this period, then so was the cricket board. A star player was forced to bend before a board for expressing dissent at not being paid a little more. The board president Purshottam Rungta had never played the game but dominated the Rajasthan cricket board for decades. This was the pre-liberalized India of shortages and tight money controls when even a 50 pence increase in foreign exchange was viewed with suspicion. 'Forget about being seen as a sportsman, I was being treated by the board as a criminal for asking for my rights as a player,' says Bedi.

By making him captain less than a year after the fracas, the board thought they had perhaps bought Bedi's silence. He would prove them wrong in his very first series as captain against Sri Lanka in 1975. During a match in Nagpur, the team stayed in an MLA hostel but only the captain and the manager were given a room with hot water. When Bedi objected, the local board official laughed it off as a 'minor' issue. An incensed Bedi shouted back, 'The crowd comes to see us play, not to see you officiate.' The aggrieved official complained and Bedi was once again hauled up before a board committee. 'The committee meeting was held in a five-star hotel to decide whether I should have protested the issue of players being denied hot water in their rooms. Can anything be more ridiculous,' says Bedi.

After the Nagpur fracas, the officials refused to book rail tickets for Bedi and some other 'dissenting' players. 'Surinder Amarnath and myself travelled in the luggage rack of the first-class compartment without any bedding in the December cold, reached Old Delhi railway station, went to the bus terminal and took a bus to Chandigarh to play

a Ranji match against Haryana barely forty-eight hours after we had
played for India. Do you think that would ever happen now?' he asks.

The events of Bedi's revolt in the 1970s must seem incongruous
in today's India where players are treated like royalty and have every
possible luxury at their disposal. But in the context of Indian cricket's
evolution, it was a landmark moment, perhaps the first public display
of player power that changed the terms of engagement between
cricketers and officials. No longer could players be taken for granted.
In an era where protests against the 1975 Emergency threw up anti-
establishment political heroes, Bedi became cricket's angry rebel with
a cause, a captain ready to fight for his players. That he was also a
world-class player only added to his stature and ability to influence
events. 'Bishan paaji empowered us, gave us hope that we could take
on the system,' says former Test player Mohinder Amarnath, who
in later years would memorably call the Indian selectors 'a bunch of
jokers'.

Critical voices have suggested that his revolt was inspired by
personal ambition and the desire for monetary benefit. 'Whenever
we ask Bedi to feature on a programme, he first wants to know how
much we'll pay him for an appearance,' a television producer reminds
me. Bedi's response is straightforward. 'I am a professional, what is
the harm if I ask for a just price?' My own experience is that while
Bedi does appear to be bitter and resentful at times over losing out
in commercial terms, his romance with cricket overrides all else.
He may have wanted more money from the sport but what he really
treasured was his self-respect and an abiding attachment to the
finer traditions of cricket. 'Remember the phrase "It's not cricket"?
We never say "It's not hockey" or "it's not tennis". Because cricket is
special,' he says, a man still in love with the game.

In 1977, for example, Bedi took on the English cricket
establishment when he accused the English fast bowler John Lever of
using Vaseline to swing the ball illegally during a tour of India. For
a country claiming to play the 'gentleman's game' by the rules, Bedi's
criticism stung. He was, after all, challenging a colonial mindset that

claimed moral superiority over Indian 'subjects'. The men in suits and ties at Lord's believed they were the last word on the sport. The Indian 'takeover' which would see the balance of power shift away from London was still some time away. 'I guess they couldn't handle the fact that an Indian was questioning the "goras"!' says Bedi.

A year later, Bedi's contract with the English county Northamptonshire was abruptly terminated. For six years, he had been a star of the county scene, his colourful headgear spreading much joy, his classical action leading to lyrical prose. Now the sardar was the local villain because he had challenged the English game. 'It was an unhappy time for me professionally. Suddenly, I felt unwanted and betrayed by people whom I had played with for years. But I have no regrets. My father had taught me to always speak the truth. If speaking one's mind is a crime, then I am guilty several times over,' he says firmly.

Bedi's conscience would be tested again when the Kerry Packer revolution threatened the future of Test cricket in 1977. Australian television magnate Packer signed contracts with some of the world's biggest cricketers to play a 'rebel' cricket tournament. Bedi was one of the few Indians who were approached with the promise of a lucrative contract. 'Packer's agent came to me thrice, each time with larger amounts on offer. The third time he pulled out a chequebook and threw it at me, saying, "C'mon Bish, fill in your price." His obnoxious attitude put me off and I threw the chequebook back and told him, "No bastard has ever put a price tag on me."' Which is perhaps why Bedi speaks out so vehemently today against the practice of auctioning cricketers during the IPL. 'You can call me old-fashioned but I just don't like players being treated like horses and sold to the highest bidder!' he responds angrily.

That rejoinder is typical Bedi – a man frozen in time and unable to adjust to the new market-driven cricket economy, almost a relic from a bygone era when the sport was primarily about honour and not bank balances. He may sound unusually harsh in his denunciation of the modern game, even hypocritical, but he isn't an impostor either.

This is after all a captain who once 'declared' an innings in the West Indies when he found that his opponents were bowling four bouncers in an over only to intimidate the Indian batsmen. 'It was worse than Bodyline. You play cricket to win, not to kill,' he says sharply.

This is a captain who once 'conceded' a match to arch-rivals Pakistan in 1978 because the Pakistani bowlers were deliberately bowling wide balls and bouncers in a one-day game. This was the first tour to Pakistan in seventeen years and it was seen as a diplomatic coup for the then Morarji Desai–led Janata Party government. But it soon became apparent that the Pakistanis, with no small help from their local umpires, were determined to win the match at all costs. An enraged Bedi told the team manager, 'If you want us to be diplomats and lose matches unfairly, ask Morarji Desai to captain the team. I am going home.'

That tour of Pakistan was Bedi's last as captain. Losing to Pakistan is the ultimate 'crime' for an Indian and Bedi was no exception. But Bedi, the boy from Amritsar, was always a huge draw across the border. In 2001, we were on the same flight to Lahore. At the duty-free shop in Delhi, Bedi picked up a few bottles of rum and whiskey for his hosts in Pakistan. 'Won't they be confiscated by customs?' I asked him. 'Don't worry, it's Pakistan. My face is my passport there!' he replied. Sure enough, he was allowed to keep the alcohol. Clearly the bond of 'Punjabiyat' could overcome customs regulations and memories of on-field antagonisms from past encounters.

It was this gregarious spirit that made Bedi so attractive as India captain. He led from the front and expected his players to show the same zest. As Bradman wrote after the 1977–78 series in Australia which India narrowly lost: 'Bishan Bedi will always be able to derive comfort and satisfaction in the knowledge that he and his men played cricket in the manner and spirit envisaged by our forebears and they will retain a warm and cherished place in the hearts and minds of Australians.'

Maybe Bedi the captain could never measure up to the skill of Bedi the player. The decision of elevating bowlers to captains has always been the subject of intense debate. Bedi in particular was sometimes accused of over-bowling himself as captain and losing more matches than he won. But to judge him by cold statistics would be a disservice to Bedi's positive impact on Indian cricket as a leader. More than anything else, he gave it a resounding voice, which even Tiger Pataudi was unable to do. In the process he also became an inspirational figure who would help change the geography of the sport in India.

~

The first twenty-five years after Independence were dominated by cricketers from the West Zone and South Zone. When India achieved its breakthrough overseas wins in 1971, there were six players from Mumbai and four from the south in the team. Bedi was the lone northern warrior. Fifteen years later, in 1986, when the Indian team won in England for the second time, there were five players from north India and just two from Mumbai. While speedster Kapil Dev has been widely credited for the geographical shift in power, the sardar from Amritsar was the pioneer.

Bedi is only the third Sikh to play for India after 1947. But just four years after he played his last Test in 1979, the Indian squad had as many as five Sikhs. It even led Mumbai-based satirist Behram Contractor (better known as Busybee) to write in a satirical column that 'If you are looking for a taxi, just ring up the Indian cricket team!' Bedi, who was by then a national selector, didn't find it funny at all. He rang up the newspaper editor and warned him that he would send the article to the Sikh militants who were then leading a violent movement for a Khalistani state. 'I have no time for anti-national elements like Bhindranwale but I also don't like anyone hitting me or my religion below the belt even in jest!' he said at the time.

Like a warrior king, Bedi saw himself as the leader of his north Indian 'boys'. He had moved from Amritsar to Delhi in 1968, just over a year after he first played for India. The lure was a job offer from the State Bank of India (SBI), one of the institutions employing cricketers at the time. The role of the nationalized banks in the rise of Indian cricket is significant. The Indian squad in the early 1970s had as many as six SBI players, a reflection of the dominance of the public sector in the economy. 'The bank gave us respect and financial security. What more could we ask for as players?' says Wadekar, who worked with SBI for four decades.

The move to Delhi gave Bedi a larger canvas to showcase his abilities. Delhi was the national capital but cricket was languishing in its stadiums. In the city of political conspiracies, Delhi's cricket corridors mirrored its byzantine netagiri. Factionalism meant that the administration rarely presented a united front. A decade earlier, Pataudi had left Delhi for Hyderabad because he didn't know how to deal with its scheming officials. Bedi, by contrast, was spoiling for a fight to change the face of cricket in the city. He set about building a team containing the best talent. The Amarnath brothers, Mohinder and Surinder, moved from Punjab as did the promising all-rounder Madan Lal. Opening batsman Chetan Chauhan relocated from Maharashtra. 'It was all about opportunity. In the West Zone, there was fierce competition for a place but in the North, Bedi was promising us a chance to perform,' says Chauhan. Madan Lal says Bedi was like a Pied Piper for youngsters from Punjab. 'Paaji was our guru, we were the shishya [students]. His single command was enough for us to follow.'

Hari Gidwani was one of the players to emerge through the Delhi University system. 'The big college match in Delhi in those days used to be St Stephen's versus Hindu. I recall Skipper [Bedi] coming to watch the game in 1972 and picking us for the Delhi team. He wasn't just a great bowler; he was captain, selector, talent scout, chief motivator rolled into one,' says Gidwani. Until Bedi's arrival, Delhi teams would be selected through competing political influences. 'When I became captain of Delhi in the 1970s, I made it clear only merit mattered. We were selecting a cricket team, not MPs for God's sake,' says Bedi.

By 1974, when North Zone won its first Duleep Trophy, it was apparent that Bedi's 'Mission Delhi' was beginning to work. At a celebratory function, Bedi turned to sports journalists from Mumbai and told them to start looking beyond the country's commercial capital to find the next cricket superstar. 'We don't just play gilli danda in north India you know,' he said sarcastically. In 1978–79, Delhi won the Ranji Trophy for the first time. The feat was repeated a year later with a defeat of Mumbai in which Bedi took five wickets. It was the fulfilment of a long-cherished dream. 'Nothing beats winning a match for your country but beating Mumbai was special too,' he says.

The rivalry between Delhi and Mumbai is now part of Indian cricketing folklore. The seeds were sown in the Bedi years. Bedi is forthright about it. 'Yes, I didn't like most Mumbai players, except your dad who was always full of fun. I found Wadekar to be negative as a captain and wanted to defeat him. This wasn't just about north versus west; it was about two different approaches to cricket. And I think my personal rivalry with the Mumbai players helped my team raise their own performance, so it wasn't such a bad thing after all!'

The personal edge to the Delhi–Mumbai battle is perhaps best reflected in the clash between Bedi and Gavaskar, the two superstars of the 1970s. The duo first met during the 1971 tour of the West Indies and became friends. So deep was the impact of Gavaskar's batting exploits on that tour that Bedi even named his firstborn Gavas Inder Singh after him. He says even now that Gavaskar is the finest opening batsman he has ever seen. 'Absolute master; once he got in, you couldn't get him out,' he says. Today the same Little Master is referred to as an SOB by Bedi in private conversation. 'Sound Opening Batsman is what I meant, what did you think?' Bedi laughs.

Why did a relationship based on friendship and mutual admiration fall away so rapidly? Bedi traces the animosity to his decision not to become part of the multimillion-dollar Packer circus in the late 1970s. Like Bedi, Gavaskar too was offered a contract to play Packer cricket in 1978. He reportedly actively considered the offer but was forced to back off because captain Bedi put his foot down.

Gavaskar offers an entirely different version. He claims that he and wicketkeeper Kirmani were the only two Indians to be offered Packer contracts for the 1979–80 season. 'Yes, I was open about it and the Mumbai Cricket Association managing committee even invited me to meet them and give details of what it entailed. I said I would be released to play for India but wouldn't be available for the Ranji Trophy. They were quite happy to let me go but there were others who manipulated to drop Kirmani from the Indian team and remove me as Indian skipper for the 1979 tour of England even though I had won a series as captain in 1978–79 and scored more than 700 runs. In the end, I didn't play for Packer since it would have meant that I couldn't play for India. I chose my country above commercial interests and yet the media called me a traitor and what not!' reveals Gavaskar.

But Bedi doesn't hold back his punches. 'Sunny once told me at a team meeting that he would stagnate if he didn't think of money. We just had a very different view of life I guess,' he says. Gavaskar strongly denies ever having made such a remark, attributing it to Bedi's 'fertile imagination' (more in the next chapter). Soon after Gavaskar took over as captain in 1978–79 Bedi lost his place in the team and this only seemed to aggravate the conflict. They even stopped talking to each other. 'I was frankly relieved to be dropped because playing under Gavaskar was torture for me,' says Bedi. In 1983 Bedi is alleged to have taken 'revenge' as part of the selection panel that removed Gavaskar as captain. 'Rubbish,' counters Bedi. 'How could one man in a five-member panel remove the captain?'

Like with ugly political leadership battles, we will perhaps never know the truth of the Bedi–Gavaskar tussle. Cricket is supposedly a team game but expecting highly talented individuals with contrasting personalities to share a common space while pursuing individual ambitions is a big ask. In a country as diverse as India it is almost impossible. Gavaskar was the tough, battle-hardened, middle-class

Mumbaikar who built his reputation on the unforgiving maidans of Mumbai; Bedi the irascible but gregarious Punjabi who didn't know how to take a step back. This pairing of two strong-headed individuals was never meant to be. As Bedi's biographer Suresh Menon writes, 'Like the poet Walt Whitman, Bedi can claim that he is large, he contains multitudes. He makes friends easily, and enemies even more easily. He can be childish and mature in the same breath, infuriating and comforting all at once.'

This could be the reason Bedi didn't make a successful transition to cricket administration after retirement. Performing on a cricket field requires pure skill while administration needs negotiation and compromise. 'With Bedi it was always "my way or the highway". You can't work like a one-man show off the field,' a Delhi cricket official tells me. Bedi was sports secretary of the Delhi & District Cricket Association for a while but eventually ended up fighting the very system he was part of. 'Look, I can never be somebody's yes-man. In cricket administration, you have to be a chamcha, and I cannot be one.' He sounds defiant but also isolated.

The image of anti-establishment hero is also what makes Bedi so endearing. At a time when most Indian cricketers are reluctant to question the board, Bedi has always stood out. Maybe he has a Don Quixote–like tendency to tilt at windmills, to see 'enemies' everywhere, but he also has a desire to push for change, to be a moral soundboard, to spell out inconvenient truths. Age has slowed his reflexes, made him give up drink and become even more spiritual. He gets up at 6 a.m. to listen to morning kirtans from Harmandir Sahib before walking his platoon of dogs and then settling down to reading half a dozen newspapers. But even age has not conquered his spirit. He still shoots from the hip, ready to answer any bouncer thrown at him with a spinning delivery of his own.

Often during a television debate Bedi will send an SMS. 'Don't let these bloody netas off the hook, they have looted the country, go for them!' When the Aam Aadmi Party first emerged as a force while playing the anti-corruption card, Bedi chose to support them.

'I like this Arvind Kejriwal guy,' he told me once. 'He doesn't mince his words.' Neither does Bedi. When he delivered the Sardesai Memorial Lecture in 2010, he stirred a controversy when he bluntly questioned Sri Lankan bowler Muttiah Muralitharan's bowling record. 'What record, the man is a chucker who has more than 800 run-outs, not wickets to his name!' He also accused the IPL of destroying the sport. 'The whole thing stinks of multimillion-dollar corruption. I can't think of more rubbish being sold at such a high price.' When it comes to life or cricket, Bedi likes to have the last word.

~

Bedi, as mentioned earlier, was one of the four 'spinning' stars whose sunshine illuminated Indian cricket for a decade and a half with a light so incandescent that it completely overshadowed many other contemporary spin talents. Which is why recounting his life and times would be incomplete without at least one reference to the poignant story of Haryana's Rajinder Goel and Mumbai's Padmakar Shivalkar, two left-arm spinners who picked up a staggering 1339 first-class wickets between them but never played for the country. The duo would have walked into any other international side but in Indian cricket there was space for only one left-arm spinner in the late 1960s and 1970s. With Bedi the automatic choice, Goel and Shivalkar had no option but to parade their skills in the domestic Ranji Trophy matches where year after year they would pick up a bucketful of wickets but still miss out on an India cap. They were arguably the best Indian cricketers to lose out on the honour.

Shivalkar was one of my early heroes. I don't recall watching one match in the 1970s when he didn't take wickets for the Mumbai Ranji team. Does he regret not playing at least once for India? 'Yes and no,' he tells me. 'Yes, I would have loved to have played at least once for India, but no, I don't regret anything because cricket has given me so much.'

Shivalkar is a case study for all talented youngsters who dream of playing for the country but eventually realize that in a tough, competitive sport only eleven cricketers in a nation of 1.3 billion can make it. Shivalkar, or 'Paddy' to his friends, started playing with a proper cricket ball only at the age of nineteen. Till then he would spin a tennis ball at Shivaji Park in local tournaments till one day in 1960 a club cricketer friend suggested he try getting a job via the cricket teams of various companies. 'I had passed out from school but had no job for three years. When I went to the cricket nets, an elderly man on a rocking chair looks at me and throws me a ball. He introduces himself as Vinoo Mankad. Just being in the presence of the greatest spin bowler of that period made me nervous and I couldn't even bowl properly at the stumps. Vinoo bhai smiles, puts his arm around me and asks, "You want to play for our office cricket side? Just be yourself, don't copy anyone." That's how I got my first job as a clerk in Bradbury Mills for Rs 125 a month!'

Over the next decade, Shivalkar was mostly in the Mumbai reserve side till in 1971 at the relatively late age of thirty-one he suddenly became the team's main bowler and spun them to victory in the Ranji Trophy. 'You could say I was a "Star-Late" kind of cricketer who started late in life!' He laughs. Shivalkar would bowl more than 34,000 balls for Mumbai, playing his last first-class game at the age of forty-eight in the 1987–88 season. With an easy rhythmic action of just a couple of steps, he could bowl tirelessly for hours in the relentless pursuit of wickets. He played in an 'unofficial' series for India against Sri Lanka in 1973–74 but that is the closest he came to an India cap. 'The Indian team had two off-spinners in Prasanna and Venkat but when it came to left-arm spinners, the selectors chose only one, who was always Bedi. So I guess I was just born at the wrong time,' he says. So what kept him going for so many years in the less glamorous routine of domestic cricket? 'You know when I first played for Mumbai in the 1960s, we were paid Rs 10 per day; when I retired, it had increased to Rs 1000, so it was never the money. What kept me going I think was the love of cricket, just the joy of taking wickets and winning matches for my team. Nothing can beat that feeling,' he says.

Shivalkar is still connected to the game he loves. As cricket secretary of the Shivaji Park Gymkhana, the spiritual home of Mumbai cricket, he still attends cricket nets in the evenings, coaching young cricketers, offering them comforting words. He continues to be a lean and energetic presence on the field. Blessed with a melodious voice, he hums Mohammed Rafi songs and has even cut his own music album. His mobile caller tune is his life anthem, a song from the 1961 Dev Anand hit film *Hum Dono*. 'Main zindagi ka saath nibhata chala gaya, har fikr ko dhuyen mein udata chala gaya.' (Ironically, it's my caller tune too.) Sahir Ludhianvi's masterful lyrics talk of the readiness to take life one day at a time, unmindful of troubles. 'I can't sing like Rafi saab or act like Dev Anand, but then they couldn't bowl like me,' says Shivalkar.

In February 2017, the BCCI honoured Shivalkar and Goyal with the C.K. Nayudu Lifetime Achievement award and a cash prize of Rs 25 lakh each. It was a great gesture, one of the best things the cricket board has done. In 2004, the award had gone to the original spin quartet led by Bedi. Now, by recognizing the duo who lived in the shadow of the legendary spinners for decades, the jury offered encouragement to the thousands of Indian foot-soldier cricketers who may never get their moment in the sun but who still uncomplainingly play on. All because of their undying passion for the game.

~

On a hot summer afternoon in May, Bishan Bedi is supervising hundreds of young kids practising in the nets at Delhi's National Stadium. Around forty of them will be taken to a summer camp in Una in Himachal Pradesh for four weeks in June. It is an annual ritual that Bedi has been involved with since 1993 when he set up the Bishan Bedi Cricket Coaching Trust. One of his founder-trainees was India's World Cup hero Yuvraj Singh. Many others have since trained under the master spinner's benevolent gaze. Mentoring the young is a long-standing passion and commitment. 'Being with them is like a tonic for the body and soul,' he says.

As the children gather around him at the National Stadium, the excitement in their eyes is palpable. Bedi looks like a large Santa Claus about to distribute goodies. 'I don't just coach them about cricket but talk to them about life. Before you become a good cricketer become a decent human being is my message!' he says.

He had a brief stint as India coach in 1990, a roller-coaster ride that was best known for his controversial remark after India's defeat in New Zealand – he declared that the team should be thrown into the Pacific Ocean. 'I didn't quite say that. What I said is that if somebody wants to commit suicide by jumping into the ocean, I won't stop them,' he clarifies. Ravi Shastri, who played in a series while Bedi was coach, describes him as the 'ultimate motivator'. 'He liked to play Big Boss but his energy is infectious.' Another player who didn't wish to be named is less charitable, claiming Bedi was more headmaster than coach. 'Bedi was obsessed with fielding practice so every time we dropped a catch, we had to run an extra round of the ground as punishment. He thought we were kids, not grown-up Test players!'

Murali Kartik, another left-arm spinner who benefited hugely from Bedi's guidance, says the 'Deadly Bedi Training Regime' was not for the faint-hearted. When a senior Delhi batsman couldn't take the strain of the laps that Bedi was making them run, he threw up. Bedi was unimpressed. Recalls Kartik, 'Paaji just told him that vomiting is a woman's problem, not a man's.' Ask Bedi about his obsession with fielding and fitness as a coach and he counters, 'Look, I wasn't the greatest athlete or fielder. But you learn from your mistakes and help others in not repeating them.'

The tough, straight-shooting approach extended to his son, Angad, who briefly aspired to emulate his father before trying his luck in the film and television industry. Angad was part of a group of young cricketers that Bedi had taken to England in 1995 and he forgot to carry his whites to the indoor nets at Lord's. Kartik offered him his extra set so that Angad could avoid the 25 pound fine Bedi had imposed on potential offenders. 'When Paaji found out, not only did he fine Angad, he made me pay 50 pounds for abetting him!' Kartik laughs. Angad admits his strict disciplinarian father did him no favours on the cricket field. 'I remember once I was late by a few minutes after a lunch break and my father yelled at me in front of everyone and asked me to run all the way from the National Stadium to Rashtrapati Bhavan and back in the Delhi heat as punishment.'

His coaching methods may have been unconventional but few would quarrel with Bedi's motivational skills. Former India player Maninder Singh, once considered a natural successor to the left-arm spin king, remembers how he was inspired by Bedi as a teenager. 'I was thirteen years old in 1978 when Bishan paaji saw me bowl for the first time. He straight away put his arm around me and gave me a pep talk about how if I worked hard I had the potential to play for India one day. Think about it, a man I idolized was telling me I could play for India. What bigger motivation can there be for a thirteen-year-old!' Maninder had another surprise waiting for him – the next morning Bedi gave him a pair of spiked shoes so he could bowl better!

It is this generosity of spirit that marks Bedi's incurable love affair with cricket. It has been tempestuous at times, even sadly acrimonious, but also laden with the joyful big-heartedness that comes with being a man who romances life as much as he does the sport. In his farmhouse on the outskirts of Delhi, he points to the fifteen cricket pitches he has prepared in the surrounding gardens. 'One day we will have a cricket nursery here, a place where you can learn the philosophy of clean, upright living via cricket with no netas and officials messing around!' What a wonderful little corner of India that would be.

4

Sunil Gavaskar

Original Middle-Class Hero

There are moments in life when time stands still, when sepia-tinted memories acquire a glow of warm and sunny permanence. There are rare occasions when a childhood hero becomes a teammate and when sport creates a magical bond of camaraderie that unites fan with champion. I enjoyed one such special day in the cricketing sun in 1991 while captaining the Bombay Gymkhana cricket team against Dadar Union in a local club match.

It was a clash of two contrasting cricketing cultures. The Gymkhana represents the old elite of Mumbai (which might also explain why it hasn't changed its original name even after the city was renamed). It was here that India played its first cricket Test at home against England in 1933. The Gymkhana at the time was a shining symbol of the Raj with its membership exclusively reserved for Europeans. That colonial legacy wasn't entirely shaken with the coming of independence. Liveried waiters still serve you pot tea and egg and chicken sandwiches, and during the drinks interval there is always fresh, ice-cool nimbu pani for the easily fatigued club members.

By contrast, the Dadar Union cricket club holds up a mirror to a city that has long since shaken off its colonial origins and seen the irresistible rise of the Maharashtrian middle class in cricket. From a tiny shed in Mumbai's central Dadar–Matunga area, the club has produced many Test cricketers. The angrezi-speaking Gymkhana amateurs versus the cut-throat aggression of the Dadar Union 'dadas' of cricket – this was clearly a no-contest.

But there was a slight difference this time. In our Gymkhana team, we had Sunil Gavaskar, the world's highest run scorer in Tests at the time. Then forty-two, Gavaskar had retired from cricket four years earlier and would come to the Gymkhana for a regular afternoon game of badminton as part of his fitness regimen. All through his cricketing career, he had played with great commitment for Dadar Union. Now, post-retirement, he just wanted to enjoy the sport. Which might explain why he chose to play a Sunday game for the Gymkhana gents rather than for the hard-edged professionals of his original club side.

Dadar Union batted first and scored 260 runs in their 50 overs. When our turn came to bat, I asked Gavaskar 'sir' with a nervous edge to my voice what number he would like to bat. 'Any number is good for me,' he said. We finally asked him to bat at number four. Predictably, we lost two early wickets and Gavaskar in his trademark floppy hat briskly walked to the wicket. For the first few balls, he played and missed. Then the opposing fast bowler bowled a bouncer that appeared to take him by surprise. The bouncer seemed to wake him up: it was almost as if his competitive instincts as well as his technical skills had been challenged and he wasn't going to allow age to be a barrier. For the next two hours, Gavaskar batted with near perfection and took us to the winning target. Awestruck, I asked him if he would be available the next Sunday as well for a game. 'Not really, the mind may be willing, but the legs are not!' he replied with a smile. After having broken every batting record for India at the time, he could afford to rest well. But he had given us a peek into his genius. And given me a story to embellish my rather average cricket career with: I once captained the legendary Sunil Manohar Gavaskar when Bombay Gymkhana defeated Dadar Union!

~

India's greatest-ever opening batsman almost became a fisherman. Of the many stories in Sunil Gavaskar's delightful autobiography *Sunny Days* it is the one of his being momentarily exchanged at birth that has stayed with me. Apparently, at the nursing home where Gavaskar was born, he was exchanged with a fisherwoman's baby while being given a bath. It was only an alert uncle who spotted this because he had noticed a little hole at the top of the left earlobe of the baby Gavaskar. 'The story is absolutely true, I haven't made up a word of it,' insists Gavaskar. And then with his trademark dry humour suggests, 'Now you know why I got caught behind the wicket so often. Because I would go fishing outside the off stump!'

The loss of the fisherfolk community was cricket's gain. Sunil Gavaskar is, and always will be, Indian cricket's original Little Master. No one before or since has played with a straighter bat. No one has been such a remorseless run accumulator. And no one has batted with greater single-minded concentration. It's a habit he inculcated when he was barely six years old and playing tennis-ball cricket in the locality. 'We would play in the street outside our building and he just wouldn't get out till finally we would either force the umpire to give him out or snatch the bat from him by threatening to break it,' says his oldest friend and neighbour Milind Rege who also went on to play for Mumbai. And when Gavaskar wasn't batting, he would take a long run-up and try to bowl fast to emulate his first cricket hero, the West Indian fast bowler Wesley Hall. But he didn't have the size or build for fast bowling: he was destined for batting greatness.

'Yes, it was in the compound of Bhagirathi buildings, a cluster of four buildings with six flats each, that I learnt my cricket. Since the buildings were so close to each other, the only way to get runs was to drive straight. The rule there to prevent windowpanes from being broken was if you hit the ball above the first floor then you were out. So one learnt to play along the ground and play straight to get any runs,' says Gavaskar. The lessons were learnt well: Gavaskar would go on to score 10,122 Test runs, then a world record.

The Chikhalwadi area in Tardeo where Gavaskar grew up is in the heart of south-central Mumbai, a congested neighbourhood that is symbolic of the rise and fall of the Maharashtrian middle class. In the cosmopolitan mix of this part of Mumbai, the Gujaratis had their jewellery stores, the Sindhis and Bohris their trading genes, and the Catholics played football while the Maharashtrians saw cricket as their escape from clerical serfdom. Today, the centre of gravity in Mumbai cricket has shifted to the distant suburbs as the Maharashtrian middle class has been gradually dislocated from its original bastion. Traffic snarls and crumbling infrastructure have made living in the heart of Mumbai an urban nightmare. But in the 1950s and 1960s, cricket was Chikhalwadi's badge of identity: young boys played the game with a fierce determination that would characterize their mantra for success. 'At one time, there were around half a dozen players from in and around the neighbourhood who were playing for the Mumbai side. It was almost as if Chikhalwadi was representing the entire city,' says Gavaskar with a touch of pride.

The sport was ingrained in the family. Gavaskar's father, Manohar, was a decent club-level wicketkeeper-batsman who played for his office team. His mother, Meenal, was also a driving force in spurring him to play cricket: she would throw a tennis ball at her little son in the veranda while his two younger sisters doted on their elder brother. 'I remember once when Sunil hit the ball so hard that his mother's nose began to bleed. But that didn't stop her from playing with us,' recalls Rege affectionately.

Meenal instilled the original middle-class values of hard work and discipline in her son, ensuring that he didn't miss out on academics while excelling at cricket. Gavaskar couldn't make one India schoolboys cricket tour because his mother insisted that he give his final exams first. 'I remember when all of us had alcohol for the first time and Sunil's mother came to know of it. She made Sunil promise that he would never touch a drink again, a promise he kept through his cricketing career,' says Rege. When Gavaskar made his Test debut, his mother promised him one rupee for every international run he made. After every tour, she would give him the money in a neat envelope. Gavaskar says he has kept the envelopes with him to this day!

But it was his mother's brother and Gavaskar's uncle Madhav Mantri who was the first major influence on his cricket. Mantri had represented India in the 1950s, as a resolute if unspectacular wicketkeeper-batsman. His Test record may have been average but he enjoyed a formidable reputation as a cricket mentor and strict disciplinarian. 'Nana mama, as I affectionately called him, had a big impact on my cricket. Being an Indian Test player, he was an early hero. Once when I was visiting his house, I saw plenty of cricket caps lying in a drawer in his cupboard, so I asked for one. He told me that an India cap had to be earned and could not just be given away, so that was a big lesson,' Gavaskar says.

That wasn't the only lesson the uncle would teach his diligent nephew. 'Once I got a double hundred in an inter-college match and had a partnership of nearly 500 runs. Nana mama asked me how I had got out. I told him that I had got bored and had tried a big shot and been dismissed. He then asked me if my batting partner was out. I told him that my partner was nearing the 300-run mark, at which point Nana mama reminded me that if I had carried on, then I too could get a triple century. "Never do a bowler any favours and give him your wicket" was his message. I never forgot it,' says Gavaskar.

From the time he began playing the game seriously at the age of twelve for St Xavier's School, and later for St Xavier's College, Gavaskar built an impressive reputation as a batsman who could bat for long hours. Xavier's was then South Mumbai's premier Jesuit institution, seeped in the best traditions of nurturing young minds to attain all-round excellence. Gavaskar points out, 'We had the freedom to play sports but not at the cost of studies so you learnt to balance the two. I had to score runs, but also had to get the marks!' While in recent years the sporting culture has faded, in the 1950s and 1960s, St Xavier's had a decent cricket team. Just next to the school and college is the vast Azad Maidan, which has played host to many political protest movements and has also nurtured cricket talent. Between Azad Maidan and its adjacent Cross Maidan, there are two dozen turf wickets; no other city anywhere in the country has a similar facility. In the city that never sleeps, cricket is played round the year, even during Mumbai's monsoon months when a unique inter-club tournament called the Kanga League is held. 'I don't remember a single weekend when I was growing up when I wasn't playing a cricket match. We played on all kinds of wickets, rain or shine. That experience is priceless,' says Gavaskar about his early years.

It was a tough education for the young Gavaskar in the hard-edged, uncompromising world of Mumbai cricket. The city had a rich tradition in the sport, especially in the art of batsmanship, and recognition had to be earned through the sheer weight of runs. Gavaskar's first break in Mumbai club cricket came when he moved to Dadar Union in 1966 as a seventeen-year-old. Dadar Union symbolized Mumbai's highly competitive middle-class cricketing ethos. Mantri was the captain of the side but would do no favours to his nephew. Nor would Mantri's successor, the more flamboyant Mumbai player Vasu Paranjpe. Such was Gavaskar's passion for local club cricket that even after becoming a star Indian player, he would still play for Dadar Union. 'He would come from a foreign tour with the Indian team at 5 a.m. and call me to say that he wanted to be included in the side the next morning. I guess the club was in his blood,' recalls Paranjpe. 'It was at Dadar Union that I toughened my cricket, knowing every run had to be earned, especially on the wet wickets of the Kanga League,' acknowledges Gavaskar.

A chronicler of Mumbai cricket, Makarand Waingankar in his book *A Million Broken Windows: The Magic and Mystique of Bombay*

Cricket writes of the city's 'khadoos' attitude as defining its cricket, a unique 'Bambaiya' word that, as mentioned in Chapter 1, reflects the metropolis's dogged, never-say-die spirit. 'Anyone familiar with the local trains of Mumbai would know that it is like a survival game in itself. To board the train in record time, push yourself through the crowds to make just 20 centimetres of space, to be able to extend your hands enough to grab the handlebars, every moment of the travel is truly a struggle. Every day on a local train going to a match makes a Mumbai cricketer a more determined player!' writes Waingankar.

He also describes the Mumbai batting 'gharana'. 'Mumbai cricket is a big family, a family which is replete with people who are happy to pass on their genius to others. This is precisely why the talent bed of Mumbai never gets barren . . . Gavaskar was a genius but his genius was not his own. He was the product of Merchant, Manjrekar and Sardesai and many other great cricketers of Mumbai who had bequeathed the legacy, the conditions, for Gavaskar to come and play.'

And play he did. With a technical finesse that has scarcely been matched. His was not to be the prodigious rise of a Sachin Tendulkar who was already playing for the country at the age of sixteen. Gavaskar was more like the fierce mountaineer who steadily moves from one base camp to the next without ever wavering from his ultimate goal of reaching the summit. Through school, college, university, club and state cricket, he kept piling up the runs, breaking batting records and waiting for the elusive India cap he had first seen at his uncle's home. 'Today, you can get an IPL contract if you score just a couple of hundreds in local cricket; then you just kept at it in the hope that you would finally get selected for India. Inter-university cricket in particular was a big boon in those days but I think it was only after I had scored my first few hundreds in the Ranji Trophy that I began to feel that I might be ready to play for the country,' says Gavaskar.

By the winter of 1970 at the age of twenty-one, he was ready and was picked for the Indian team to tour the West Indies. His father had promised to give him ten rupees for every hundred he scored as a teenager, a promise that had already sent the household budgets awry through the 1960s! The young Gavaskar didn't need any incentive to score runs though. 'His obsession with run-making in local cricket convinced us that he was special,' says Paranjpe. Just how special the world was about to find out.

~

Sunil Gavaskar left for the West Indies in December 1970 as a talented young cricketer with stars in his eyes; he returned four months later, as the brightest star in the sport. Translating potential into success can take years but Gavaskar was the meteorite who bridged the gap between domestic and international cricket with dazzling ease. A mighty 774 runs in the five-match series made it the most productive debut in the history of the game. India defeated the West Indies in the Caribbean for the first time and Gavaskar was a name that was literally on everyone's lips: a Trinidadian musician even composed a Calypso song in his honour. 'It was Gavaskar, the real master, just like a wall, we couldn't out Gavaskar at all,' the words reflecting the jaw-dropping feats of the debutant.

'I went to the West Indies excited but apprehensive at the same time. My career had progressed steadily from schools cricket through to playing for Mumbai. But I was picked for India without even playing for West Zone, so it was a big leap forward and naturally I was concerned whether I would make the grade,' says Gavaskar, a trifle modestly. He needn't have worried: from his very first game at the Queen's Park Oval in Trinidad, Gavaskar showed that the years spent in the maidans of Mumbai had more than prepared him for the rigours of international cricket. 'There are plenty of memories from that first tour of the West Indies but my favourite is hitting the winning boundary in my first Test; that was a very special moment that will always stay with me,' he says.

The Indian team under Ajit Wadekar had a nice blend of experience and youth: four of the team members had toured the West Indies in 1962 when they had been routed 5-0. They included my father and M.L. Jaisimha, an early hero of Gavaskar. 'I was a huge fan of Jaisimha for his elegant batting and the way he carried himself on the field. To be sharing dressing room space with him was like a dream. The West Indies also had players like Garfield Sobers, Rohan Kanhai, Lance Gibbs, players whom I had only seen in photo albums and long admired. Now, to be playing against them was unforgettable. It was a tour that I just didn't want to end!' recalls Gavaskar.

In 1971, the West Indies team led by Sobers, the world's greatest all-rounder, was a team in transition with many of its best players nearing retirement and the fast bowlers not quite so threatening. And yet, past scars of heavy defeats in the Caribbean loomed large over the Indians. My father hit the first high note for Indian self-confidence with a double century in the opening Test in Jamaica and then boosted the morale of the young Gavaskar. 'I didn't play the first Test because of a finger injury. Sardee [as my father was affectionately called in the West Indies] is sitting in the dressing room and turns to one of the West Indian players and tells him, "This young man will also score a double century against you." It just lifted my spirits and made me feel as if I really belonged,' says Gavaskar.

My father's words would prove prophetic. In the last Test, Gavaskar scored a match-saving 220 runs, following up a century in the first innings. Many years later, I asked my father what had led him to predict a glorious future for Gavaskar even before he had played his first game for India. My father's explanation: 'Sunil's bat was always so straight and he just had this hunger for runs which all of us could see. Most of us would be happy with scoring a century every few games, Sunil wants centuries for breakfast, lunch and dinner!'

The appetite for runs against the formidable West Indies in particular was insatiable. In 27 Tests against them, he scored 13 centuries at an average of more than 65 runs per innings. And while his average dips to a more modest 45 when facing the four-pronged West Indies pace attack in the latter part of his career, he still managed to score 5 centuries and average higher against the most intimidating bowling in the history of the game than any other batsman in that period.

I ask Gavaskar to explain his formula for success against the West Indies. His response: 'I don't know whether I have a rational explanation, it's just something that happened. Maybe, since I am a short man, the new-ball bowlers right from my schooldays thought they could bounce me out. So I was well prepared to play the short balls which the West Indies fast bowlers would throw at me. I saw the bouncer, especially in my debut series, as a scoring opportunity and that maybe helped me to succeed against the West Indies.'

In a sense, that first series against the West Indies in 1971 set the template for future generations of Indian cricketers when playing fast bowling. As his contemporary and another batting great Gundappa Viswanath puts it, 'Sunny's biggest contribution is that he gave all of us the self-belief to take on the fastest bowling in the world.'

Indeed, until Gavaskar burst on to the scene, Indian batsmen had a reputation of shying away from playing the short ball, of showing a lack of courage when confronted with quick bowling. His arrival signalled the start of a new era where Indian batsmen were encouraged to look at the fiercest of opponents squarely in the eye. With his unflinching obduracy, he ended decades of an inferiority complex that had troubled Indian batting. And he did it, as my father would often point out, without wearing a helmet or the protective equipment that today's batsmen are blessed with. My father's constant refrain was, 'Never compare Gavaskar or any player of my era with today's batsmen. Today's batsmen don't have to fear getting hit because they wear helmets. We learnt our technique without any helmet.'

The 1970s was a glorious period for fast bowling with every international side having at least one genuinely quick bowler and there were no restrictions on the number of bouncers in an over. Didn't Gavaskar ever fear for his life? 'No, I never ever feared a cricket ball. I always saw playing fast bowling as a challenge and felt that if you kept your eye on the ball, no fast bowler could hit you,' he says.

In 1980, Gavaskar got a skullcap designed for himself purely as a precautionary measure, that too on the advice of the Pakistani paceman Imran Khan. 'Imran kept urging me to wear one because as he rightly said, there is always one ball that even the best batsmen can lose sight of and it's for that one ball that you need to wear some protection. It was sound advice,' says Gavaskar. The only time Gavaskar was hit on the head in his career was in 1983 when a Malcolm Marshall bouncer struck him. And even then he did not flinch.

Which is why the Gavaskar era that began in 1971 marks a turning point in Indian cricket. In 1962, the Indian team had gone to the West Indies and been battered into submission. The captain Nari Contractor had almost died after being hit by a bouncer and many of the players were actually scared of facing up to the West Indians. Then, almost a decade later, a pint-sized opening batsman emerges and shows that it is possible to face up to the West Indians and defeat them in their own backyard. A major psychological boundary was conquered: tenacity had triumphed over timidity.

If a Gavaskar-inspired cricket team provided hope in the first half of 1971 with victory over the West Indies, the Indian army and the political leadership of Indira Gandhi would win a major battle of its own in December that year by forcing the Pakistani army to surrender and liberate Bangladesh. The decisive triumph on the battlefield laid to rest the ghosts of the 1962 Sino-Indian war, which had left the army bruised and humiliated. Indira Gandhi led from the front, demonstrating admirable courage in the face of adversity. Through the 1970s, Indira would tower over all her rivals; there was an authoritarian streak to her personality that was deeply problematic but she was also a staunch nationalist who would never back off from a fight. Patriot and putative dictator, Indira did not see politics as a morality play like her father, Jawaharlal Nehru, but there was a fierce desire to survive and win at all costs. The toughness of her character would make her an inspirational figure for millions; India's political leadership was acquiring a more ruthless edge and so slowly would its cricket.

Indeed, Indira's combative, if controversial, style would typify the politics of a turbulent decade just as Gavaskar's stoic determination would shape Indian cricket. Both would have their detractors but few doubted their patriotism and commitment to the cause. Both were raised in an India which was insecure about its true place in the world, where socialistic economics, public sector monopolies and high tax rates held out limited opportunities for economic growth and social mobility and where hope and despair were conjoined twins. But in 1971, an air of defeatism was being replaced by a future pregnant with renewed expectations, where self-reliance was the new credo.

~

After instant success in 1971, it took Gavaskar another three years to notch up his next hundred, leading some critics to wonder whether he was a one-series wonder. This is why he rates his century against England in 1974 as one of his best knocks. 'That century at Old Trafford was a turning point because it brought back my self-belief which had taken a beating and also because it was scored on a green pitch against some really fine fast bowling,' he says, although he rates a 50 on the same ground in 1971 as his best Test innings.

From that point on, there was no turning back. Between January 1976 and January 1980, Gavaskar scored 18 hundreds in 45 Tests at an average of just under 60 runs per innings. It was almost Bradmanesque, and Gavaskar was firmly established as one of the all-time greats of the game. Indeed, in his first 62 Tests, Gavaskar scored as many as 23 hundreds. He then appeared to slow down: in his last 63 Tests he managed only 11 hundreds. 'I think a batsman peaks between the age of twenty-four and thirty-two years and that's when you will find that most batsmen have their most productive period,' says Gavaskar.

The statistics also suggest the gradual evolution of Gavaskar as a batsman. In the first half of his career, Gavaskar, along with Gundappa Viswanath, carried the Indian team on broad shoulders.

'You got Gavaskar and Viswanath out and you knew the Indian team was almost done and dusted,' is how Sir Vivian Richards, another great player of the 1970s, puts it. The pressure to score runs and hold the team's batting together meant that Gavaskar almost completely eschewed all risks while batting. He was like a monk in a monastery, engaged in a personal battle of constant self-denial, while putting the team's interests above his own. It was almost as if Gavaskar's batting reflected the values of the salaried Indian middle class in the 1970s, which placed a premium on thrift and abstinence. This was a generation that was wary of any form of extravagance, where hard-earned money in the bank mattered far more than any flirtation in a nascent stock market.

As a teenager growing up in a middle-class family in the 1970s, I recall there being little time or money for any personal indulgences. A school friend shared a WhatsApp message that sums up the period well: 'The [19]70s were of an India where a Camlin geometry box and a Natraj pencil were prized possessions, ice cream meant an orange stick or a chocolate bar, holidays were spent with grandparents and an HMT watch was a "gift" only if you passed your final school exam.' Gavaskar was our hero because his fortitude at the crease offered comfort in times of scarcity.

Explaining his approach to batting, Gavaskar says, 'I was actually a very aggressive batsman when I started off playing the game, loved to hook and cut. But after my first series, I realized that the team needed me to stay at the wicket and score big runs, so I tried to eliminate the risky shots, but when the bad ball came along I invariably scored off it.'

It was only towards the end of the 1970s that Gavaskar finally felt that the time was ripe for him to liberate himself from the self-contained cage in which he had imprisoned himself. By then, Indian batting had found a steel that went beyond just two short men. 'Now, it was no longer just Vishy and me, there was Chetan Chauhan, Mohinder Amarnath, Dilip Vengsarkar, Sandeep Patil and Kapil Dev who could share the burden of run-making. I now began to take a few more risks. It meant, of course, I scored fewer hundreds but I enjoyed my cricket much more in the second half of my career,' he says.

An epic innings of 221 at the Oval in 1979 when India almost chased down an improbable 438 runs to win a Test was perhaps the moment when Gavaskar discovered a new-found freedom. Chetan Chauhan was Gavaskar's opening partner in that fourth innings chase and remembers how effortlessly his colleague shifted gears. 'I think we were 200-odd runs for no loss soon after lunch. Suddenly, Sunny became the aggressor and started even hitting the odd lofted stroke. It was flawless batting and just a joy to watch from the other end. The English didn't know what had hit them,' recalls Chauhan. On a sunlit Oval evening, Gavaskar had played a heroic innings whose afterglow would shine for years as a monument to the art of batsmanship.

Four years later, in 1983, Gavaskar would play a similar attacking innings, this time against the mighty West Indians in Delhi, a century which would equal Bradman's record of 29 Test hundreds. The hook, one of cricket's most audacious shots, which he had kept locked in his kitbag for over a decade, was now suddenly back on display. 'I found that ducking and weaving from the bouncer were restricting my scoring opportunities, so I decided that if they bowl short, I will not hesitate to play the hook,' he says.

Two Tests later in Chennai, he would score another classic double century, this time to cross the Bradman record for most Test hundreds. 'Look, breaking Sir Don's record was never a goal because he got his hundreds in less than 70 innings and just 52 Tests. My thirtieth hundred was a statistical achievement, but not a record,' Gavaskar says modestly. In 1986, Gavaskar would scale another mountain by scoring his 10,000th run, becoming the first batsman to reach that landmark, one which he again brushes aside as 'a statistic, not a record as such'.

And yet, as the first cricketer to get to 30 centuries and 10,000 runs, Gavaskar's achievements must be seen as more than just any other statistic milestone in the record books. Others have since crossed those marks, but at the time this was the first major world record held by an Indian sportsperson. For a nation still struggling to make its mark globally, Gavaskar became a badge of middle-class pride. Yes, we had our Olympic hockey golds, and had produced world champions in billiards, but while hockey was trapped in black-and-white images from a glorious past, billiards had a limited audience. Cricket was India's mass sport and Gavaskar was the first Indian cricketer whom one could argue was the 'best' in the world. The West Indians would claim Viv Richards was the dominant batsman of the 1970s era, the Pakistanis might point to the artistry of a Zaheer Abbas and the Australians will remind you of the style and authority with which Greg Chappell batted. And yet, many years later when I asked Pakistan's captain Imran Khan in a television show which cricketer he would choose to bat for his life, his answer was illuminating: 'Well, Viv was the best player I bowled to because he would intimidate you with his shots, but Gavaskar was the one who gave the least chances. To save my life, I will probably plump for Sunny.' Imran's assessment is probably accurate. Gavaskar once batted left-handed for the first time in his life in a match against Karnataka in 1981–82 to counter the opposition spin bowlers and, quite remarkably, still didn't get out!

~

Is there a Gavaskar school of batsmanship that defines Indian cricket? Almost every modern great Indian batsman, including Sachin Tendulkar, pays tribute to Gavaskar as an inspiring role model. When Tendulkar was yet a teenager Gavaskar gifted him his leg guards, making him feel on top of the world. 'I slept with the leg guards next to me. It was like being given a gift from God!' Certainly, every Indian opening batsman, till Virender Sehwag changed the rules of the game, has been judged by the lofty standards that Gavaskar set. 'He is the gold standard for batting and the inspiration for me to play the game. I don't think there is a batsman who watched him play who wasn't influenced by his style,' former Test player Sanjay Manjrekar says.

Shishir Hattangadi, a former Mumbai captain who opened with Gavaskar, recalls how he was nervous when he went out to bat with him for the first time as a twenty-one-year-old in 1981. Says Hattangadi, 'He was a cult figure for all of us and we just wanted to seek his approval. Everyone in the dressing room wanted to copy him, not just his batting style and how he prepared for a game, but even what he wore and what music he listened to. When Gavaskar hummed a ghazal, then everyone in the team wanted to also sing the same tune.'

To appreciate the Gavaskar batting masterclass, I turned to Viswanath, his soulmate on the field, and also his brother-in-law. Married to Gavaskar's younger sister Kavita, Viswanath quips about the family relationship, 'Moral of the story: never introduce your friend to your sister!' On a balmy evening in his home town of Bengaluru, he tells me just why he believes Gavaskar is in another league as a batsman (Gavaskar, on the other hand, insists Viswanath is the superior batsman and the best player he has seen, a belief shared by most Bengalureans in particular). Both Gavaskar and Viswanath are short men. Gavaskar is five foot five inches, Viswanath half an inch shorter. If you were to pick an all-time great Indian team, the only pure batsman above six feet who might push for a place would be V.V.S. Laxman and even he is unlikely to make the cut. Is there something about short Indian men that makes them better batsmen? 'We might be short in height, but we are quick on our feet,' says Viswanath, whose rasping square cut was a signature shot.

He then analyses Gavaskar's game: 'I think what makes Sunil stand out is his judgement of line and length and just how still his head was when standing at the crease. As an opener, he played the fastest bowling in the world and never seemed to be caught in no man's land. But above all else, his biggest quality was his concentration. When you were batting with him, he was so focused that it was difficult to even talk to him. It was as if he was in another world.'

The concentration powers, Gavaskar claims, are a 'gift of God'. 'Even today, I can read a book in a crowded room full of noise,' he says. Gavaskar at the wicket was like a sage seeking nirvana under a banyan tree. Nothing it seemed would affect his concentration (except once a dog running on to the pitch!). The art of batting for him was a process of meticulous preparation, which would begin the moment he arrived at the ground. 'I might crack a few jokes, or hum a song during practice but the moment I put on my box [abdomen guard] and heard the bell to signal the start of the game, I would stop talking to anyone and my teammates would also respect my need to be left alone. I just wanted to shut everything out and focus on the battle ahead,' he says. Such was his concentration at the wicket that he didn't even look at the scoreboard to see how many runs he had scored.

Gavaskar's batting genius lies then in the conquest of the mind: there might have been better shot-makers than him but no one has probably self-analysed and worked on his batting with the mental discipline that Gavaskar brought to his game. The likes of Viswanath or Tendulkar would leave you awestruck with the boldness of their strokes but Gavaskar was like the artisan who keeps chiselling away at a sculpture till he achieves perfection. His straight drive and square cut were classical shots as was his flick off the hips to the pacemen and on drive to the spinners, but like a singer doing riyaz all his life, he never stopped learning. 'The rest of us could make the same mistake twice, but Sunil would never give the bowler a second chance,' says Viswanath.

He didn't have one single coach to guide him but would keep imbibing new lessons. Whether it was making a slight adjustment in his stance or grip, or a gentle modification in the length of his bat handle or even using lighter pads, Gavaskar was the professor of batting with an encyclopaedic knowledge of the game. In his first series for India in the West Indies, for example, he stood outside the crease to narrow the swing for the bowler and didn't ask the umpire for a leg guard. By the time he played his last game, he was playing more strokes than he ever had as a twenty-one-year-old. He might not run the 100 metres in under 12 seconds or even race the marathon, but he would spend the off-season in leg-strengthening exercises by running up and down the stadium stairs at the CCI. And where once he was an average fielder, he worked at his game to become a first-rate slip catcher. Today's cricketers are brawny athletes, spending hours in the gymnasium to build muscle or else using computer technology to analyse their batting. Gavaskar's mind was a computer, his body an able ally. 'I made sure I was fit enough to bat all day, that's all that really matters in cricket,' he says.

In 1975, in the first World Cup, he scored a tortoise-like 36 not out in 60 overs against England, an innings he says remains a 'regret': 'I didn't know how to score runs quickly that day, nor how to get out.' But in the 1987 World Cup, he was good enough to score a one-day century in just 85 balls against New Zealand in his penultimate one-day match. The fastest then was an 82-ball century by Clive Lloyd in the 1975 finals. 'I was 99 in 80 balls and maybe if I had known of the record earlier, I would have gone for it,' says Gavaskar.

'Sunny made use of every ounce of talent he had to keep getting better. He was a genius, but someone who never took his talent or success for granted,' says Mohinder Amarnath, another contemporary. Chauhan, who saw Gavaskar at close quarters as his most successful opening partner, says every day of batting with him was an education. 'I remember once I refused a single and almost got him run out. He wasn't happy but just turned to me and said, "Chetan, 99 singles will get you close to a hundred, so let's not miss the singles." Taking singles became the secret of our success as a pair,' points out Chauhan.

Each of these formidable qualities were on display in Gavaskar's last Test innings against Pakistan in 1987 at Bengaluru. It was a mini-epic: he scored 96 runs in an innings where the next highest score was extras with 27. On a vicious turner, Gavaskar brought all his skill and experience to the game, defending the dangerous deliveries with soft hands, watchful eyes and a straight bat, but never missing a scoring chance. He had planned to retire a year earlier but had been persuaded out of it by the Pakistani captain Imran Khan. 'Imran and I were at a lunch in England in 1986 when I told him of my decision to retire because I wasn't enjoying the game any more. He was horrified at the idea saying, "You can't retire now. Pakistan is coming to India early next year and I want to beat India in India and it won't be the same if you are not part of the Indian team. Let's have one last tilt at each other." That's how I decided to carry on for one last series,' says Gavaskar.

Imran got his wish: Pakistan defeated India in India in 1987. But it was Gavaskar's batting in Bengaluru that provided the enduring memory: a master playing one final symphony before his admirers. That very year, Gavaskar played his last first-class match. This time, Imran and he were on the same side as the Rest of the World played the MCC in a bicentennial match at Lord's. Gavaskar had turned thirty-eight a month earlier but technique is ageless and he batted with the spirit of a much younger man against an attack that included the two best bowlers in the world at the time, Malcolm Marshall and Sir Richard Hadlee. He had never scored a hundred at Lord's, but now in his final game he filled that blank too. It was a perfect ending to a near-perfect career. You wouldn't have expected it any other way from the ultimate cricket perfectionist. As Gavaskar would later say, quoting India's other great opening batsman, Vijay Merchant, 'Retire when people say why, and not why not!'

~

Sunil Gavaskar would have been acknowledged as an all-time great just for his run-making feats. But what sets him apart is the leadership that he provided to the game, on and off the field. If Pataudi was the charismatic captain and Bedi provided the rebellious streak, Gavaskar had the stature to redefine the concept of 'player power'. The intelligence which he brought to his batting is reflected in almost every aspect of his life. 'When Sunny talks, you listen. He has that kind of articulate and authoritative voice which no one else can match in Indian cricket,' says Ravi Shastri, who made his Test debut under Gavaskar's leadership.

Gavaskar captained a series for the first time in 1978–79 against a weakened West Indies side. India had just been defeated in Pakistan and there was an urgent need to repair a faltering ship. As captain, he would take some tough steps initially, including dropping Bedi, a move that ruptured an already difficult relationship between the two Indian stars of the game. 'Look, I didn't drop Bedi, the selectors did but they didn't have the courage to inform the great man about it. So I went to his room to inform him about it before he heard it from the media. It is fashionable to blame me for every selection or omission,' says Gavaskar.

But it was the sheer weight of the runs he made that instantly earned Gavaskar his captaincy spurs. In the first Test he made a double century on a difficult wicket, confirming that the burden of captaincy wouldn't affect his batting. In fact, as captain Gavaskar averaged 50.72 per innings in 47 games with 11 hundreds as against 51.33 in 78 Tests when he was not captain. 'I think I was able to compartmentalize my cricket. Once I had a bat in hand, my job was to stay at the wicket and score runs because that's what I was selected to play for the country for,' says Gavaskar.

As captain, Gavaskar won more Tests than he lost: winning 9 and losing 8, including a memorable 'revenge' series win against Pakistan in 1979 that he describes as his finest victory as skipper. That was the series where Gavaskar used Kapil Dev as a strike weapon, the first time that an Indian captain made pace and not spin his calling card. Recalls Madan Lal, Kapil's new-ball partner, 'Before Gavaskar became captain, people used to laugh at us and say, oh, here come India's spin bowlers. It was Sunny who gave us the respect and the confidence that we could also take wickets,' says Lal.

Leg-spinner L. Sivaramakrishnan fondly remembers playing as a nineteen-year-old one-day debutant under Gavaskar's captaincy during the 1985 World Championships of cricket in Australia. 'Just before the first game when I was bowling in the nets, Gavaskar comes to me and tells me quietly, "Listen, don't reveal your bowling variations in practice, these Australians have cameras everywhere." He was the best captain I played under, clear-headed and methodical, someone who knew exactly what he wanted,' says Sivaramakrishnan. The mystery spinner would go on to play a key role in India's victory in the tournament, which would end up being Gavaskar's last as India captain.

But as a strong-willed, at times stubbornly unbending, man, his tenure as captain was not without controversy. In 1981, for example, he led his partner Chetan Chauhan off the field in Australia after being wrongly given out. It was a bizarre scenario, a captain forcing a reluctant partner to leave the field, almost forfeiting the match in the process. It is, Gavaskar says, his biggest regret in cricket. 'It wasn't the fact that I had been given a bad decision that prompted the walkout but the abuse and intemperate language used by the Australian players as I was making my way from the crease that led me to lose my cool. Had I not been abused, I would have gone back to the pavilion and vented my anger in the privacy of the dressing room,' he claims. Chauhan, who ultimately came back to bat after the team manager intervened, says it was one of the few instances where Gavaskar who had been struggling for runs in the series seemed to crack under pressure. 'We were 200 runs behind on the first innings, we had a strong partnership going and then Sunny gets a terrible leg-before-wicket (LBW) decision. Naturally, he was angry,' says Chauhan. Yet, in typical Gavaskar fashion, he bounced back with his shrewd captaincy just a day later to lead India to a famous last-day win.

In 1981–82, Gavaskar was again in the eye of a storm, this time being accused by the English of deliberately slowing down the game after winning the first Test. 'Even the spinners would take five minutes to bowl an over,' accused former England captain David Gower. It led to the charge against Gavaskar that he was a 'negative' captain who played for a draw and not to win. Gavaskar has a firm response to his captaincy critics: 'We Indians have too many set ideas about life and cricket. Just because a player hits the ball in the air, he becomes an aggressive batsman and captain and if you play along the ground you are a defensive, risk-free captain. I never once went into a Test match with the intention of playing for a draw, but yes, if the team was not in a position to win, then I wanted to ensure we didn't lose either. Nobody likes to lose, surely.'

A similar controversy erupted three years later when Gavaskar was accused of not declaring soon enough as India's batsmen crawled for two long days in Kolkata in the 1984–85 series against England. A volatile Eden Gardens crowd, already upset that Kapil Dev had been dropped for the game, vented their ire on Gavaskar, chanting slogans against him and even pelting fruits in his direction when he tried to pacify them. An angry Gavaskar vowed never to play at Eden Gardens again, and he actually dropped out of a Test in 1986. The fact that fruits were even thrown at the stand where his wife was sitting was apparently the last straw. 'I won't tell you what really happened, let's leave some things for my own biography,' says Gavaskar, laughing. 'I think he was more hurt than angry at the crowd's behaviour,' says Debasish Dutta, a Kolkata-based cricket journalist who has tracked Gavaskar closely for years.

Gavaskar's relations with Kolkata do have a happier ending though: his son, Rohan, played successfully for Bengal in the Ranji Trophy and, in 2016, Gavaskar was felicitated by the Cricket Association of Bengal (CAB) along with other Indian and Pakistani legends ahead of the World Twenty20. However, there is no life-size portrait of Gavaskar on the Eden Gardens walls as there are of some other Indian greats. 'I hope the error is rectified soon,' says Dutta. 'Gavaskar deserves the honour.'

The Kolkata incident highlights how cricket fandom can easily descend into nasty rowdyism, a fickleness that suggests a fragile relationship between player and fan. Or maybe it just reflects how Gavaskar was perceived as cussed and dogmatic by a section of Indian cricket watchers. A Kapil Dev was a folk hero as later a Sachin

Tendulkar would also become; they brought a childlike exuberance to their game which made them instant crowd favourites. By contrast, Gavaskar was the steely middle-class workaholic; his cricket was classical but not flashy. For a long time, he appeared to mask his emotions on the field, making him seem a distant, inaccessible figure. The multitudes admired and revered him but the spontaneous affection was sometimes missing.

Perhaps Gavaskar's uncompromising spirit was often falsely interpreted as arrogance. Which might also explain why Gavaskar often found his actions under greater scrutiny than some of his peers'. For example, he was even accused of actively promoting fellow Mumbai cricketers at the cost of talented players from other regions. When a nineteen-year-old Mumbai collegian Ravi Shastri was flown down to New Zealand as a replacement bowler, there was criticism that Gavaskar had influenced the decision. When fringe players Ghulam Parkar and Suru Nayak, both from Mumbai, were picked for the 1982 English tour, Gavaskar was again in the line of fire.

The charge of parochialism ill fits a cricketer of Gavaskar's standing. 'Would any captain be so foolish as to promote players only because they come from his home state?' asks an irate Gavaskar. 'The India captain doesn't have a vote in the selection committee and if you see, the selectors at the time, they included some of the biggest names in Indian cricket. To suggest that I muscled my way over them is to do grave injustice to them. Please look at the record of Shastri and look at the number of non-Mumbai players who made their debut under my captaincy.'

Gavaskar sparked off another controversy when he dropped fellow Mumbaikar Dilip Vengsarkar, who also played for the same club, Dadar Union, during a Ranji Trophy match in 1985–86. 'We had gone to play a charity game the day before in Jamshedpur and landed back in Mumbai at midnight. I told the players that they needn't come for the warm-up the next morning but had to be at the ground before I went for the toss. The other players like Ravi Shastri and Sandeep Patil were there in time, but Dilip didn't land up even though I went about five minutes late for the toss and even walked slowly to the pitch in the hope that he would turn up before I exchanged team names. Unfortunately, he didn't, leaving me with no choice but to leave him out,' claims Gavaskar. Did it rupture his relationship with the Indian team's other star batsman? 'No, I think he understood the discipline that Dadar Union players were taught,' says Gavaskar. The incident typifies Gavaskar's no-nonsense approach to the game, which allowed for no shortcuts to success.

A more familiar charge against Gavaskar is that he is Indian cricket's original money-minded mercenary. Bedi has, as mentioned in the earlier chapter, accused him of claiming at a team meeting that he would 'stagnate' if he didn't think of money. It's an accusation that infuriates Gavaskar. 'Mr Bedi is the finest left-arm spinner I have seen but he is also a terrific spinner of yarns and one of them is this so-called statement of mine. I would like him to produce even one witness to back up his statement,' he says angrily. 'I simply articulated the Indian cricketers' views about the fees they were getting, fought for better compensation and for that I got branded money-minded.'

Ironically, for a while, Bedi, the instinctive rebel, and Gavaskar, the more artful practitioner of cricketing realpolitik, formed the perfect pair in negotiating with the cricket board on behalf of the players. On the 1976 tour of the West Indies, the duo was instrumental in forging a players' association, the first move towards pushing for greater equality between players and board officials. 'Do you know, on my first tour to the West Indies in 1971, we were made to blindly sign a contract at the airport by the board under which we would be paid Rs 500 during the tour and another Rs 500 at the end of it depending on the manager's report on our behaviour. It was an unequal contract and we made a strong case for changing it, and I am glad to say the board responded positively,' says Gavaskar.

It was Gavaskar again who would lead the players' demand to allow their wives to travel with them on tour. 'We would go on long tours for several months and it could get very lonely. My reasoning was simple: if having our wives made the players happy, they were likely to perform better,' points out Gavaskar. Again, the board relented, confirming the belief that the master batsman from Mumbai was more than just a run machine; he was someone who got what he wanted off the field too. Gavaskar had changed the image of the middle-class salaried cricketer – his was not to be a life of servitude; he expected to be adequately compensated for his skill.

In a historical context, Gavaskar is arguably the first Indian cricketer who understood his true worth as a player in monetary terms, fought for his rights and thereby transformed the player–board relationship forever. 'He is probably the only cricketer who the board officials were actually frightened of,' says Madan Lal. In the early post-Independence years, some of the great Indian cricketers like Vijay Hazare and Vinoo Mankad relied on the patronage of princely families for sustenance. When Mankad played in a professional league in England in 1952, he was not selected for the Indian team as a 'punishment'. In the 1960s and 1970s, it was public sector companies like the State Bank of India and a few private companies like Tata and Mafatlal which gave cricketers job security. Despite their stardom and mass following, the cricketers were lowly paid, mostly salaried employees. The advertising industry too offered limited incentives: for his first advertisement in 1972 for a Tata soap, Gavaskar was paid just Rs 2000!

But the hard-nosed man from Mumbai was determined to change the rules of the game by looking the cricket board in the eye and demanding a fair share for the players. 'I think every cricketer owes Sunny a huge debt,' says Shastri. 'He was the first cricketer from the subcontinent to make the cricket board and all of us realize the value of a professional cricketer.'

But above all else, Gavaskar, like many special cricketers before and after him, wore the India cap with great pride. 'I was very clear that I didn't want to be a one-Test or even five-Test wonder. I wanted to play for India for many years and that's what was my sole aim every time I wore the India cap: to perform to the best of my ability and do my country proud,' he says. His sense of Indianness was reflected in his refusal of a life membership of the MCC at Lord's after an altercation with a steward who had denied him entry into the ground in 1991. He subsequently took a strong 'nationalistic' position, questioning the alleged double standards of the English. 'The English media could come to India and say what they wanted about our facilities, umpires, pitches and get away with it. But as a proud Indian, I wasn't going to take things lying down. Tell me, would any English cricketer have been denied entry into an Indian ground?' he asks.

Having won the World Cup in 1983, India had taken the first tentative steps to becoming the home of international cricket by hosting the 1987 World Cup. Gavaskar as the symbol of Indian cricketing pride was conscious of his role as the flag-bearer of the sport. He had the image and the intellect to defy the stereotype of the submissive Indian cricketer. And he wasn't going to back off from a verbal joust if the occasion arose.

Here is a story which is part of Gavaskar folklore. During India's tour of Pakistan in 1982–83, the Indian team manager Fatehsinghrao Gaekwad was hosting a dinner in Lahore when the legendary Pakistani singer Noor Jehan arrived. 'I am sure you know our captain, Sunil Gavaskar,' Gaekwad said while introducing the singer to the players. Noor Jehan replied, 'Nahin ji, I only know of Imran Khan and Zaheer Abbas!' Gavaskar was miffed but got his chance to hit back soon enough when Gaekwad turned to him and said, 'Sunil, surely I don't need to introduce Mallika-e-Tarannum Noor Jehan.' The immediate quick-witted response from Gavaskar: 'No, sir, I only know of Lata Mangeshkar!'

As always, Gavaskar had the last word.

~

'My father is a much misunderstood man,' says Rohan Gavaskar, who played 11 one-day internationals for India. He may not have inherited all his father's batting skills, but Rohan has imbibed the ready wit. 'I guess my sixes per first-class match ratio is higher than my father's!' he says. As a young boy, Rohan would scurry around the Indian dressing room and also watch his father play. But there was no attempt made by Indian cricket's most influential player to push his son into the sport. 'I think the first time my father saw me actually play a match, I was already into my teens,' Rohan tells me.

The image of a stern, singular, self-obsessed run machine on the field is seen to contrast with the reality of a more relaxed, fun-loving individual off it. On university tours by train, teammates remember him as a prankster and a natural mimic. 'When we were in college, Dev Anand once came to cast young students in a role for his film. Sunil may not remember it, but he dressed up in a nylon Dev Anand–like shirt for the trials,' says college mate Rege, laughing. Gavaskar also acted once in a Marathi film, a tepid debut which was in sharp contrast to his stunning rise on the cricket field.

In his cricketing years, Gavaskar lived in a self-contained bubble, a man in constant battle with his mind and the bowler. Post-retirement, he has brought the same focus to a career as a media professional; perhaps no other Indian cricketer has made such a smooth and successful transition to a cricket afterlife. Travelling the world as a highly paid commentator and columnist, Gavaskar has built a successful business model around Brand Gavaskar. 'Watching and commenting on cricket has been my way of staying in touch with the game I love,' Gavaskar says. He hasn't coached, which might seem surprising given his immense knowledge of the game. 'If someone comes to me for advice, I am happy to share it,' he says.

As with his batting, he has always adapted to changing times. Even the emergence of Twenty20 cricket, seen by many old-timers as a bastardized version of the sport, has not fazed him. 'I enjoy watching Twenty20 cricket, it has brought new excitement, more money and audiences to the sport,' he says. And so it isn't unusual to find Gavaskar in a Twenty20 match studio doing a jugalbandi with television's motormouth funny man, Navjot Singh Sidhu. 'Sunny bhai can be a laugh riot in the studio because he can laugh at himself,' says Sidhu.

Critics have suggested that the twenty-first-century Gavaskar is now an 'establishment' man who will not question authority because of a conflict of interest as a result of having a lucrative commentary contract with the board. The charge doesn't impress Gavaskar. 'Can anyone show me a clause in my contract which says that I have to say what the BCCI wants me to say. Don't make allegations without proof. And those who accuse me of not speaking out against the BCCI, would they speak out against their employers? I have my own business and will not be dictated by anyone,' he says firmly. In 2014, he was even briefly appointed interim cricket board president by the Supreme Court, a choice that reflected his stature in the sport and one he deems as a 'great honour'.

Maybe the passing years and the riches that have come with being part of the multimillion-dollar professional cricket industry have softened Gavaskar's outlook, made him more amenable to compromise where he once would have been itching to confront. Where he once petitioned the board for higher fees, he can now demand his price for a television appearance or for being a member of the IPL governing council. 'Why should I pick a fight without reason?' he argues.

He may have become an NRI, spending half the year out of the country for tax purposes, but he fundamentally remains the middle-class boy from Chikhalwadi who grew up in an age of austerity. You won't see him driving a glitzy car or wearing expensive suits and watches (his first car, he reminds me, was a Premier President Fiat, well earned after his 1971 debut series). On a cricket tour, he will often be seen shopping from a local convenience store and will rarely party or have a late night out, preferring to read a book instead. He isn't a foodie and remains fitness conscious. One of the few indulgences he allows himself is the occasional glass of red wine. His best partnership, he says, has been his marriage to Marshneil, who travels almost everywhere with him. He is a staunch Sathya Sai Baba devotee and says he is at complete peace with the world. 'I don't think I have to prove anything any more to anyone,' he says, summing up his frame of mind.

An intensely private man with strong likes and dislikes, he never forgets his friends' birthdays or anniversaries. When cricket journalist Dutta's daughter got married in Kolkata, Gavaskar spent three days at the wedding. 'He mingled with everyone without acting like a celebrity while enjoying his favourite mishti doi,' recalls Dutta. 'He may be a great cricketer, but he is an even finer human being.' My mother tells me that Gavaskar will always message her on my late father's birthday with a note to say, 'Remembering my friend Sardee today!'

Indeed, old cricket friendships remain Gavaskar's bedrock, the anchor around which he can connect to a lifetime of passion for the sport. Once a year, he hosts a party for all the people he has played cricket with right from his early club cricket days. Rege is charged with organizing the event. 'No expense is spared and we prepare an exhaustive list of invitees. Sunil just wants to be around his cricket friends and sing, laugh and crack the same jokes we did when we were playing the game all those years ago,' Rege says.

And yet, the Gavaskar story that I find most appealing isn't related to the game. During the 1992–93 post-Ayodhya communal riots in Mumbai, he spotted a Muslim couple in a taxi fleeing from a mob below his apartment building. He rushed down and stood between the mob and the taxi. 'You will have to kill me first before you touch them,' he warned. The mob melted away and the couple was saved. 'It was simply a humanitarian thing to do; which religion tells you that it's okay to kill another person?' he asks me now. In a city divided by religious violence, it was an act that defined the original spirit of Bombay before the ugly provincialism of Mumbai took over.

For decades, Mumbai has been ruled by the Shiv Sena, a party whose rise and influence are built around a nativist identity and an anti-Muslim plank. It was the Shiv Sainiks who had been involved in the communal violence on Mumbai's streets. When he wasn't playing the political demagogue, the Shiv Sena supremo Bal Thackeray prided himself on being a cricket enthusiast – the sport is intimately connected to the party's idea of Maharashtrian asmita (self-respect). And yet, here was arguably the city's most famous Marathi manoos standing up to the street thugs from the Sena, at risk to his own life. Gavaskar is a proud Mumbaikar but also a product of the city's more genteel cosmopolitanism that is the antithesis of what the Shiv Sena stands for. He had faced many bouncers on the cricket pitch, but standing up to a mob during a riot was easily the most courageous act of a true son of the soil.

5

Kapil Dev

Superman from Haryana

In 1975, Indian cricket had its Oliver Twist moment. A tall, wiry teenager representing Haryana was participating in a national under-19 coaching camp at the CCI in Mumbai's scorching summer heat. The camp was being run in true military style by Colonel Hemu Adhikari, former India player and one of the few armed services officers to represent the country. The players weren't even allowed drinking water during the practice. The young man had bowled four hours on the trot on a hot and humid morning and was famished. When lunch was served, there were two chapatis and dal kept in the plate. The sixteen-year-old turned to the CCI secretary, Keki Tarapore, with a request: 'Sir, these two chapatis are not enough for me, I am a fast bowler and need more food.' Tarapore looked at him and laughed. 'Young man, there are no fast bowlers in India so please don't give me this bullshit about wanting to be a fast bowler.'

Sometimes, a stray remark can become a base camp to motivate an individual to reach the summit. Tarapore, a genial Parsee, had played one Test for India in 1948 as a left-arm spinner and was conditioned to believe that this was a land of spinners only. The desire to prove him wrong became a driving force for Kapil Dev Nikhanj. Not only did he get the full meal he asked for but he also achieved the seemingly impossible: he bowled fast for India. Barely four years later, as he became the youngest to take 100 wickets for his country, Kapil Dev sought out Tarapore at a function. 'I just went up to him and said thank you. He had given me a goal in life by almost challenging me to bowl fast,' he says.

Till Kapil Dev arrived, Indian cricket's tryst with pace had been more in the nature of footnotes in history. In its first Test in 1932, the Indian team was blessed to have a pair of new-ball bowlers in Amar Singh and Mohammad Nissar, both well over six feet. The England star batsman Walter Hammond had remarked of Singh that he was 'as dangerous an opening bowler as I have ever seen, coming off the pitch like the crack of doom'. Nissar was reputedly even faster, his broad chest and rippling muscles giving him the physique of a genuine quick. But by the time India achieved freedom in 1947, the fast bowlers, including Nissar, had mostly migrated to Pakistan. Partition divided the subcontinent but it also split the cricket talent by physical traits. The brawny Pathans were well equipped to bowl fast while the relatively smaller Indians produced the slow bowlers. As Vinoo Mankad and Ghulam Ahmed spun India to its first Test wins in 1952, the die had been cast: India would be typecast as the land of spin. The one exception was Ramakant Desai, who was India's premier new-ball bowler in the early 1960s, but even he was short of height (his nickname was 'Tiny') and not really express pace. In 1967 in England, India's new-ball bowling was bizarrely handled in the fourth Test by Budhi Kunderan who had been chosen on the tour as a wicketkeeper. Kunderan ran in from a few steps and rolled his arm over in the gentlest possible manner, bowling 4 overs and conceding 13 runs. The Indian team had selected four spinners for the Test and Kunderan's task was to ensure the ball lost its shine in the fastest possible time so that the spin quartet could take over. In fact, just before the game when captain Pataudi asked Kunderan what he bowled, his cryptic response was: 'Skipper, to be honest, I don't really know!'

It was in this spin-friendly environment that Kapil Dev was being asked to make a mark. 'I guess those who controlled cricket at the time thought that if you are from Haryana then you must drive a tractor, not bowl fast with a cricket ball,' says Kapil Dev. Which is why his journey from the cricketing wilds of Haryana to becoming India's fast bowling icon is like no other in Indian cricket: his rise would defy every stereotype that existed at the time. This was a sport which till the early 1970s was primarily defined by the deeds of the batsmen from Mumbai and the match-winning spinners. It was an upper-caste, Brahmin-dominated sport played mainly in the country's big cities (Only seven cricketers in the first fifty years of Indian cricket were born in rural India, three of whom played in the 1930s, and all of whom had to move to a metro city to learn the game.) To truly democratize the sport, Indian cricket needed a small-town hero to emerge, one who could become a potential trendsetter.

A political parallel can perhaps be drawn with the Green Revolution in the country in the 1960s and 1970s that exponentially increased agricultural productivity and empowered the farm community in rural India. Until the Green Revolution gathered momentum, Indian politics was ruled by an upper-caste, metropolitan elite. It was only after the 1967 elections that a middle-caste, agrarian leadership began to assert itself, thereby effecting a dramatic change in the character of Indian assemblies and Parliament. If the Green Revolution (and later the Mandal Commission report giving reservations to backward castes) changed the face of Indian politics, one man with his stirring deeds would trigger Indian cricket's biggest revolution, one that started with a simple desire for a meal of more than just two chapatis.

Located in the foothills of the Shivaliks, Chandigarh is among India's most liveable cities: neatly divided into sectors, with wide roads, gardens and a lake. Designed by the renowned Swiss–French architect Le Corbusier, the city was part of the Nehruvian project of creating a new capital for post-Partition Punjab. In 1966, with the carving out of Haryana state, Chandigarh became a joint capital for Punjab and Haryana and was designated a union territory. 'We have more bureaucrats per square kilometre than in any other part of the country,' is the standing joke among Indian Administrative Services officers. In recent years, the city has developed satellite townships, populated by retired civil servants and military officers, attracted by the fine weather and even better golf courses. Olympic gold medallist in shooting Abhinav Bindra is from Chandigarh, yet the city's most famous son of the soil remains Kapil Dev.

The Chandigarh that Kapil Dev, born in 1959, grew up in was a small town with no big-city pretensions. The decision to make it a joint capital for two states though had spurred rapid construction activity. Dev's parents, from a Punjabi Khatri business family, had moved from Sahiwal in Pakistan after Partition and relocated to Chandigarh in the 1950s. Kapil's father, Ram Lal Nikhanj, was a timber contractor, his mother, Raj Kumari, a housewife raising a large family. 'My parents had no clue of cricket, and had never seen a cricket match till they saw me play one on television,' says Kapil. The family was relatively prosperous and doted on the young Kapil, the sixth of seven siblings. His elder brother Bhushan was an early influence, encouraging him to pursue his dream. 'I remember when my cricket coach met my brother and told him that I had the talent to play cricket but needed to become stronger, my father who was overhearing the conversation bought two buffaloes and kept them in the backyard so that there was never a shortage of milk in the house. The milk would be given to me by my mother in a large military mug and I was literally pestered to guzzle it by the gallon,' he recalls.

Small towns in India have plenty of open spaces, very few entertainment options, and a neighbourhood which can be like one large extended family. Chandigarh was no different in the early 1970s. Kapil Dev had enrolled in the DAV School, an education institute like many others in Chandigarh that was blessed with a large sports ground. 'I used to play every sport since there was little else to do in the town and I wasn't very good at studies. In fact, when my daughter once came home depressed after getting 95 per cent in her exams, I told her that I didn't even get half your scores in school and I wasn't complaining,' says Kapil Dev with typical candour.

The image of 'daredevil' Kapil was cemented in his youth. Ashok Malhotra, the former Indian cricketer who is his schoolmate from Chandigarh, says that there was no sport that Kapil didn't excel in. 'Kuckoo [Kapil Dev's pet name] was our football goalie, volleyball captain, athletics champion and always full of mischief. He would untie the police horses and ride them bareback even as the police would be searching for them. The only thing he didn't do was study, so the entire class and even teachers got together to ensure he at least passed the tenth standard exams,' says Malhotra with a grin.

Less than a kilometre from Kapil Dev's home was another sports facility: the Sector 16 ground where a cricket coaching camp was being run by Desh Prem Azad, a former Haryana first-class player. It was here that Kapil enrolled himself in 1971 as a twelve-year-old (North Indian cricketers are often accused of fudging their date of birth to play age-group cricket but Kapil insists that he wasn't a day older than his birth certificate claims). Azad was an old-style coach who placed emphasis on discipline and mental toughness. The camp would begin at 6 a.m. all through the year with another round in the evening at three. 'If you were five minutes late for practice, then you had to run five rounds, or were banned from the nets for a week,' remembers Chetan Sharma, another Team India fast bowler to emerge from the Azad school. 'Once when Kapil took us to a movie instead of going to practice, Azad sir came to the movie hall, gave us a tight slap and kept us away from the nets for fifteen days,' recalls Malhotra.

While Kapil Dev was a natural athlete, it was Azad who encouraged him to bowl fast. 'With my height and build, I guess it was expected that I would turn out to be a fast bowler. In those days, if you were short, you wanted to bat like Sunil Gavaskar, if you were tall, then you were supposed to bowl with the new ball,' says Kapil. But there were no Indian role models for anyone aspiring to bowl fast, no fast bowling equivalent of a Gavaskar. Maybe it helped then to be in a town like Chandigarh with no cricket lineage, where every teenager could dream to script his own history. 'Do you know the first Test match I saw was the one I played in,' says Kapil with a smile.

The absence of any obvious hero to emulate meant that the small-town cricketer could develop his own distinctive style, free from the burdens of the past. Kapil Dev's run-up to the crease was like a 400 metre runner, robust and powerful, before he burst on to the batsman with a big leap. The jump became Dev's signature image, one that would be engraved on Indian cricket walls forever. 'In hindsight, that jump was a mistake. My coach thought it would give me greater speed, but it actually ended up putting a lot of pressure on my knees and wasn't ideal for hard Indian wickets,' Kapil analyses.

And yet, what would stand out through Kapil Dev's career was his remarkable physical fitness – he ended up playing 131 Tests over a fifteen-year period, missing just one match when he was dropped in a Test game in 1984 for playing an 'indisciplined' shot. Of all his records, this is probably the most impressive: for a fast bowler not to break down over an extended period while bowling in the heat and humidity of India makes Kapil Dev Indian cricket's marathon man. And it is here that the long hours of training in Chandigarh as a teenager made the difference. 'We used to bowl at least six hours every day, summer or winter. And when I wasn't bowling, I was running all the time which made my legs strong. You can't be a fast bowler without strong legs,' says Kapil, explaining his longevity in the sport.

His partner in training in Chandigarh was another physically strong specimen, Yograj Singh, whose son Yuvraj would later go on to play for India with distinction. If Kapil had the build of a decathlete, Yograj had the muscles of a javelin thrower. 'I was two years older, but we were like blood brothers. Every day, I would pick him up and we would go together to the ground and terrorize the batsmen by bowling fast. Once when we went to Patiala to play a match, some of the batsmen didn't want to play the game when they heard that Kapil and I were in the opposing side,' says Yograj.

If Kapil was focused, Yograj was seen as a bit of a wild child. (In later years, his name would crop up in the Jessica Lal murder case for allegedly helping the accused destroy evidence.) But in the 1970s, they were united in their dream of playing for India as a fast bowling partnership. They would train for hours together, even run around Chandigarh's roads like, to use Yograj's words, 'two complete mad men'. If Kapil had asked for more than two chapatis, Yograj too wanted the diet of a fast bowler. 'Kapil and I went to the same under-19 camps in Bengaluru and Mumbai. I also made it clear that a sher [lion] can't be made to eat ghaas [grass]. We needed our meat and chicken. If they didn't give it to us, we would eat it when no one was noticing,' he says.

Yograj claims that he got his father, who was a wealthy businessman, to send him Rs 5000 during a training camp to satiate their large appetites. 'I divided the money between Kapil and me so that we could eat all the tandoori chicken we wanted. And when once during the Moin-ud-Dowla tournament we were told that the food was on the house, we ate so much that our captain Anshuman Gaekwad called us "man-eaters",' he says.

But the dream that Kapil and Yograj had of bowling together for India quickly fell apart. While Kapil was making his Test debut at nineteen and was a household name by his twenty-first birthday, Yograj would play just one Test in 1980 and then fade away. In an almost mirror image of what happened in later years to Sachin Tendulkar and Vinod Kambli, single-minded determination scoring over raw talent. Their personal relations also fell apart, Yograj even accusing Kapil of being 'envious' of him. And yet, the fact that Chandigarh, a town that didn't even have a turf wicket and had never produced a cricket star, was suddenly blessed with not one but two potential superstars, suggests a mini-revolution was in the making. While the 'Punjab da Puttar' Yograj would never fulfil his promise (he ended up acting in films), Kapil Dev extracted every ounce of potential from his six-foot frame to become the 'Haryana Hurricane', a cricketer who would change the face of Indian cricket forever.

~

In early 1978, my father Dilip Sardesai had his post-retirement benefit match in Ahmedabad. The star attraction were three Pakistani players, the first to play in India in seventeen years. They included the burly fast bowler Sarfraz Nawaz, the man whose thick moustache made him look like a Pakistan army general. The teams were being taken from Mumbai to Ahmedabad by train. While autograph hunters were chasing Nawaz, Kapil Dev was sitting quietly in a corner. 'You must take his autograph also,' Ashok Mankad, the former India player, said, pointing to Kapil. 'He is a fast bowler who will soon play for the country.' Nawaz smirked. 'You mean India now produces fast bowlers also?' A mild-mannered and nervous Kapil Dev didn't say a word. By the end of that year, he was playing for India against Pakistan.

Kapil Dev's debut series in Pakistan was hardly spectacular. The Pakistani batsmen destroyed the Indian spinners while Dev picked up just 1 wicket in 3 games. But there were flashes of promise. In one Test match, he bowled a sharp bouncer that forced Pakistani opening batsman Sadiq Mohammad to wear a helmet. 'An opposing batsman wearing a helmet to an Indian fast bowler was unheard of; Kapil was already changing the rules of the game for us in his very first series,' says former India opener Chetan Chauhan.

The young Haryanvi was making a mark not just with the ball but with the bat too. Team captain Bishan Singh Bedi relates one incident that stands out. In the second Test in Lahore, Bedi asked Kapil Dev to go in as nightwatchman. 'Just play out the day, puttar,' he told Kapil. Kapil went in and smashed 20-odd runs in 12 balls and came back to the pavilion smiling. 'Arre, I told you to play carefully, not to hit boundaries,' Bedi reprimanded the young Kapil, who half-smiled. 'But Paaji, I only know how to hit the ball, not to defend it.' The entire dressing room was laughing: Kapil had never heard the term 'nightwatchman' in cricket! Kapil had started his cricket career batting at number eleven for Haryana. Now he was suddenly being spoken of as a potential all-rounder. 'I became a batsman only after I started playing Tests. Till then, I saw myself purely as a bowler. Bowling for me was serious business, batting was just fun,' he says rather modestly.

In the next Test in Karachi, as the Pakistani fast bowlers led by Imran Khan tried to bounce him out, Kapil Dev hammered his first 50 in just 33 balls. He even hit Sarfraz for a six, perhaps retribution for the Pakistani's dismissive remarks on a train journey only months earlier. 'I don't think the Pakistani pacers had ever been confronted with an Indian batsman who was ready to hook their bouncers. I think that day in Karachi, I knew I belonged in Test cricket,' says Kapil. A medium fast bowler and batsman who was ready to fight fire with fire, he was an uncut diamond discovered by Indian cricket.

India lost that series in Pakistan 2-0. But just over a year later, Kapil had his revenge: the uncut diamond was now a well-polished, finished product. In the home series against Pakistan in 1979–80, Kapil Dev took 32 wickets and hit important runs, while becoming the youngest player to achieve Test cricket's double of 1000 runs and 100 wickets. In the oppressive Chennai heat, he took 11 wickets and scored 84 runs. If the Pakistani batsmen had decimated the Indian spinners in 1978, now Kapil Dev's pace and swing would hasten the retirement of their star players. 'In that series, Kapil made great players like Zaheer Abbas and Majid Khan look mediocre,' says Syed Kirmani, who as wicketkeeper was experiencing the joy of finally getting to keep to a genuine Indian quick bowler, the kind that opposing opening batsmen would actually fear. Remarkably, in Kapil Dev's first 34 Tests for India, the opposition did not have a single century opening partnership.

What made Kapil stand out? His new-ball partner Madan Lal says it was his perfect side-on action and natural outswinger. 'In Test cricket, a good outswinger is a lethal weapon and Kapil had it,' says Lal. I asked Kapil how he developed the outswinger. Like so many other greats, he offers a prosaic answer: 'I guess it was God's gift!' And yet, there is method that lies at the heart of divine genius. The outside world saw Kapil Dev as this brilliantly talented cricketer who could bat and bowl with ease, the boy from Chandigarh who effortlessly made the transition to Test cricket. Truth is, he was a thinking cricketer all the time. 'I knew, for example, that the Pakistani batsmen were strong on the back foot, but struggled if you drew them forward around their off stump. I made a plan to get them out and it worked,' he says. In later years, Kapil would add a sharp inswinger to his repertoire, a skill he learnt while playing county cricket in England, making him an even more difficult proposition to face as a batsman.

Another of Kapil's pace partners, Karsan Ghavri says Kapil's refusal to give up on a cricket field was his biggest strength. 'I have never seen a greater trier than Kapil Dev. He could bowl 10–12 overs at a stretch in the midday sun without complaining and then come back at the end of a long day and bowl even more – now that requires extreme fitness and commitment,' says Ghavri.

Those qualities were in full evidence during a remarkable Indian victory in Australia in 1981 at Melbourne. In the fourth innings in that match, Australia required 143 runs to win but were bowled out for just 83. Kapil took 5 wickets for 28 runs off 16 overs. But statistics don't reveal the real story. On the fourth day of the match, Kapil couldn't walk because of a strained thigh muscle. On the fifth morning, he went out to play after taking painkillers. 'I knew the team needed me so I thought I would bowl a few overs on the fifth day. After five overs, Gavaskar, who was captain, asked me if I wanted to take rest. I said, "No, I will endure the pain as long as we win the match."' After the victory, Kapil collapsed in the dressing room in agony; his talent was never in doubt, now he was seen as the epitome of raw courage. Till this day, Ghavri is astonished by Kapil's performance: 'He bowled us to a win on one leg!'

The legend of Kapil was growing: he was now rated as one of the top all-rounders in the world. The early 1980s saw four great all-rounders dominate the world game. England had Ian Botham, a larger-than-life figure who emptied the pubs every time he held bat or ball in hand. New Zealand had Richard Hadlee, on whose broad shoulders the hopes of a tiny cricket nation often rested. Pakistan had the charismatic Imran Khan, cricket's poster boy with his tigerish good looks. And we had our Haryana Hurricane to cheer. Comparing their merits became a favourite topic for cricket fans: a Pakistani friend and I almost stopped talking to each other after a heated debate on the skills of Imran versus Kapil. Kapil himself is honest in his assessment of the four men competing for the top spot: 'Botham was the best batsman, Hadlee the best bowler, Imran the best captain, and I guess I had the most natural talent.'

If the 1970s had been shaped by the batsmanship of Gavaskar, it was Kapil who defined Indian cricket in the 1980s. If Gavaskar had given self-belief to Indian batsmen that they could take on the fastest bowlers in the world, Kapil had come to symbolize a new aggressive, never-say-die spirit in Indian cricket. If Gavaskar was breaking every batting record, Kapil was now climbing mountains of his own as a bowler and all-rounder. One was the technical genius who would charm the purists, a master of his craft whose batting was akin to Mohammed Rafi singing a ghazal. The other was a fearless free spirit who could do the unexpected, a bit like Kishore Kumar's rollicking song in *Padosan*. Gavaskar was the nation's pride, the kind you went to watch with the luxury of an expensive dress circle seat. Kapil was the favourite of those who could only afford to be in the first row of the stalls in a cinema house. Gavaskar's forward defensive shot might be a picture on your mantelpiece, a poster of Kapil Dev's leap while bowling would be found in your local paan–beedi shop. In the power shift from the suave, convent-educated, middle-class Maharashtrian to the earthy Haryanvi from

DAV School, Chandigarh, Indian cricket was finally breaking the class and regional barrier.

Just how Gavaskar and Kapil Dev were received by audiences is best captured by their contrasting roles in advertisements for Palmolive shaving cream. The Gavaskar ad in the 1970s has him playing a square drive with the tag line 'As Gavaskar was perfecting his square drive, Palmolive was perfecting his shaving'. The brand then was seen to represent a certain classical quality as reflected in Gavaskar's quest for perfection. The Kapil Dev ad had the star flashing a toothy smile with the tag line 'Palmolive da jawaab nahin'. The transition from the metropolitan sophisticate to the small-town hero, from English to the vernacular, was slowly being recognized.

It was a power transfer that was taking place in the politics of the 1980s too as the genteel, English-speaking Nehruvian elite of the early post-Independence years was swept away by a new breed of regional politicians who were unchained by class and caste privilege. The rise of netas like N.T. Rama Rao in the south and Lalu Prasad Yadav and Mulayam Singh Yadav in the north symbolized a new democratic empowerment of social groups that had remained on the periphery till then. As the inimitable Lalu once told me in an interview, 'Tumhare pass angrezi class hai, hamare pass Hindi mass hai!' (You may have English-speaking classes with you, I have the Hindi-speaking masses with me!)

Kapil says he was never overawed or embarrassed by the fact that he couldn't speak perfect English and was more comfortable in his Haryanvi-accented Hindi. He recalls, 'I remember when I was first made India captain, one of the board officials told me that I might not want to do the customary press conference since there will be questions in English. I told him, "You have chosen me to captain because I play cricket well, not because I should have gone to Oxford university to speak English."' Even his future in-laws were initially reluctant to allow him to marry their daughter because he was seen as the rustic boy from the boondocks. 'Romi comes from a sophisticated, English-speaking family in Mumbai, while I was seen as the outsider who offered no financial stability. But in the end, love conquers all,' Kapil, who was married at just twenty-two, says with a smile.

Romi Dev, who confesses to not being a cricket fan, says she first met Kapil in August 1978 when he hadn't even played for India. 'I was not at all embarrassed that he couldn't speak English like my Mumbai friends. I think our times were simpler and in any case Kapil's self-confidence was such that it surpassed any sort of drawbacks he may have faced on any front. As for overcoming parental opposition, we just stuck to our guns,' she tells me.

Within days of their marriage in 1981, the couple flew to England where Kapil was to play in the Lancashire League. In those days even the top Indian cricketers spent summers in England to earn a few thousand extra pounds as 'professional' cricketers. 'We initially shared a countryside cottage with Jimmy [Mohinder Amarnath] and his wife since they were accustomed to life in England. For the first time ever, I had to do my own cooking. It wasn't easy, and when I first tried to cook rajma, the cover of the cooker wasn't fitted properly with the result that everything in it splashed all over the kitchen!' recalls Romi. 'She started crying,' says Kapil, 'but I told her, "Don't worry, you've made a flying start, now things can only get better."'

Today, with most Indian cricketers staying in luxurious accommodation, the idea of a star player and his wife sharing a home with another cricket couple in a small English village and doing their own cooking sounds unusual. Cricket in the early 1980s was still a few steps away from becoming a big-money sport, but as Kapil puts it a little dramatically, 'There were some uncertain times but "pyaar kiya toh darna kya" was our motto.' It was this uncanny ability to hit opponents for a six with an easy smile, on and off the field, which made Kapil such a folk hero for millions. From 1978 to 1983, in the space of just five years since his debut, Kapil brought an irresistible dynamism to Indian cricket. But his moment of truth which would become the next big turning point for the sport in the country was yet to come.

Any history of modern Indian cricket needs to be classified as BWC (Before World Cup 1983) and AWC (After World Cup 1983). Indian cricket was transformed on 25 June 1983, the day India under Kapil Dev's leadership lifted the World Cup at Lord's. Till then, India had won just one World Cup match spread over two tournaments, that too against no-hopers East Africa. Its greatest batsman Sunil Gavaskar had once scored 36 not out in a 60-over game, an innings that typified how India struggled with one-day cricket. Barring the odd win, India had been timid performers outside the subcontinent. Cricket was a national craze but the players remained glorified amateurs, dependent on the cricket board's largesse for monetary benefits. Seven memorable hours in the sunshine at Lord's changed all that.

Reams have been written on the World Cup victory, a David versus Goliath battle between rank outsiders India and the greatest ever one-day team. The West Indies in the early 1980s were a cricketing juggernaut, a team that combined Caribbean flair with a ruthless streak. They didn't just defeat their opponents, they pummelled them like heavyweight boxers taking on scrawny pretenders. They had won the first two World Cups, on the back of an intimidatory fast bowling attack and a power-packed batting line-up led by the greatest one-day player of his age, Sir Vivian Richards. No one expected them to lose, not even the most loyal Indian supporter.

I was at the ground at Lord's that day, one which would turn out to be among the happiest in my life. We had obtained tickets from distraught English fans who had seen India defeat their team in the semi-finals. Accompanying me was former India player Yajurvindra Singh, a joint record holder for most catches by an outfielder in a Test match. When India, batting first, scored just 183 runs, Singh decided to leave the match. 'My wife wants me to go shopping with her. There is no point staying back and watching India lose,' he told us. Even Kapil's wife, Romi, left the match midway when it appeared that the West Indians were running away with the game. 'Every time Viv Richards hit a four, the West Indians around me would jump and scream. It was all very depressing so we thought we might as well go to our hotel room,' she says.

It would turn out to be a bad call as India didn't lose. Instead, the mighty West Indians were bowled out for just 140 runs and it was Kapil Dev, not Clive Lloyd, who lifted the cup. 'I guess if we played the West Indians ten times, we would probably win only once. We just picked the right day to win,' says Mohinder Amarnath, who was chosen the man of the match. Another World Cup winner that day, Kirti Azad remembers Kapil's words to the team at the halfway mark: 'Jawaanon [soldiers], we may not have a winning total but we have a fighting one. Let's fight.' It was a typically defiant Kapil Dev remark: his body language was of a warrior who just wouldn't give up.

Kapil Dev has his own favourite World Cup final day story. After the game, he went to the West Indies dressing room to shake hands with their players. There was an eerie silence in the room, almost disbelief. 'I saw these champagne bottles which had been bought in preparation of a West Indian win. I just requested Lloyd if I could take a few since we hadn't bought any. He mumbled something, and we quickly took the bottles and celebrated all night. It was only when we read the morning papers the next day that it sunk in that we were actually World Cup champions,' recalls Kapil. That night, the Westmoreland Hotel near Lord's where the team was staying became a 'mini-India'. 'I think there was bhangra music playing all night in the lobby and laddoos being served by the dozen,' remembers Romi Dev.

As captain, Kapil Dev became the face of the World Cup triumph. He wasn't seen as a great tactician, but his positive attitude was infectious. 'From day one, all I would tell the team was to enjoy the game and try our best because we had nothing to lose,' he says. Starting the tournament 66 to 1 rank outsiders, some of the players had even booked holiday flights to the US after the end of the first round. 'We didn't expect to be in the semi-finals, forget about winning the tournament, so we had planned to go on a holiday with our families. But after we defeated the West Indies in the first

preliminary game, we felt confident that we could make an impact,'
is how Kapil describes the 1983 journey.

The real turning point though was a match against Zimbabwe
where Kapil Dev showed his match-winning skills. On a slightly
green wicket in Tunbridge Wells, the Zimbabwean bowlers had
reduced India to a miserable 17 for 5 when Kapil walked in to bat.
He remembers, 'I was in the shower after a morning workout and
was still wrapped in a towel when the third wicket fell. I rushed to
change and put my pads on. When we lost the fifth wicket, I just
told my partner Roger Binny to hang in there and play out the overs.
It is only in the last 10 overs that I actually decided to start taking
chances and hit out. I guess it was just my lucky day.'

It was more than just luck. Kapil Dev made a record-breaking
175 runs, with 16 fours and 6 sixes. Madan Lal, who batted with
him that day, says, 'Each six was a clean hit, each one crossed the
boundary by several yards.' That innings symbolized what Kapil
Dev meant to Indian cricket at the time. Only he could have played
an innings where attack was seen as the best form of defence. From
Gavaskar's painful 36 not out in 1975 to Kapil's blitzkrieg in 1983,
Indian cricket had finally found its feet on the one-day stage, a new
self-belief was coursing through the team. 'That one innings changed
the mood in the dressing room,' says Azad. 'The captain had shown
the way, we just had to follow.'

Sadly, the Tunbridge Wells innings isn't captured on camera
because there was a BBC strike and there was no camera crew at
the ground. 'I guess I could have shown it to my grandchildren,
now they will have to read the scorecard,' says Kapil. There is one
moment though which is etched in memory and is replayed every
time the 1983 World Cup victory is shown on television. It is the
catch Kapil took in the finals that dismissed Viv Richards. 'Richards
was in prime form and hitting me all over the ground. I felt he was
overconfident and asked Kapil for an extra over,' recalls Madan Lal.
'That is when Richards miscued a pull and Kapil took the catch.'
The catch was taken by Kapil running backwards, his eyes firmly

on the skied ball even as a nation held its collective breath. When he caught it, he appeared almost nonchalant, with the look of a man wondering what the fuss was all about. He only allowed himself a hint of a smile when his teammates and fans rushed towards him. A difficult catch had been made to look ridiculously simple: again, only Kapil in that Indian team could have done it.

That catch and the image of Kapil Dev lifting the cup are embossed in memory because they were among the first 'live' moments captured on colour television in India. Colour television had come to India only a year earlier when the 1982 Asian Games were held in Delhi. To acquire a colour TV set was a big middle-class aspiration, the sight of Kapil Dev lifting the cup gave that early consumerist dream a huge lift. Sales of television sets registered a quantum jump in the aftermath of the World Cup win.

It was also a period when the country was in turmoil: militancy in Punjab, massacres in the northeast, trouble in Kashmir – it seemed as if the Indira Gandhi government was presiding over the unravelling of the nation state. In a time of growing depression, Kapil Dev and his team provided a rare sunshine moment, a triumph of cricketing nationalism that the country could celebrate. India desperately needed inspiration: in Kapil's 'Devils' a nation had found its heroes.

It isn't as if the team members became millionaires overnight after the World Cup win. The BCCI still hadn't made the transition to running cricket like a commercial enterprise and the players were not yet accustomed to demanding their rightful share. The consumer market was small: most middle-class household gadgets didn't go beyond a refrigerator, a small television and a mixer, so potential sponsors were tough to find. During the entire World Cup, the players were paid just around Rs 20,000 and their daily allowance of 20 pounds included laundry. 'We didn't get any big prize money after the 1983 World Cup. It is only when a Lata Mangeshkar music concert was organized that we were given Rs 1 lakh each from the proceeds,' claims Kapil.

And yet, the players did get a permanent place in the hearts and

minds of every Indian cricket fan which they could cash in on post
retirement. Which is why every four years when the World Cup is
played, the 1983 winners are wheeled into television studios as experts
and their achievements are celebrated. In 2008, we had organized a
television event to mark twenty-five years of the win. At least half a
dozen corporates immediately agreed to sponsor the event and the
players were laden with gifts. As one of the sponsors told me, 'You
know, I was eighteen when we won the World Cup and since that day
I have wanted to take one picture with Kapil Dev and his 1983 team.'
For an entire generation, Kapil Dev was the ultimate teenage folk
hero. And the 1983 win a coming-of-age moment for Indian cricket.

~

Kapil Dev was only twenty-four when he was crowned captain of a
World Cup–winning team just five years after his international debut.
It seemed as if he had climbed Mount Everest without even travelling
to base camp. Instant success can be dangerously intoxicating and
hazardous. Just a year after the glorious Lord's moment, Kapil was
stripped of captaincy and even dropped from the team. It was typical
of whimsical Indian cricket selection: a 5-0 defeat at home against
the mighty West Indies, out to avenge their World Cup defeat, was
seen as reason enough to show the door to Kapil. 'I think I was
made captain too early in life, and removed from it also in an unfair
manner,' he says.

After the heady achievement of 1983, suddenly 1984 became a year
of failure. From a brief moment of triumph it seemed the nation too
was being pushed back into a slough of despondency, even fear. It was
the year of Operation Blue Star – the storming of the Golden Temple
in Amritsar – the assassination of Prime Minister Indira Gandhi and
the horror of the anti-Sikh riots in Delhi. Amid the bloody violence,
cricket seemed to be little more than a momentary distraction.

A series was played in the winter of 1984 against England, which
India surprisingly lost and Kapil became the fall guy for the defeat.

One bad shot in the Delhi Test match, and he was dropped from the team. At the time, it was widely speculated that Kapil had been targeted by the Mumbai 'lobby' led by Gavaskar, who had returned as captain. 'Not true,' says Kapil Dev. 'I played badly and was dropped, let's not blame anyone.' Bishan Singh Bedi, who was a national selector, claims that the decision was taken purely on disciplinary grounds. 'We were looking to save a Test match and Kapil plays a poor stroke and, what is worse, comes into the dressing room whistling as if it didn't matter. A message had to be sent out that no one is greater than the game,' emphasizes Bedi. It would turn out to be the only time in a Test career of sixteen years that Kapil Dev would not stride out to play for the country.

The controversy over the dropping of Kapil (a cricket board official even claimed that he had been 'rested') was the first of many in the second half of the all-rounder's career. If between 1978 and 1983 he could do no wrong, post-1984, Kapil Dev had to come to terms with the highs and lows of international sport. In 1986, for example, he would return to England as captain, this time leading the team to an emphatic 2-0 win, the first Test series success for India on English soil since the breakthrough win in 1971. While Dilip Vengsarkar's splendid batting was the turning point, Kapil Dev's captaincy too seemed to have matured. Significantly, there was also a major geographical power shift in Indian cricket. In 1971, the victorious Indian team had six players from Mumbai, and just one, Bedi, from north India. In 1986, the winning team had five players from the north, just two from Mumbai.

One of Kapil's north Indian 'boys' to make a mark that year was fellow Haryana player Chetan Sharma. Sharma was just eleven when Kapil Dev spotted him for the first time. 'He had come to watch a local under-12 match in Chandigarh, took me aside and told his wife that this boy can bowl faster than Ian Botham. Can you imagine what that did for my confidence?' asks Sharma. It was that positive spirit, Sharma says, which made a difference on the 1986 tour. Just ahead of that series, Sharma had been hit for the

most famous sixer in Indo-Pak cricket history: last-ball heroics by
Pakistan's Javed Miandad in Sharjah that had led to India's defeat.
'It was a nightmare for me. Everywhere I went, I was abused and
reminded of the Miandad six. In the first game in England, I was
so nervous that I couldn't even hold the ball. That's when Kapil paaji
came and put an arm around me and said, "Arre, you have been
abused so much, ab kya pharak padta hai [what difference does it
make now], just bowl as if you have nothing to lose,"' says Sharma.
The young Haryanvi would end up as India's highest wicket taker
in the series and, for a brief while, be seen as a successor to Kapil
Dev as India's new-ball spearhead.

Still, a year later, Kapil Dev lost the Indian captaincy yet again,
this time after a defeat at home in the 1987 World Cup. It was the
first World Cup to be played outside England, marking an important
step towards future subcontinental domination of the sport. The
move to take the World Cup away from England and bring it to
India was sparked off when Siddhartha Shankar Ray, former West
Bengal chief minister and a close aide of Indira Gandhi, failed to get
a ticket to watch the 1983 World Cup finals. An irate Ray complained
to Prime Minister Gandhi who asked the then BCCI president and
a Congress MP, N.K.P. Salve, to intervene. Salve agreed to bid to
host the World Cup but needed a sponsor. That is when Reliance
Industries, also close to the Congress government, agreed to acquire
the title rights for just over 2 million pounds. Reliance's chairman
Dhirubhai Ambani had only one condition: he should be seated next
to the prime minister during an India–Pakistan exhibition match that
was being played just ahead of the World Cup and being broadcast
on national television.

But even though the 1987 World Cup saw the first major injection
of domestic sponsorship, the Indian players were not the direct
beneficiaries. The players were still paid only around Rs 75,000 each
for the entire tournament. 'Some of us wanted to put a sponsor logo
on our shirts to get additional money, but the board refused. When
I defied the board diktat and refused to sign the contract along with

a few other players, a board official warned me that I was making a huge mistake. Sure enough, when we lost in the semi-finals, the board had its revenge by sacking me as captain,' recalls Kapil.

His ouster from captaincy hurt him and post-1987 Kapil Dev was not the same. The happy-go-lucky persona of the early years would now be replaced by a less effervescent presence – the knees were beginning to wobble, the spirit and the body were at odds with each other. Kapil Dev was still Indian cricket's brightest star but a new sparkling light was about to burst on to the scene. The emergence of Sachin Tendulkar in 1988 signalled the gradual end of the Kapil Dev era. And yet, there would still be an occasional reminder of just what the Kapil brand of vibrant cricket meant for the sport, most notably when Kapil hit 4 sixes in an over to save India from a follow-on in 1990 against England at Lord's. 'I was batting with the number eleven batsman Narendra Hirwani and I told him to just defend, the rest I would handle. Eddie Hemmings, the off-spinner, flighted a few balls and I hit three of them for six. On the sixth ball, I had planned to take a single to keep the strike but then I was in the flow, so I just hit it for six again,' he says, smiling, as if to suggest that he could hit sixes for fun. It's the same toothy smile which had bewitched a generation. 'Only Kapil Dev could hit 4 sixes in a Test to save a follow-on, he was the ultimate bindaas boss of cricket,' says an awestruck teammate Ravi Shastri. It was the classic 'Kapil Dev da jawaab nahin' moment, perhaps the last his fans will remember him for.

In 1994, Kapil Dev would retire but not before becoming the world's highest wicket taker. He was accused of chasing Sir Richard Hadlee's record of 431 wickets and thereby prolonging his career by at least two extra years at the cost of team interest. Fast bowlers like Javagal Srinath were emerging but Kapil hung on till the record was broken. 'Why two years, maybe I played five years more than I should have,' he says sarcastically. In his office in central Delhi, there is a framed picture that marks the moment Dev broke the Hadlee record with the signatures of his teammates. 'Who doesn't like to break records? It felt good to have the most wickets, but I played cricket because I was passionate about the game, not because I wanted to become the world's highest wicket taker one day.'

Kapil Dev's career statistics are a monument to his hard work, especially in hot, unforgiving Indian weather and on dry pitches. He bowled 27,740 deliveries in Tests, took 434 wickets, and hit 5248 runs in 131 games. A further 253 wickets and 3783 runs in one-day internationals and he is easily ranked as India's finest all-rounder. In 2002, Kapil Dev was chosen the Wisden 'Indian Cricketer of the Century'. But to judge him by statistics alone would do injustice to his massive contribution to Indian cricket. For almost the first fifty years of Indian Test cricket, the star cricketers were all either batsmen or spin bowlers. There were great players but they were all seen to represent a 'non-violent' Brahminical tradition that didn't see cricket as a macho, aggressive sport but rather as one that was played in the mind, not in the body. Kapil Dev with his athleticism and muscular fast bowling energy changed the very image of the Indian cricketer. In the thirty years from Independence to Kapil Dev's debut in 1978, Indian spinners took 1462 wickets while the new-ball bowlers took 423 wickets, or barely 22.4 per cent of the total. From Kapil's arrival to 2016, spinners have taken 2534 wickets while pace bowlers took 2364 wickets, or 47.6 per cent of the total. 'As a young boy in Mysore, I saw Kapil Dev bowl on television and was hooked,' says Srinath, who eventually took over the mantle of pace kingpin from Kapil.

Indeed, even beyond the fast bowling revolution, Kapil Dev's biggest achievement perhaps is his role in inspiring young Indians from small towns to take to the game, thereby setting it free from its elitist, metropolitan origins. If Indian cricket now has star players from Ranchi to Rajkot, it is Kapil Dev who must be seen as a pioneer. He was, in a sense, India's first truly mass cricket hero, encouraging the boys on the street to bowl fast and hit the ball hard. If Gavaskar brought 'sunny days' to Indian cricket, Kapil Dev injected thunder and lightning into the sport. 'I would like to believe that I instilled self-belief in small-town families that if a non-English-speaking boy from Chandigarh could become India's cricket captain, then everyone can aspire to reach the top,' he says with a grin.

Kapil, more than anyone else, shattered the Mumbai monopoly over Indian cricket once and for all. Which is why one of his favourite moments on the cricket field came in May 1991 when Haryana defeated Mumbai at the Wankhede stadium by just 2 runs in an incredible match to win the Ranji Trophy for the first time. 'I don't think I have ever seen Paaji as excited as he was that day,' recalls Chetan Sharma. 'When the umpires didn't give a Mumbai batsman out, he even threw his shoes in the dressing room in anger during the tea break. And when we won, he just sat in a corner and got very emotional.'

'To defeat Mumbai in Mumbai was a dream come true. Yes, I might have shed a tear that day on the field,' says Kapil. As it turned out, less than a decade later, the whole country would see their icon sob, this time in very different circumstances.

~

Of the many dramatic images in Indian cricket, few can match that of Kapil Dev sobbing away in a television interview in May 2000. Here was a national folk hero whose broad smile every time he took a wicket or hit a six left cricket fans pleading for more. Kapil Dev represented happiness and the gay abandon of youth, not anything remotely connected with grief. Which is why the sight of him crying left a nation numb.

The interviewer was Karan Thapar, one of Indian television's most recognizable faces, someone acknowledged for his tough, well-researched interviews. Thapar had lined up Kapil for an interview for a BBC programme, *Face to Face*, a show which focused on interesting trivia around an individual's life story. But just days ahead of the interview, Kapil Dev's name surfaced in the match-fixing scandal that was swirling around Indian cricket. Indian all-rounder Manoj Prabhakar had sensationally claimed in 1997 that a former Indian cricketer had offered him Rs 25 lakh to underperform in a match in Sri Lanka in 1994. Prabhakar wouldn't reveal the name till a cricket board official, I.S. Bindra, claimed that it was Kapil Dev who, Prabhakar had told him, was the offending player.

Recalls Thapar, 'Suddenly, we had this huge story before us. So I rang up Kapil again and asked him if he would still do the interview, only this time it wouldn't be on his life but on his alleged role in match-fixing. To my surprise, Kapil readily agreed.'

Even so, when Kapil arrived at Thapar's office studio in Delhi's Jamia Nagar, no one was quite prepared for the high drama that was to follow. 'I remember he came in a blue collarless shirt and short pants. We began the interview and then suddenly about ten minutes into it, he began literally bawling and wouldn't stop crying. We didn't even have a handkerchief to offer him as he kept sobbing. When we finished the interview, I said to him, "Thank you, Kapil, that was a great interview." He replied, "Yes, but my career is destroyed," and then cried even more as we drank coffee,' remembers Thapar.

The next day, a screen grab photograph of a sobbing Kapil Dev was splashed across the front pages in all newspapers. Thapar had his 'scoop'; Kapil Dev had to deal with the aftermath of the public breakdown. Kapil's critics saw it as 'stage-managed', a move designed to garner audience sympathy at a tough moment in his life. 'If it was orchestrated, then all I can say is that Kapil Dev is a Shakespearean actor. I certainly didn't get that impression; he seemed genuinely disturbed,' says Thapar.

When I asked Kapil Dev about the interview and the match-fixing allegations, there was a flash of anger: 'What do you want me to clarify? I know who I am and what I have achieved. Why should I have to explain myself? Only because television journalists want TRPs?' I even referred to a match against New Zealand in 1999 when Kapil Dev was coach and there were allegations that he had forced the captain Sachin Tendulkar not to enforce the follow-on, a move that resulted in the match being drawn amid allegations of fixing. 'Anyone can make any allegation. It hurts when people accuse you of something without any evidence,' says Kapil. (When I asked Sachin later about this match he claimed that it was a 'collective decision' not to enforce the follow-on.)

A year later, Kapil was exonerated by the CBI, which was inquiring into the case even as a life ban was served on Mohammed Azharuddin while other cricketers named too received tough penalties. Did Kapil Dev get away because of his iconic status, or was he wrongly accused in the first instance? The cricket world seemed divided but in the court of the public, there was less doubt: this was a cricketer who had given his heart for Indian cricket, why would he sell his soul for a few extra dollars? No one is above the law, but in the public imagination, a cricketer of Kapil Dev's stature is always larger than life. The match-fixing controversy did scar Kapil's reputation and he had to resign as Indian coach less than a year into the job. But for a generation which had grown up celebrating his achievements, he will always be Captain Marvellous who led us to a World Cup win against all odds, not the grown man who cried like a child on television.

~

After finishing with cricket, Kapil Dev has become a successful businessman. He has several offices in the National Capital Region, and has interests ranging from media to real estate to providing lighting equipment for stadia. He says the transition from cricketer to businessman was driven by a desire not to be dependent on the cricket board for anything. 'I remember once during a Test match against New Zealand in the 1980s, we finished the game early. Chandu Borde, a great player in his time, was our manager and I saw him sitting in the dressing room hours after the game was over. I asked him why he wasn't going home like the rest of us. He told me, "I have to wait for the board secretary for my daily allowance and he is having an afternoon nap." That day, I decided that I would always be financially independent,' says Dev.

A wealthy man now, Kapil Dev clearly enjoys living life king-size.

'You know, when I was playing cricket, I had to live a disciplined life. Now I just want to enjoy: bungee jumping, horse riding, I am ready to try it all,' he says enthusiastically.

One of his passions is golf, a sport where his ability to hit a ball long and hard is an advantage. He plays golf three to four times a week, and briefly even considered taking it up professionally. 'Then I realized it would be too much work after a long cricket career, and decided it's best to play it for leisure,' he says, laughing.

But even on the golf course, the competitive spirit and self-belief are intact. A golfing partner tells me that Kapil and he were once playing a foursome against a very good team. 'We were three down with four holes to play. I was ready to give up, but Kapil said we have to keep trying. And you know what, we won on the 18th hole!' gushes Kapil's friend. It was, one guesses, a bit like hitting 4 sixes at Lord's to avoid a follow-on. Which is why as Indian cricket's first superhero, someone straight out of the comic books who could do the improbable, Kapil Dev will always be in a league of his own. Or as they would say in Haryana: 'Kapil paaji da jawaab nahin.'

6

Mohammed Azharuddin

Destiny's Child

It is the summer of 2009 and I am on the campaign trail with former India captain Mohammed Azharuddin in Moradabad in western UP. He is contesting an election for the first time on a Congress ticket. An election in India's most populous state, Uttar Pradesh, is like no other. Politics is the heartbeat of the Indo-Gangetic plain and almost everyone has an opinion on the poll arithmetic. In the caste and communal cauldron, whipping up election frenzy isn't difficult. 'Kaante ki takkar hai par Congress nikal aayegi [It's a close contest but Congress will win],' says the local paanwallah, often the most accurate barometer of the prevailing election 'hawa' (breeze).

For Azhar, the western UP town is a long way off from the genteel environs of Hyderabad, the city he grew up in. Moradabad is a hot and dusty provincial district along the banks of the river Ramganga (a tributary of the Ganga) which prides itself as 'Pital Nagar', home to the country's brass industry. But even the brass factories are experiencing a slowdown: irregular power supply and a hostile economic environment have meant shrinking revenues. In the midst of gloom, the arrival of Azhar and his actor-model wife

Sangeeta Bijlani has created a real buzz in every mohalla. Everyone wants a piece of the star couple.

As Azhar's SUV winds through the potholed roads of the township, the crowds get larger. It is noon and the May sun is oppressive but that hasn't stemmed the enthusiasm. A Congress party worker seated next to Azhar suggests that the roof of the car be opened. 'They all want to see you, Azhar bhai,' he says. Azhar looks nervous – an introvert by nature, he has been pulled out of his comfort zone. Like a tense batsman about to take guard, Azhar gets up slowly and along with Sangeeta awkwardly waves to the crowd. Dozens of people clamber around the slow-moving car to clasp Azhar's hand or just gawk at his stylish wife. Dressed in a collared Lacoste shirt and blue jeans, Azhar lifts his Ray-Ban glasses, looks nervously at the audience and raises his hand. The crowd goes delirious and shouts slogans in support.

This could have been Eden Gardens in Kolkata, where a twenty-one-year-old first dazzled the world with a debut century; it could be Lord's, where he made a frenetic hundred with an array of strokes; it could be Cape Town, where he scored a century at more than a run a ball. It could even have been the benign fields of Nizam College, Hyderabad, where it all began for a young middle-class boy. But this is a completely different pitch, one where Azhar has no control over his destiny. The Congress, after all, has been a party on the decline in UP, once its bastion and the karmabhoomi of the Nehru–Gandhi family. While the Bharatiya Janata Party (BJP) has targeted the Hindu vote, the Samajwadi Party and the Bahujan Samaj Party have appealed to caste affiliations, leaving the Congress in a quandary.

'Will you win?' I ask Azhar. 'Winning and losing is for Allah to decide but I am confident,' he says with a typical shy smile and that unique Hyderabadi drawl which is never easy to follow. It's the same quiet confidence that saw him become the first cricketer to score a century in each of his first three Tests in 1984–85. Now, he is hoping to score in his opening innings in politics. His speeches on the campaign trail are short and amateurish. Azhar has always been a soft-spoken man of few words, a mumbler more than a speech-maker. However, people haven't come to listen to a fiery orator but to catch a glimpse of a former India captain in a new avatar. The best one-liner Azhar comes up with has a cricketing analogy: 'I am here to play a Test match, not a Twenty20 contest, I will always be there for you!'

The evolution into a political role has come at a time in his life when Azhar appears to have little to look forward to. His first marriage has fallen apart. Charged with match-fixing, he was banned from all forms of cricket in October 2000; many of his teammates have shunned him; the cricket board is reluctant to invite him to their official functions. 'I am innocent, there is no case against me, no charges proven in any court,' he keeps reminding me as his political opponents rake up the issue. The man who has urged him to enter politics is his old school friend and a former Nizam College and Hyderabad University captain, Kiran Kumar Reddy. Reddy, who would later become chief minister of Andhra Pradesh before it was split into two states, says he wanted Azhar to originally contest from Hyderabad. 'He is our pride, naturally we wanted him here, but the central party leadership decided otherwise,' he tells me later. One meeting with Congress president Sonia Gandhi and Azhar was happy to try his luck in UP.

It's a wise choice as it turns out. The 2009 general elections see a sudden, if temporary, as it turns out, revival of the Congress fortunes in UP: the party wins twenty-two of the eighty seats, its best showing since its 1984 sweep. The victory is attributed to Manmohan Singh's stable leadership at the Centre along with Rahul Gandhi's youthful appeal. At the core of the triumph lies the shift in the Muslim vote towards the Congress. Moradabad, for example, has a 45 per cent Muslim population and this becomes the cornerstone of Azhar's comfortable win by over 48,000 votes. While Azhar appears to get support from across communities, it's in the Muslim areas that the backing for him is strongest.

I get a sense of this when a young man invites me to his house while I am covering the Azhar campaign in a predominantly Muslim locality. In the small two-bedroom house, the furniture is sparse while the hospitality is large-hearted. 'You must try our korma and biryani,' he tells me. 'It's as good as what you will get in Hyderabad.' Over dinner, he excitedly brings out his album of photographs. He shows me one picture he has taken with Azhar. And then points to another photo he managed to click with actor Salman Khan in Mumbai. 'Dekhiye sir, Azhar bhai and Salman bhai, donon mere hero hain [Azhar and Salman are both my heroes].'

Azharuddin, former India captain, and Salman Khan, the big boss of Bollywood: both controversial and yet both wildly popular. Azharuddin may have been haunted by match-fixing while Salman has faced serious charges in a hit-and-run accident and a blackbuck poaching case. Yet, the taints have not affected their standing, especially amongst Indian Muslims in small towns. They are the heroes of the back streets, the men who have risen to the top in their respective fields but never lost the common touch. To the young man in Moradabad, the future is uncertain, perhaps even hopeless, but Azhar bhai and Salman bhai are his icons, two public figures, both Indian Muslim achievers who are helping him live out his dream of wealth, fame and success through the country's two biggest passions: cinema and cricket.

~

In the lives of our Democracy's XI, there is the familiar pattern of a family member who steps up to help young, talented men realize their ambition. A doting mother, a helpful elder brother, a supportive father or uncle. In Azhar's case it was his stern but caring maternal grandfather who became his life compass. Azhar was just forty days old in March 1963 when his grandfather Mir Vajehuddin approached his son-in-law and Azhar's father Mohammad Azizuddin with an unusual request. 'My daughter Sultana lives with you. But I have grown extremely attached to your little son. If you have no objection, I would like to take him to live with us,' he said.

It was a request which would change Azhar's life forever. From that day on till his late teens, Azhar would live with his maternal grandparents. Vajehuddin was a deeply religious man who lived by a credo of discipline and hard work. A school headmaster, he taught mathematics and had a deep knowledge of the scriptures. In the middle-class heartland of Hyderabad's congested Musheerabad area, Vajehuddin was a revered figure. 'My grandfather was like a Sufi saint, he was my guide and mentor. He never taught me cricket, but I learnt everything about life from him,' says Azhar.

His grandfather wanted Azhar to excel in maths but destiny would take him in a different direction. Vajehuddin's son and Azhar's uncle Abid Zainulabidin was a good local cricketer and there would be a few cricket bats in their house. Inspired by his uncle, Azhar would occasionally pick up a bat and play imaginary strokes. In the street games in the city's crowded lanes, Azhar had his first taste of cricket. 'The other boys were much bigger than me but I just loved being in the thick of the action,' says Azhar.

By the time he was eleven years old and a student of All Saints High School, the early flirtation with the sport was turning into a full-blown romance. The school, like many Jesuit institutions, was run by benevolent priests who nurtured young minds with tender care. One of them was Brother Joseph, a schoolteacher who doubled up as cricket coach. Every evening after school, Azhar would attend cricket practice on the school's matting pitch with his priest-coach looking on. 'Brother Joseph was like a father figure to me, he taught me the basics of cricket and would always encourage me,' recalls Azhar. One of those early cricket lessons was to take a hundred catches every day, a ritual that would eventually help make Azhar one of the finest fielders the country has ever seen. That he was also the fastest runner in the school was a bonus – 100 metres in just over 11 seconds.

Slowly, Azhar began to make a name for himself in school cricket.

Hyderabad cricket may not have been as competitive as Mumbai or even Delhi, but the city had a rich tradition of producing talented players. Azhar's own school had produced Indian cricket stars like Syed Abid Ali and, later, Venkatapathy Raju. If Mumbai cricket was defined by the grit and determination of catching the 8 a.m. local train, Hyderabad cricket was seen to mirror the soul of a more laid-back city: the city of the Nizams, of tehzeeb, of grace and elegance. From M.L. Jaisimha through to V.V.S. Laxman, the Hyderabadi cricketer prototype has been of the cricket stylist, soft-spoken gents who play the game with rare finesse. Azhar, with his wristy strokeplay, would soon become part of the city's folklore.

His first break came when he was picked to play for the Hyderabad under-19 team as a fourteen-year-old schoolboy. Saad Bin Jung, who captained Azhar in under-19 cricket, says there was something special about Azhar right from his schooldays. 'He was thin and lanky, but he used to hit the ball with power and precision. Whenever he went to bat, we marked at least a half-century to his name,' says Jung, who once scored a century in a first-class game against the West Indies but never played for India.

Jung and Azhar, in a sense, represented the two poles of Hyderabad society: one the nephew of the Nawab of Pataudi with royal lineage and the other the son of a lower-middle-income group state electricity board official. 'I guess we princely types were lazy amateurs, but Azhar had a real hunger to succeed and he did it without any godfather; else he would have played for India much earlier,' says Jung.

The ambition to play for the country was hidden under a quiet resolve: his cricket may have been flamboyant, his early persona never was. Harsha Bhogle, cricket commentator and a contemporary of Azhar in Hyderabad university cricket, says the first time he saw Azhar play, he was bowling medium pacers with his sleeves rolled down. 'He came across as a shy, self-effacing teenager without any airs about him,' Bhogle tells me. In his authorized biography of Azhar, Bhogle writes: 'To understand Azhar is also to breathe the air of his city, to drink the water of the Gandipet as they say in Hyderabad. It is a charming city with a delightfully unhurried air to it . . . To the average Hyderabadi, time is something to be savoured, not lost to the dizzying speed of modern life. He's a left-lane man, the Hyderabadi, driving his scooter contentedly while the limousines hurry past.'

Kiran Kumar Reddy says that even on long train journeys as part of an under-19 or university team, Azhar would be mostly silent. 'The rest of us would play cards or sing, Azhar would sit quietly in a corner. The one thing he was very good at, apart from cricket, was that he knew all the capitals of every country in the world,' says Reddy. Perhaps it was the austere, orthodox upbringing in the Vajehuddin home, but Azhar was allowed few indulgences in his teenage years. He would travel to matches on a cycle, never have a late night or touch a drop of alcohol, and rarely ever watch a movie. His grandfather was his moral tutor, guiding his every move with an unseen hand. 'Whenever Azhar was not scoring runs, his grandfather would come to watch the game, and somehow Azhar would be back in form,' remembers Reddy.

One such inter-college match was played in 1981 between Hyderabad's two oldest cricket rivals, Nizam College and Osmania University. Bhogle remembers the game well: 'I was playing against Azhar for Osmania University. We had in our ranks Arshad Ayub who would later play for India as an off-spinner. When Azhar came in to bat, we packed the leg-side field to contain his run flow. I was fielding at deep long-on and we had a deep midwicket also. And yet, he kept hitting the ball in a manner that made us look helpless. Arshad even said, 'Yeh bachcha aisa khelinga toh ball dalna bhi kidhar? [If the boy bats like this, where am I to bowl?]'

An eighteen-year-old Azhar made 97 runs that day. Sitting under a tree lining the ground was an old man with a lunch box. Vajehuddin had come to see his grandson at the crease. The day before the game, Azhar was morose because he hadn't been scoring runs. The grandfather had put a comforting arm around Azhar and promised him: 'Kal main aoonga, dekhte hain duniya ki kaunsi taakat tumhareku rokengi [I'll be there at the ground tomorrow, let us see what power on earth stops you].'

His words would prove prophetic, as if there was a kismet connection between grandson and grandfather, a kind of deeper connect that was truly inexplicable, almost mystical. In later years, when his grandfather was no more, Azhar would suddenly play a blindingly magical innings in the middle of a patch of bad form; it was like he was constantly by his grandson's side, ensuring he kept his appointment with run-making. 'Yes, whenever I am in trouble, be it on the field, or off it, I think of my grandfather. If he is with me, no one can touch me,' is how Azhar describes the special bond.

And yet, there is a poignant twist to this chapter in Azhar's life. In the 1983–84 season, his breakthrough year in Ranji Trophy cricket, he was on the verge of an India cap after scoring a bagful of runs. Azhar had been chosen for the India under-25 team to play the visiting Englishmen in Ahmedabad in 1984. As he was preparing to go in to bat, Azhar received a telegram from Hyderabad that said tersely: 'Grandfather serious. Start immediately.' A worried Azhar told his captain, Ravi Shastri, that he needed to rush home. Shastri rang up the senior Hyderabad cricket official P.R. Mansingh, who told him that Azhar's grandfather had passed away. Shastri chose not to give Azhar the grim news but instead lectured him on how crucial the game was for his career. Azhar scored 151 runs, an innings played in a tortured mental state but one which sealed his place in the Indian team.

'All his life my grandfather had waited to see me play for the country but he died just before my first Test,' recalls a misty-eyed Azhar today. But there is another twist to this unique kismet connection. Every time Azhar went to play outside Hyderabad, his grandfather would accompany him till the railway station. It was no different in 1984. 'I had scored runs in the Ranji Trophy, and Symonds, the bat manufacturers, had given me a bat contract for Rs 5000 and two bats a year. I showed the bats to my grandfather as we were leaving for the station. He asked me which bat I was going to use. When I showed him one, he turned to me, "No, don't use this one, use the other one, it will be better." I used the one he wanted me to use and scored all those runs against England.'

Vajehuddin's premonitions may be dismissed as superstition but Azhar insists it was based on an 'ilm', an Islamic term for knowledge. 'I have always believed my grandfather could predict the future, don't ask me how, but he could,' he claims. But could Vajehuddin really have predicted the kind of topsy-turvy life that Azhar was about to embark upon, or indeed that his grandson would make a Test debut the likes of which Indian cricket had never seen? Azhar may have been destiny's child, but a man makes his own luck in the end.

~

Eden Gardens, Kolkata, is Indian cricket's ultimate stage, a colosseum-like amphitheatre that at one time would accommodate almost one lakh people. It is where men are separated from boys, where dreams are made and broken. It was here that Azharuddin made his debut on New Year's Eve in 1984, just weeks before his twenty-first birthday. The match was being played against the backdrop of a defeat to the English in the previous Test, a result that had led to two stalwarts, Kapil Dev and Sandeep Patil, being dropped. The intimidating presence of a large crowd had almost convinced captain Sunil Gavaskar not to pick the young man right away but the chairman of selectors Chandu Borde was insistent. 'I had seen enough of Azhar's batting and athletic fielding to be convinced that he could make the transition to Test cricket and told Sunil not to worry about the age factor; there was something special about him as a batsman and an outstanding fielder,' Borde says.

The wise cricketing head of Borde would be proven right. Azhar came in to bat with India 4 wickets down and with just over a hundred runs on the board. He had barely scored half a dozen runs when he stepped out to off-spinner Pat Pocock, missed the ball, and should have been stumped. Wicketkeeper Paul Downton missed the stumping and Azhar survived. Destiny's child had got another lucky break. 'It is kismet you know,' he tells me now. 'If I had been out early in my first Test, who knows what would have happened.' As it transpired, Azhar took full advantage of the missed chance and went on to score a century on Test debut in a big partnership with Ravi Shastri. 'When I took the single to reach the hundred, I don't think I realized just what I had achieved. My only thought was for my grandfather; I just wished he had been there watching me,' says Azhar.

What stood out in that first innings was how nerveless Azhar seemed at the crease. Here was a twenty-one-year-old playing with some of the biggest names in Indian cricket and yet it appeared as if he had been born for the big occasion. Maybe he was able to make the leap to Test cricket so effortlessly because right from his first tryst with cricket in the galis of Hyderabad, he had always played with boys much older than him. Interestingly, he had only worn a helmet once in his career till the first Test in Kolkata. Just before the Test, he borrowed one from a friend in Hyderabad, Chamundeshwarnath, who had played Ranji cricket for Andhra. The helmet was oversized but it didn't seem to bother Azhar too much. 'Do you know that just before he made his Test debut, he came to me on a cycle and took a fresh kit that I had just bought in Australia,' recalls Reddy. Even the shirt he wore in the first game was a Fred Perry shirt gifted by captain Gavaskar. 'I guess I was just so excited to be in the same dressing room as these great players that nothing else really mattered,' says Azhar.

Colleagues in the India team recall the young Azhar as being the silent man in the background, humble and respectful of his seniors. 'He always had this shy smile but barely said a word,' remembers Mohinder Amarnath. Azhar was letting his bat do all the talking, no special celebrations after achieving a milestone, just a toothy grin and monosyllabic responses to the media. He followed up his debut century with another century in his second Test in Chennai and then capped it with a third ton at Kanpur. He had achieved what no cricketer before or since has ever done: centuries in each of his first three Test matches. A star had not just been born, he had exploded on the Indian cricket scene with a cosmic force that has scarcely been matched. 'It was all a bit of a fairy tale for me. And I have always believed that it was not just me scoring the runs, it was my grandfather's spirit that was driving me forward. His duas [wishes] were with me,' says Azhar.

It was not just the runs he had scored which made Azhar a superstar but the way he made them. He didn't have the technique of a Gavaskar or the classical strokeplay of a Viswanath but he had his own original style, one that was built around a keen eye, powerful wrists, the ability to play the ball as late as possible and a street-smart approach to batting. His footwork wasn't always his best ally, he seemed to slouch at the crease, looked awkward when facing bouncers, his bat came down almost from third man, he had a strong bottom hand but even at the age of twenty-one, he seemed to understand his strengths and limitations as a batsman. One of those strengths was a shot he played through the leg-side off even the most perfectly pitched deliveries on the off stump. From the days of Ranjitsinhji, Indian cricketers have been known for their leg-side strokes; Azhar simply took the aura of wristy oriental sorcerers to another level. 'I grew up on matting wickets, so I could hit off the back foot through the off-side. And on the leg-side, I guess I always felt at ease,' he says.

Above all else, there was the seemingly calm, unflappable temperament, someone never too carried away by success or dismayed by failure. It was almost as if the taveez (amulet) around his neck was his good luck charm. 'I think some of us obsess about technique all the time,' says Sanjay Manjrekar, another contemporary. 'Azhar didn't get too caught up with achieving perfection. When he was in bad form, he would often go for his shots almost as if he was on a lottery ticket that he knew he could win.' And yet, what might seem hara-kiri to an external eye worked remarkably well for Azhar: he would end his Test career with more centuries (22) than fifties (21), an impressive conversion rate that suggests when Azhar was on song he was virtually unstoppable.

In that glorious winter of 1984 that's exactly what his batting was like, a magician dazzling the world with his craft. It also meant that his days as the anonymous bashful young man from the bylanes of Hyderabad were now well and truly over. Five weeks of cricket had turned his world upside down: he wasn't just a star, he was already a superstar at the age of twenty-one. When he returned to Hyderabad, there were a thousand people waiting for him on the tarmac and he was taken in a motorcade to his home in the Vithalwadi area. Everyone wanted a slice of Indian cricket's new hero. When he went to a local mosque for namaz, there was such a stampede that the traffic police had to block the road. Almost every evening, he had to attend a celebratory function in his honour. For an introvert and intensely private man, the public adulation wasn't easy to handle. 'It was nice to be given such a grand reception but, honestly, I was never carried away,' he says.

Proof that Azhar was still the boy next door with his feet on the ground comes from the fact that he still wanted to cycle to matches in the city. Bhogle recalls how he saw Azhar arrive for a Ranji game after his Test success riding on the pillion of a friend's scooter. He had achieved fame but he still hadn't got financial security. His first modelling assignment for a clothes company got him the princely sum of Rs 25,000 and he looked very awkward posing in a suit. In fact, the bicycle was still the only mode of transport he owned. 'We used to call the cycle Azhar's "Honda"; it was his constant companion,' says Reddy. So he could travel easily to every function, a family friend finally arranged for a taxi to be kept at his disposal. The luxury cars would come much later and change Azhar's life dramatically. But in the 1984–85 season and for many years later, Azhar was simply a national hero, the young man from a nondescript middle-class home in Hyderabad who played the game with a dash and flair that brought the crowds flocking to watch him wherever he played.

~

Like many cricketers who get off to a spectacular start, Azhar soon found that sustaining rising public expectations was not easy. Bowlers looked for his technical weaknesses and he suddenly found himself going through a difficult period in Test cricket. His fielding was consistently brilliant and kept him in the side even when the runs appeared to dry up. His one-day form was much better: in 1987 he scored a century off just 62 balls against New Zealand, the fastest by an Indian. But by the time he arrived in Pakistan for a series in 1989, his Test career was truly at the crossroads. He wasn't due to play the first Test, but like always, kismet was on his side. On the morning of the match in Karachi, Raman Lamba dropped out with a finger injury and Azhar was drafted in as a last-minute replacement. That wasn't the only lucky break. The Pakistani master batsman Zaheer Abbas had been watching Azhar play in the nets and suggested a small change in his grip. 'The one change he made was enough, suddenly I felt more comfortable,' Azhar recalls. (Interestingly, years later, Azhar would provide similar help to the Pakistani batsman Younis Khan when he was struggling for runs.) Azhar scored 35 runs in each innings of that game and took five catches, some of them truly special. It was enough to give him another Test match chance.

In the second Test in Faisalabad, Azhar was out for a duck in the first innings. As he walked back, he thought his career was over. That evening, he rang up his mother in Hyderabad in a mood of utter depression. His mother comforted him: 'Don't worry, son, you will score a century in the second innings, God is with you.' And then she told him the reason for her confidence. Apparently, her sister, that is, Azhar's aunt, had told her that their father (Azhar's grandfather Mir Vajehuddin) had come in her dreams the previous night and told her that Azhar should play freely and without fear. The same words which had been uttered to the young teenager at Nizam College years ago were apparently repeated by the fond grandfather: 'Dekhte hain, kaun taakat use rokti hai! [Let's see what force stops him].' He was right. With the divine force of his grandfather behind him, Azhar scored a fighting century, one that saved India from defeat, and revived his career. 'I am telling you my grandfather could predict the future,' he reiterates.

Not only was Azhar's career back on track, he was made India captain a few months later as India toured New Zealand. Here too, there is a twist in the tale. Raj Singh Dungarpur, the chairman of the selectors, had a special fondness for Azhar. A cricket romantic, Dungarpur felt that at the start of a new decade, the 1990s, Indian cricket needed a fresh face at the top. Having just about convinced his fellow selectors, he travelled to Bengaluru, where Azhar was captaining the South Zone team. 'Miya, captain banoge? [Will you be captain?],' he famously asked Azhar. 'But I am already captain, sir,' said Azhar, thinking Dungarpur was referring to the South Zone team. Dungarpur laughed. 'Not captain of South Zone, but of India.' 'It was crazy,' says Azhar in hindsight. 'Just weeks earlier, I was almost out of the Indian team in Pakistan, now I was captain.'

Captaining India is not easy at the best of times. But when you are leading a team that includes three former skippers – Kapil Dev, Ravi Shastri and Dilip Vengsarkar (and later a fourth, Krishnamachari Srikkanth) – the task becomes even more difficult, especially for a mild-mannered person like Azhar. It seemed at first a strange choice: the coy, inarticulate Azhar was always seen as one of the backstage artistes, now he was being asked to be lead actor. 'Yes, I was initially scared to tell a legend like Kapil Dev what to do. I preferred to just listen and allow them to have their say,' says Azhar.

On his first two overseas tours, Azhar had Bishan Singh Bedi as the team's coach. It was a curious case of contrasting personalities that was destined to fail: Bedi the outspoken, rumbustious character; Azhar the cautious introvert. The arrangement quickly unravelled when, on the 1990 tour to England, Azhar defied Bedi's advice and chose to field at Lord's, a decision that backfired badly. Bedi was fuming. 'We had agreed to bat first, then Azhar consults some senior players and reverses the decision at the last minute. It was a compromise that I was not willing to be part of,' says Bedi, who lost his job soon after.

For the first few Tests, Azhar's captaincy limitations were cruelly exposed. India was defeated in New Zealand, England, Australia and South Africa. By the time the team returned from South Africa in January 1993, it seemed that the Dungarpur experiment had failed. But yet again, the wheel of fortune would turn dramatically in Azhar's favour. Just as the selectors were about to appoint Kapil Dev as captain for a home series against England, the team's new cricket manager Ajit Wadekar suggested that Azhar be given one last chance in home conditions. 'I have always believed that captains deserve to be given an extended period to learn on the job,' says Wadekar, one of the country's more successful Test captains.

Kismet was on Azhar's side yet again: the last-chance series would see a sudden turnaround. In the very first Test in Kolkata in February 1993, Azhar scored a superb hundred at Eden Gardens, the ground where he had scored his debut century. Azhar has a special affection for the venue – among batsmen with more than 400 runs scored at Eden Gardens, he has the second highest average of 107 runs per innings with five centuries. Only fellow Hyderabadi V.V.S. Laxman has a slightly better average.

The Kolkata Test against England would mark the beginning of a run where for a decade India did not lose a series at home. The Azhar partnership with Wadekar appeared to be the perfect match: both were reticent individuals with sharp cricket minds, better listeners than talkers. Wadekar was the chief general manager with SBI, the same place where Azhar had got his first employment. Like a good banker, Wadekar had a safety-first approach, which suited Azhar too. In Indian conditions, the duo was comfortable with pushing for turning wickets and then unleashing three spinners on the hapless opposition. 'It isn't as if some magical new formula was discovered by us,' says Wadekar. 'We were just playing to our strengths, and on Indian pitches, spin will always be our trump card.'

So, was Azhar a good captain, or a bit like Wadekar, a lucky one? In 47 Tests as captain, Azhar won 14 and lost 14, a winning percentage of just under 30 per cent. But just one of those wins came overseas, against Sri Lanka in 1993, confirming the stereotypical image of the Indian team being 'tigers at home but lambs abroad'. His one-day record is far more impressive – he led India to victory in 90 out of 174 internationals, a win percentage of more than 50 per cent. His one-day form as captain stands out too: he averaged just under 40 runs in 174 one-day internationals as captain. As a brilliant fielder and stroke-filled batsman, the one-day format allowed him to lead from the front, a task he was not always up to in the more rigorous Test match set-up.

The Azhar–Wadekar combine helped nurture the careers of several of India's gen-next cricketers in the 1990s who would go on to become true champions of the game. The great Sachin Tendulkar flourished under Azhar's captaincy as did the spin leader Anil Kumble and the paceman Javagal Srinath. Other future giants like Sourav Ganguly and Rahul Dravid also found their international cricket feet in the Azhar era. Maybe they had enough class and pedigree to make it even without the captain's support but to completely discount Azhar's role in building a solid base for Indian cricket in the 1990s would be unfair. 'My captaincy theory was simple: once you are playing for India, you don't need to be told what to do. Kumble, for example, knew where to bowl; you don't teach Sachin how to bat. Even in field placing, I was happy to allow the bowlers to decide,' says Azhar. The strategy may have been limited, and in overseas conditions the team was badly exposed, but he did pull off some famous wins, most notably in the Hero Cup semi-finals in 1993 in Kolkata (where else?) against South Africa when he backed his instincts to give Tendulkar the last over of the game. 'It was the wicketkeeper Vijay Yadav who suggested to me that Sachin might confuse the batsman with his change of pace. Besides, Sachin loved to bowl, and I have always believed that in a pressure situation, best to have someone who enjoys the pressure,' is Azhar's explanation for a move that worked like a charm.

Maybe it was the kismet connection that had worked again. Like his grandfather, Azhar too was convinced that his future was written in the stars, a fable-like story that had seen a young man being plucked from the anonymity of Hyderabad's back streets and become one of India's most successful cricket captains. And yet, kismet is a double-edged weapon: it can bring unexpected rewards but also push one to doom. Through his cricket years, Azhar had been blessed by kismet, but destiny's child was about to embrace life's darker side.

~

In April 2000, a friend in the Delhi Police called to suggest that I might wish to meet the Delhi police commissioner, K.K. Paul, and that there was a big story brewing that might interest me. I was a bit surprised: I had never covered the crime beat in the capital and had only a passing acquaintance with the commissioner who wasn't the most media-friendly police officer. (Paul would later become governor of several states.) When I arrived at the police headquarters, I was taken to Paul's office where the commissioner in a very businesslike manner said that there was a phone conversation I might want to listen to. A transcript was also thrust in my hand. What followed left me stunned. The Delhi Police had stumbled upon a phone conversation between the South African cricket captain Hansie Cronje and a bookmaker-businessman Sanjeev Chawla where they were discussing match information. The transcript concerned a South Africa–India one-day international in Nagpur that had just concluded where the South African players had reportedly been offered money by Indian bookies to fix the performance. I was allowed to take notes amidst gathering excitement over what was obviously a huge story. That evening, we tried to piece it together for the NDTV night news (Star

News was the channel's name at the time). The next morning, the
explosive news was a screaming banner headline across all national
dailies. And yet, somehow, I wasn't fully convinced of all the details.
Surely Cronje, the man who had led a post-apartheid South Africa
with such courage and conviction, couldn't be a match-fixer? And if
he was, then he certainly wasn't alone.

A few months later, Cronje's guilt was confirmed when he
broke down in court in South Africa. Not only did he admit to
fixing matches but he also named Azhar as a key collaborator. My
initial reaction was again disbelief. Those who tracked the cricket
circuit had periodically whispered about possible match-fixing. As
mentioned earlier, former India all-rounder Manoj Prabhakar had
claimed in 1997 that he had been offered Rs 25 lakh by a fellow
player to fix his performance in a match in Sri Lanka in 1994. Even
Pakistani cricketers were being accused of match-fixing. But now,
the name of Indian cricket's biggest icons had been dragged in: could
Azharuddin, the self-effacing icon from Hyderabad, grandson of the
God-fearing Vajehuddin, be part of this match-fixing ring?

I recall contacting Azhar for a reaction when the story broke:
'Lies, all lies,' was his short, terse response. Years later, in 2011, in a
television programme after teammate Vinod Kambli suggested that
Azhar may have fixed a World Cup semi-final in 1996 against Sri
Lanka by choosing to bat second after winning the toss, I asked him
the question again: 'Will you swear on the Quran that you didn't
fix matches?' It was the only time I saw Azhar lose his cool: 'What
kind of question is this, please don't ask me questions like this, this
is not done.' When I interviewed him for this book, he sounded more
composed: 'The High Court has exonerated me, no evidence has been
found against me. Please look at my performances and tell me how
I could fix a match.' (His average before 1995 as captain was 47.63;
it dropped to 36.19 after 1995.)

So, did Azhar fix matches? No player who has played with him
is willing to speak on record to provide evidence that he had. But
several of his teammates I spoke to say they felt 'betrayed' by what

Azhar was accused of doing. 'We always had our suspicions. I am afraid Azhar wasn't entirely honest with us,' one of them told me. Another player made it clear he would never appear on a television show with Azhar. Saad Bin Jung, his teammate from their Hyderabad school days, recalls meeting former Pakistan captain Salim Malik ahead of an India–Pakistan World Cup quarter-final in Bengaluru in 1996. 'He was clear that many players were involved in fixing, it was a global epidemic,' says Jung. Malik would later be given a life ban for match-fixing by the Pakistan Cricket Board. K.K. Madhavan, the CBI officer whose report held Azhar guilty, insists that the former India captain had much to answer for even though he says that the reports claiming Azhar broke down and confessed to the crime are untrue. 'He seemed to be scared and wanted to avoid being questioned by me,' says Madhavan.

In December 2000, Azhar was banned for life by the BCCI along with Delhi all-rounder Ajay Sharma. Others like the original whistle-blower Manoj Prabhakar, who ironically was also found guilty of match-fixing, were given lesser sentences while Kapil Dev was exonerated. In 2012, the Andhra Pradesh High Court granted relief to Azhar, lifting the BCCI ban on him, and claimed there was no evidence to link him to match-fixing. Was Azhar then the fall guy in the BCCI's attempt to cleanse the sport, or was he just lucky not to get a jail sentence because the evidence against him could not be corroborated? Did he deserve to be given the benefit of doubt or had he fallen prey to the most basic human indiscretion: greed?

We will probably never get the exact answers but what is clear is that the young man who would happily ride his Honda 'cycle' to matches was taken into a different social orbit by cricket stardom. The turning point came in the mid 1990s. Until then, Azhar was still very much the reluctant hero in the shadows, someone who remained wrapped inside the game that had given him so much. Asaduddin Owaisi, the high-profile Hyderabad MP who was a friend of the family, recalls visiting him in 1993–94 when he was playing county cricket for Derbyshire. 'I was studying for my bar

at law at Lincoln's Inn in London and on weekends we would go
to Derbyshire with Azhar's brothers. His wife Naureen would cook
for us and Azhar would be in bed by 9 p.m. while we would take
a spin in his BMW. He was almost a recluse, never going out to
party,' recalls Owaisi.

Maybe the starry life of being an India captain finally turned
his head: he suddenly began flaunting expensive watches, designer
clothes, flashy cars. It was almost as if without the benevolent gaze
of his grandfather to guide him, Azhar chose to 'break free' by
embracing the material pleasures denied to him in childhood. His
marriage to Naureen, which had been arranged by his parents, broke
down in 1996; he left his Hyderabad home for Mumbai, entered into
a relationship with Sangeeta Bijlani (they would later get married)
and slowly began drifting away from many of his friends. 'Divorcing
Naureen was the biggest mistake that Azhar made,' says Owaisi. 'She
was a lovely simple girl who was devoted to her husband.' Another
Hyderabad friend insists that Bijlani 'trapped' Azhar. 'She cast a
spell on him by enticing him into a world of glamour that he was
not used to,' says the friend.

In his 1994 biography, Bhogle had written about Azhar's 'trusting'
nature, about how despite the trappings of wealth, he remained an
extremely simple, rooted human being, generous to a fault. 'When I
first started ghostwriting columns for Azhar as part of a newspaper
syndication service, he didn't even ask me what his fee would be. I
guess somewhere along the way it was the prospect of big money
that changed his life,' says Bhogle.

Azhar insists he hasn't changed. 'When I was playing cricket and
had several brand contracts, I would give away my shoes and clothes to
any of my teammates who wanted them. And even today, if someone
needs help, I will be there for them,' he says. His long-time friend and
business associate Anas Baqai says Azhar has a 'heart of gold'. He
recalls that even after the match-fixing scandal broke, when Manoj
Prabhakar, the teammate who accused him of fixing games, needed
help, Azhar readily obliged. 'Unka dil bahut bada hai [His heart is

very big], he can never say no to anyone and bears no grudges,' says Baqai, one of Azhar's last 'loyalists'.

Maybe then Azhar just chose the wrong company to enjoy his new-found riches with. One such controversial individual was Ashraf Patel, a Mumbai businessman with alleged links to the Dawood Ibrahim gang. Patel, who held a dealership for the watch company which had Azhar as a brand ambassador, was gunned down in April 2000 in a contract killing near a South Mumbai shopping complex. He was reportedly seen with Azhar just two days before the killing and would often be spotted hanging around the Indian cricket team. 'It was Ashraf who was a link between cricketers and the Dawood gang in Sharjah,' claims a Mumbai police official. Sharjah was then seen as the hub of the cricket betting business. 'How was I to know of Ashraf's underworld connection? I knew him as a watch dealer only. And if people click photos with the Indian cricket captain, am I to be held guilty by association?' asks Azhar today.

Whether others took advantage of his gullible nature, or he consciously got entangled in the murky world of match-fixing, the harsh reality is that one of India's greatest cricketers had to quit the game in disgrace. The BCCI ban meant that Azhar's 99th Test in March 2000 against South Africa would be his last: he scored a century in his final Test as he had in his first, the only Indian to achieve this rare feat. It is a pity that Azhar couldn't complete a century of Tests for the country, falling just one short of the landmark. Maybe this script too was written in the stars; it was his kismet that ruled him out on the cusp of another century.

～

Azhar made his Test debut exactly two months after Indira Gandhi was assassinated by her bodyguards, sparking off the grisly anti-Sikh pogrom in the national capital in which more than 3000 Sikhs were killed. It was a debut made while India was being torn apart by the worst sectarian violence since Partition. The 1984 tour of England, where Azhar achieved instant superstardom, came close to being called off and was eventually played amidst heavy security presence. The 1980s would be pockmarked by communal conflagrations from Bhiwandi to Bhagalpur, Meerut to Moradabad. As a cricketer, Azhar was insulated from the communal tension spiralling around him but as a devout Muslim he would become a symbol of Indian Muslim aspirations in a period of religious conflict. 'I never saw myself as a Muslim playing for India; I was just like any other young man with a dream to play cricket for the country,' he tells me.

Indian cricket in its infancy endured a troubled relationship with the country's multiple religious identities. In the pre-1947 period, in keeping with the colonial tradition of 'divide and rule', the sport was organized along stark communal lines with teams like the Hindus, Muslims, Parsees and the Rest competing in the original Quadrangular and Pentangular tournaments. As a 'national' eleven though, the Indian team always presented a more unified front. The first Indian Test team in pre-Partition India in 1932 had four Muslims, four Hindus, two Parsees and a Sikh. After the bitter divide of Partition many Muslim Test cricketers left for Pakistan (three of them, Gul Mohammad, Amir Elahi and A.H. Kardar played for both countries as a result). And yet, independent India was not a 'Hindu Pakistan', and cricket came to represent the best of the country's secular traditions: faith was never an obstacle to wearing an India cap. Three Muslims captained India before Azhar, including the Pataudi father-and-son duo and fellow Hyderabadi Ghulam Ahmed. Almost every generation has produced at least one Indian Muslim cricket star from Mohammad Nissar (who later migrated to Pakistan) and Mushtaq Ali in the 1930s, Ghulam Ahmed in the 1950s, Pataudi and Salim Durani in the 1960s, Syed Kirmani and Abid Ali in the 1970s, Azharuddin through the 1980s and 1990s, Zaheer Khan and Mohammad Kaif at the turn of the century to Mohammed Shami today. Hyderabad itself, a city with a 40 per cent–plus Muslim population, also has a robust tradition of Muslim community participation in the sport; a few players went on to play for the country. Azhar's school senior Syed Abid Ali, for example, was a hero in the early 1970s, a combative all-rounder with the heart of a lion.

And yet, there was always a sense that Azhar's religious identity coexisted at times uneasily with his fame and status as an Indian cricketer. He could have made his Test debut against Pakistan in the tour preceding the England series but wasn't picked because the selectors felt it might be too much pressure on the young man. The subtext, although never explicitly spelled out, was that of an Indian Muslim being put through a 'patriotism' test every time he played Pakistan. In 1991, when he got out for two consecutive ducks against Pakistan in Sharjah, there were whispers that Azhar had failed because he was a Muslim. It was an unkind, hurtful campaign but one which even political parties like the Shiv Sena never hesitated to publicly voice. 'I had scored runs against Pakistan and yet every time I went out to play against them, I had to almost prove myself all over again,' is his lament.

Azhar is a pious Muslim: he prays five times a day, doesn't touch liquor and cigarettes, eats only 'halal' meat. 'In his hotel room, amidst the Ralph Laurens and the Reeboks, at a distance and always on a pedestal, lie a mat, a cap and a lungi: the common man's prayer kit,' writes Bhogle in Azhar's biography. Religion perhaps was his safety valve, his private cocoon where he could hide from the turbulence swirling around him.

The decade of rising communal antagonism resulted in the demolition of the Babri Masjid in Ayodhya in December 1992 and bloody rioting in several parts of India. Azhar was captaining India in South Africa when the masjid was demolished. Bhogle recalls how in a match that was played soon after, Azhar rather uncharacteristically dropped two catches. 'He may have been affected, but if he was, he clearly didn't try to show it,' says Bhogle.

Two weeks later, I was in South Africa covering the 'historic' tour – the first official visit to that country in over two decades of a global boycott over apartheid – and I tried to get a reaction from Azhar to the political developments at home. 'Can we talk cricket, please?' was his slightly irritated response. When I persisted, he would only say, 'Jo hua achha nahin hua [Whatever happened was not good].' Later, I asked myself whether I would have ever asked any other Indian cricket captain to respond to the Babri demolition. Had I too chosen to see Azhar through the prism of the Indian Muslim predicament? Perhaps I had, but then again in an acutely depressing period where my home city of Mumbai was being torn apart by communal violence resulting in several hundred deaths, Azhar appeared to me to be the most striking badge of a plural, secular Indian identity, one that had risen above narrow religious barriers to scale new peaks.

Indeed, when in February 1993 Azhar scored a big Test hundred in Kolkata, I wrote an effusive column in the *Times of India* in praise of the India captain: 'The importance of being Azharuddin is that he gives us all hope that we will reach out to discovering the finest values in all of us, that we will not define our sense of Indianness by which community we belong to but by the opportunities this great country offers, to become what we choose to be. Every time Azharuddin hits a boundary, he is scoring runs for all of us against bigotry, against those who portray the Indian Muslim as anti-national.' A spectator during the Mumbai Test that same month put it more simply but far more tellingly with a poster: 'Mohammed Azharuddin. Made in India'.

Which is also perhaps why I felt more depressed and let down when Azhar was charged with match-fixing. It almost seemed as if all the romantic fantasies one had woven around a cricketer's impact beyond the boundary had suddenly come crashing down. Worse, it seemed to only confirm the malicious anti-Muslim propaganda of groups like the Shiv Sena and the Sangh Parivar, the worst stereotypes of the Indian Muslim as 'untrustworthy' and 'anti-national'.

Maybe we had put too much of a burden on one cricketer to lift us out of the slough of despondency which the communal politics of the 1980s and 1990s had pushed India's unique liberal, multi-cultural ethos into. Azhar was human, with frailties that afflict all of us. He was probably still Mr India to his fans, heroic with many of his deeds on the cricket field but also cursed with the infirmities that can afflict the soul. In cricket, a batsman doesn't get a second chance. In life, maybe Azhar deserves a break, if only because in the terrible winters of 1984–85 and 1992–93, he came to the rescue, not just of the Indian cricket team, but the collective spirit of a nation that was shaken by communal violence. It is perhaps those who lived through the times who will recall with some affection the importance of being Mohammed Azharuddin.

~

I am sitting in Azhar's rented apartment in a multistorey building in Hyderabad's Banjara Hills in October 2016. He has just returned from two hours in the gym: even in his fifties, Azhar is still supremely fit. His elder son Asaduddin is at home, reading a Khalid Hosseini novel. Well-built and taller than his father, he was picked for the UP one-day side but didn't play a game. Azhar's other son Mohammad Ayazuddin had passed away in a bike accident in Hyderabad at the age of nineteen in September 2011. The death was doubly tragic for him: the super-bike which the teenager was riding had been a gift from father to son. Azhar's nephew Ajmal-ur-Rahman, who was riding pillion, also died in the accident. Ajmal's father Khaleeq-ur-Rahman says Azhar was a pillar of strength for the family in its darkest hour. 'When we broke down, it was Azhar who would comfort us,' he recalls. When I met Azhar to offer condolences, he was typically stoic. The eyes were moist as he mumbled, 'Kya karen, Allah decides.' Like in his cricket career, it was almost as if Azhar believed his life off the field too was preordained.

The house is sparse with a large-sized television dominating the room. On the wall, there is a picture of Mir Vajehuddin. Azhar still seems to derive strength from his grandfather's benign presence. He lost the 2014 elections after shifting constituencies to Tonk in Rajasthan; he lives apart from his second wife Sangeeta; his business ventures have met with little success; he was denied permission to contest the Hyderabad Cricket Association elections in 2017; and many of his former cricket colleagues still shun him. And yet, there is no trace of rancour or bitterness. 'My grandfather always told me, if you have no expectations, there will be no hurt,' he says, fiddling nervously with his shoelaces.

A young nephew has dropped in. 'You must bat like your uncle, he was a great batsman,' I tell the little boy. A man of old-style Hyderabadi courtesy, Azhar comes to drop me to the car when I am leaving. With a familiar shake of the head, he remarks, 'Thank you for coming, kuch achha likhna [write something nice].'

In 2016, a biopic was released on Azhar, the first of its kind on an Indian cricketer; not surprising given the dramatic, roller-coaster ride he has been through. The film flopped: it was badly made and glossed over the match-fixing issue. Maybe the producers got the title wrong. They should have taken a cue from a previous Hindi film hit and named it 'Kahani Kismet Ki' (a story of fate). To continue the film analogy, perhaps Azhar should be seen as a muqaddar ka sikandar (someone who wins against all odds) who ends up as a tragic hero.

7

Sachin Tendulkar

Boy Genius

In 1988, the world geared up for the end of history. The Berlin Wall, symbolic of the division between communism and capitalism, looked as if it was about to collapse. India too was in turmoil. The Rajiv Gandhi government, hobbled by the multi-crore Bofors gun payoff scandal, teetered as a new anti-corruption messiah, V.P. Singh, offered to clean up Indian politics. The saffron army led by the BJP and the Vishva Hindu Parishad (VHP) was preparing to embark on a Ram Janmabhoomi movement to assert its Hindu identity. A sense of disquiet spread through the land. It had been a decade of turmoil and bloodshed. India was looking for a guiding light, a fresh-faced hero who could provide hope. Into the breach stepped a fifteen-year-old who would change the life of a country and, in a small way, my life too.

I had joined the *Times of India* in Mumbai in October 1988 and was struggling to find my young feet in the Old Lady of Boribunder. Having returned from Oxford as a law graduate and spent a few eminently forgettable months in the Bombay High Court, I was a disoriented twenty-three-year-old looking at journalism as my window to the wider world. This was the pre-breaking-news television era, and the *Times of India* moved at the pace of a tortoise with its hind legs tied up. As a trainee assistant editor, my job was to write the occasional opinion piece: it was a pretty cushy existence and by 1 p.m. I was already making plans for a long lunch. But what I was itching for was to be a reporter and to get a front-page byline. In a rigidly hierarchical structure of a newspaper imbued with feudal colonial traditions, this wasn't easy. And then a miraculous December day just six weeks into the profession changed everything.

The editorial meeting on 11 December 1988 was over by noon and I was at a loose end. Mumbai was playing Gujarat in a Ranji Trophy match at the Wankhede stadium, a few kilometres from office. In normal circumstances, a domestic cricket match would hardly attract any attention. But this match was not routine: a fifteen-year-old was making his first-class debut for Mumbai, the youngest to play for a city with proud cricketing traditions. Which is why I suggested to my editor, the very amiable Darryl D'Monte, that maybe I could be sent to cover the game. 'But we already have a sports reporter at the ground,' he reminded me. 'Yes, but maybe I could do a colour story around the teenager making his debut,' I sputtered. Darryl wasn't much of a cricket aficionado but reluctantly agreed, perhaps more out of pity for a young journalist stuck with writing editorials on famine in West Africa.

When I reached Wankhede stadium, Sachin Ramesh Tendulkar was striding in to bat for the first time in a first-class match. The stands were mostly empty but there was a distinct buzz in the air. Next to the press box is the VIP enclosure, occupied by many former Mumbai and India players. Sunil Gavaskar was in the stands – he had been the sole divinity of Mumbai cricket for almost two decades, now he was about to witness the birth of a new God of cricket. Tendulkar's school buddies from Sharadashram Vidyamandir were also there: they had been given the day off to cheer their classmate. 'Sachin nakki shambhar karnar [Sachin will definitely score hundred],' they all exulted confidently. 'Shambhar', the Marathi word for century, has echoed through the city's maidans for decades, the ultimate marker of cricketing excellence.

The Gujarat bowling attack wasn't too special but they weren't going to do any favours to the teenager either. In the first over, Tendulkar was struck on the pad, a close LBW decision which went in his favour. Perhaps the umpire too wasn't keen to give up his chance to watch the teen prodigy. Once he settled in, Tendulkar began to treat the bowling with the same aggressive spirit that had seen him break batting records in school cricket, hitting the ball to all corners of the ground. It was almost as if making the transition from the maidan to the big stage was the easiest thing in the world. His batting partner in that game, Alan Sippy, recalls being awestruck by Tendulkar's calm demeanour at the crease. 'The day before the match I remember telling my dad that I don't know why the selectors have picked a fifteen-year-old, he may get hurt,' remembers Sippy. 'Next day, I realized that Sachin was from another planet!'

When he came to bat, Sippy as the senior player went across to Tendulkar and told him, 'Relax, aaram se.' 'I thought he would be nervous but Sachin just said one word to me in response, "Bindaas", and then went and hit the first ball so hard that I didn't know what to say,' says Sippy. Indeed, the teenager with the curly locks and rosy cheeks who had barely had his first shave was truly 'bindaas', a unique Mumbai word suggesting a fearless approach to life. With every shot he played, the cheers of his school friends intensified, and as the score began to mount, the stadium began to slowly fill up.

Just before the day's play ended, Tendulkar reached the almost inevitable shambhar: at fifteen years, seven months and seventeen days, he had become the youngest centurion in the first-class game in India in his very first match. Gavaskar and the few thousand spectators stood up to applaud, astounded by the strokeplay of an adolescent for whom the bat was a sword in a knight's hand, flashing through the air with deadly intent, even as his peers sweated over their school maths. Australia could never find the next Bradman; India

had found its new batting icon less than a year after Gavaskar retired
from the game. And yet, while we were captivated by Tendulkar's
magical batsmanship, the teenager was unfazed by the adulation.
Shishir Hattangadi, the former Mumbai captain, recalls Tendulkar
coming to the pavilion with barely a hint of a shy smile on his face.
'It was almost like another day in the office for him, as if he knew
he would score a century since that is what he had been doing in
schools cricket from day one,' says Hattangadi. Indeed, when I
rang up Tendulkar's coach, Ramakant Achrekar, for a reaction, his
response was equally unruffled: 'He has a long way to go, this is only
the beginning.'

I returned to office, only to be accosted by my editor. 'So, how
was your afternoon out at the cricket game?' he asked with a hint
of sarcasm. 'Well, sir, I think I have just seen the birth of the next
cricket superstar,' was my excited response. The next morning, I found
my article on Tendulkar with a byline on the front page with the
headline 'A New Dawn in Indian Cricket'! It was my first front-page
article. Little did I know that the dawn of a new age I had predicted
would spread the most glorious sunshine across the cricket world for
the next twenty-five years.

~

We don't know just when Sachin Tendulkar began his romance
with cricket but there are pictures of a chubby little boy holding a
cricket bat at the age of three. By the age of six, he was playing with
the boys in the Sahitya Sahawas colony in Bandra where he lived.
At the age of eleven, he began his formal coaching at Ramakant
Achrekar's camp at Shivaji Park. At the age of twelve, he played
his first junior cricket match for Sharadashram Vidyamandir. At
fifteen, he was playing for the Mumbai Ranji Trophy team and
a year later he was playing for India. It is quite simply the most
remarkable example of a child prodigy in Indian sport, maybe even
in global sport.

Rajdeep Sardesai

Sharmila Tagore

op, left to right: S. Venkataraghavan, P. Krishnamurthy, Eknath Solkar, Dilip Sardesai and K. Jayantilal
ding in an open-top Buick during a victory procession in Mumbai after India won its first overseas series
England in 1971. Sardesai recalled, 'the English in their jackets and ties couldn't believe that the Indians
hom they had taught the game had defeated them at home'.

ottom: Mansur Ali Khan Pataudi, chief guest at an event in Mumbai in April 1969. In 1962 when skipper
ari Contractor was hit in the head in the West Indies by a bouncer that ended his career, Pataudi, 21,
as made the youngest ever captain of the side. 'I was thrown into the deep end and asked to swim from day
ne,' he said.

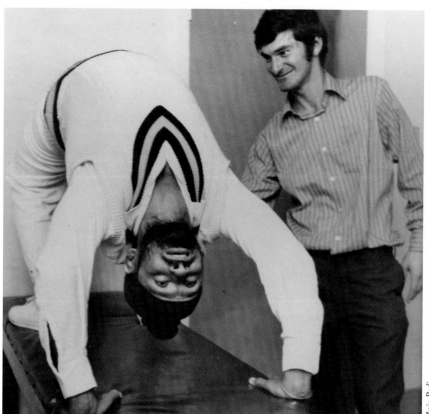

Anju Bedi

Anju Bedi

Left: Sunil Gavaskar batting left-handed for the first time in the Ranji Trophy semi-final between Mumbai and Karnataka in March 1982. Gavaskar batted left-handed to counter crafty left-arm spinner Raghuram Bhat. Such was Gavaskar's skill that he still managed not to get out.

Below: Kapil Dev in a Nippo Batteries advertisement from the early 1990s. Kapil was India's original small-town folk hero, never embarrassed that he couldn't speak perfect English. 'I wasn't picked for India for my English,' says the 1983 World Cup–winning captain.

The Hindu *Archives*

Facing page, top: Bishan Singh Bedi showing England wicketkeeper Alan Knott a yoga pose in 1971. Bedi was an outspoken upholder of player rights at a time when they were treated as subordinate to BCCI officials. During his captaincy, in 1975, he shouted at a BCCI official, 'The crowd comes to see us play, not to see you officiate.'

Facing page, bottom, left to right: G. Viswanath, Syed Kirmani, B.S. Chandrasekhar and Bedi celebrating after Chandrasekhar bowled India to a famous win against Australia in Melbourne in 1977–78. Chandra, Bedi, Venkataraghavan and Erapalli Prasanna, the 'spin quartet', took more than 800 Test wickets between them.

Romi Dev

Top, left to right: Chetan Chauhan, Dilip Vengsarkar, Karsan Ghavri, Kapil Dev, Yashpal Sharma and captain Gavaskar celebrating India's first series win against Pakistan in Chennai in January 1980. India–Pakistan matches have been described as 'war minus the shooting'.

Bottom, left to right: Cricket writer Harsha Bhogle, captain Mohammed Azharuddin and chairman of selectors Raj Singh Dungarpur at the release of Bhogle's book *The Joy of a Lifetime* in 1990. It was Dungarpur who made Azhar captain, asking him, 'Miya, captain banoge?'

Prakash Parsekar

young Sachin Tendulkar at the Cricket Club of India, circa 1989. Tendulkar made his India debut at age 16
a series against Pakistan in 1989. In the fourth Test at Sialkot, his nose was bloodied by a Waqar Younis
ort delivery, but 'Tendlya' refused to retire hurt. 'I didn't want anyone to feel I was scared,' he says.

Top: Sourav Ganguly, New Delhi, October 1997. The 18-year-old Ganguly was first picked for the side as a reserve batsman for the 1991–92 tour of Australia. But 'Maharaj', as he was then called, was branded lazy and arrogant, unwilling to do the drinks-trolley duties of the twelfth man, and dropped from the team. He made a sensational comeback in 1996.

Bottom, *left to right*: Sachin Tendulkar, Sourav Ganguly, Rahul Dravid, V.V.S. Laxman and Virender Sehwag at a fitness camp in Bengaluru in June 2004. Between them these five Pandavas of Indian batting in the 21st century have more than 50,000 Test runs to their credit.

Deccan Herald

Sunil Kumar

Above: Anil Kumble (*left*) and Dravid (*right*), beloved icons of Karnataka, at a felicitation ceremony in Bengaluru in May 2006. Their great Indian cricket dream included a balance between sport and academics. Kumble studied engineering and Dravid did a one-year correspondence MBA course as a back-up.

Left: Mahendra Singh Dhoni, circa 1995, with Ranchi University in the background. When Dhoni was born in 1981, his father was a pump operator with the public sector firm MECON, and they lived in a one-bedroom house in Ranchi. Dhoni's first salary, playing for the SAIL team, was Rs 625 per month.

Top: A chubby Virat Kohli (*centre*), then captain of the under-19 team, flanked by his coach Rajkumar Sharm
(*left*) and Suresh Batra (*right*) of the West Delhi Cricket Academy in March 2008. When Kohli's father pass
away one night in 2006, in the middle of a Test match, Kohli phoned Sharma to ask for advice. He ended up
playing the match. 'That's what my father would have wanted me to do,' Kohli says.

Bottom: Kohli (*left*) and Dhoni (*right*) share a light moment ahead of their World Cup quarter-final against
Bangladesh in March 2015. Dhoni retired from Test cricket in 2014 and stepped down from the one-day an
Twenty20 captaincy in 2017. Kohli is now India captain in all three formats and arguably the best batsman i
the world.

Yes, we know of a few Pakistani cricketers who have played at similarly young ages but there has always been a question mark over their birth certificates. (Was Shahid Afridi, for example, really sixteen when he made his debut for Pakistan?) Yes, we have had gymnasts like Nadia Comaneci who dazzled the world with a perfect 10 at the 1976 Montreal Olympics as a fourteen-year-old but then gymnastics is a sport where nimble, youthful feet are a huge advantage. Not so with cricket: this is supposed to be a 'grown-up' sport, where you have to confront a hard cricket ball that can really hurt you. Even a tennis prodigy like Boris Becker, who quite incredibly won Wimbledon at the age of seventeen, didn't face the same physical threat from a tennis ball that Tendulkar did when he had to face up to the fastest bowlers in the world while still in his early teens. At home, he was a mischievous teenager who plucked mangoes from trees and relished his mother's fish curry rice; on the field he was a grown-up batting assassin.

I have tried to find a rational explanation for Tendulkar's prodigious feats. His elder brother and friend and guide, Ajit, tells me how from the age of seven Sachin had this wonderful hand–eye coordination with an extremely relaxed backlift and a calm, nerveless temperament. 'When he hit the tennis ball in our colony garden, he always did it with minimum effort and no fuss,' he points out. But then that may well be true of thousands of young children who throng the maidans and galis of the country to play cricket. What was so unique about Sachin that enabled him to play the sport at the highest level at such an early age? Ajit offers another interesting insight. Sachin, he says, was blessed with unusual power from an early age. Sachin's pals in the colony recall how even as a young boy he could hit the ball harder than others twice his age. 'You know, my mother, Rajni, used to go to Talwalkars Gym in the 1960s when weight training for women was unheard of. Her brother was a weightlifter while another uncle was a long-distance swimmer. Maybe Sachin got his early power and muscle from our mother's side of the family,' suggests Ajit. Ironically, Ajit, a good junior cricketer himself, is thin and wiry; he was a technically correct batsman but struggled to hit the ball with any real power.

The truth is, rationality has no answers when confronted with pure genius. The idea that talent is 'God-given' may be a trifle exaggerated and fails to recognize the human effort that goes into shaping success but it is probably the best way to understand the Tendulkar phenomenon. Few who saw Tendulkar bat in his early years would not say that he was touched by divinity, almost a supernatural force that seemed to drive him forward. Indeed, anyone who saw Tendulkar bat for the first time was convinced that he was destined to play for India. When Tendulkar attended an under-15 national camp in Indore in 1987, coach Vasu Paranjpe introduced him to Indian cricket legend Mushtaq Ali: 'Meet the young boy who is the second-best batsman in the country after Gavaskar.' This at the age of fourteen.

Milind Rege, the former Mumbai captain, recalls how Sachin in his very first match for the CCI in 1988 stepped out and lifted the fast bowler Pradeep Sunderam for six at the Brabourne stadium. Sunderam was no slouch with the ball, having once taken 10 wickets in an innings in a Ranji Trophy game for Rajasthan. 'It was the most unbelievable shot for anyone to hit, leave aside a fifteen-year-old,' says Rege.

Ajit recounts an anecdote of how his younger brother's future as a potential India cricketer never seemed in doubt right from his early teens. Having first been picked for the Mumbai under-15 team as a thirteen-year-old, Tendulkar was being dropped off at the station by his father, Ramesh, a Marathi poet and professor. The father expressed his concern to another parent, Vilas Godbole, about how cricket was affecting his son's studies. Godbole, a handy club cricketer whose son was also in the team, laughed. 'Ramesh bhau, you don't have to worry about any of this. Your son will be playing for India one day, it's the rest of us who have to ensure our children balance cricket with academics.' (Tendulkar would eventually drop out in junior college, after class eleven.)

And yet, every talent needs a nurturing umbrella, a protective environment that allows it to flourish. There are innumerable stories in Indian cricket of record holders in school cricket fading away when having to take a step up. Tendulkar never faced that problem because his path to the top was smoothened by a caring family and a selfless coach who became a father figure. Tendulkar would probably have played for India one day in any case, but his spectacular early rise owes much to his father Ramesh, brother Ajit and coach Achrekar: they were the triumvirate that allowed Tendulkar to express his unique talent on the cricket field, were there to guide him when he could have faltered, to support him when he was thrown into the deep end.

Ramesh Tendulkar was a scholar, not a sportsman. He could have easily pushed his son into spending more time on school work, yet he chose to allow him to chase his dream. 'My father never put any pressure on me, he just let me play,' acknowledges Tendulkar. 'He would only keep reminding me that whatever you achieve in cricket, always be a good human being first.'

An early test of the father's willingness to allow his son to fly came when Tendulkar was twelve and had moved to Sharadashram Vidyamandir to play cricket. The school was a little far away from their Bandra home and closer to Shivaji Park. So it was decided to allow Tendulkar to stay with an aunt and uncle who lived near the school. 'I think my father missed having Sachin around the home but he just wanted what was best for Sachin at the time,' recalls Ajit. It was from his father perhaps that Tendulkar inherited his calm temperament. 'Even when Sachin was first picked for India or scored his first hundred, there was no special celebration at home. My father didn't want Sachin or any of us to get carried away,' says Ajit.

What his father managed to ensure at home, coach Achrekar was able to achieve on the cricket field. Tendulkar first came under Achrekar's tutelage at the age of eleven in 1984. It was a summer cricket camp at Shivaji Park and was the first time that Tendulkar got a chance to play on a turf wicket with a hard ball. 'I was very excited, but nervous also to play with the big boys,' recalls Tendulkar. 'It was just something to keep me occupied in the holidays.' It would mark the beginning of an intense love affair that would last a lifetime.

The start wasn't exactly auspicious. Tendulkar scored a duck in his first practice game in the camp. It was only in the third game that he reached double figures, hitting the ball with the same vigour that he had shown in his colony. 'I remember sir telling me that day, this is your game and this is how you have to always play, attacking cricket,' says Tendulkar. He also made it clear that Tendulkar would always bat at number four.

What did Achrekar see in an eleven-year-old that prompted him to bestow extra attention? 'All the boys were special for my father but I guess Sachin was always a bit extra special,' says Achrekar's eldest daughter, Vishakha. She recalls how after Tendulkar had scored his first 50 in a school match at the age of twelve one of the officiating umpires rang up her father excitedly to say that he had seen a future Indian batting star. Talent spotting is an art which sometimes isn't given enough recognition in sport, but clearly Achrekar had a rare gift which might explain why he coached a dozen young cricketers who went on to play for the country. Employed with SBI, he had been a more than useful club cricketer. Coaching was a passion for him: his nets would be conducted round the year for a fee of just Rs 7 a month (later raised to Rs 11). The bank was most obliging. He would be at the nets at 6 a.m., go to office, sign in and then be back at the ground at 2 p.m. 'For my father, it was never about the money, it was simply that he just loved coaching children,' says another daughter, Kalpana.

Achrekar's coaching style was less driven by a search for technical excellence than by a conviction that the best cricketers needed to be match-hardened. He initially tried, for example, to change Tendulkar's firm bottom-handed grip where both hands were close to the lower end of the bat in defiance of conventional cricket wisdom but relented when he saw that his young ward's unique style didn't stop him from scoring runs. 'I started by using my brother's bat which was slightly heavy for me which is why I felt more comfortable holding it a little lower than normal,' says Tendulkar. In the year

1985–86, Tendulkar recalls playing more than a hundred matches in a season, often batting twice in a day, once in a morning game, and then in a late afternoon match. He would also bat in four to five different nets at practice, often batting till it was too dark to spot the ball, and then be made to run two rounds of Shivaji Park with his pads on, which helped strengthen his legs from an early age. 'We would finish practice around 7 p.m. and then sit on the Shivaji Park benches and eat vada pav, sing songs and talk cricket all the time,' says Tendulkar.

It was a happy time but there were no short-cuts either. 'I was slapped on more than one occasion by sir. Once when I went to see a senior school match instead of attending practice, sir saw me and slapped me so hard in front of everyone that my tiffin box fell from my hand. That day he told me, "You aren't supposed to see others play, the world must watch you play." On another occasion, when I dropped a catch in practice, he slapped me again,' Tendulkar remembers. During a match, Achrekar would take notes and after the game was over point out the mistakes and seek immediate redressal. The tough, no-nonsense coach had a softer side too. Taking his young ward to play matches on his Lambretta scooter, he would stop at a bhelpuri stall and treat his teenage prodigy if he scored a hundred. 'It was his way, I guess, of saying "well played",' says Tendulkar.

The first century came in 1986 in an interschool match against Don Bosco. Tendulkar remembers it well. He had been batting 94 overnight and next day in the first over hit two fours to reach his century. That day, his 'sir' visited his house for the first time. 'I had always been pestering sir to come home and he insisted that he would come only after I had scored a hundred, so it was a special moment for me,' says Tendulkar. That morning Tendulkar had visited a local Ganesh temple to pray for success. It would mark the beginning of a ritual before every cricket series: a visit to a temple and then a trip to his coach's house to seek blessings. In 1993, Achrekar suffered a paralytic attack that left him immobile and brain-damaged. He could no longer advise Tendulkar on his game but he didn't need to. His shishya, by then India's champion batsman, had more than handsomely repaid his guru by giving him the ultimate guru-dakshina: scoring runs by the bucketful.

If Ramesh Tendulkar was the role model and Achrekar the guru, Ajit was the guide and mentor, the compass who made sure that the single-minded focus on the game was never shaken. I knew Ajit well: we were contemporaries in club and age-group cricket. We once even had a century partnership together for Jolly Cricket Club. Ajit had a good defensive technique but limited strokes. What he did possess though was a stoic calmness and an obsession with the game, qualities he would pass on to his younger brother. Sachin was ten years younger, an age difference that defined the relationship. 'I trusted him completely, never questioned his judgement, whatever he said, I did,' Sachin tells me.

I have often thought that Ajit and Sachin were soulmates, almost like conjoined twins chasing a common goal. Ajit lived vicariously through Sachin's bat, his younger brother's success being the driving force of his life. 'I realized that he had a special talent and wanted him to succeed where I had failed,' Ajit says. Which is why he took an eleven-year-old Sachin to Achrekar's camp for the first time, changed his school to Sharadashram Vidyamandir, sat with him after every game to analyse his innings and was always at hand to answer his queries. Other family members chipped in too. Sachin's sister, Savita, for example, bought Sachin his first Kashmir willow bat while his eldest brother, Nitin, would sometimes drop him to the bus stop or railway station.

There were other benefactors too. Hemant Kenkre, a useful club cricketer, gave him the extra-light pads that Gavaskar had used while scoring a double century in the 1979 Oval Test when he found out that Sachin had lost his pads during an under-15 camp. Madhav Apte, the former India player, as CCI club president, changed the rules to allow a fourteen-year-old playing membership of the prestigious club. And Hemant Waingankar, another club cricketer, got him early sponsorship for cricket equipment from Sungrace Mafatlal, the corporate house. 'When you see magic in front of you, you want to embrace it; we all wanted to be part of the magical journey of Tendulkar in some small way,' says Kenkre.

And yet, in the end, it was the will and skill of one prodigiously talented teenager that was the deciding factor in his amazing rise. Tendulkar tells me the story of how he was once injured in a match while wicketkeeping as a thirteen-year-old and his nose was bleeding. Since he didn't have a change for his blood-soaked shirt, nor money for a bus ride, he went on a cycle with a friend from Shivaji Park to Bandra, a fair distance away, lugging the kitbag, while trying to hide his injury from onlookers. 'I guess all the rides in crowded buses and trains toughened me up at a young age,' he says.

Ajit recalls how Sachin as a twelve-year-old would sometimes wake up at night and practise his strokes. He even cut a golf ball at the edges into an oval shape and asked his aunt to throw it at him in her living room so his reflexes would sharpen. 'With the edges cut, the ball would keep changing direction but I made sure that I always hit it with the middle of the bat and nothing in the house was damaged,' says Sachin. Another contemporary, Jatin Paranjpe, remembers how at age fourteen Tendulkar was captaining an under-17 team and once went up to the manager and threatened not to play if he was not given the team of his choice. 'Right from the start, he had a mind of his own,' says Paranjpe.

Former Ranji player Kailash Gattani recalls taking Sachin on a cricket tour to England as a fourteen-year-old, his first trip abroad. 'In the first match, he got out playing on the rise on a green, seaming wicket. When I explained where he had gone wrong, he promised never to repeat the mistake, and he didn't,' says Gattani. On that tour, when he wasn't batting, he would happily do the scoring, a mark of his desire to stay involved in the game. Former India captain Dilip Vengsarkar invited Sachin to the India nets as a fifteen-year-old and got Kapil Dev to bowl to him. 'He wasn't at all intimidated by having to face Kapil; in fact, he asked me if he could come the next day to bat again,' recalls Vengsarkar.

It was almost as if Sachin was born to play cricket from the time he learnt how to walk. As Hattangadi says, 'A cricketer takes years to get skilled in his craft, but Sachin was ready for the big stage almost right away, he was like a Ferrari from day one with no obvious defects.'

~

'When I was twelve and playing my first school match, I knew I would play for India one day,' Tendulkar says. It's a remark made without the slightest hint of arrogance but with an intense self-belief in his ability. And yet, even he could not have dreamt that he would play his first Test for India at the age of sixteen against the mighty Pakistanis led by Imran Khan. It was baptism by fire. The selection meeting that chose him was headed by Raj Singh Dungarpur who, as mentioned in the previous chapter, was determined to engineer a generational change in the sport. At the meeting, one of the selectors reportedly warned that sending Tendulkar to Pakistan was a bad idea: 'He is only sixteen, he may get injured facing the Pakistani quicks and a failure will haunt him for the rest of his career.' The West Zone selector and former India wicketkeeper Naren Tamhane countered, 'Don't worry, Tendulkar never fails.'

He was right. Even though Tendulkar didn't set the Indus aflame on his first tour, there were two moments that offered a glimpse into the future. The first came in the fourth Test at Sialkot. Tendulkar had scored a fifty in the second Test but was still coming to terms with the pace of the Pakistani attack led by Wasim Akram when he was hit on the nose by a Waqar Younis short delivery. The ball hit the flap of his helmet before thudding into his nose. As Tendulkar fell to the ground, it seemed as if the selector's warning had proven prophetic. There was blood all over his shirt and the combative Javed Miandad suggested he be taken to hospital because he was a 'kid'. But Tendulkar says, 'I just felt that if I left the ground, I would be dubbed a coward. Tea was a few minutes away and I was determined to stick on and prove a point.' Ajit, who was watching the match at the ground, recalls seeing him near the dressing room during the tea break. 'He looked at me and said, "I am fine, don't worry." That was enough for me,' says Ajit. An injury from a bouncer can destroy a player's self-confidence, but the blow on the nose only seemed to make Tendulkar more resolute. He had never feared a cricket ball from the day he put bat to ball. He batted after tea and into the next day to score a match-saving half-century. At sixteen, Tendulkar was already Indian cricket's macho saviour.

A week later, Tendulkar produced another little gem of an innings, this time hitting the champion Pakistani leg-spinner Abdul Qadir for 4 sixes in an over in a one-day exhibition game in Peshawar. In the build-up to that over, Tendulkar had smashed another leg-spinner, Mushtaq Ahmed, fifteen years Qadir's junior, for six, prompting Qadir to taunt Tendulkar: bachche ko kyon maarta hai, dum hai to mujhe maar (why are you hitting a child, if you have the guts, hit me). The Indian captain Kris Srikkanth was the non-striker and recalls going up to Tendulkar after the second six and asking him to calm down a bit. 'He just nodded his head, didn't say a word, and then hit the next two deliveries for six again. Pure genius,' exclaims Srikkanth. Twenty-eight runs in an over against one of the game's most feared bowlers: Tendulkar had made the transition from maidan to the big stage with ease.

Playing against Pakistan is the ultimate skill test for any Indian cricketer: it is almost like war without weapons. Cricket between the two countries could not be distanced from its fractious politics and competing nationalisms. My father and Pataudi, for example, played for India through the 1960s but never got a chance to play Pakistan because there were no cricket matches between the two countries for seventeen years between 1961 and 1978, an unsettled period which saw two wars between the countries. The 1980s were a more congenial decade for Indo-Pak cricket: six Test series were played in ten years. In 1988, Rajiv Gandhi and Benazir Bhutto had a one-on-one meeting in Islamabad, two inheritors whose youthful energy offered hope for a future. Barely two years later though, Pakistan-backed militancy in Kashmir would rear its menacing head and dash any optimism about peace; conflict would rupture cricket ties once again.

The 1989 tour to Pakistan, Tendulkar's first, would be the last between the two countries for a decade. 'I always enjoyed playing Pakistan; yes, there was pressure, but there was also the challenge of raising your game and being remembered forever,' says Tendulkar. Then, be it a century while batting through cramps in the Chennai heat in 1999 or a match-winning knock in a World Cup semi-final in 2003, Tendulkar's mastery shone through against the men in green.

Three other standout performances in the early years confirmed Tendulkar's extraordinary skills. The first came in England in 1990 when he scored his maiden Test century at Old Trafford to help India draw a Test they looked like they would lose. Not only did he become the youngest Indian to score a Test hundred that day, but he proved to himself that he could play a defensive innings when required. 'That was an important innings for me because my natural game was to attack,' says Tendulkar. 'I now knew I belonged to Test cricket.'

What struck observers on that England tour was just how a seventeen-year-old Sachin relished the challenge every time he went in to bat against more experienced cricketers. Bishan Bedi, who was the team coach, says that when he asked the team to run half a dozen rounds of the ground, Tendulkar was always enthusiastic to run an extra round. 'He was this fair, energetic boy who spoke very little but just let his bat and cricket do all the talking,' recalls Bedi. He was rested, for example, in a county game against Derbyshire whose pace attack included West Indian quick Ian Bishop. On the night before the match, he went to the manager Madhav Mantri and insisted he be allowed to play. 'I want to test myself against the pace of Bishop,' he told Mantri in a soft but firm voice. Sure enough, he scored a hundred the next day.

The second Tendulkar special came against Australia in the long and difficult 1991–92 series Down Under. The Perth wicket is considered the fastest in the world, the steep bounce having undone many an Indian batsman. And yet, even before his nineteenth birthday, Tendulkar scored a hundred there which he rates as possibly his best. 'I guess all those years playing against a bouncy rubber ball in the colony with friends helped me,' he says. Indeed, Australia would prove a happy hunting ground for Tendulkar, leading even the most parochial Australian fans to draw comparisons with Sir Don Bradman. 'I never saw Bradman play but I doubt he could have batted better than Sachin on that tour. He was standing out of his crease and hitting the likes of Craig McDermott and Merv Hughes on the up,' recalls Ravi Shastri, who shared a big partnership with Tendulkar in the Sydney Test.

The third Tendulkar moment that stands out is a little more unusual. It came in the Hero Cup one-day semi-final against South Africa in Kolkata in 1993. It was the last over and South Africa needed just six runs to win. As mentioned in the previous chapter, skipper Azharuddin was mulling his options when Tendulkar offered to turn his arm over. 'I just went by the hunch that if someone was so keen to bowl then maybe it was best to give him a chance, we had nothing to lose!' All through his schooldays, Tendulkar had enjoyed bowling: he once even went for a trial to a Dennis Lillee fast bowling camp in Chennai. Now he had a rare opportunity to show off his bowling skills. 'I bowled mainly slow leg-cutters in that over, taking out all the pace. The South African batsmen struggled to hit me, maybe because they didn't know what to expect from my bowling,' says Tendulkar. Only two runs were scored in that over and India won the game. Tendulkar had shown that he was not just fearless with the bat, but nerveless with the ball too. Well before his twenty-first birthday, he had displayed the cricket brain of someone much older. Most of us search for maturity all our lives; Tendulkar arrived into adulthood by living his teenage years in the nursery of a cricket field.

Sachin Tendulkar was always destined to be a cricket great. Even so, I believe that his cricketing life changed dramatically after he decided to open the innings in one-day cricket for the first time in 1994 in New Zealand. The regular opener Navjot Sidhu was injured and Tendulkar put up his hand to replace him. 'I went to the coach Ajit Wadekar and captain Azhar and told them to give me one chance. "If I fail, I won't ask you again," was my promise,' he says. That day, taking full advantage of the field restrictions in the first 15 overs – only two fielders were allowed outside the inner 30 yard circle – Tendulkar scored 82 off 48 balls, his natural attacking instincts being tailor-made for the shorter format. In Test cricket, Tendulkar was conscious not to take any risks and loft the ball early in his innings; in one-day cricket, he had a licence to hit over the in-field from the outset. 'It was like I was back to my schooldays when the idea was to attack the bowling from the very first ball,' he says. India's permanent number four in Test matches was now its star opener in limited overs cricket.

The move would have an impact beyond the boundary too. By the mid 1990s, the equation was rapidly changing between one-day and Test cricket: the players and the aficionados still valued Test performances but the crowds were flocking to 50-overs cricket. By opening the batting in one-dayers, Tendulkar got a chance to showcase the full range of his skills before newer, younger audiences. He was already the world's number one Test batsman along with West Indian Brian Lara; he would now become the undisputed king of the one-day game. Tendulkar in white flannels was revered; in the blue Indian colours he became a folk hero for a gen-next audience who, with shorter attention spans and a premium on time, were thirsting for a more aggressive brand of cricket.

A year after Tendulkar opened for India in one-dayers for the first time, cable and satellite television in the country crucially also got a big boost. The 1993 Hero Cup in Kolkata had seen the CAB give the telecast rights to a private broadcaster, Star TV, for the first time, effectively ending the monopoly of state-run Doordarshan over the airwaves. When Doordarshan protested, the Supreme Court in a landmark order in 1995 ruled that the right to broadcast cricket matches was not a government preserve but the airwaves belonged to the people. Suddenly, every match could be beamed live across the country on satellite television. It was just the trigger the sport needed to link cricket to the expanding consumer marketplace – Manmohan Singh's 1991 budget had already opened the door for multinational brands to discover the Indian market. 'It is a happy coincidence that when cricket entered the satellite television age, the country had a hero who had already won our hearts and multinational companies had a vehicle to advertise their brands. Sachin was there at the right place at the right time,' is how cricket commentator Harsha Bhogle puts it.

With Brand Tendulkar as its presiding deity, cricket was now finally married to commerce. In 1990, when Tendulkar was starting off, a player earned Rs 10,000 a day for a Test match and just Rs 6500 for a one-day match. By the time, he retired in 2013, Rs 7 lakh was the Test match fee with Rs 4 lakh for a one-dayer, apart from a hefty annual retainership. My father's era where cricketers were glorified amateurs who were paid Rs 250 per Test with no extra allowances was finally over. At a BCCI function in the late 1990s, my father joked, 'If only we were born in the age of colour TV, we would have also been crorepatis, but we sadly couldn't go beyond being radio stars.'

If Tendulkar's batting exploits were the catalyst for change on the cricket field, the 1996 World Cup in the subcontinent was a turning point off it. The harnessing of the Marwari business instincts of BCCI secretary Jagmohan Dalmiya and the flamboyance of Punjab bureaucrat and board president I.S. Bindra saw the World Cup become an occasion to showcase a new post-liberalization India, one that brought together multinational cola brands and desi upwardly mobile companies like ITC and Hero. Delhi-based businessman Lokesh Sharma, who was handling Pepsi's cricket account at the time, remembers the fierce bidding war that broke out between the two cola majors for tournament sponsorship. 'Coke outbid Pepsi as one of the official Cup sponsors, so Pepsi started its own campaign "Nothing official about it". Cricket had never seen anything like it before,' he recalls.

The board sold the telecast rights to WorldTel, a private company headed by a Connecticut-based tycoon of Indian origin, Mark Mascarenhas, for $10 million, including a $2.5 million down payment. Mascarenhas decided to cover the World Cup on a grand, multi-cam scale: eight TV cameras and four video tape machines along with OB vans were criss-crossing the subcontinent. 'Mark was a giant of a man who did everything king-size,' says Shastri, who was on the global commentary team.

It was Mascarenhas again who that year offered Tendulkar what seemed at the time a staggering amount of money for an Indian sportsman: a five-year management fee contract worth Rs 25 crore. Cricket was finally a crorepati sport in India. And Tendulkar its first big beneficiary. 'Mark saw the future before anyone else,' says Shastri, who introduced the businessman to Tendulkar. Mascarenhas was tragically killed in a road accident near Nagpur in 2002. Only a year earlier, he had renewed his contract with Tendulkar, this time reportedly for Rs 100 crore.

Tendulkar though insists that money was never his motivation to play the game. 'Do you know that in the 1996 World Cup I was the only Indian to play without a bat sponsor? The rest of the team had either Four Square or Wills on their bats but I had promised my father I would never endorse a tobacco or a liquor brand,' he says. It's a promise he has kept: Tendulkar has been the face of many major advertising campaigns but never a cigarette or a liquor company. He has, however, realized his market value: his agent drives a hard bargain and his fee for a TV commercial has at times matched that of a top film star. (In 2013, the year he retired, he was ranked 51 in a list of the highest paid global athletes with his net worth being pegged at $160 million.)

Truth is Tendulkar never consciously chased money when playing the game; money chased the biggest superstar of the most watched sport in the country. He was, after all, the quintessential middle-class boy next door who had achieved global recognition, the perfect symbol of hope for an increasingly aspirational India. Ad-film-maker Prahlad Kakkar, who did the first Pepsi ad with Tendulkar as a teenager, remembers how shy and awkward the cricketer was when facing the camera: 'I remember once jokingly telling him that he might have to put his arm around a young girl in the ad, and he suddenly became very nervous till I told him that I was kidding! On another occasion, he saw the entire crew having a Pepsi during the break, and innocently asked me if he could have one too!'

For Kakkar, Tendulkar's brand value was commensurate with his meteoric run-making rise. As he puts it, 'His was simply the greatest story of our times. A middle-class boy with no godfather becomes a world-beater through sheer talent and thereby offers a dream of succeeding in life to millions. Plus, he looked so cute and vulnerable as a teenager that every mother in the country wanted to embrace him! He was the ideal son of every Indian mother, the classic combination of someone who was tough and aggressive on the field, but polite and calm off it.'

In the final analysis, what really mattered was not the dollars to be earned off the field but the runs to be made on it. Between the world cups of 1996 and 2003, Tendulkar was the master of the game: he was the top run-scorer in both those tournaments, scoring 523 and a whopping 673 respectively in the marquee events. In Test cricket, between 1993 and 2002, he hit an astonishing 27 centuries at an average of more than 60 runs. In between, he had an incredible year in 1998 when he scored a record-breaking 9 one-day hundreds in a year, including a stirring performance in Sharjah against Australia. It was described later as the perfect Desert Storm with two consecutive centuries against a bowling attack that included Shane Warne, the dazzling array of stroke-making taking Tendulkar's batting to another level. 'I guess I was in the zone; as an international sportsman you go through periods when you feel that you can't do anything wrong, that was one such moment,' he says.

Tendulkar would end his one-day career in 2012, having played 463 games, scored 18,426 runs at an average of 44.83 with 49 centuries, including the first double century in the format. To put those staggering achievements in perspective, the next highest centurion is Ricky Ponting with 30 one-day hundreds and the next highest run-scorer is Kumar Sangakkara with 14,234 runs. It is possible that other players, most notably Virat Kohli, will one day overtake Tendulkar's one-day record, but the fact is that Tendulkar was the first to scale the Everest of batting when it came to the 50-over game. And it all started with a simple decision to open the batting (Tendulkar as opener averages over 48 in one-day cricket as against 33 runs as a non-opener). As Tendulkar puts it, 'I had been a number four all my life, so opening the batting did require making some adjustments while playing the new ball but I guess I did manage to do it successfully in the end.' You bet he did!

~

On 17 October 2008 in Mohali against Australia, Sachin Tendulkar broke Brian Lara's record to become the highest run scorer in Test cricket and the first to cross 12,000 runs. Tendulkar had promised me an interview to mark the momentous occasion. We had also contracted Gavaskar for expert comments on the series. Which is how one evening during the Mohali Test I came close to achieving cricket nirvana as Gavaskar and Tendulkar sat down together to talk cricket: Gavaskar dressed in a traditional collared shirt, Tendulkar in a more casual polo-neck T-shirt, their sartorial differences reflecting the generational shift.

Gavaskar and Tendulkar, two short men with tall achievements: 85 Test hundreds between them, and more than 26,000 Test runs. They are the twin towers of Indian batting, one is the classicist, the other the more versatile; both all-time greats. More than the sheer volume of runs, it is what they represented to two generations of Indian cricket fans that sets them apart: if Gavaskar gave Indian cricket dignity and self-respect, Tendulkar brought energy and excitement. When Gavaskar first saw Tendulkar bat, he immediately rang up his wife to say he had seen something 'special'. When Tendulkar was growing up, Gavaskar was a role model along with the West Indian Sir Vivian Richards. 'I was a huge fan of Sir Viv but Gavaskar's 10,000 runs and 34 centuries was always the benchmark for cricket greatness,' says Tendulkar. 'It wasn't a conscious target but I guess it was always there somewhere at the back of the mind.'

Tendulkar eventually went past Gavaskar's records but a pure statistical comparison isn't easy. They both averaged more than 50 in Test cricket, but Gavaskar was an opening batsman, Tendulkar played at number four. One was nurtured in the pre-helmet era, the other had the benefit of batting with a helmet. Gavaskar played for a long time with the knowledge that the entire Indian batting performance was dependent on him while Tendulkar had the benefit in the latter half of his career of being part of a rare assemblage of Indian batting stars from Sehwag to Dravid to Laxman in one team. Gavaskar was reared in an age where there was a premium on defensive batting; the Tendulkar period saw a transition to the more attacking game. Gavaskar scored only one limited overs international century whereas Tendulkar hit an incredible 49 one-day centuries. Like all great players, they could adapt to any situation. Tendulkar once batted with grim determination for more than 600 minutes to make an unbeaten double century against Australia at Sydney in 2004 without hitting a single off-drive in anger. Meanwhile, Gavaskar changed gears on his way to a double century at the Oval in 1979, attacking the English bowling and taking India close to an incredible last day win.

Tendulkar played almost 1500 days of international cricket in a career spanning twenty-four years; Gavaskar played less than half that number over sixteen years. Both were outstanding performers against the top sides of their generation: Gavaskar scored a staggering 13 Test centuries against the fearsome West Indian pace attack, arguably the most hostile the game has ever seen, while Tendulkar scored 11 hundreds against Australia, the premier team of his era.

Gavaskar's average in the fourth innings of a Test match is much
higher than Tendulkar's, suggesting that he had a superior technique
in match-saving situations but he also had a lower strike rate, making
Tendulkar potentially the match-winning batsman.

Both had very distinctive batting styles: Gavaskar more upright
in stance, using a much lighter bat, feet closer together with a slight
shuffle before the bowler delivered, while Tendulkar, with the heavier
bat and unconventional bottom hand grip, crouched a little more and
the feet were wider apart. Gavaskar was probably the better cutter,
Tendulkar the more effective puller; a signature Tendulkar back foot
cover drive was as delightful to watch as a Gavaskar late cut. Both
were masters of the straight drive, the leg-side flick and judging a
single. Indeed, the precision of their movements, the stillness of
the head, the straightness of their bat and, above all else, the fierce
determination and hunger for runs were a common thread: Gavaskar
had simply passed the baton to Tendulkar just as a previous generation
had relayed the torch to him. 'I remember when Gavaskar gifted his
pads to me, I slept with them next to me because it was like a piece
of priceless treasure for me,' recalls Tendulkar.

At the turn of the century, Tendulkar received the ultimate
compliment when the Australian batting legend Sir Don Bradman,
widely regarded as the greatest-ever batsman, claimed to have
seen distinct similarities between Tendulkar's compact, aggressive
batting style and his own. I interviewed Tendulkar a few months
after the Bradman comment and he was clearly overwhelmed by
the comparison. 'I don't think I can ask for more as a batsman, can
I?' he said proudly. In 2001, Bradman's own greatest all-time eleven
selection saw Tendulkar figure as the only Indian in the side but the
fact that there were as many as seven Australians in Bradman's team
suggests that cricket selections are often dictated by parochialism.

For a more nuanced assessment of their art of batting, I turned
to Rege, the veteran Mumbai cricketer who played with Gavaskar
right from their schooldays together and was one of the first to spot
Tendulkar's talent. 'Very difficult to compare the two greats from

different generations,' he says. 'But what I will say is that Tendulkar was a prodigy, Sunil was not. Gavaskar worked at his game and through amazing powers of concentration became an all-time great while Tendulkar was already a finished product by the time he was fifteen. Gavaskar never gave you a chance once he was set while Sachin was always looking to attack and so was more fallible. In a sense, Sachin was more like Viv Richards in his desire to dominate the bowling while Gavaskar was the traditional error-free opening batsman.' So who would you like in your team, I ask Rege. 'Can't I have both?' He winks, adding, 'Let me put it this way, I would love to have Sachin in my team but I would hate to have Gavaskar in the opposition.'

Kapil Dev who bowled to both says that Gavaskar was the more difficult to get out but Tendulkar was the more talented. 'Gavaskar would always hit the bad ball for four, but with Sachin, he could even hit the good deliveries for a boundary,' says Kapil. India's premier all-rounder believes Tendulkar should actually have scored even more runs than he eventually did. 'With his skills, he should have actually scored triple centuries and quadruple centuries in Test cricket, Sachin was that good,' Kapil argues. That Tendulkar's highest Test score is 248 not out against Bangladesh is perhaps a slight statistical blip, especially when you consider that a contemporary like Virender Sehwag hit two Test triple hundreds. It perhaps suggests a mindset that was risk-averse even when the opposition bowlers had tired and wilted. When I ask Tendulkar to respond, he smiles. 'You can't have everything in life, but nearly 16,000 Test runs isn't too bad, is it?'

Gavaskar has a better captaincy record but then Tendulkar, one could argue, didn't get enough opportunities to lead the team in more familiar home conditions. 'Yes, not getting to captain a successful side is a big regret,' he once told me. The more articulate and cerebral Gavaskar has spoken out in public on cricket issues far more often than the more introverted and diplomatic Tendulkar, who has never expressed himself strongly on even, say, the match-fixing controversy.

'I have spoken when I needed to but I don't believe in loose talk based on allegations,' he tells me.

During the joint interview in Mohali when I asked Gavaskar and Tendulkar who was the better player, each pointed immediately to the other. 'I would go miles to watch Tendulkar bat but am not sure I would do that for me,' said Gavaskar self-deprecatingly. He said Tendulkar's 'balance' was a true measure of his success, 'balance on the field, balance in life'. Tendulkar said Gavaskar's professional work ethic was inspirational for his generation.

The mutual respect, in a sense, is reflective of a similar Maharashtrian middle-class background, of being part of a shared heritage of Mumbai cricket that was nurtured on the city's maidans and toughened by the crowded bus and train rides to matches. Gavaskar started playing in the narrow lane of a crowded colony in south-central Mumbai where the focus was on keeping the ball along the ground so that no windowpanes were broken. In the leafy Sahitya Sahawas colony in suburban Mumbai, Tendulkar had a little more freedom: you could actually hit a lofted shot, strike a tree and still not be out, which might explain his more effervescent strokeplay.

Perhaps one way to contrast Gavaskar and Tendulkar is to view them as pre- and post-liberalization batting heroes. Gavaskar grew up in 1960s India when the country was still unsure of its place in the world. His debut series in 1971, as mentioned in an earlier chapter, was a breakout year, one that instilled hope in the future of Indian cricket. But through much of Gavaskar's career, India was growing at a slow 'Hindu' rate of growth and cricket mirrored the frugal times: this was not an India that allowed for extravagance. By the time Tendulkar made his mark on the game, India was a nation on the move: the 1991 opening up of the economy was seen as unshackling the 'animal spirit' of Indian entrepreneurship. Tendulkar's batting epitomized this spirit of greater freedom and risk-taking.

That they both come from Mumbai only shows how the city has been at the heart of Indian batting for the greater part of the first sixty years after Independence. However, there have been distinct signs in the past decade that show the glory days of Mumbai cricket are over as other regions of the country throw up their own heroes. (In 2016, the first Test played at Mumbai's Wankhede stadium after Tendulkar's retirement didn't have a single player from Mumbai.) But the reverence for the Gavaskar–Tendulkar batting legacy is unshaken in India's original cricket capital. For my generation, Gavaskar was a cricketing God. For the 1990s generation, it is Tendulkar. The Siddhivinayak temple in the heart of Mumbai attracts lakhs of devotees, as does the Haji Ali dargah. Different religious groups come to worship here. But in cricket, there is no religious barrier when celebrating our divinities – in Mumbai, we venerate Gavaskar and Tendulkar with equal fervour.

~

In Tendulkar's long and distinguished career there are very few low points. One of the first was being stripped of captaincy in 1998 barely a year into the job. 'When I was removed as captain, the BCCI did not have the courtesy to inform me; I found out through the media. That was hurtful,' he recalls. Was he too absorbed in his own striving for batting excellence to make the successful transition to captaincy, I ask him. 'No, I enjoyed captaincy and think I did a good job with the Mumbai team that included many senior players,' he counters. 'He deserved a longer run as captain, he was just twenty-five then and was slowly growing into the job,' says Madan Lal, who was the coach when Tendulkar captained the Indian team to the West Indies in 1998. On that tour India was bowled out for 81 while chasing just 120 for victory in the Barbados Test. That defeat still rankles with Tendulkar. 'I didn't sleep for days after that loss. It was a real nightmare,' he says.

Tendulkar experienced even more misery in the West Indies when the Indian team was knocked out of the 2007 World Cup in the group stages. At thirty-four, Tendulkar feared his World Cup dream was over and he was depressed. Not just depressed, he was angry, having been pushed out of the openers' slot to accommodate 'younger' batsmen by coach Greg Chappell. I went to interview Tendulkar one evening at his home soon after the World Cup defeat and sensed that the quiet composure that had marked his entire career was deserting him for the first time. There was a lava within that was waiting to explode. As we talked, Tendulkar made it clear that Chappell had played dirty and sown seeds of dissension within the team. 'Whatever is said in the dressing room is being leaked to the media by Chappell, it is totally unethical,' he told me angrily. In his 2014 autobiography, Tendulkar would make an even more sensational allegation, claiming that Chappell had visited his home in 2006 and offered to remove Dravid and make him captain. Chappell has denied making any such offer but Tendulkar is adamant. 'My wife Anjali was there, she heard everything, Chappell was playing divide and rule,' he says.

My 2007 interview with Tendulkar was recorded on audio tape, not on video camera, and later Tendulkar, normally very careful with his words, asked me to edit out some of the more explosive parts. But what he was willing to say on record was enough to become a front-page headline the next morning: 'Chappell has not treated us fairly, Team India is being divided'. In his autobiography, Tendulkar is even more scathing, describing Chappell as a 'ringmaster who imposed his ideas on the players without showing any concern whether they felt comfortable or not'.

The anger over the Chappell episode left Tendulkar contemplating retirement for the first time. He had already been out of the game for almost five months in 2005 with a tennis elbow surgery and the years of lifting a heavy bat were beginning to take a toll on the body. He had told me in the interview that maybe winning a World Cup was not in his 'naseeb' (fate). The World Cup had been a long-cherished ambition from the day that, as a ten-year-old, he saw Kapil Dev lift the cup at Lord's. 'That was the moment I knew I wanted to play cricket and do nothing else,' he says. In 1992, his first World Cup had a few bright moments but, as a nineteen-year-old, he could bide his time. In 1996, he was at the peak of his form but one bad day in Kolkata in the semi-final against Sri Lanka was enough to end the dream. In 1999, he scored a hundred in the World Cup after he had flown back to Mumbai to attend his father's funeral. 'That was the most difficult moment for me personally, but I knew my father would have wanted me to go back and play the game,' he says. From that day on, he would always look to the heavens after every century, in eternal gratitude to the father who had allowed him the freedom to play. And yet, even the emotional hundred wasn't enough to win a World Cup.

Four years later, in 2003, he went to South Africa and came within one match of lifting the trophy. He scored heavily right through the tournament but missed out in the finals against Australia. In one memorable game against Pakistan, he played one of the great innings in World Cup history. India versus Pakistan is always a marquee contest but the game in 2003 had an extra edge. It was the first match up between the two countries after the 1999 Kargil war and the game was played amidst a jingoistic subcontinental frenzy, blue and green pitted against each other in a noisy, colourful clash. 'I don't think I have felt the kind of pressure I did that day, wherever we looked there were Indian supporters waving the tricolour,' says Tendulkar. His opening partner Virender Sehwag didn't want to face the first over to be bowled by the Pakistani captain and premier bowler Wasim Akram and left it to Tendulkar to take guard. 'I was nervous and didn't want to get out first ball against Pakistan so I pleaded with Sachin paaji to take first strike. He just smiled and didn't say anything till we actually reached the crease and he took guard, it was his way of teasing me,' says Sehwag.

Sehwag needn't have worried. In the first over bowled by Akram, Tendulkar stroked a confident boundary. In the next, he hit Pakistan's fastest bowler Shoaib Akhtar for 18 runs, including an incredible slashed six over backward point. It was a shot which ended any Indian inferiority complex of past battles when facing up to Pakistani fast bowlers. 'I guess I was just charged up that day and wanted to make a point,' says Tendulkar. He would end up scoring an exhilarating, match-winning 75-ball 98, an innings that was a firm rejoinder to the critics who claimed that Tendulkar would sometimes fail in crunch match situations.

And yet, even the Tendulkar blitz wasn't enough to win the cup: Australia in the finals was too good for India. So would Tendulkar for all the individual acclaim end up without the one big team prize in the sport? 'That's what I told him when he was depressed after the 2007 World Cup defeat. I just created an image for him of the 2011 World Cup final being played in Mumbai and Sachin lifting the trophy,' says brother Ajit. Tendulkar had trusted his brother implicitly all through his career and this moment would be no different. 'I guess I didn't want to retire from the game a loser,' he says.

Twelve months after the despair of 2007, Tendulkar was back in the groove, the gloominess having been wiped off. Chappell had been sacked after the World Cup defeat and the South African Gary Kirsten was brought in his place. Kirsten was a similar personality to Tendulkar: a quiet man but a skilful motivator. The pressure was lifted and Tendulkar felt liberated. In 2008, he would go on to play what he describes as his most important Test innings, a match-winning century against England at Chennai within weeks of the 26/11 Mumbai terror attack. 'That was a special moment, one where I felt that maybe I had brought a smile back to my city which was so badly affected by the killing of innocents,' he says.

I was among those millions of Indians who had been scarred by the terror strikes in Mumbai in which 166 people were killed. I was, after all, an archetypal South Mumbai boy: the always buzzing Leopold Café along Colaba Causeway was where I first tasted alcohol and the Taj Mahal Hotel was within walking distance from the building where my parents lived. Places that I identified with cheery college memories were under attack. From the veranda of our house, my mother even heard the gunshots at Nariman House, where a Jewish couple was killed by the terrorists. South Mumbai represents Mumbai's original open and liberal cosmopolitanism which the terrorists clearly wanted to destroy. And yet, the city was back on its feet within twenty-four hours. It was this undaunted spirit of Mumbai which Tendulkar, in a sense, also symbolized. For a grieving nation, his hundred in Chennai was comforting: Tendulkar scoring runs always offered hope and joy even in melancholic times.

That sense of elation would reach new heights in April 2011 when Tendulkar finally fulfilled his dream of winning the World Cup. That tournament too was played against the backdrop of galloping public cynicism: the ruling Congress-led United Progressive Alliance was ensnared in several corruption scandals. People were losing faith in the political leadership and success on the cricket field was the perfect antidote to the mood of scepticism. In fact, a week before the World Cup, a Delhi-based political activist, Arvind Kejriwal, had come to our newsroom to reveal his intention to start an agitation for an anti-corruption ombudsman with the help of an ageing but upright Gandhian crusader from Maharashtra, Anna Hazare. 'Look, Arvind, I think you are better off postponing your campaign. The World Cup is about to start and I don't think the country is interested in anything else at the moment other than winning this tournament,' was my sincere advice. Sure enough, Kejriwal's India Against Corruption 'andolan' which would eventually propel him into the Delhi chief minister's chair started just days after India had won the World Cup.

Tendulkar didn't hit the winning shot in the 2011 World Cup but it was otherwise pretty much the perfect script. A victory in front of adoring home fans in Mumbai, it couldn't have been a more fitting climax to a glittering career. 'When Dhoni hit the winning shot, I first screamed in delight but then went to a corner in a dressing room and shed a tear before composing myself and running excitedly on to the ground. Yes, I did cry,' admits Tendulkar.

'This is for Sachin paaji,' man of the tournament Yuvraj Singh said at the trophy presentation. Virat Kohli and Yusuf Pathan lifted Tendulkar on their shoulders for a victory lap, the tricolour fluttering in the Mumbai sea breeze. Yuvraj was eleven when Tendulkar played his first World Cup, Kohli just four years old. Tendulkar had defied

Father Time to become a World Cup winner at age thirty-eight. As Kohli would poignantly remark, 'Sachin paaji has carried the burden of the nation for twenty-one years, it is time we carried him.' Yes, the baby-faced boy who started his career with the nickname 'Tendlya' had now graduated to being Paaji, or elder brother in Punjabi.

'It was Harbhajan who first began calling me by that name and it stuck,' says Tendulkar. Harbhajan Singh, who was just nine years old when Tendulkar made his international debut, describes him as a father-like figure for his generation, a cricketing God on the field but the friendly elder off it, a prankster and storyteller in the dressing room but always available for help and advice when needed. 'I remember when we won the famous 2001 series against Australia, Sachin paaji told me, "I will gift you whatever you want," and I asked for two pairs of new spiked cricket shoes which he happily gave me. Maybe I should have asked for a Ferrari!' he says. (In 2003, Tendulkar received a Ferrari as a gift from Fiat for crossing Sir Don Bradman's tally of 29 centuries, a gift that landed him in an unsavoury controversy when he sought a duty waiver to import the car.)

For Tendulkar too the eternal respect of his teammates is a fond and lasting memory. At Tendulkar's residence, pride of place in his bar is given to a champagne bottle with the signatures of the entire World Cup–winning team. 'It's the first bottle we opened after we won,' he recalls. It is a permanent reminder of that glorious evening in Mumbai when a childhood dream was realized on cricket's biggest stage, a dream belonging to a little boy with a supernatural big bat.

~

Tendulkar should probably have retired that April night in 2011 after winning the World Cup. He had no mountains left to climb, no peaks left to conquer. Yet, he chose to play for two more years, a decision that in hindsight is questionable. Yes, he did still score centuries, including achieving a landmark 100th international century against

Bangladesh in 2012, but somehow he gave the impression of an ageing master who was beginning to play from memory rather than instinct. When the English swing bowler Jimmy Anderson troubled him in the 2011 series, there were even harsh suggestions that a weakness had been discovered in Tendulkar's technique. And when he was bowled a few times while appearing to lose balance, critics were actually asking the unthinkable question: 'When will Tendulkar retire?'

'Look, when to retire is a personal choice. I remember talking about this to my childhood hero Sir Viv at the time and he told me that no one else can make the decision for you. I was still passionate about the game and was enjoying my cricket so why should I have stopped?' he says. It was, Tendulkar says, only in September 2013 that he finally felt that he had lost the edge. 'There was a Champions League Twenty20 game being played in Delhi and for the first time I felt like I didn't want to go to the gym to train, didn't even feel bad about missing a practice session. That was the moment when I decided that I was ready to leave the game,' he says.

He spoke to the two people he trusted the most, wife Anjali and brother Ajit and they supported his decision. The original plan was to travel to South Africa and play his final series there, including an unprecedented 200th Test match. But the BCCI suddenly announced a two Test series against the West Indies, the second of which would be at the Wankhede in Mumbai. It appeared as if the entire move had been designed to enable Tendulkar to play his 200th and final Test in front of his home fans, making it almost an extended farewell journey. Critics might argue that it was a bad precedent to organize a series only to enable a player to fulfil a personal milestone. And yet, Tendulkar was no ordinary player but a unique cricketer who had become a cricket immortal by defying traditional notions of age and time; India, after all, had seen as many as eight prime ministers between Tendulkar's first Test and last!

I travelled to Mumbai for that game. For millions of Indians this was a sentimental journey, a chance to be part of history, an opportunity to hear an entire stadium erupt one last time to the chant of 'Sachin! Sachin!', a roar that united the country in good times and bad, and made us all feel part of something special. He was 38 not out at the end of day one, leaving open the tantalizing prospect of a century in his last innings. It wasn't to be – he was eventually out for 74, caught Darren Sammy bowled Narsingh Deonarine, hardly names that will resonate in cricket's history. As he walked back, head slightly bowed, acknowledging the applause, one knew that this was the final walk. Twenty-five years ago, on that very ground he had given me my first front-page byline; he was now leaving me with a lump in my throat. When the match ended, his last act was to pick up a piece of grass from the Wankhede stadium pitch before walking away into the sunset, leaving me teary-eyed once again. 'With Tendulkar no longer playing, I might just age even faster,' I told a friend wistfully. After all, when I had first seen Tendulkar play, the hair was jet black; now I had fully greyed.

And yet, the standout moment was not what Tendulkar achieved with the bat in that final game but how he delivered a thank you speech with grace and warmth, remembering all the people who had supported him in his rise. Every word was measured and truly heartfelt. 'I had jotted down names and points on a piece of paper while travelling from Kolkata to Mumbai for the last game, I just didn't want to miss anyone out,' he says. As he spoke, one realized just how far he had travelled in the journey of life – when I first met Tendulkar, he was shy and inarticulate, preferring to speak in Marathi. Here he was now delivering a fine speech in English without any hesitation. As he posed with Anjali and his children, Sara and Arjun, one was also reminded that the boy wonder was now a father of two teenagers and we had, in a sense, all aged with him. Family has been a crucial part of the Tendulkar story. He had met his doctor-wife as a seventeen-year-old and she had been by his side all the way through, even giving up her medical practice as a consequence. If his brother had been his guide in the early years, Anjali has given Tendulkar the support he needed in his adult life. 'She is not just my wife but has also been my best friend,' he says.

The family now lives in a four-storey bungalow on a relatively quiet, leafy lane in Bandra. The opulent, high-ceiling house acquired from an old Parsee family is dotted with paintings, Ganesh idols and eclectic designer furniture. A multimedia entertainment 'den' coexists with a puja room. A fleet of cars is lined up in the garage: Tendulkar has a fascination for fast cars and occasionally zooms off for a drive on his own. 'Driving relaxes me and maybe if I had not been a cricketer, I would have been a Formula One or a go-kart driver,' he says with a laugh. He has a home in London too, and is spotted every summer at Wimbledon, where he is treated as sporting royalty.

The luxurious lifestyle symbolizes how a modern-day cricketer can acquire riches beyond the imagination of the stars of an earlier era, of how cricket has redefined social and economic mobility. And yet, the vast material rewards have not really changed Tendulkar's core middle-class value systems. Old friendships, for example, do matter: his schoolfriend Atul Ranade tells me that for his 'gang', he is still 'aapla Sachin [our Sachin]'. 'In school, we shared vada pav at Shivaji Park, now we share doner kebabs in London,' remarks Ranade. When I was setting up a news channel in 2005, I requested Tendulkar for an on-air endorsement. He instantly obliged, no questions asked. When a book on the late Raj Singh Dungarpur was being released in Mumbai, Tendulkar was stuck in Hyderabad because his flight was delayed. 'Please keep the function going till I come. I want to be there for Raj bhai,' he told me. Sure enough, he arrived in the nick of time.

Cricket remains his calling card even after retirement. In the garden at his Mumbai home, there is a floodlit cricket practice pitch. Son Arjun is passionate about the game and plays junior cricket. He bowls and bats left-handed but Tendulkar is keenly aware of the pressure on him. 'My message to him is the same that my father gave me: enjoy the game but be a good human being first,' he says. The pressure of being Sir Don Bradman's son forced John Bradman to change his surname to Bradsen. Hopefully, the boy blessed with

Indian cricket's most famous surname will be allowed to play the game in peace.

~

As the country gave a befitting send-off to Sachin Tendulkar, one man who knew the master batsman better than most was sitting quietly in a corner in the Wankhede stadium. For many years, Vinod Kambli was seen to be Tendulkar's left-handed partner in batting crime as much as his school friend. It was, after all, their record-breaking partnership of 664 runs for Sharadashram Vidyamandir in a school match in February 1988 that catapulted the duo into the national headlines for the first time. Tendulkar played for India a year later and Kambli followed a few years later. In 1993, Kambli hit two double centuries and three centuries in a row in Test matches even before his twenty-first birthday. 'I have taken the stairs to success while Sachin took the elevator,' he proclaimed. And yet, while Tendulkar would play an incredible 200 Tests, Kambli lost his place after just seventeen Tests. And where Tendulkar received every possible accolade in the sport, Kambli faded out into an abyss of alcohol and controversy.

One Sunday morning just before I interviewed Sachin for this book, I decided to call on Kambli. He lives in an apartment block in Bandra, not far from Tendulkar's residence. I ring the doorbell to find two adorable little children greeting me. 'Meet Joanna Cristiano and Jesus Cristiano,' says Kambli's lovely wife, Andrea, while doing the introductions. It's twelve noon and Kambli has just surfaced. He comes out a few minutes later in a black sleeveless T-shirt and shorts. He is in his early forties, but a grey beard makes him look much older. He meets me with a cheery spirit. 'Welcome to my kingdom.' He laughs, and then pointing to his black shirt hums an old Hindi film tune, 'Hum kaale hain to kya hua dilwale hain! [We may be dark-skinned, but are large-hearted].' Clearly, the sands of time have not dulled his sense of humour. But I also smell alcohol on his breath, see a sadness in the reddened eyes. The mischievous twinkle has gone. A touch of pathos has set in.

I ask him to turn the clock back to the famous school match of 1988. It brings an instant smile to the face. 'Sachin and I were enjoying the game so much that we could have got a 1000-run partnership and scored 500 runs each. That would have been some record,' he says with a grin. If it hadn't been for coach Achrekar's insistence that the innings be declared, maybe Kambli would have got his desire. Such was the abandon with which he played the game as a teenager that he once stopped the bowler in his run-up to fly a kite during a school game. 'The kite was coming on to the pitch, so I thought that rather than allow it to stop the game, might as well fly it for a bit. It was all a bit of fun,' he says.

The fun continued for a while as Sachin and he destroyed bowling attacks together as teenagers. 'We were like brothers, you know, and when we were batting, we didn't even need to call for a run, there was mental telepathy between us,' he says. So why did Kambli, despite his undoubted talent, never come close to achieving the success of his school friend? 'You must not compare anyone to Sachin, he is in a league of his own, a genius,' admits Kambli.

And yet, Kambli still carries a sense of grievance that he didn't play longer for the country. 'I made nine comebacks to the Indian team, averaged more than 50 in Tests, played more than a hundred one-dayers, and yet, every time I was dropped, no selector gave me a rational explanation for dropping me. I was once told that I was being dropped on disciplinary grounds. Just because I liked to have a drink after the game with my opponents, does that make me indisciplined?' he asks with a flash of anger.

The fact though is that Kambli's performance dropped after his initial success in 1993. In Test cricket, fast bowlers began to pitch short and target his leg stump and he struggled to find an answer. New middle-order batting talents like Rahul Dravid, V.V.S. Laxman and Sourav Ganguly emerged in the latter half of the 1990s to lead a renaissance in Indian batting. Kambli was left behind. While Tendulkar's technique never let him down, Kambli was never quite able to find a way to overcome his flaws.

And yet, there is a sociological as much as a cricketing explanation for Kambli's failure to handle success. While Tendulkar came from the middle-class Maharashtrian heartland, Kambli was born in a low-income Dalit family, living in the distant Mumbai suburb of Kanjurmarg. To travel to school near Shivaji Park, he would take a 6 a.m. train and often return home only at 1.30 a.m. because the evening trains would be too crowded for a little boy with a kitbag. The oldest of four brothers, he fought with his father, a useful club cricketer, at the age of twelve and went to live in a chawl in Worli in central Mumbai with a friend. Where Tendulkar's success was almost a family mission, Kambli had to fight a lonely battle, with himself as much as with a hostile environment. Achrekar was possibly the only person to bring some sense of permanence to his unsettled childhood years. 'Sachin always had stability in his life, I just lived on the edge,' Kambli says candidly.

It's that life on the edge that has seen him go through more tumult than most. A first marriage that ended badly, a heart condition that suddenly surfaced and sent him to hospital for days, a failed attempt at electoral politics and the lure of alcohol have meant that life after retiring from the game in 2000 hasn't been easy for Kambli. In 2014, he married Andrea, converted to Christianity and now seeks solace in God. A large glass painting of Christ dominates his living room. 'Our local church priest comes and spends time with Vinod, fingers crossed he is now much better,' Andrea says.

Does he meet Sachin, I ask. The relationship had reportedly been strained when in a 2009 reality television show Kambli suggested that he had been abandoned by Tendulkar during his dark days. 'I shouldn't have said it. It was a mistake. We don't meet much, but are in regular touch on SMS,' he says. Tendulkar did not mention

Kambli in his farewell speech after his last Test, an omission that stung his schoolmate. 'I guess it is my fault,' Kambli says. Again, the hint of melancholy returns, a desire to rewind the clock to happier times if he could. He tried his hand at cricket commentary for a while but it didn't quite work out. 'If only I was playing cricket now, I would have been in the IPL, earned in crores and wouldn't have had to worry about the future,' he says.

Kambli did make an attempt in 2008 to get himself fit for an IPL franchise but a shin surgery ended that dream. He was a made-for-Twenty20 cricketer, an aggressive batsman, a handy fielder but most of all a colourful character, a good singer and an even better dancer, the kind who would have been a big draw in cricket's entertainment age. 'You know I was the first Indian cricketer to wear an ear stud and have tattoos on my arm, now everyone does it. Then, it was frowned upon, but I guess I was a trendsetter,' he says.

As I leave the house, I spot his three-year-old hitting a ball with the left hand. 'He is a leftie like the father,' Kambli says. Maybe life hasn't been entirely fair to him, but at least his children won't have to make the long journey from Kanjurmarg to Shivaji Park by local train. He may not have fulfilled his potential, he may be guilty of taking his talent for granted but the fact that a Dalit boy from a slum colony could play successfully for the country, despite enduring many hardships, is proof that the great Indian cricket dream is alive. 'Jai Bhim!' he shouts out as a parting shot with fist raised. This is the rousing war cry of political groups in Maharashtra that swear by Dr Bhimrao Ambedkar.

A few days later, I get a phone call from Kambli: 'Don't forget to tell Sachin when you meet him I still love him very much!' I promise him I will. Yes, we all love Sachin for the sheer joy he has given us on the field. But we should embrace Kambli too: his is a poignant story, yet another reminder of the vulnerability of a sporting life, but also a celebration of how a cricketer through sheer talent can break caste and income barriers to represent the country. Cricket, once a preserve of the elite, has at least partly fulfilled the Ambedkarite dream of a more equal and merit-driven society. 'Jai Bhim!' I say to myself quietly.

~

On his final day in international cricket in November 2013, Tendulkar was conferred India's highest civilian honour, the Bharat Ratna. I was driving to the airport after the Wankhede game when I got an SMS from a source in Rashtrapati Bhavan: 'Bharat Ratna for Sachin!' I excitedly rang up Sachin to convey the news and Anjali picked up the phone. 'Are you sure?' she asked me. Shortly afterwards, the news was official – at the age of forty, Sachin Ramesh Tendulkar was India's youngest Bharat Ratna, but also the first sportsperson to be so honoured. For years, there had been a campaign to give the award to Dhyan Chand, the hockey wizard; now Tendulkar had been given the honour instead. It was, to my mind, the right decision. Dhyan Chand was a hockey legend, the first global Indian sports star but he had died in 1979 and a posthumous award often means little. Tendulkar, by contrast, was the most visible, durable and inspiring living symbol of sporting achievement in the country. Sepia-tinted nostalgia may have chosen Dhyan Chand; a new India in the age of satellite television rooted for Tendulkar.

If Bharat Ratna musicians like Lata Mangeshkar and M.S. Subbulakshmi had touched the soul with their singing talent, Tendulkar had captured our hearts. For twenty-five long years, he had been the ultimate entertainer who had thrilled us, but even more crucially, offered hope, a beacon of positivity in dark and cynical times. A young man from Bihar's Muzaffarpur, Sunil Gautam, who has Tendulkar's name along with the tricolour tattooed on his chest and follows the Indian team across the country, is typical of the Tendulkar fandom. 'Jab Sachin khelta hai, hum saare dukh dard bhoolte hain [when Sachin plays, we forget all our troubles],' he says. On Tendulkar's birthday every year, Gautam gifts him a box of his town's world-famous litchis. 'He is like part of our family,' says Tendulkar.

An architect friend of mine, Anish Shah, tells me how he would slip out of office every time India was two wickets down only to watch Tendulkar bat. 'He was just simply someone who was an integral part of our lives, someone who made us feel so proud as Indians,' says Shah. Perhaps only Amitabh Bachchan among contemporary Indians has received the kind of public adulation that Tendulkar has. The fan frenzy for Bachchan is driven by the mighty appeal of cinema stars, the razzle and dazzle of the big screen. In Tendulkar's case, there is reverence for him as a genuine national folk hero, the sense of pride he gives us in being Indian – when we call out his name, we are bonded by a truly uplifting connection with our Indian identity. When Bachchan performs an exceptional film role, we clap and applaud in admiration. When Tendulkar scores a hundred, we want to wave the national flag and celebrate with patriotic fervour. If Bachchan is about fame, Tendulkar is about glory. What takes the duo into another orbit above all others in their respective spheres is their sheer longevity. To play international cricket for a quarter of a century with the composure that Tendulkar showed and without buckling to pressure from fans or opponents is truly mind-boggling, as indeed is Bachchan's fifty-year career in cinema. 'For me, every day on the cricket field was like a new day, a new challenge, such was my passion for cricket that I have never felt bored on a cricket field ever,' says Tendulkar.

Interestingly, while Bachchan was a failure in politics, Tendulkar too hasn't distinguished himself as a nominated MP in the Rajya Sabha. He has barely attended Parliament and asked his first question in the Upper House more than three years after joining it. It was, on reflection, a bad call to become an MP in 2012 when he was still playing cricket. Maybe Tendulkar too erred, like many other high-profile MPs before him, in viewing the nomination as yet another honour rather than a responsibility. 'Parliament is not a social gathering but a place for serious discussion, if celebrities don't want to attend, why do they get nominated? It is better they should resign,' argues the Samajwadi Party's garrulous MP Naresh Aggarwal, who first raised the issue of Tendulkar's prolonged absence from Parliament.

Tendulkar supporters point out that the cricketer has spent almost 100 per cent of his allotted MP fund on different social projects, and contributed to states hit by natural disasters like floods. He has lent his name to Prime Minister Narendra Modi's Skill India and Swachh Bharat campaign and supported toilet-building initiatives in remote areas. He has also adopted villages in Andhra Pradesh and Maharashtra as part of the prime minister's Adarsh Gram Yojana. 'Don't judge him only by how many times he has been seen speaking in Parliament, please see the projects he has supported as MP,' says a friend of the cricketer. He also supports Apnalaya, an NGO which works to educate slum children, and visits cancer patients supported by the Make a Wish foundation.

And yet, as a Bharat Ratna, the expectations are greater. For example, one hopes that Tendulkar will one day set up a charitable foundation of his own, like many international sporting legends have, which will be involved in major social initiatives. 'I do a lot of charity work quietly, but setting up a foundation will mean I will have no time for anything else,' says Tendulkar. Even after retirement Brand Tendulkar is a huge draw: he appears in advertisement campaigns, part-owns football and badminton franchises, is a mentor for the Mumbai Indians IPL cricket franchise and there is a successful biopic that has been made on his career. Could an iconic champion who has the capacity to change the lives of millions perhaps show a greater philanthropic zeal? Or does Tendulkar remain trapped in his own celebrityhood and the whirl of commerce?

Maybe we expect too much of our sporting icons; having played the first innings of life with such aplomb on the field, perhaps it's too much to ask of them to play a similar larger-than-life role beyond the boundary too. For the hours of pleasure he has given us, the blissful moments of pure magic which took our breath away and gave us reason to hope and dream when all else appeared bleak and doomed, Tendulkar has earned the right to live life on his terms. A poster at his farewell game read, 'Thank you, God!' As a friend reminds me, you don't ask God too many questions. He is right: Sachin Ramesh Tendulkar is the God of Hope.

8

Sourav Ganguly

Dada of Bengal

It may have been spun as a myth in history textbooks, but it was only in April 1994 that I realized just what Bengali 'exceptionalism' was really all about. A hardened Mumbaikar, I had just got married and suddenly found myself in a universe which had a distinct Bengali identity. My mother-in-law, Chitra Ghose, in particular, resonated with the sights and sounds of Bengal. A gourmet chef, she introduced her jamai babu to the delectable world of hilsa, macher-jhol and prawn malai curry. 'So much better than the pomfret you get in Mumbai, no?' she would half-tease me. I didn't want to set off a fishy battle between the east and west coasts, but learnt to instead slowly appreciate the sheer diversity of the Bengali palate and their sense of local pride. In the mind of the average Bengali, mishti-doi tasted better than shrikhand, Park Street was way more cosmopolitan than Colaba Causeway, Satyajit Ray was several notches above V. Shantaram, Suchitra Sen was more beautiful than Nutan, and Tagore was a greater intellectual than Ambedkar.

There was one area though where my mother-in-law would concede to Maharashtrian superiority: the world of cricket. An avid cricket fan, she would reluctantly admit that Mumbai was the cricket capital of the country. In the first seventy years after Independence, Mumbai has produced 60 Test cricketers, or more than 20 per cent of those who had represented the country in Test cricket. Bengal, by contrast, had thrown up just sixteen Test players, of whom only four – P. Sen, Pankaj Roy, Sourav Ganguly, Wriddhiman Saha – played more than ten Tests, and both Ganguly and Saha made their debut after my wedding in 1994. Two other Bengal players, Dattu Phadkar and Arun Lal, with more than ten India appearances, had learnt their cricket in Mumbai and Delhi respectively while a third, Dilip Doshi, was a Gujarati whose family lived in Kolkata. Yes, Eden Gardens could house one lakh cricket crazy fans, but it was Mumbai which dominated the sport on the field. Mumbai has won the Ranji Trophy forty-one times while Bengal has won it just twice.

Where did the Bengal presidency lose out to Mumbai? The Calcutta Cricket Club, after all, is the second oldest in the world, founded in 1792, just six years after the Marylebone Cricket Club was set up at Lord's. Cricket matches were played regularly in Kolkata's clubs and gymkhanas – the archetypal British sport and leisure institutions – from the early nineteenth century. And yet, it was in Mumbai that the first competitive structure for Indian cricket blossomed with the Parsee community leading the way. While the anglicized, business-oriented Parsees saw cricket as a passport to upward social mobility, the Bengali bhadralok turned to football to assert their sporting identity. In his book *Nation at Play: A History of Sport in India*, Ronojoy Sen suggests that Bengalis took to football to overcome the slur of physical inadequacy foisted on them by the British ruling class. Football, after all, is seen as the macho, working-class sport unlike cricket's more aristocratic lineage. Sen quotes Horatio Smith writing in the *Calcutta Review* in the 1850s: 'The most superficial observer of Bengali manners must know that their games and sports are, for the most part, sedentary . . . the maxim being that walking is better than running, standing than walking, and lying down best of all . . .' Interestingly, Swami Vivekananda, an early inspiration for Bengali Hindu nationalism, is quoted as having said, 'You will be nearer to heaven through football than through the study of the Gita.'

In 1911, Mohun Bagan defeated the East Yorkshire Regiment of Faizabad to win the prestigious Indian Football Association shield: it was a seminal moment for Indian sport, one which sparked off a wave of Bengali subnationalism, best captured by a report in a newspaper, *The Bengalee*, proclaiming that the Bengali is 'no longer the timid and weak-kneed representative of the race whom Macaulay so foully libeled', while another newspaper, *The Englishman*, commented that 'Mohun Bagan has succeeded in what the Congress and the Swadeshiwallahs have failed to do so far: explode the myth that the Britishers are unbeatable in any sphere of life'.

What Mohun Bagan achieved on the football field in Kolkata, India's first cricket superstar, C.K. Nayudu, would accomplish with the willow in Mumbai. In a match between MCC and Hindus (a team of the Hindu community; cricket teams were organized entirely around religious lines at the time) played at the Bombay Gymkhana in December 1926, Nayudu blazed his way to 153 runs in just 116 minutes, with 13 fours and 11 sixes. It was an inspiring innings, watched among others by a fifteen-year-old Vijay Merchant, later to become India's first great opening batsman, who describes it as the best he had ever seen. From that moment on, Nayudu came to embody the hopes of a nation in the making, a nationalist cricket hero in an age of anger against the Empire. The die had been cast: Kolkata would be the football capital of India, Mumbai would be the home of cricket. If Mumbai looked to dominate the Ranji Trophy domestic cricket tournament, Kolkata had its Santosh Trophy football to aspire for, and if Dadar Union versus Shivaji Park was the great Mumbai cricket maidan battle, then East Bengal versus Mohun Bagan was the ultimate football fight.

Not that this stopped many Bengali cricket fanatics from nursing a sense of permanent grievance. So, when Gopal Bose, the Bengal opening batsman, was not selected for a tour in the mid 1970s, irate

Bengali fans accused the selectors of partisanship. 'From Netaji Bose to Gopal Bose, I think the Bengali has always seen conspiracy theories in politics and cricket,' jokes Kishore Bhimani, veteran Kolkata-based cricket commentator. Bhimani recalls a Ranji match at the Wankhede stadium in 1982 between Mumbai and Bengal when Gavaskar scored his highest first-class score of 340, but the Bengal players were convinced he was out LBW early in his innings. 'I was in the commentary box and got so carried away that I even said that maybe no umpire in Mumbai dared give Gavaskar out LBW,' he admits. 'It was a close call but I wasn't out,' says Gavaskar. 'But I knew that the argumentative Bengalis would spend the entire day grumbling about it so much that they forgot to focus on the game,' he says with a laugh. The parochial edge appeared to blight Bengal cricket for years, a sense that the entire world was ranged against Bengalis.

Historian Ramachandra Guha in his cricket book *Wickets in the East* draws a comparison between Bengal's cricketing and political fortunes, the rise of the Marxists in the mid 1970s coinciding with a sharp decline in cricket standards. Celebrated Afro-Trinidadian Marxist C.L.R. James wrote emotionally on cricket in the West Indies, but the fact is, as British politician Woodrow Wyatt acutely pointed out, no country which has cricket as one of its national games has turned communist. Cricket for many communist writers was a metaphor for elite decadence. A section of the Bengali communists, infused with revolutionary zeal, perhaps saw the game as an unwanted colonial legacy but there were also Bengali communist leaders like former Lok Sabha speaker Somnath Chatterjee who were passionate about the sport. We once went to the Speaker's chamber and found a 'do not disturb' sign on his door. Chatterjee's assistant told us, 'Boss is in an important meeting.' We later found out he was watching an exciting one-day match on television!

What is undeniable is that as a left coalition under the CPI(M)'s Jyoti Basu came to power in West Bengal in 1977, the state was slowly distancing itself from the national 'mainstream' and building an alternative 'ekla chalo re' (go your own way alone) narrative. The energies of an entire generation of Bengali youth were spent in fighting time-worn ideological battles with political rivals rather than winning on the sports field. And yet, the truth is the Bengalis who thronged Eden Gardens by the thousands to watch any international match were always searching for a local cricket hero, someone who could be a cricketing equivalent of a Netaji, an individual who would become a badge of self-respect for an entire community. 'We were looking for just one spark to light a fire,' says Bhimani.

Which is why the emergence of Sourav Ganguly was so crucial to Bengali self-esteem. I shall never forget my mother-in-law's reaction when Ganguly scored a debut Test hundred at Lord's: 'I told you, didn't I, we Bengalis are good at cricket, it's just that we have never had the chance to prove ourselves,' she said excitedly. Later, when Ganguly was dropped, she was infuriated: 'You should ring up these selectors, what do they know of the game, it's all one big conspiracy, how can they just drop the pride of Bengal?'

The pride of Bengal indeed: there have been greater Indian cricketers than Ganguly but perhaps no other player has so strongly and passionately defined the hopes and aspirations of his local community as the 'Prince of Kolkata'. Call it Bengali subnationalism, but every time Ganguly played for the country, he was not just representing Team India but the dreams of every cricket-mad Bengali. Until the advent of Ganguly, only nostalgic images of Pankaj Roy dotted the Bengali cricket imagination. Now they had their very own modern cricket hero to celebrate, a symbol of their cricketing rebirth. Once during a Tendulkar–Ganguly opening partnership, the commentator was euphoric over Tendulkar's strokeplay, prompting my mother-in-law to remark, 'I think Sourav is playing just as well as Sachin.' Bengali exceptionalism was alive and well.

~

Behala in south-west Kolkata is not a particularly sought after address like Alipore which is dotted with tree-lined bungalows and fancy apartments now owned mainly by the Marwari business community. Behala is old Kolkata, a crowded Bengali enclave, whose markets are heavily laced with the sights and smell of fresh fish and traditional sweet shops. Travelling through its winding lanes, every taxi driver will easily identify Sourav Ganguly's house there. Four large red-brick three-storey buildings make up the residential complex: three generations of the family have lived here. Ganguly's grandfather started a flourishing printing business which has stood the test of time.

'We were a large joint family and lived a life of relative luxury,' says Ganguly, as we chat in his 'den' on the ground floor. The room is littered with trophies and pictures from Ganguly's cricket career. It was his father, Chandidas, an avid sportsman who would later become a Bengal cricket official, who was an early inspiration. 'My father was a good club cricketer and crazy about the game, so cricket was always played and talked about at home,' says Ganguly. His father had three brothers, so there was never a problem of putting together a cricket team to play in the garden outside their home. 'In fact, we were six cousins in our generation who all played cricket, and interestingly all were left-handed.' Ganguly was a natural right-hander who chose to bat with the left hand, mimicking his family members.

The best of them all was elder brother Snehasish, five years senior, good enough to hit six first-class centuries for Bengal. If Sachin Tendulkar's elder brother Ajit looked to fulfil his dreams through the bat of his precociously talented younger brother, there was an element of sibling rivalry between the two Gangulys. 'I guess there was some competition later, but my brother was the original first-class cricketer in the family so we all looked up to him. In fact, in my school years in St Xavier's, Kolkata, I was the footballer and he was the cricketer,' says Ganguly. It was only at the age of thirteen when his father pushed him into a summer cricket camp that Ganguly discovered the joys of the game. His first big break would come when a local coach invited him to play in a Bengal versus Orissa under-15 friendly match at Eden Gardens because the team was short of a player. 'I scored a hundred in my first game and after that it was cricket over football,' he says.

The enthusiastic father had already kept a personal coach, Debu Mitra, for Sourav's elder brother. Now Mitra had two Ganguly boys to train. Two concrete pitches were laid out near the residence for the Ganguly boys to practise alongside a multi-purpose indoor gym. While Snehasish was making his way into the Bengal Ranji team, Sourav made his mark in junior cricket, his peer group including the likes of Tendulkar, Anil Kumble and Rahul Dravid. A new generation of Indian cricketers was being shaped by India's well-structured junior cricket programme. Ganguly, born in 1972, and Tendulkar, 1973, would attend a national under-15 camp in Indore together in 1987 and travel to England a year later as part of a private cricket tour organized by veteran Rajasthan cricketer Kailash Gattani. 'The bonds of friendship between Sachin, Rahul, Anil and I were sown in our teenage years which only grew stronger when we played international cricket together,' says Ganguly.

On that tour, Tendulkar and Ganguly opened together for the first time in a match. 'A strong Sussex juniors' team scored around 270 runs and left us 30 overs to get the runs. Both Sachin and Sourav put up their hands to say they wanted to open and then went and smashed the bowling around to enable us to win the game,' remembers Gattani. It was a sign of even happier times to come.

While Tendulkar would make a sensational Test debut in 1989 at the age of sixteen, Ganguly was still proving himself in junior cricket. Picked for the India under-19 team against Pakistan in 1990, he scored a century in the fourth Test in Mumbai. 'We were three wickets down very early when I went to bat, and the batsman before me had been hit in the face and I could see blood on the wicket. The Pakistani junior side had the likes of Waqar Younis playing for them so it wasn't easy. But that hundred showed that I could play at a higher level,' says Ganguly.

Weeks later, Ganguly was making his first-class debut for Bengal against Delhi, albeit in controversial circumstances. Bengal had reached the finals, hoping to win the Ranji Trophy for only the second time in history. Brother Snehasish had played for Bengal through the season but was dropped for the finals. Replacing him was Sourav, still four months short of his seventeenth birthday. 'Being dropped from the finals was shocking and hurtful and it took me time to get over it, but to suggest that I resented my brother taking my place or we didn't talk to each other for months is false,' says Snehasish.

Sourav scored 22 in the finals, batting at number three against a strong Delhi bowling attack and bowled six overs without taking a wicket. Bengal won the game and the trophy, but it wasn't a debut that set the Hooghly aflame. The pundits though were impressed with a rising new talent. 'There is always something special about a left-hander, and Sourav had this amazingly natural ball-striking skill that stood out; he could almost hit sixes at will as a teenager,' says Arun Lal, the Test player who shepherded Bengal cricket through this period.

A year later, Sourav had scored his first century in first-class cricket for East Zone against a powerful West Zone side, and also taken four wickets with his gentle medium pace. He was now being pitched as an all-rounder ('I always loved to bowl,' he says) and not just as a batsman. His one-day form was particularly solid: in a Wills Trophy one-day match against West Zone, he hit Test left arm spinner Ravi Shastri for a six that hit the clock at Mumbai's Brabourne stadium. Shastri was impressed enough to recommend him to his employers, the Tata Group, who were always on the lookout for young players to strengthen their cricket team. 'He had this free-flowing bat swing which stood out,' says Shastri. In later years, Sourav would be devastating against left-arm spinners, a skill Shastri had spotted early on.

And yet, when Ganguly was picked for the India team to tour Australia in 1991–92 more than a few eyebrows were raised. Was one first-class century enough to throw an eighteen-year-old into the deep end of a tough tour? There were familiar accusations of a quota system in Indian cricket, of Ganguly being accommodated to complete the East Zone 'quota'. 'When a talented player from East Zone gets picked, the press shouts quota system, but when someone is picked from any other part of the country, everyone is silent,' is Ganguly's terse response to his selection.

The four-month tour was a disaster. Ganguly hardly played any cricket as a reserve batsman and was picked for only one international game. Worse, there were persistent reports that Ganguly wasn't willing to do the chores of a twelfth man and had an 'attitude' problem. His original pet name, Maharaj, didn't help: he was branded as a lazy, arrogant cricketer. He was promptly dropped from the 1992 World Cup squad and banished to return to play for Bengal. 'It is rubbish to say that I didn't want to get involved with the team or didn't want to carry the drinks trolley as twelfth man,' retorts Ganguly. 'But it was a very strong Indian batting line-up that had no place for me in the final eleven and I just had to accept that.'

A blighted history of misfortune, it seemed, was dragging down yet another aspiring Bengal cricketer: would he end up like many before him as yet another Kolkata boy who couldn't make the leap from 'para dada' (Bengali for neighbourhood bully) to the big league? In hindsight Lal believes the dropping of Ganguly was the best thing to happen to him. 'When Sourav started off, he appeared to doubt his own ability and was actually a little weak in the mind. Having to fight to return to play for India really got Sourav's competitive juices going and helped him mature as a person and a cricketer,' feels Lal. Sourav was determined not to be the next Gopal Bose, a talented Bengal cricketer who toured with the Indian team but never played a Test. He would instead be what Bengal was craving for: a cricketing Netaji who would carve out his own unique place in Indian cricket, bravely leading the men in blue like an Azad Hind Fauj of the twenty-first century.

～

Sourav Ganguly's 'vanvas' from international cricket lasted over four years. New players, like Mumbai's left-hander Vinod Kambli, dazzled in the early 1990s where Sourav had failed. It seemed as if it would take a real twist of fortune for Sourav to return to the Indian team. 'I never gave up, I knew I was good enough to play for India,' insists Sourav with the self-confidence that would become his trademark. After a strong 1995–96 domestic season, his moment would come when he was picked for the Indian team to tour England in the summer. Once again, his selection drew criticism: this time, there were allegations that the all-powerful cricket board secretary from Bengal, Jagmohan Dalmiya, had pushed Sourav's case. Lal says the virulent criticism smacked of a bias against players from the east. 'I remember being part of a commentary panel before the England tour and being asked who I would pick. When I said Sourav, the others laughed at me. I am glad he proved all the critics wrong,' says Lal.

Like in Australia in 1991–92, in 1996, Sourav was again a reserve batsman on the England tour. Only this time, kismet was on his side. The senior batsman on the tour, Navjot Singh Sidhu, controversially walked out of the team just ahead of the series after an alleged run-in with skipper Azharuddin while another Test regular, Sanjay Manjrekar, was injured. Having lost the first Test badly, India turned to a new generation of batsmen: Sourav and Rahul Dravid were picked for the first time for the Lord's Test. 'I had seen both of them play well in the lead-up games; they had talent no doubt but whether they would perform at the highest level, no one could be sure of that,' is how the team skipper Azharuddin explains the selection.

Azhar needn't have worried. In 1984–85, the India skipper had dazzled the cricketing world with a debut century against England. Now Sourav would emulate him, arguably in more difficult circumstances. It was a green-tinged wicket; England had scored 344 in their innings and dismissed the Indian openers cheaply. 'I came in to bat with about an hour to go for stumps and really began to hit the bat smoothly from the very first ball. Honestly, I didn't feel any pressure of this being my first innings because I felt I had nothing to lose,' is how Ganguly remembers the early part of his debut innings.

Undefeated on 26 overnight, he spoke to his parents on the phone from the hotel, had an early dinner and felt even more relaxed. The next morning, India lost Tendulkar and skipper Azharuddin and were in trouble at 202 for five. Ganguly was then joined by Dravid, a comrade in junior and India-A cricket. Two debutants were being asked to save the reputation of Indian cricket at the intimidating gates of Lord's. What followed can best be described as a resurrection of Indian batting: Ganguly's flowing drives, especially through the off-side, and Dravid's sturdy defence and leg-side play would come to define a partnership that not only saved the game for India but gave fresh hope for the future of Indian cricket. 'There are days when you are in the zone, that was my day, I don't recall getting beaten even once on a tough pitch,' says Ganguly.

The nightmare of Australia 1992 had been replaced by a steely self-belief in England 1996: 'Maharaj' was now transformed into 'Dada' (elder brother). On a Saturday afternoon in glorious London sunshine, Sourav would hit his seventeenth boundary to reach a debut hundred. As he raised his arms in joy, he wouldn't have known that he had become only the third cricketer in history to score a debut century at Lord's and the first non-Englishman to achieve the feat (three Englishmen, Harry Graham, John Hampshire and, in 2007, Matt Prior, have done so). 'I was happy but also relieved to have proven a point, to have shown that I had it in me to become a successful Test player for India,' he says.

Nine Indian batsmen had scored Test debut hundreds before him, but only two, Azharuddin and Viswanath, had gone on to score more than the solitary century. Two previous Indian left-handers with Test hundreds, Deepak Shodhan and Surinder Amarnath, had brief Test careers. Ganguly wasn't burdened with history: he would score a hundred in his second Test match too, another rare feat achieved by only eight others in Test history. His skipper, Azharuddin, who, as mentioned earlier, holds the unique record of three hundreds in his first three Tests, believes Sourav's performance was even more impressive. 'I made my centuries at home, he scored his in foreign conditions against a moving ball when everyone had written him off. To achieve what he did requires talent and courage,' is how Azhar looks back at Ganguly's remarkable English summer.

Back home, his parents were ecstatic, the Bengali newspapers were euphoric and Kolkata finally had a cricketing knight to celebrate. 'I was on the flight home via the Netherlands when my brother rang me up to say that a special celebration and a motorcade was being planned on my return. I asked him not to do it, saying I wasn't comfortable. But when I landed in Kolkata, I had no choice – from the airport to Behala there was a sea of people who wanted to meet and greet me,' Sourav says with a smile.

That year, Ganguly would be named in Wisden's list of cricketers of the year. But even more significantly, he was responsible for what Arun Lal describes as a 'watershed' moment for Indian cricket. 'Sourav's success ensured that cricketers from the east would now be taken seriously, it was our cricketing renaissance moment,' he says. Bengal had produced great social reformers like Raja Ram Mohan Roy, Nobel laureates like Rabindranath Tagore and Amartya Sen, actors like Uttam Kumar, Suchitra Sen and Soumitra Chatterjee, celebrated film directors like Satyajit Ray, freedom fighters like Subhas Bose, but they hadn't thrown up a global sporting superstar: the rise of Sourav meant that a yawning gap had been filled in the Bengali pantheon of icons, a yearning for a truly homegrown cricket hero had been satiated.

Interestingly, the year of Ganguly's ascent could well have also seen a Bengali become prime minister for the first time. In 1996, as the general elections led to a hung Parliament, then Bengal chief minister Jyoti Basu was propped up as a potential prime ministerial candidate of a non-Congress, non-BJP third front at the Centre. But the Delhi-based CPI(M) national leadership blocked his nomination on the grounds that the party was not in a position to implement its ideological agenda in a coalition government. 'It was a historic blunder,' Basu would later lament. While a 'regional'

Bengali strongman could not impose his writ on Delhi, a cricket hero from Bengal faced no such opposition – on the cricket field, the gap between Kolkata and the rest of the country had finally been bridged.

The year 1996 though was only the beginning; over the next decade, Sourav Ganguly would become one of the most charismatic and controversial cricketers of his generation, leading Indian cricket on an exciting, roller-coaster adventure.

~

While attempting to explain the Bengali elite's fascination with Marxist philosophy, Ramachandra Guha in his book *An Anthropologist among the Marxists and Other Essays* suggests that the British had constantly denigrated the Bengali bhadralok's lack of physical prowess, leading them to turn to political radicalism. A British colonial official had once remarked that the Bengali 'has the intellect of a Greek and the grit of a rabbit'. The stereotypical image of a docile, file-pushing Bengali babu or a chain-smoking ideologue in a coffee adda was caricatured in popular culture: the Bengali was seen to talk more than act.

All this changed rather dramatically on 13 July 2002 when India won a remarkable NatWest trophy one-day final against England at Lord's. The victory, sparked off by a valiant partnership between two young players, Yuvraj Singh and Mohammad Kaif, is perhaps best remembered for Sourav Ganguly, then skipper, taking his shirt off at the Lord's balcony and waving it triumphantly in the direction of the English players. Lord's hadn't seen anything like it before – or since – but purely as a statement of intent it seemed to reflect the changed body language in Indian cricket: an Indian captain was defying the traditions of the gentleman's game by doing an impersonation of a bare-chested Salman Khan. 'Look, I regret what I did that day, but maybe it was part of the football culture I had grown up in as a teenager in Kolkata,' is Sourav's explanation. 'Besides, I also don't have a six-pack like Salman,' he adds with an embarrassed smile.

Truth is Sourav saw it as payback time for the English. Months earlier, England's star all-rounder Andrew Flintoff had pulled off a similar shirt removal act at Mumbai's Wankhede stadium after England levelled a one-day series. Ganguly had shared an uneasy relationship with Flintoff when playing together for Lancashire in county cricket in 2000. (In his biography, Flintoff claims, 'Ganguly turned up like he was royalty: it was like having Prince Charles in your side.') 'I guess somewhere in the back of my mind was a desire for revenge, to show that we weren't going to take it lying down any longer,' admits Sourav.

A year earlier, in 2001, he had shown a similar combative attitude when leading India in a historic series against Australia at home. By keeping Australian captain Steve Waugh waiting at the toss, Sourav was once again playing mind games with the leader of the best team in the world. 'It isn't cricket,' is how an irate Waugh described Sourav's actions. Sourav has his own explanation: 'Before the second Test in Kolkata, I was speaking to the groundsman on the mobile and asking him to make sure that the wicket suited our spinners. Steve overheard my conversation and wrote a column criticizing me. That's when I decided that if he could try and intimidate me, then I was also going to keep him guessing at the toss.'

It is this defiant edge, the refusal to take a step back, that would come to define Sourav's captaincy and persona. It wasn't just on the field: Sourav could be rebellious in his personal life too. Within months of his debut century, he married his childhood sweetheart, Dona Roy. It was a marriage that had a Romeo–Juliet script to it but with a happy ending this time. The Gangulys and Roys had been business partners initially, even acquiring large plots next to each other in Behala. When the business relations soured, a high wall came up between the two feuding homes, but it didn't stop Sourav from meeting Dona secretly. When Sourav acquired sudden fame and began travelling the world, Dona told him that she was worried that he would now forget her. 'That's when we decided to have a registered marriage quietly because we knew our parents wouldn't approve,' says Sourav.

But when you are Bengal's lone cricket superstar, nothing can be hidden from the media gaze. 'A friend of mine went and leaked the story to the Bengali press and all hell broke loose. My parents were very angry but eventually came around to accepting it. I guess when you are in your twenties, there is always a streak of the rebel in you!' he says.

It was, perhaps, just the kind of non-conformist attitude that Indian cricket was looking for in its captain. After all, Sourav had taken over captaincy in early 2000 just when the match-fixing controversy erupted. Tendulkar had given up the job after being appointed captain a second time just months earlier amid growing reports of intrigue in the dressing room, Azharuddin and Ajay Jadeja had been banned and fans had lost faith in the team. Indian cricket was in disgrace. In this dark hour, Ganguly was being asked to lead a young team into an uncertain future. 'It wasn't easy but I told the team that we had to live by the old saying "when the going gets tough, the tough get going",' recalls Sourav.

The new captain was lucky: a group of senior players with similar core values would come together at just the right time to rescue Indian cricket from the abyss. 'Rahul, Sachin, Anil, V.V.S., Srinath, these are men of character, without them I would have achieved nothing,' admits Sourav. Srinath, the spearhead of the pace attack, says the team felt a 'collective pain' after the match-fixing scandal broke. 'That pain I think made us more determined to prove ourselves to the world.' Allied to the senior players were a group of talented youngsters like Zaheer Khan, Virender Sehwag, Yuvraj Singh and Harbhajan Singh, imbued with small-town energy, hungry for opportunity, desperate to make a mark.

It was the perfect mix, one that would radically transform Indian cricket in the space of a few years: between 2001 and 2005 under Sourav's leadership, India won Test series not only at home, but also overseas Test matches against the mighty Australians and the English and a historic series win over Pakistan in Pakistan in 2004. The team would also reach the finals of the 2003 World Cup in South Africa. As captain, Ganguly would lead India to 21 wins out of 49 Tests, second in terms of wins only to Mahendra Singh Dhoni. Importantly, his record in terms of away Tests is better than Dhoni's with 11 wins to 10 losses as against Dhoni's 6 wins to as many as 15 losses.

The turning point, according to Sourav, was the 2001 home series against Australia. Playing a near-invincible team that had won 16 consecutive Test matches and after losing the first Test in Mumbai and being made to follow on in the second at Kolkata, Sourav's men scripted one of cricket's great turnarounds. An epic partnership between V.V.S. Laxman and Rahul Dravid that changed the course of the Kolkata Test and possibly Indian cricket (more on this in the next chapter) was followed by a magical spell by a twenty-one-year-old spinner from Jalandhar, Harbhajan Singh. 'The day we beat Australia, we had the self-belief that we could beat anyone. And yes, if we could do it at home, we resolved to do it abroad too,' says Sourav, recalling the dressing room mood after the game. Harbhajan's spell also benefited from an instinctive move by the captain. 'He was bowling well but the umpire wasn't giving any LBWs when the batsman stretched forward, so I just changed his bowling end and suddenly he was a match-winner!' is how he explains the Kolkata magic.

Harbhajan was just one of the young cricketers to blossom under Sourav's leadership. A new order was emerging in Indian cricket, cricketers like Yuvraj and Sehwag in particular becoming torchbearers of a brand of refreshingly aggressive cricket that won hearts and minds. Zaheer Khan, who gradually replaced Srinath as the team's fast bowling leader, recalls making his debut under Sourav's captaincy in the ICC Knockout Trophy in Kenya in October 2000. 'I was the juniormost pacer in the team and yet in the first game against Kenya Sourav gives me the new ball ahead of the more experienced Venkatesh Prasad and Ajit Agarkar; imagine what that one move on his part did for my confidence. That was Sourav's ability – once he had faith in you, he backed you till the end,' says Zaheer.

Sehwag, in particular, hugely benefited from Sourav's keen eye for talent. Initially drafted into the Indian one-day side as a part-time off-spinner and hard-hitting lower order batsman, Sehwag was put on a new career path when Sourav pushed him into opening the batting. 'I just felt that he had the skills to take the attack to the bowlers from ball one,' says Sourav. The experiment was first attempted in a tri-series in Sri Lanka in 2001. 'I remember Viru asking me what would happen if he failed as opener. All I said to him was, "Don't worry, whether you succeed or not, you will play the entire tournament." Just three matches later, Sehwag scored his maiden one-day century from 69 balls.

A year later, Sourav pushed Sehwag to open in Test cricket too, this time on green wickets in England. 'Everyone thought I was crazy, but I was convinced Viru had the game to be a match-winner in all forms of the game,' he claims. Once again, Sehwag came to Sourav with his concern over being dropped if he failed. Pat came the response again: 'You will play the entire series, don't worry.' The rest is history: Sehwag would go on to become one of India's most successful openers, the only one to score two triple centuries for the country.

Sehwag, like many gen-next cricketers of the early twenty-first century, acknowledges Sourav's contribution to his career. 'In cricket, confidence is key. Sourav as captain always backed me, so I could play my natural game without any concern of failure,' he says. Indeed, just before the Pakistan series of 2004, I had interviewed Sourav and asked him how he intended to take on the pressure of captaining an Indian team in Pakistan. His response was interesting: 'When you have young players like Viru who will hit the first ball of a Test match for six, where is the question of pressure?' Sourav was spot on: in that series, Sehwag would score a belligerent triple century that would earn him the title 'Sultan of Multan'.

In a sense then, one of Sourav's big contributions as captain was to remove the senior–junior divide that had afflicted Indian cricket for decades. 'I had suffered on my first tour as an eighteen-year-old and didn't want anyone else to go through a similar feeling. I do believe that once you have been picked for India, you are one of eleven members, no one is senior or junior any more,' reasons Sourav.

Importantly, while he was adored by his fellow Bengali fans, Sourav never played the parochial card when leading Indian cricket. In politics, the rise of regional leaders to fill the vacuum left by a declining Congress had created political instability through the 1990s. Many regional bosses in politics chose to pander to narrow caste and local identities to cement their vote base. H.D. Deve Gowda, who became prime minister in 1996, the year of Sourav's debut, was encircled in his brief tenure in the Prime Minister's Office by Kannadiga aides. The likes of Lalu and Mulayam Singh Yadav played the caste card to boost their support, Dravidian party leaders were happier in Chennai than in Delhi and even a powerful chieftain like Sharad Pawar couldn't entirely shake off his Maharashtrian roots after moving to the Centre. Sourav, to his credit, always kept country above Bengal, more evidence of cricket's growing democratic impulses.

Making Sourav's task easier was the gentle presence of the team coach John Wright, a quiet New Zealander with a strong work ethic. It was a classic case of contrasting personalities working in near-perfect harmony: Wright was the silent, ever-smiling, behind-the-scenes figure, who when he was not talking cricket would be strumming his guitar, while Sourav was the excitable, argumentative Bengali who loved the arc lights and a good fight. The relationship, says Sourav, was based on mutual respect. 'I remember just before the NatWest trophy in 2002, I had a big bust-up with John in the dressing room. He had shouted at Viru for coming late by a few minutes to a team meeting and I told him that no one could shout at my players. He just walked away and we didn't talk to each other for twenty-four hours. But when we won the match, John just came up to me and gave me a big hug. In the end, our goal was the same: make Indian cricket stronger!'

And yet, not everyone would be as accommodating of Sourav's mood swings. When Wright relinquished the coach's position in

2005, there was a distinct feeling that life would not be the same again: like good openers, a captain and coach are also a partnership. Wright gave the space to Sourav to express himself as leader, to engage in the occasional bout of gamesmanship, yes, to even bare his chest at Lord's. The man who would take over from him wasn't going to be nearly as obliging: one of the more grim chapters in Indian cricket history was about to unfold.

~

Greg Chappell is a cricketing legend: a former Australian captain who with Viv Richards and Sunil Gavaskar could legitimately claim to be the three best batsmen of the 1970s. John Wright had been a cricketing journeyman, someone who had to work diligently to succeed. Chappell, by contrast, was a star from the very moment he scored a debut hundred: he walked on to the cricket field with a regal swagger, played shots of power and elegance and had the record to back the claim of being one of the sport's all-time greats. It was perhaps his stature in the game that first attracted Sourav to Chappell. 'I had trained with him before the Australia tour of 2003 and had been impressed with his knowledge of the game, so when the BCCI was looking to replace John as coach, I suggested Chappell's name,' he says.

It was to prove a grave error of judgement. Chappell was a man of strong views who wanted to 'revolutionize' Indian cricket; Sourav was not one to be easily bullied. Two tough characters, Chappell and Ganguly could never have an easy relationship. It started badly when, just ahead of a Test match in Zimbabwe in September 2005, Chappell suggested to Sourav that he step down from captaincy to concentrate on his batting. 'I was taken aback. Here I was a successful India captain for five years, and now the coach instead of backing me was asking me to exit without any proper explanation,' says Sourav. A hurt and enraged Sourav hit back: after scoring a century in the Test, he went ahead and told the media in a post-match interview that he had been 'extra determined to succeed' because Chappell wanted him out of the captaincy. The conflict was out in the public domain and would only get worse.

A few days later, a controversial email from Chappell to the BCCI damning Sourav was leaked to the media. Sourav was accused of having a 'fragile mind' and playing politics in the dressing room. 'Everything he does is designed to maximize his chances of success and is usually detrimental to someone else's chances . . . this team has been made fearful and distrustful by the rumour-mongering and Sourav's modus operandi of divide and rule. Certain players have been treated with favour, all of them bowlers, while others have been shunted up and down the order or left out of the team to suit Sourav's whims,' wrote Chappell. The gloves were off: never before had an India captain been so publicly targeted by a coach. Sourav suspected that the email had been leaked by Chappell in cahoots with a BCCI official and a senior journalist. 'I don't have any proof against anyone, but there is little doubt that Chappell for some reason wanted me out,' Sourav says testily.

Barely a month later, Sourav was out of the captaincy, replaced by Rahul Dravid and dropped from the one-day squad. By early 2006, he had been removed from the Test squad too. Intrigue and musical chairs had been part of being an India captain, especially in the 1950s (as mentioned in an earlier chapter the 1958–59 series had seen four captains in five Tests) In the 1980s, Kapil Dev and Gavaskar had also alternated in a bizarre fashion while S. Venkataraghavan was famously told of his sacking as captain while on a flight back from England in 1979. By 2005, most cricket observers believed that Indian cricket had acquired a reassuring stability: a captain wasn't always on test. And yet, the Ganguly episode proves that opaqueness in decision-making is part of Indian cricket culture: no one till date has clearly explained the real reason for Ganguly's abrupt removal.

There may be a cricketing explanation for Sourav's dropping from the side: 2005 wasn't his best year in international cricket, with the century against Zimbabwe being his sole hundred that year. Not the best athlete, his fielding came under fresh scrutiny and his batting seemed to have lost its edge. He had also been captain for five years, which is just about par in the contemporary game. But if he was to be dropped, then surely as a senior cricketer he deserved a more honourable exit. Years later, when I asked Chappell, he wouldn't offer an explanation beyond reiterating that he was 'acting in the best interests of Indian cricket'. A selector claims that Chappell wanted to encourage young talent with an eye on the future. This was a period when other left-handers like Yuvraj Singh were pushing their claims for a Test spot. 'Greg told us that we needed a younger, fitter team if we were to raise the bar and that Sourav was an impediment in that transition,' says the selector. Sourav's fitness had at times been questioned as was the charge that he wanted to pick and choose his opponents: in 2004, he had dropped out of the Nagpur Test against Australia, allegedly because there was too much grass on the wicket. 'This is pure rubbish, I was injured. Don't forget, I scored a century just a year earlier against Australia on a more difficult wicket in Brisbane; I have never shied away,' he angrily counters.

It is also possible that Sourav, like many Indian captains before him, was a victim of board politics. The removal of Sourav as captain coincides with an intense fight in the BCCI where eventually Jagmohan Dalmiya lost out to Mumbai's heavyweight politician Sharad Pawar. Sourav had shared a blow hot, blow cold relationship with Dalmiya. The rise of Sourav to captaincy corresponds with the dominance of the Dalmiya faction in the BCCI in the early 2000s. Together, it marked the distinct shift of the power base of Indian cricket from west to east, from Mumbai to Kolkata. But while Dalmiya may have encouraged Sourav in his early years, by 2005 the equation was strained. 'Look, you can't have two Dadas in the same neighbourhood, and Dalmiya was convinced by 2005 that Sourav had grown too big for Bengal and Indian cricket,' a Bengal cricket official says, explaining the fallout. Without Dalmiya's sheltering presence, Sourav became vulnerable to the board's machinations: when he was dropped as captain, Dalmiya did not stand up for him.

By 2006, with Pawar firmly in control of the BCCI and also now an influential minister at the Centre, the balance of power had shifted away from Eden Gardens once again.

During a year of exile from the team, an insecure and anxious Sourav would often call up to find out if I knew more of what was going on in the minds of the new power axis in Indian cricket. I would in turn ask him if he planned to retire. 'No way, why should I give up, are you telling me I am not good enough to be in the top six batsmen in the country,' was his defiant response. In a strange way, his removal from the side only seemed to strengthen his resolve: it was almost a rerun of the early 1990s when he bounced back after being written off by the critics. The never-say-die rebellious spirit has always been Sourav's ally in dark days, and this time was no different. He even did a tongue-in-cheek Pepsi ad where he smiled into the camera: 'My name is Sourav Ganguly, I hope you have not forgotten me!'

He had not been forgotten: he would return to the Indian Test team for a difficult tour of South Africa in 2006–07, ironically with Chappell still the team coach. He would score a match-winning unbeaten half-century in his first comeback innings on a difficult pitch in Johannesburg. He would end the series as the most successful Indian batsman with 214 runs at an average of 42.8, thereby ending the speculation over his future. 'I don't think I have been as determined as I was in that series,' he tells me. 'I guess I had a point to prove to my fans, but especially to Mr Chappell.'

Barely a few months later, Chappell was gone, a casualty of India's failure to qualify for the knock-out stages of the 2007 World Cup. More players, including Tendulkar, as mentioned in the previous chapter, began to speak out against what they called the coach's autocratic and divisive style of functioning. Sourav felt vindicated: 'He just wasn't a nice human being,' is his final verdict. An ugly episode in Indian cricket had concluded with the public slanging match benefiting no one. Maybe Chappell's inflexible professionalism was ill-suited for the more laid-back Indian style of playing the game: he might have been a better coach for the Indian junior team than he was for senior, experienced cricketers who were loath to be taken out of their comfort zone. Maybe Sourav should have learnt to adjust his temperament to a new coach or risk being left behind. Personally, I would rather not remember Sourav from the rancorous Chappell era but celebrate the captain who led India with pride and passion to lift Indian cricket from the debris of the match-fixing controversy. That will perhaps be his most durable legacy in taking Indian cricket forward.

~

Sourav Ganguly retired from international cricket in November 2008, almost achieving the rare distinction of scoring a century in his first and last Test (85 and 0 in his last game against Australia at Nagpur). He had little left to prove: his comeback had been way above expectations, two centuries against Pakistan, including a career-best 238, being a highlight. And yet, typical of the man, he was hungry for more, choosing to play in the first four editions of the IPL, initially as captain of the Kolkata Knight Riders (KKR), later with the Sahara Pune franchise. Given Sourav's inextricable connect with Kolkata, it was tough to visualize a city team without its ultimate icon. I recall interviewing the KKR owner, Bollywood superstar Shah Rukh Khan, and his reaction was typical: 'Can anyone but Dada be our captain?' he had gushed.

In hindsight, it was probably a mistake for Sourav to take the pressure of the IPL captaincy in the autumn of his career. A year into his KKR tenure, he was made part of a unique 'multiple captain' system and was eventually offloaded (under the 'multiple captain' system, captaincy would rotate between the senior KKR players for each game, a strange decision taken by another Australian coach, John Buchanan). There were reports of discontent and murmurs of a standoff between Sourav and Shah Rukh. Explains a KKR official, 'Sourav made little effort to integrate with the younger players and those from other countries; he chose to stay at home in Kolkata rather than the team hotel.' It almost seems as if the ghosts of the Chappell years had returned. When Sourav moved to the Pune franchise after being passed up by KKR in the 2011 auction, there were reports of more trouble. Some Pune players reportedly felt that Sourav was past his prime and didn't deserve a place in the side even as the team owner, Subrata Roy, would reportedly ring up Sourav late into the night to question team selection.

'Just look at my IPL numbers. I was one of the highest scorers for the KKR franchise,' says Sourav defending his decision to play in the IPL. As always, he wasn't short of confidence, convinced that he was still good enough to play Twenty20 cricket. But it wasn't just about the cricket: as an iconic player, Sourav got a million-plus dollars for a six-week cricket season. The money was too good to refuse. On his first tour to Australia in 1991–92, Sourav had signed a bat contract for Rs 10,000 and got just Rs 50,000 for an arduous four-month tour. (Rs 25,000 paid before and the balance amount on return.) The world had now changed dramatically and Sourav didn't want to be left out. 'Yes, the money was something I couldn't have imagined when I started playing, but remember, I came from a wealthy family, money was never my motivation, it was always the challenge of performing under pressure,' he claims.

Indeed, few Indian cricketers have relished the spotlight as much as Sourav: at times, it seemed as if he almost relished controversy, living by the dictum 'like me, hate me, but you can't ignore me'. 'It is wrong to suggest that I took pleasure in being controversial, I guess controversy chased me,' he says.

Controversial he may have been, but how good a batsman was Sourav Ganguly? Statistically, he must rank as India's finest left-handed batsman by some distance with 16 Test centuries in 113 Tests at an average of 42.17. The remaining Indian left-hander centurions have 33 centuries between them (as of August 2017), with Gautam Gambhir the next highest with 9 centuries. Significantly, his average never dipped below 40 runs an innings throughout his career, a mark of consistency. Captaincy may have affected his batting figures though: only 5 of his 16 centuries came as captain and his average as captain fell to 37.66 in 49 tests. His Test average is the lowest of the big five who were part of the best batting side India has produced (Tendulkar, Dravid, Laxman and Sehwag being the others), maybe the result of struggles against the short ball in overseas conditions. 'I scored hundreds in Australia and England, got runs in South Africa, how can you say that I was uneasy against fast bowling,' he rebuts.

What stands out is his one-day aggregate (11,221 runs) and 22 one-day centuries, well ahead of all his contemporaries barring Sachin. 'He was a very fine Test player but a truly outstanding limited overs cricketer,' is how Shastri assesses Sourav's career. His 31 Man of the Match awards in this period rank second only to Sachin. The Sachin–Sourav opening partnership was often match-winning, with 26 century partnerships in the 8227 runs they put on together. 'I loved batting with him,' says Sachin. 'Sourav was great at pacing his innings, he knew which bowlers to target, when to attack.' He may not have been the classical left-hander in the David Gower mould, but he was blessed with wonderful timing and shot-making skills. When in form, his cover-driving could be imperious, hand, feet and eyes in perfect tandem. 'On the off-side, first there is God, then there is Ganguly,' is how Dravid famously described Sourav's batting once.

And yet, it would be unfair to judge Sourav's contribution only in terms of statistics. For over a decade, he was 'Mr Bengal', carrying the hopes of an entire state every time he wore the India cap. Youngsters across India may have idolized Sachin, but in Bengal, it was 'Dada' who became a true folk hero, inspiring an entire generation to embrace cricket. Arun Lal, who runs a coaching centre in Kolkata, says that hundreds of youngsters, especially from the districts, took to cricket after Sourav made his mark. 'We have a tournament in which more than 150 coaching academies now compete, many of them from far-flung areas. The kids dream of becoming the next Dada,' he says.

Not surprisingly, the most successful Bengal cricketer since

Ganguly's retirement has been a small-town boy, India wicketkeeper Wriddhiman Saha, who was born in Siliguri in north Bengal. 'Of course, watching Dada play as a young boy was a big motivation for me,' says the soft-spoken Saha, who was a footballer in school before enrolling in a local cricket academy as a thirteen-year-old in 1997. Indeed, the 'democratization' of cricket, which has ended the monopoly of the Kolkata clubs over the sport and seen cricket academies mushrooming across district towns, is a major factor in Bengal's cricket mini-revolution. 'Today, go into any district in Bengal and you will find as many young kids playing cricket as football,' says Kolkata-based sports historian Boria Majumdar, adding, 'Sourav's achievements and the popularity of the KKR team in the IPL have been the major catalysts in this dramatic change.'

While Saha may be the latest Bengali to have made a mark in Indian cricket, Sourav remains the original 'Dada' of his state. In 2016, when India played its 500th Test, I was asked on a TV show to pick an all-time Indian Test eleven. I didn't include Sourav in the side, my number five being a toss-up between Laxman, Viswanath and Kohli. An irate Bengali sent me a long mail accusing me of being biased and 'anti-national'. While I had been used to such comments after a political programme, I didn't think a cricket show would generate such extreme emotions. The English opening batsman Sir Geoff Boycott was right: Sourav Ganguly was, and always will be, the Prince of Kolkata for his legion of Bengali fans.

~

In September 2015, Sourav Ganguly became the CAB president. Jagmohan Dalmiya had just passed away and Sourav who was then joint secretary was chosen to take over, again not without controversy. The appointment was not made after a proper election, but was instead unilaterally announced by Bengal chief minister and Trinamool Congress chief, Mamata Banerjee, now the undisputed monarch of Bengal politics. 'Make no mistake, yes, I am making a decision for CAB. It is my way of supporting cricket,' she said emphatically. Bengal watchers believe that Mamata's true agenda was political: she wanted to ensure that Sourav was seen to be on her side in the state elections that were to follow in the summer of 2016. 'There were some ambitious Trinamool Congress men who were eyeing the post, but Mamata wanted to keep them out. By making Sourav president, she killed two birds with one stone,' claims a CAB insider.

Unlike many of his peers, Sourav is also genuinely keen on cricket administration. 'He is the one person from our generation who knows how to deal with board officials and their politics,' is how a teammate describes Sourav's role as a cricket administrator. When I attended the India–Pakistan game during the World Twenty20 in March 2016, the stamp of the new CAB president could be seen. Brand-new covers and an effective drainage system ensured the match could go ahead despite heavy rain. Only eighteen months earlier, a match in Kolkata had been washed out after only a light shower. 'I was sitting with Sourav that day and he promised me he would never allow this to happen again at Eden Gardens and he lived up to his promise,' says Majumdar.

Ahead of the India–Pakistan match, Sourav had rung up to ask me if I could put him in touch with A.R. Rahman because he wanted the music maestro to sing the national anthem at the venue. We couldn't get through to Rahman but Sourav managed to connect with Amitabh Bachchan and got him to kick-off the match with a rousing rendition of 'Jana Gana Mana'. 'I want Bengal to have the best of cricket facilities, make Eden Gardens the best place to watch cricket in the world,' he says.

That Sourav's ambitions extended beyond the cricket pitch was obvious when the Justice R.M. Lodha panel was appointed to reorganize Indian cricket administration in 2016. With the panel ruling against several long-serving board members, there was talk that Sourav might be elevated to board chief. Often when there was some breaking news about the Lodha panel, Sourav would call up to find out more details. When we met once, I teased him, 'Get ready to be the first Test cricketer to be board chief.' He shook his head and then said with a hint of a smile, 'Arre, I am too young, no?'

Navigating the maze of board politics may test Sourav's skills, but he has the makings of a future politician. Both the left and the ruling Trinamool Congress at various times have reportedly offered to make him a Rajya Sabha MP while the BJP was keen to have him contest the 2014 Lok Sabha elections from Bengal. 'He would be the ideal new clean face for us in Bengal to attract young voters,' a BJP leader tells me. With support for the once-dominant left rapidly shrinking, the BJP is pushing to occupy the opposition space in the state. Mamata, who has vanquished the left, is equally keen to keep Ganguly within her tent of supporters. Mamata's populist Bengali subnationalism agenda has seen her identify with local sporting and cultural icons, a few of whom have even been sent to Parliament. 'To become a political leader would be a natural progression for Sourav; his popularity amongst the masses is undiminished even after retirement,' says Gautam Bhattacharya, the joint editor of the Bengali news daily *Pratidin*. 'No, no, I am not interested in electoral politics,' insists Ganguly. But there is a glint in the eye when I suggest that he could be a future chief minister of Bengal.

The idea of Sourav as Bengal chief minister is improbable but worth fantasizing about. He is, after all, the ultimate Bengali son of the soil. For all his achievements, he is in the end the boy from Behala who made his people proud, who showed guts and character to take on the world's best teams. He wears his Bengaliness on his sleeve and palate. Visit his house and tea is served with fish cutlets and mutton chaap. He loves Kolkata's Nizam kathi rolls and the biryani from the city's famous Arsalan restaurant. Every Durga Puja, dressed in dhoti-kurta, he leads the celebrations along with his entire family at the local pandal. He has hosted a popular Bengali TV quiz show, *Dadagiri Unlimited*, and even anchored *Kaun Banega Crorepati* in Bengali. He now co-owns a football franchise, Atletico de Kolkata, and has even wooed investors to the state at the Bengal investment summit. On the road from Kolkata airport to the city, there are numerous hoardings of a beaming Sourav advertising a range of products. Only life-size portraits of Chief Minister Banerjee offer serious competition to him across the Kolkata skyline. 'There are three Bengalis who are global brands who will stand the test of time – Rabindranath Tagore, Satyajit Ray and Sourav Ganguly,' says Majumdar on Sourav's standing in Bengal.

Indeed, in a state which has had little to celebrate in recent years, where social and political unrest have erupted frequently, Sourav remains a beacon of hope for the future, a symbol of untapped potential waiting to take flight. Controversial but courageous, Sourav's success is seen to have buried the stereotype of the silent, effeminate Bengali babu once and for all. Which is why when, just before the 2016 Bengal elections, I rather mischievously asked young boys playing cricket on Kolkata's maidan who they would prefer as their future leader, opinion was divided between Mamata and Sourav. 'Didi in politics, Dada in cricket, both are our leaders,' is how one youngster put it diplomatically. Sourav 'Dada' and Bengal will always be inseparable.

9

Rahul Dravid

Indian Cricket's Conscience-Keeper

India is playing Pakistan in a rare Test series at home in 1999 at Delhi's Feroz Shah Kotla, a ground where new India clashes awkwardly with the old, where the crumbling remains of Feroze Shah Tughlaq's impressive fortress are now shaded by a less striking concrete stadium.

Built in 1883, this is the second oldest international stadium in the country after Eden Gardens and has played host to many memorable cricket encounters. This is where Sunil Gavaskar equalled Sir Don Bradman's record of the most Test centuries in 1983–84, and where Sachin Tendulkar overtook his hero in 2005–06. Now my four-year-old son Ishan – watching a Test match for the first time – and I are about to witness yet another slice of history.

India–Pakistan encounters always have an added edge, cricket the hostage to the bloody scars of a divided subcontinent. But this 1999 series is different. Pakistan has won the first Test in Chennai in a thrilling finish, receiving a standing ovation from the crowd. Meanwhile, Delhi's audiences, embittered by Partition, are less forgiving of defeat to Pakistan.

We have got complimentary VIP passes for the main enclosure, a perennial badge of influence in the city of a 'don't you know who I am' swagger. The cool February breeze is comforting as is the gentle winter sun. It is the fourth innings of the game and the Indian spin bowlers led by the redoubtable Anil Kumble are on the prowl. The morning is dominated by the Pakistani openers who put on a century stand in their chase of 420 runs. At lunchtime, the crowd is silent and the tension palpable.

'Will the Pakistanis win?' Ishan asks innocently, tricolour in hand. 'No, no, they won't, we have Kumble to spin them out,' I say, offering him some fatherly reassurance. For once I am right. Between lunch and tea, Kumble – nicknamed 'Jumbo' because of his ability to get a ball to lift from the wicket like a jumbo jet – has the Pakistanis in a real spin, taking wicket after wicket, eventually leading India to a great win by picking up a record-equalling 10 wickets. It is only the second time in the history of cricket that a bowler has picked up all 10 wickets in an innings. (England's Jim Laker was the first to do so in 1956.)

My excited boy now wants to get an autograph of Kumble but the surging crowds make it impossible to get close to the players. In any case, I have to rush back to office. We are doing a special studio show to celebrate the historic achievement. Kumble's fellow Bengalurean and India colleague Rahul Dravid has been contracted as our expert for the series and we have sent a car to the team hotel to pick him up. But the car is waiting when I get a phone call. Dravid is on the line. 'Look, Rajdeep, I don't think I should be your guest on the show today. After all, it isn't every day that a bowler picks up 10 wickets in an innings, is it. This is Anil's big day, you should be interviewing him, not me.'

'But how do I get through to Anil? We go on air in an hour and his number is busy,' I ask anxiously.

'Don't worry, I will arrange this,' he tells me.

Sure enough, that evening Kumble is in our studio, we get our exclusive interview, and my son his precious autograph. Kumble is the star but in his own modest, unobtrusive way. Dravid is our silent hero, the rare cricketer who is happy to stay in the shadows and bask in the glory of a friend and colleague.

Just days after watching the Test, I'm reporting on an Indo-Pak encounter of a very different kind. Prime Minister Atal Behari Vajpayee has decided to embark on a bus yatra to Lahore, possibly the boldest initiative by an Indian prime minister to rebuild ties with our difficult neighbours. It is a courageous act of a true statesman, a goodwill gesture that gets instant support from the citizenry in both countries. It doesn't please the Pakistani army, though, which once again betrays India's trust. In June 1999, it sends its men to capture the Kargil heights along the Line of Control. War breaks out and Kumble and his 10-wicket haul are forgotten in the bloodletting.

Soon after the successful conclusion of the Kargil war, Vajpayee gives me an interview. I ask him about his Lahore yatra and whether he has any regrets. 'Nahin, nahin, hamnein shanti ke liye puri koshish ki [No, we made every effort for peace],' he says. I congratulate him on the success. 'It has nothing to do with me, congratulate our soldiers,' he insists with typical Vajpayee charm. I am bowled over much in the manner that Dravid's civility had gratified me earlier. Vajpayee and Dravid, two men I have grown to admire because they represent a precious and increasingly scarce human trait – decency in public behaviour. In contemporary India where politics and cricket seem trapped in squabbling and petty ego battles, where narcissism seems to have replaced niceness, those 1999 memories now seem to be from another age.

~

'Why is it that the heroes of Karnataka, be it in business or sports, are so soft-spoken and humble?' I ask. 'It must be the Bengaluru weather,' says N.R. Narayana Murthy, the founder of Infosys. I am in conversation with him and former All England badminton champion Prakash Padukone for a television show on leadership in the sprawling, verdant Infosys campus.

The ever-smiling Padukone concurs. 'We have the best weather so it helps us stay calm.' My producer helpfully reminds me that Vijay Mallya, the controversial and flamboyant Kingfisher boss, is also a Bengalurean and a stark exception to the rule of modest and self-effacing famous Kannadigas. But despite the awkwardness of sweeping generalizations, there is some merit in the proposition that fine weather can be a recipe for good conduct; far too many Kannadiga icons fit the bill to dismiss this as a fanciful thought.

Cricket has been no exception to the rule even though Karnataka (then Mysore) struggled to make a mark in the sport right after Independence. Unlike the Bombay and Madras presidency towns, the old Mysore state didn't have a cricket tradition. Madras, in fact, was the capital of cricket in south India in those days. Bengaluru (then Bangalore) was a sleepy cantonment town and a pensioner's paradise with limited cricket facilities. For years, the city had just one turf wicket, at Central College, and it was only in 1974–75 that the first Test was played at the newly built Chinnaswamy stadium. In the 1960s Mysore began to make a mark in the Ranji Trophy, twice reaching the semi-finals under the captaincy of V. Subramanya. (They lost both times to Mumbai.) 'Subbu gave Karnataka cricket a competitive edge and uncovered new talent,' says veteran sports journalist Vedam Jaishankar. 'Until then, there was a feudal, leisurely attitude to our cricket, almost as if the maharajas had never left.'

This was also the period when Karnataka produced its first major national cricket stars in the shape of the two spin bowling legends Erapalli Prasanna and Bhagwat Chandrasekhar. The duo were genteel sons of the soil, happy to talk cricket over a plate of idli vada and filter coffee with locals in the neighbourhood. Under Prasanna's leadership Karnataka would win the Ranji Trophy for the first time in 1974, ending Mumbai's fifteen-year monopoly. 'One of the happiest days in my life,' says the off-spinner.

By the end of the 1960s, another local hero would emerge. Gundappa Viswanath came to typify the wristy artistry of Indian cricket, a pocket-sized genius blessed with unmatched technique and skill. 'Vishy' was an iconic figure on the field but the most unassuming gent off it. He was the original nice guy of Indian cricket, nice enough to once recall Bob Taylor after he was wrongly given out in a Test match against England in 1980. 'For at least two decades, while he played the game and after, everyone who played cricket for Karnataka wanted to emulate Viswanath,' says historian Ramachandra Guha, a long-time Karnataka cricket fan.

The two 1983 World Cup winners from Karnataka, Syed Kirmani and Roger Binny, carried forward Viswanath's fine tradition of sportsmanship. Kirmani had a ready infectious smile while Binny would appear almost apologetic when he swung out a wicket. The next generation led by bowling champions Kumble and Javagal Srinath were more expressive on the field but still very much in control of their emotions off it. 'We played cricket hard but fair and with utmost respect for its traditions,' Kumble says. He and Srinath would later become Karnataka cricket administrators and contribute significantly to the sport's expansion in the state, especially with turf wickets put up in every district.

But, arguably, no one has exemplified the quintessential Karnataka cricket character better than Dravid, of whom Australian cricket historian Gideon Haigh writes, 'For most of the fifteen years at the top, Dravid was the most immaculate cricketer in the game, a batsman of preternatural serenity and a sportsman of model decorum . . . He batted as a river runs, at an immemorial pace. You could tune into an innings of his at any time and be unsure whether he had batted six hours or six minutes. He carried himself with the same easy dignity in success and failure . . .'

I first got to know Dravid when we were putting together a television series ahead of the 1999 World Cup. It was his first experience in the rapidly evolving 24x7 electronic media world and his innate curiosity and studious mind were apparent. Even before the shoot he was keen to know how many changes of clothes he should bring along, how long he should speak, what would be the nature of the questions. After every show, he would unfailingly ask, 'Was that okay?' He was attempting to do in a television studio what he had trained himself to do on the field: achieve excellence by working hard at making the best possible use of his talents.

In 2014, two years after his retirement, I invited Dravid again, this time to deliver the annual Dilip Sardesai Memorial Lecture. He came with a prepared text to speak on the oral traditions of Indian cricket, of how the age-old guru–shishya 'parampara' had seen one generation pass on the baton of cricket knowledge to the next simply by word of mouth. Dressed impeccably as ever in jacket and tie, he floored the audience with his erudite wisdom. As he finished and the audience applauded, he smiled shyly, took a few obligatory photographs and then gently turned to my mother. 'Thank you for inviting me, ma'am, I hope that was fine.' It was said with unpretentious refinement, like a student who strives to get better even after an A-plus grade. It was vintage Dravid, a gentleman who fulfils his duties with a sense of propriety, whose common courtesies and understated charm stand out in a universe of endless marketing and constant self-promotion. His is a story of grit and discipline, of hunger and ambition, but above all else a story that is reassuring as it confirms that nice guys do win sometimes.

~

Born in 1973, Dravid grew up in an upper-middle-class home in Bengaluru. His father Sharad was a food scientist in Kissan, a popular brand making jams, squashes and ketchups (hence Dravid's early nickname 'Jammy') and his mother Pushpa an art lecturer in a leading college. A double-income family living in Bengaluru's Indiranagar colony – a parallel could perhaps be drawn with the Gavaskar home in Mumbai. But while Mumbai's Maharashtrian colonies were the heart of Indian cricket and Gavaskar had an uncle who played for the country as an early guide, middle-class Bengaluru was less of a natural cricket nursery. Indiranagar in the 1970s was a distant suburb with wide open spaces, ideal for tennis-ball cricket; today, it is the heart of the Bengaluru construction boom. Living in the neighbourhood were the likes of former India wicketkeeper Sadanand Viswanath and Prasanna. 'As a kid just to watch Prasanna walking his dog in the locality was pretty special for us,' recalls Dravid.

The family did not have a legacy in the sport but Sharad was definitely a cricket enthusiast. 'My father loved cricket and would spend hours listening to the radio commentary. When there was a Test match in Bengaluru, he would try and at least get tickets for the weekend so he could take my brother and me to the game. I guess that's where my cricket dream was first nurtured with Gavaskar and Viswanath as early heroes,' says Dravid, adding that a picture of the beaming Dravid boys with Gavaskar is a cherished memory. But cricket's role was always secondary to education. 'My parents were very clear: first came studies, then cricket,' he says.

Like Gavaskar, Dravid also went to an elite Jesuit institution, St Joseph's Boys' High School. The school had a sporting ethos that wasn't confined to cricket. 'Our number one sport was hockey. We had peers like Sandeep Somesh and Anil Aldrin who played for India and even I was good enough to be in the reckoning for the Karnataka junior hockey team. Cricket was seasonal, played for a couple of months in the year, nothing like Mumbai where you play round the year. I often joke with people that when Sachin Tendulkar was practising seven hours a day in Mumbai as a thirteen-year-old, I used to practise three times a week for fifteen minutes batting in the nets and the rest of the time I would play hockey, badminton or study,' remembers Dravid.

Schools cricket in Bengaluru was also not as competitive as in Mumbai. As mentioned earlier, there was only one main turf wicket at the Chinnaswamy stadium, so Dravid grew up playing cricket on the matting wickets in the city. The practice made him a strong back-foot player from an early age, but while he scored runs at the under-15 level in Karnataka, it was nowhere near what his contemporaries were achieving in other parts of the country. In 1987, fourteen-year-old

Dravid travelled to Cuttack as a backup wicketkeeper-batsman for the South Zone team to play West Zone. 'That is when I saw Sachin for the first time and was simply awestruck with the way he played. He was the same age as us but batting on a different planet,' he says.

A year later, when Dravid attended a national junior camp in Kolkata, he was again made aware of the gulf between the cricket in Bengaluru and the level of the more well-trained boys from Mumbai. 'Vasu Paranjpe was the coach and I doubt if you had asked him who out of the thirty kids at the camp would play for India he would have mentioned my name. I was simply a big fish in a small pond called Bengaluru and had a long way to go,' says Dravid.

Dravid's school and club coach Keki Tarapore was an early mentor. The two had first met when Dravid was a thirteen-year-old; his father had taken him to a Karnataka State Cricket Association (KSCA) summer camp. Like many coaches of top cricketers, Tarapore himself was an average player, having briefly represented Mysore in the Ranji Trophy in the 1940s. But he had a passion for teaching cricket. 'He was a classical old-world coach who instilled values of discipline and hard work and taught me the basics of the game, especially the need to hit straight and keep the ball on the ground at all times,' says Dravid. Hours would be spent on shadow practice or with a ball hung up on a string to ensure the bat came down straight, copybook training right out of an MCC coaching manual. This would stand Dravid in good stead in the future, as would Tarapore's insistence that his students always be perfectly attired cricketers right down to polished white shoes.

Among Dravid's schoolmates was Fazal Khaleel, who also played for Karnataka. 'The first thing that struck us about Rahul was how focused he was even as a teenager. When he went out to bat, it was as if nothing else mattered but staying on the wicket and scoring runs. He could be boring to watch but his appetite for run-making even at the under-15 level was insatiable. I remember him scoring a double century once against Kerala as a fourteen-year-old and it looked like he was never going to get out,' says Khaleel.

The parallels with India's original run machine Gavaskar are uncanny. If Gavaskar could sit in a crowded train and read a book with utmost concentration, Dravid could do the same in a cramped local bus on his way to practice. 'He was a damn good student, someone who could compartmentalize his life; he was able to juggle his life between cricket and academics with ease while the rest of us struggled,' remembers Khaleel. When other teenagers in their group would party, Dravid would prefer an early night and an extra half-hour in the nets the next morning. 'Rahul told me once, "I just want to give the next five years to becoming the best cricketer I can be." He wasn't the most talented junior cricketer but he had an extraordinary level of commitment to the sport,' says Khaleel.

His school principal Father Dennis Coelho remembers Dravid as a model student, studious and self-motivated. 'We even let him miss classes when he had a major cricket tournament because we knew he would always catch up with his studies,' Coelho says. It wasn't easy, though, especially in a family where both parents were working. He would have to get up at the crack of dawn to take the bus or cycle to the KSCA nets which were five or six kilometres away, finish at 8.30 a.m., then eat breakfast on the run (sometimes just an apple!) and rush to school with his kitbag, school books and lunch box. 'I guess I just wanted to play cricket badly enough not to think about any of this as hardship,' says Dravid.

But the first major transformation in his cricketing life would come only at St Joseph's, the result of something as simple as finally buying a motorcycle. 'In school, I used to travel by bus or bicycle to practice, which was never easy while carrying a heavy kitbag. In junior college, it became easier because I was suddenly more mobile as a result of the motorcycle.'

His parents had enrolled him in commerce, itself a difficult decision since most Bengaluru students with an interest in cricket usually opted for an engineering course. 'Engineering colleges used to actively support cricket since you had only one yearly exam and you could play cricket round the year and then mug for the exams in the last two months,' says Dravid. Many Karnataka cricketers including Kumble studied engineering. Dravid chose commerce instead with the clear understanding with his parents that if he didn't succeed in his cricket dream by the second year of his B.Com. course, he should be ready to apply for a chartered accountant degree or an MBA programme.

But his parents needn't have worried. At seventeen, barely a year into college, Dravid made his first-class debut for Karnataka. He scored 82 in that match and followed it up with three consecutive centuries. His boyhood hero Viswanath had retired and was now a selector. His first captain, Kirmani, was hugely encouraging, and he was surrounded by other talented young men like Kumble, Srinath and Venkatesh Prasad, all of whom shared that fierce ambition to succeed. 'I think it helped to have many senior cricketers around us in club and first-class cricket who were always available to guide us,' says Kumble. 'When I first played for Karnataka as a nineteen-year-old, my captain was Roger Binny who smiled, put his arm around me and said "Call me Roger".'

A golden cricket period was about to unfold in Karnataka, culminating in three Ranji titles in a decade. As many as eight players from the state represented the country in the 1998–99 season. Karnataka had lived under the shadow of Mumbai for years but was now the new powerhouse of Indian cricket. 'Dravid was the key factor in our rise because he gave our batting the solidity it needed so our strong bowling attack always had runs to play with,' points out Kumble.

It wasn't just on the cricket field that the balance of power had shifted by the late 1990s. Mumbai was the country's undisputed commercial hub while Bengaluru was typecast as the somnolent garden city, ideal for retirement. But through the decade, as the IT revolution gathered steam, the laid-back city of pensioners was embraced by the innovative vigour of the young. The Infosys and Wipro of India's Silicon Valley were ready to challenge Mumbai's hegemony over the stock market numbers' game just like Karnataka's cricketers dared Mumbai on the field. Entrepreneurship, like cricket, was bridging the geographical divide and Bengaluru was refashioned as India's start-up capital.

However, breaking into a strong India side wasn't easy for Dravid, who played more than 50 first-class matches over five years and scored more than 15 centuries before finally edging closer to an India cap. He even did a one-year correspondence MBA course as a backup just in case he couldn't fulfil his Indian cricket dream. But such was his desire to play cricket and for constant self-improvement that he never let his guard down. He spent two summers in Chennai in the mid 1990s, playing for India Cements and living in rented accommodation with five other cricketers – his singular ambition of getting more exposure to turf wickets in the city. 'In hindsight, I guess the extended grind in first-class cricket helped improve my game and made me mentally stronger and more mature. I was ready as ever to play for India at twenty-three as I would have been as a teenager,' he says.

The long apprenticeship was finally over when Dravid was picked for the Indian team to tour England in 1996. But even he couldn't have anticipated the journey ahead. The shy, scholarly boy from Bengaluru was about to pass his most rigorous exam yet.

~

Like all cricket fans, Dravid's father Sharad had paid homage at Lord's on a visit to London, taking a picture of himself in front of the pavilion. Young Dravid had been reared on cricket nostalgia, on stories not just of the 1983 World Cup triumph at Lord's, but also the folklore of the world's most famous ground. 'I went to Lord's knowing that these were the gates through which Bradman and Gavaskar had walked, that this was the ground which had been witness to some of cricket's great moments,' he says.

As a student of the game's history, Lord's was perhaps an appropriate place for Dravid to make his Test debut. His first Test cap was serendipitous. On the eve of the match, senior batsman Sanjay Manjrekar suffered an ankle injury and pulled out. 'If Sanjay had not been unfit, I doubt I would have ever played the Lord's Test or any Test in that series since I was only a reserve batsman. I guess it was pure destiny,' reminisces Dravid.

When he walked out to bat for the first time, the team was in deep trouble. At 202 for 5, India was still well over a hundred runs behind England. Dravid was the last recognized batsman, a twenty-three-year-old batting at number seven since the team had picked an extra batsman after the batting collapse in the first Test. If he had any reason to feel reassured it was the fact that there was another Test debutant at the other end. Six months his senior, Sourav Ganguly was already on his way to a remarkable debut century. Dravid had known Sourav since their under-19 days, and the duo had batted together for India-A as well. 'I guess having Sourav as a partner on debut who was himself batting so well increased my comfort factor and helped settle the nerves,' says Dravid.

For the next few hours, the debutants restored Indian pride. Sourav scored a majestic 131 as the duo added 94 runs. Dravid himself missed out on a century, scoring 95 before being caught behind the wicket. He walked without waiting for the umpire's signal, an early measure of the man's value system. He had missed out on a slice of history, a debut century at Lord's, but 95 wasn't a bad start. 'I guess there was a bit of disappointment at coming so close but also the realization that I had managed to take the first step up,' says Dravid. His innings had been trademark Dravid, built on firm defence and strong on-side play with a display of unflappable temperament. 'I think the first thing that struck anyone who watched Dravid bat that day was just how calm he was. It was as if he was born to play Test cricket,' says Sandeep Patil, then the Indian team coach.

Dravid did not look back from that day in Lord's. He may not have scored a hundred on debut but he had begun a flirtation with England that would blossom into a full-blown romance. In 13 Tests in England spread over four series in the next fifteen years, he scored

6 Test hundreds and 4 fifties at an average of almost 70 runs an innings. That is easily the most impressive performance by an Indian batsman in the original home of the game.

If Gavaskar built his reputation in the West Indies, it was in the English summers that Dravid carved a special place in the hearts of connoisseurs. His technique, built on a big strike forward and assured back-foot play, was ideally suited to handle the vagaries of swing and seam in English conditions. He played the ball late, knew exactly where his off stump was, and was rarely caught on the crease.

'I guess I just fell in love with England from the very beginning,' Dravid says, explaining his success in the British Isles. The English way of life seemed to suit his temperament and quest for privacy – he could soak in the game's ethos, go for long quiet walks in parks and relish London's cultural cosmopolitanism. In 2000, he even signed up with English county Kent and three years later spent his honeymoon playing cricket in Scotland.

His Kent colleagues have fond memories of their Indian visitor. As Ed Smith, his county colleague, wrote in a tribute on Dravid's retirement, 'When Rahul Dravid walked into the dressing room of the St Lawrence ground in Canterbury on a cold spring morning, you could tell he was different from all the others. He did not swagger with cockiness or bristle with macho competitiveness. He went quietly round the room, shaking the hand of every Kent player, greeting everyone the same, from the captain to the most junior. It was not the mannered behaviour of a seasoned overseas professional but the natural courtesy of a real gentleman. We met a special human being first, an international cricketer second.'

Dignity with timeless steel, as Smith puts it, came to define the Dravid persona. A year after his memorable debut, he had scored a maiden Test century in the 'bullring' of the Wanderers stadium in Johannesburg, South Africa, again in difficult conditions. Mental toughness was already his calling card. In a one-day game on the same 1997 South Africa tour, he smashed Allan Donald, arguably the world's fastest bowler then, over his head for a six. It was an

incredible stroke of courage and audacity from a batsman supposed
to be a strokeless wonder. As Donald let off a string of expletives,
Dravid looked on impassively. That was the moment the world knew
they were watching the rise of a special cricketer.

'Did you know that Rahul's father was undergoing a serious
operation in Chennai when he was playing that game in South Africa?
But such was his focus that not only did he play the game, he was
our highest scorer. He took the evening flight out to Chennai after
the match. That is when we knew what true courage in adversity is
all about,' recalls Srinath, his Karnataka and India senior.

Dravid's performance in that South Africa series set a new
template for Indian cricket, the beginning of the era of batting
glory, no longer defined by the dependence on a single individual but
thriving on durable partnerships. The 1990s had seen the ascendance
of coalition politics at the Centre where no one major party could
run a government without the backing of smaller groups. On the
cricket field, Sachin had been the lone ranger so far but now he had
a comrade to share the burden, a cricketer blessed with similar guts
and commitment. Jammy was now rechristened 'The Wall', solid,
immovable and impenetrable.

~

Less than five years after his Test debut, Dravid's career was at the
crossroads. Pigeonholed initially as a Test batsman, he was even
inexplicably dropped from the one-day side in 1998 before going
on to score nearly 500 runs in the 1999 World Cup. He hit half a
dozen Test centuries, including one in each innings of a match in
New Zealand. He scored at an average of more than 50 runs an
innings, and was seemingly established as India's number three
batsman. And yet the pundits were not convinced, suggesting that
his defensive technique and tortoise-like pace of run-making was not
good enough to take on quality attacks. When the all-conquering
Australians under Steve Waugh came to India in 2001, there were

even calls to drop him. He had had a bad tour of Australia in 1999–2000 and when he failed in the first Test in Mumbai, critics were ready to push the knife in.

All that changed over two and a half remarkable days at Eden Gardens in Kolkata in the second Test. India were following on and seemed to have little chance of survival against a team that had won sixteen Tests in a row when Dravid joined V.V.S. Laxman a few overs before stumps on the third day. He had been dismissed early in the first innings and pushed down the order to number six in the second with Laxman taking his regular number three spot. 'I remember when I walked in to bat in the second innings, the first thing Steve Waugh said to me was: "From number three down to number six, one more failure and you will be out of the side,"' recalls Dravid. Waugh was guilty of playing the usual Australian mind games but he couldn't have chosen a more ill-timed moment to rouse a sleeping Indian giant.

For the next day and a bit more, Dravid and Laxman stitched together the most memorable partnership in Indian cricket history, scoring a record 376 runs, batting all of the fourth day and taking India to safety. Harbhajan Singh then spun the Australians out in the last session to pull off an astonishing comeback win. Dravid had batted for 353 balls and 446 minutes and hit 20 fours before being run out for 180. Laxman batted for 452 balls and 631 minutes to score a mammoth 281 runs with 44 fours. It was a batting marathon that defied the best bowling attack in the game led by Glenn McGrath and Shane Warne.

Dravid and Laxman had batted together for years, two gentle souls from the south in a similar age bracket (Laxman is 22 months younger) and from similar middle-class backgrounds. Laxman's parents were doctors in Hyderabad, and like Rahul he too had been faced with a familiar dilemma at one stage to choose between cricket and higher education. Laxman had first seen Dravid play in an under-19 match and had always admired his Karnataka counterpart's single-minded focus. 'I guess we are soul brothers with similar value systems but when you are batting together, all that matters is scoring runs and not getting out,' says Laxman.

That fourth day in Kolkata, the refusal to back down in the face of adversity was the hallmark of the partnership. While Dravid initially struggled, Laxman was in the form of his life, the bat a sitar string in the wristy hands of a maestro. 'It took me a while to get going but Laxman at the other end was in the zone from the start and timing the ball with such ease as if he was batting on a different wicket,' says Dravid.

Laxman adds, 'You know, this is typical Rahul, he will always underplay his role.' The truth is the duo had shared a sacred space where sport was an enchanting, almost spiritual exercise. 'We set ourselves small targets,' says Laxman. 'Let's bat out an over, an hour, a session, we kept telling each other. We didn't speak much, our focus was simply on not getting out.'

Like a meditative monk, Dravid was totally absorbed in his art. Time was reduced to irrelevance, the cheering crowds a blip in the distance as his serene batting skills took over. When he finally got to a century, he did something very uncharacteristic – he punched the air, bat pointing ferociously towards the press box, with a touch of anger in his eyes. He was physically drained but needed to find release from the heat of battle, having finally settled all arguments over his mental strength and batting skills. 'I guess I need not have reacted the way I did but it was obviously very satisfying to win that battle against very tough opponents,' says Dravid.

When the duo returned to the pavilion unbeaten on the fourth day, the magnitude of the achievement began to sink in. 'The battle we had that day was mental as much as physical. I had a back problem and almost didn't play the match while Rahul had a slight fever, so batting through it all required us to keep the mind strong,' says Laxman. The Australians too knew they were witnessing something special, which was why the on-field chatter quickly subsided. 'By the end, Adam Gilchrist behind the stumps was more intent on admiring our shots than saying anything to us,' remembers Laxman.

Typical of the two unassuming individuals, there wasn't much time or need for celebration either. The evening of their record-breaking partnership, the duo went to skipper Sourav Ganguly's home for a quiet dinner. The next day, having secured a famous win, they were on a flight to Chennai for the final Test. 'Rahul and I got on to the flight and suddenly we saw all the passengers stand up and applaud us, that was pretty special,' says Laxman with a smile.

Most cricket observers believe that the Dravid–Laxman partnership was a defining moment in Indian cricket. 'It gave us enormous self-belief that transformed us as a team and individuals,' says Ganguly. Just before the series, India had appointed the Kiwi John Wright as their coach, the first foreign coach of the Indian team, chosen amidst controversy. Only a year earlier, the scourge of match-fixing had shamed Indian cricket and led fans to lose faith in their icons. The Eden Gardens partnership and the victory over Australia restored trust in the sport and allowed the rejuvenation of Indian cricket. 'I guess that win was crucial because if we had lost, people may have lost confidence in what we were attempting to achieve with a new coach and a fresh philosophy,' says Dravid.

Which is why along with India's twin victories in 1971 and the 1983 World Cup, the 2001 Kolkata Test must be seen as truly ground-breaking. It revived Indian cricket when the stench of corruption was threatening its future. In 2001 the BJP president Bangaru Laxman was caught on tape in a sting operation accepting a bribe in a fictitious defence deal. The revelation only confirmed the widespread suspicion that Indian politics was a cesspit of sleaze. Cricketers were revered because the adoring fans were convinced they were not like our netas. But match-fixing had punctured cricket's claim to be 'pure' and 'unpolluted'; the sport's reputation was in tatters and disillusionment had set in. What match-fixing destroyed in 2000, an incredible forty-eight hours in Kolkata helped restore – a belief in the inherent goodness of sport and its skilled practitioners.

Eden Gardens didn't just resuscitate Indian cricket, it altered the careers of its two central heroes forever. Laxman had been in and out of the Indian team but was now established as a 'Very, Very Special' cricketer. Dravid's cricket achievements moved into another orbit. Between April 2002 and July 2006, he played 49 Tests and scored 4720 runs at an average nudging towards an astounding 70 runs an innings (68.40) with 14 hundreds and 22 fifties. In that period, India won Tests in Australia, Pakistan, South Africa, England and the West Indies. It was arguably the most glorious period in Indian cricket history and Dravid was its central pillar. 'Until 2001, we would rely on Sachin to win us games. For the next five years, it was Rahul whose batting took us to another level,' says Ganguly.

In the golden years, Dravid scored match-winning centuries while batting first on a green wicket at Headingley, and a double century and an unbeaten half-century against Australia at Adelaide. Then he made a career-best 270 against Pakistan in Rawalpindi that propelled India to a historic first ever series win in Pakistan. 'In those four–five years, I don't think anyone in the history of Indian cricket batted better than Rahul; he just raised the bar for himself when the team needed it the most,' says Aakash Chopra, the former India opener, now a cricket commentator-writer.

So what changed in Dravid's batting to make him the world's number one player in that period? 'I guess I was just more mature, more in control of my craft and most importantly more relaxed in my mind,' he says. Laxman, who had watched Dravid from close proximity since his under-19 days, believes that the 2002 England tour was the turning point. 'Look, Rahul has always had a great work ethic and technique but he could get very intense and put a lot of pressure on himself. But after his success in England, I got the sense that he felt more secure and was now free to express himself without obsessing about his game,' he says. A predominantly on-side player, Dravid became more of an all-round batsman, dominating attacks in both Test and one-day cricket, scoring runs with robotic consistency. 'I guess I was at my peak as a batsman,' says Dravid.

What also helped was the benign presence of Wright. The two had met at Kent and struck up an instant rapport. Like Dravid, Wright had worked hard at his game. He was an old-fashioned cricket journeyman who was passionate about the sport. 'John's passion and knowledge helped inculcate a confidence in the team, setting new targets for us, helping us realize our individual and collective goals without any feeling of insecurity,' says Dravid.

Dravid, though, wasn't the sole shining star on the pitch. Indian cricket was experiencing a batting renaissance – Dravid, Laxman, Tendulkar, Ganguly and Virender Sehwag were now the Fab Five, the best-ever run-scoring juggernaut Indian cricket has witnessed. Between them they added over 50,000 Test runs. 'We enjoyed each other's company. There was healthy competition but never any rivalry,' says Dravid. 'We just inspired each other to do better by our performance.'

Adds Laxman, 'Sachin was the original leader, he set a certain benchmark and slowly we all realized the need to take greater responsibility and aim higher.' Sourav adds, 'I think it helped that we were all actually very different kinds of players so we could express ourselves very easily without trying to copy the other.' Dravid is more modest. 'Of all the five, I guess I had the least natural talent since talent is often measured in terms of strokeplay. But maybe I did have a different skill, the ability to concentrate and push myself just that bit harder to get the best out of my talent.'

Sportswriter Rohit Brijnath puts it brilliantly while paying fulsome tribute to Dravid on his retirement. 'Laxman offered me art, Sehwag liberation, Tendulkar consistent genius, but Dravid taught us that the ability to reassure is a gift. For such a neat man, he loved an ugly scrap. Runs might emerge in unsightly dribbles – sometimes it was as if to be uninhibited was an act of immodesty for him – but he'd keep going. A leave, a block, a block, a leave, and this should have been boring – and well, yes, sometimes it was – except, by the end he'd built a lead, or rescued a situation, or offered India a winning chance, and you'd look at this man, shirt bound by sweat, ferocious in his concentration, and just think, bloody hell. Struggle, in all its forms, was his hymn.'

∼

Dravid stayed away from controversy through his long and distinguished career like a careful batsman ducking bouncers. The one occasion he was reprimanded for his on-field conduct was in 2004 when he was fined 50 per cent of his match fee for alleged ball-tampering. Fragments of an energy lozenge he was chewing were found mixed with saliva on the shiny side of the white ball. 'It was an innocent mistake,' says Dravid apologetically. 'Using saliva to shine the ball is a long-held practice; it was never my intention to gain any unfair advantage.' You believe Dravid because his personal ethical code has always been a badge of honour.

Ironically, it was the appointment of Dravid as India captain in the winter of 2005 that dented his 'nice guy' image. He replaced Ganguly in controversial circumstances, with an outraged Bengali media suggesting their Dada was the victim of a 'conspiracy'. Greg Chappell had just become the India coach and the charge was that Chappell had ousted Ganguly.

Dravid was caught in the crossfire and his well-preserved reputation became collateral damage. Years later Ganguly even claimed in a television interview that 'Rahul was aware of what was happening but could not control Chappell'. Tendulkar in his biography chose to attack Chappell, accusing him of being a dictatorial 'ringmaster' who wanted to replace Dravid with Sachin as captain.

Dravid has maintained a studied silence on the Chappell issue, refusing to join the acrimonious player exchanges. 'Look, it is not for me to judge another individual. I am sure Greg himself must have introspected and realized that in hindsight he could have done a few things differently. Maybe I could have done things differently. We all need to turn the gaze inwards, become better individuals,' he says philosophically, clearly not wanting to stir the pot.

However, the Dravid–Chappell partnership did flourish for a while. As captain, Dravid led India to series wins in England and the West Indies, Test victories in South Africa and Pakistan. The Indian team under him held the one-day record for the most wins while chasing a target. His captaincy was imaginative and forward-looking with a focus on blooding young cricketers and raising fielding and fitness standards – a template for the future. 'I think all of us, including Greg, wanted to take Indian cricket forward. He had some good ideas, some worked, some didn't, but there was no lack of effort,' says Dravid, looking back on the turbulent period in Indian cricket.

Sadly, Dravid's tenure as Indian captain was defined by a World Cup exit in 2007 in the qualifying rounds after a shocking defeat to Bangladesh. The image of an ashen-faced Dravid desperately chewing his fingernails in the dressing room became the enduring image as the Indian team tumbled out of the tournament of a disastrous campaign. 'We had worked hard in the lead-up to the tournament but it just didn't happen for us when it mattered. I guess you are judged by how you perform in World Cups and we didn't do well enough,' he says. Again, no excuses, no recrimination, no finger pointing, no anger; in the calm, philosophical attitude, you sense an inner peace, possibly a consequence of his experiments with meditation.

That defeat led to the sacking of Chappell as coach but Dravid stayed back to lead India to a series win in England in 2007, the first since 1986. He wasn't at his run-making best but that didn't stop him from putting the wounds of the World Cup debacle behind him. Within days of the triumph, Dravid dramatically announced his decision to stand down as captain. 'I think I just stopped enjoying the job, maybe it was the traumatic World Cup exit, or just being on the road playing and captaining non-stop. I think to be a successful India captain, you need to get up every morning feeling excited about the challenge, and maybe during that England tour, I just didn't feel like that any longer,' he reflects.

It was, in hindsight, a strange but courageous call. In India, you don't give up any position without kicking and screaming, certainly not the captaincy of the Indian cricket team, and certainly not just after winning a series. Sunil Gavaskar was the previous Indian captain to step down after winning a one-day tournament in Australia in 1985 but even he did so at the very last stage of his career. Dravid made his exit when he was under no immediate pressure, when he could have easily carried on for a few more years. Maybe the dressing room politics weighed him down, maybe he never got over the Chappell saga or maybe his own dip in form troubled him. Or maybe he was just being archetypal Dravid: an intense but always honourable man who felt it was time for someone else to drive the team. After all, putting team before self has been a lasting legacy of Dravid's career.

Perhaps Dravid's decision to quit the captaincy could have been emulated around the same time by another figure in public life blessed with similar attributes. Like Dravid, Dr Manmohan Singh was a man of uncommon dignity and integrity. He too could have resigned as prime minister in 2009 when he was forced to compromise under coalition pressures and accommodate tainted ministers in his cabinet after being re-elected. Like Dravid, he could have bowed out with his upright image intact. Instead, by hanging on for another five-year term, he was perceived as a political survivor instead of a role model. A leaf from Dravid's book could have enhanced Dr Singh's stature.

The best example of Dravid's selfless attitude to the sport is reflected in his decision to declare the Indian innings in the 2004 Multan Test with Tendulkar batting on 194 and in sight of a double century. In a country obsessed with statistical milestones and where the people accorded a special divine status to Tendulkar, this was as tough a call as any for an Indian captain. It left Tendulkar fuming, the fans fretting, and the media speculating. But the man who took it was convinced he had done the right thing for the team. 'We were reaching the end of the third day, the Pakistani fielders were tired after being on the field for so long, we were a bowler short [Zaheer Khan was injured] and we needed time to bowl out the Pakistanis again. In hindsight, if I had known the match would be over by the fourth day, I wouldn't have taken the decision and perhaps batted longer. But at the time it seemed the right thing to do in the team's interests,' says Dravid.

The controversy simmered for years even though Dravid had a long chat with Tendulkar the next morning to clear the air. Critics of the decision even mention that India won the game to pave the way for a historic series win in Pakistan. Protective coach Wright described it as a 'collective' team decision to reduce pressure on the skipper. Dravid, though, is clear that as captain, the final call was his alone. 'Look, the buck stops with the captain and I take full responsibility for the Multan declaration,' he says emphatically. India has become notorious for the presence of men in powerful positions routinely passing the buck with little accountability but Dravid once again showed himself to be remarkably different. Possessed with rare courage of conviction, in Dravid's moral universe the buck for his actions, good or bad, stops with him. While many contemporaries sought short-cuts to success, he consciously chose to take the longer road, to become Indian cricket's conscience-keeper.

~

Dravid announced his retirement on 9 March 2012, just weeks after turning forty. He had endured a difficult tour of Australia, struggling to score runs and more worryingly being dismissed after getting bowled in six of the eight innings on tour. It seemed that the wear and tear of playing international cricket continuously for sixteen years (he played his first 93 Tests without a break till he had a bout of viral fever before a match) had finally taken a toll on his body and mind. 'I was still enjoying the game but it obviously becomes tougher as you get into your late thirties and I didn't want to ever be a liability to the side,' he says. The poor run in Australia had convinced him his time

was up. He had, in fact, planned on retiring after the England tour
of 2011. 'I was taking it series by series and had told my wife Vijeta
to be prepared to come to London for the final Test of the tour. As
it turned out, I had a great series, a kind of last flicker of the candle,
which tempted me to play for another year,' he says.

In that England series, as the rest of the Indian batsmen
struggled, Dravid hit 3 centuries in 4 Tests, and filled up one of the
few remaining blanks in his hugely impressive CV – a hundred at
Lord's. 'I had just missed out being on the Lord's honours board in
my first Test there but I got it in my last,' he points out. The circle
of his cricketing life was now complete.

He announced his decision to retire without any fanfare at a press
conference where he was, as always, impeccably dressed in a full suit.
A few months later, when India played a Test match in Bengaluru,
Dravid and his family were felicitated by the BCCI. A wave to the
crowd, a few obligatory photographs, and he was gone. Contrast this
to the manner of Tendulkar's extended and rapturous farewell a year
later when he completed his 200th Test in front of his adoring fans
in Mumbai.

Tendulkar's role in the Indian team through much of his career
was like Amitabh Bachchan's in a multi-starrer in the 1970s where
the other actors would be pushed into the role of supporting artistes.
Dravid had his legion of fans too but the man himself was always
a reluctant public figure. 'Rahul is a very private man who likes to
hang out with a few friends. He has never been a showman,' says his
school friend Khaleel.

Being away from the arc lights suited a person like Dravid, who
was so immersed in his own personal quest to achieve excellence.
'Look, Sachin is in a league of his own. When the rest of us were
struggling to make a mark in junior cricket, he was taking on Waqar
and Wasim in a Test match. He was a phenomenon,' says Dravid
candidly. He says he once told Tendulkar's wife Anjali in jest that
their son Arjun had a long way to go to emulate his father. 'For that,

he will have to not play in local schools' cricket but will have to face Dale Steyn at fifteen years old instead.'

His career record is second only to Tendulkar's, and way superior to any other Indian batsman of his generation. A mammoth 13,288 runs, with 36 hundreds and 63 half-centuries at an average of 52.31 puts him second only to the Master Blaster. A silver medal in any sport is often seen as a missed opportunity but in Dravid's case his runs were truly worth their weight in gold. His Test statistics reveal his value to the team – more century partnerships (88), more balls faced (31,258) and the most runs made at the crucial number three position (10,524) than any other player in the game's history are confirmation of the fact that if Tendulkar was the emperor who left Indian cricket fans in awe with his regal splendour, then Dravid was the general who constructed the fortress that defiantly guarded the palace at all times.

Nothing illustrates this better than his performance overseas. He is the only major Indian batsman to have a better average outside India than in more familiar conditions. In fact he was often India's 'go to' man and match-winner in overseas Tests. India won 15 Tests abroad during Dravid's career (excluding Tests against Bangladesh and Zimbabwe) and in those games he scored 1577 runs at 65.70, outscoring even the mighty Tendulkar. 'I remember Javagal Srinath telling me when I was starting off my career that the true test of a batsman is to score runs abroad. I think I just liked to embrace the culture of whichever country I played the game in, to find out more about its food, its history, its society. In India, you often end up sitting in the team hotel and ordering room service because you'll be surrounded by fans wherever you go. While touring you can switch off and just enjoy new experiences.'

The other feature that stands out in Dravid's career is his constant evolution as player and person. He started off as an average fielder but ended his career as the most successful outfielder in the history of the sport, the first to take more than 200 catches, most of them at first slip, a position that requires enormous concentration. 'I think it helped that I have big hands,' he says in his understated manner even while admitting to spending hours practising slip-catching as a young man playing for Karnataka.

When he started playing the game, he was dubbed a boring strokeless wonder. By the end of his career, he had played 344 one-dayers, scored 10,889 runs and struck 12 hundreds and 83 fifties, including one off just 22 balls, the second fastest by an Indian. The streak of adaptability saw him eventually embrace even Twenty20 cricket where, after a slow start, he enjoyed a fair amount of success in the IPL with Rajasthan Royals. 'I guess I learnt to play a few more shots along the way. I can reverse sweep the spinners but I'm not brave enough yet to try to scoop and sweep even the fast bowlers like the new-generation cricketers can,' he says with a laugh.

Through all the highs and lows, Dravid remained a committed team man. This was reflected in his willingness to keep wickets for India in as many as 73 one-day matches. He had kept wickets for his school and at the junior level because there was a vacancy for a wicketkeeper in the first coaching camp he attended in Bengaluru. He then gave it up to focus on his batting. But years later when coach Wright and skipper Ganguly suggested he keep wickets so that the team could fit in an extra player, he readily agreed. Being a premier batsman and also keeping wickets requires an extremely high level of fitness but Dravid agreed to do it in the team's interests. 'Cricket is a unique sport, it is a team game located in the context of individual achievement. You need to do well individually, but you also need to imbibe the team ethos. Maybe that's why I loved it so much,' he explains.

That also might explain why he would often celebrate more on the cricket field when he took a catch than when he scored a century. 'My wife often tells me that she has seen me at my happiest on the ground when I took a good catch. Maybe that's because when you take a catch, it's not just about what you've done as an individual but also how you've contributed to the bowler and the team's success that makes you feel nice,' he says. This approach to the game can only be endorsed by a highly evolved individual like Dravid.

Which is why when I ask him the inevitable question about how he would like to be remembered as a cricketer, his answer is fascinating. 'I am not much of a numbers person. It's nice to have achieved statistical landmarks but I'm not going to sit here and say that I'm a permanent number three batsman in an all-time great India eleven. Who knows, with time there will be others who will achieve even more. What I will say though and what gives me a sense of pride and satisfaction is that I gave my hundred per cent at all times and tried to make the utmost use of the abilities I had to become the best cricketer I could be!'

This attitude has earned Dravid the unstinted respect of his peers. Aakash Chopra is a self-confessed Dravid fan. 'The greatness of Rahul Dravid is that he never stopped working at his game,' he says, pointing out how he made technical adjustments through his career to become more than just a defensive 'wall' with a strong bottom-hand grip that initially limited his shot-making skills. Chopra comes up with a classic one-liner to explain the Dravid–Tendulkar comparison. 'Sachin was born to play cricket; Dravid made himself good enough to play the game, which is why I bow to his genius.' Manjrekar, who, like Dravid, was once seen as too absorbed in his own technique, describes the Karnataka man's success as the 'ultimate triumph of the mind in sport'.

Kumble first saw Dravid while playing junior cricket in Bengaluru, and he believes that no one has worked harder and with more discipline at bettering his game. 'I remember in 2007 when he was bowled by a Shoaib Akhtar yorker in a Test, he went immediately to the nets to see if his bat was coming down properly or not. I had to tell him to relax and remind him that he had scored a hundred only one Test earlier! Even in the nets, he just didn't want to get out or play a bad shot,' says Kumble. When he was out for 82 on his

Ranji debut, Srinath recalls Dravid being disconsolate all evening. 'A seventeen-year-old has scored 82 which is pretty good and yet he is upset that he didn't get a hundred and is constantly berating himself, but then that is Rahul for you, he is never satisfied till he has achieved perfection,' says Srinath.

A few years ago at a cricket conclave, I asked Steve Waugh, the former Australian captain and someone whose raw courage and defiant spirit Dravid says he learnt much from, which Indian cricketer he admired the most. 'Look, Sachin is probably the greatest Indian cricketer ever. But if you asked me for an Indian cricketer to bat for my life and someone I respect the most, then I would go with Rahul.' When I told Dravid about this, he gave a faint smile and blushed.

He blushes again when I refer to him as cricket's 'last gentleman' who has never let his guard down on or off the field. 'Look, I have got angry and thrown my bat in the dressing room. I once blew up at the team when we lost a Test under my captaincy to England in Mumbai. I have even thrown my cap on the ground when the Rajasthan Royals lost a match and we failed to qualify for the IPL knockouts,' he reminds me. My response is that gentlemen are entitled to lose their cool once in a while. The lasting image of Dravid the cricketer will be of someone who carried himself with dignity at all times, a throwback to an age when the sport was played with poise and pride.

~

For Indian cricket's modern greats, an afterlife in the media – doing television commentary or writing columns – is an obvious and lucrative option. Retired cricketers are paid handsome amounts as television pundits. Dravid's original hero Gavaskar in particular has set the benchmark as a media professional. With his easy articulation, Dravid could have chosen the same path but he decided not to after a brief initial flirtation. With his clean-shaven good looks, he could also have been an advertiser's dream but instead he is extremely selective about the brands he endorses. He might even have considered a career in cricket administration given his stature in the game. Again, he has stayed away, maybe because he feels ill-suited to the hurly-burly of cricket politics.

Instead, Dravid has stepped out of his comfort zone and is doing the things that give him real satisfaction. He is on the board of the Bengaluru-based non-profit group GoSports Foundation, where he helps mentor and raise money to support Olympic and Paralympic hopefuls. 'Rahul is fully committed to helping these young sportspersons realize their dream,' says Nandan Kamath, the founder.

In 2014, Dravid's advice helped Sharath Gayakwad, a Bengaluru-based para-athlete, in winning a record six medals in swimming at the Asian Games. 'I had almost given up on the sport when Rahul motivated me through mails and conversations on how to stay focused,' says Gayakwad. Dravid has also chaired the selection board for Rhodes Scholars, perhaps the first cricketer to lead the prestigious panel.

He does do the odd advertisement but there is often a public service edge to it; an anti-tobacco campaign being a recent example. He lectures management professionals on leadership skills as well; perhaps he could have just as easily been a corporate CEO instead of a cricket icon.

But most of all, he has chosen to do what he says he couldn't accomplish in two decades on the road as an international cricketer – spending more time with his family. 'My wife Vijeta sacrificed her medical career to stay with our two sons because I was constantly travelling. Now, it's my turn, and yes, I do try and drop the children to school and play cricket with them,' he says. His priorities reflect a mindset that seems untouched by fame and fortune, one that places core family values above all else.

His value system was shaken when in 2013 it was revealed that a few of the Rajasthan Royals players under Dravid as captain-coach were allegedly involved in spot-fixing matches. 'It shook me up for sure, you don't expect to be let down by your own players,' he admits.

It was a period that left him disillusioned but did not turn him into a cynic, reinforcing his belief that the easy money which now comes with professional cricket demands a greater focus on 'moral' education.

Zubin Bharucha, former Mumbai first-class player who was part of the Royals backroom team, recalls how Dravid pulled the team out of the crisis. 'He and the team owner Manoj Badale told the team that the players were free to leave and the franchise would pay their entire salary if required. Basically he only wanted those players to stay back who were fully committed to the team, and not just because of the money. He spent hours with each player reassuring them of his faith in them; it was a case of true mentorship.' The guidance worked. Despite the controversy, Rajasthan made the IPL knock-outs that year.

Maybe imparting advice on cricket and life skills suits Dravid. He is the mentor-coach of the Delhi Daredevils franchise in the IPL, and has been coach of the under-19 and India-A teams. He can seek the more high-profile role of coaching the senior side but he isn't quite ready to spend extended spells away from home. 'It's a great learning experience to work with the next generation of cricketers; they are hugely talented and I just want to give them the space and freedom to express their skills,' he says of his coaching mantra. His assistant Bharucha says that the secret to Dravid's success with the young is his eye for detail. 'He is a nuts-and-bolts coach for whom plans are nothing but planning is everything, someone who is totally hands-on. If one is playing an opposition with left-arm fast bowlers then he ensures his batsmen get enough practice against left-armers in the nets. Nothing is left to chance,' says Bharucha.

Watching him sweat it out in the heat with junior players, his commitment to the task is unmistakable. 'You need a lot of energy to keep up with the young cricketers, they are much fitter, stronger than we were,' he says. And while he is happy to join the juniors in the gym for training, he also knows where to draw the line. 'Somehow I don't think you will see me with tattoos on my arm or a pierced ear,' he says, laughing.

And when he tires of talking cricket, he has his own private universe of books that he happily retires to. A genuine bibliophile, Dravid's intellectual pursuits were apparent in his masterful speech at the Bradman Oration in Canberra in 2012, a cricket lecture that has since become a reference point for erudite commentaries on sport. Meticulous as ever, he reportedly spent weeks preparing for it, scouring through books and taking notes. He reminded his mainly Australian audience that the Indians and the Australians had fought battles together, most notably during the First World War in the famous battle in Gallipoli. 'It was a lecture in history, sport, life skills; the audience was dazzled. I doubt any cricketer in the modern era could have spoken with more authority and scholarship,' an admiring Australian lawyer friend tells me.

So what book is he reading now? 'I'm reading *The Geography of Genius* by Eric Weiner. It's a great book that takes you through a sweep of history, linking ancient Greece to Silicon Valley, telling us how creative geniuses like Plato and Steve Jobs flourished in a specific place and time,' he says. Which other cricketer, I ask myself, would venture into the rarefied world of Plato. Dravid is remarkably different, a cricketer with the mind of a philosopher.

It is his status of being a 'cricketer-gent with a difference' that might explain why he turned down an honorary doctorate offered to him by Bangalore University in 2017. 'I have been offered honorary doctorates by other places too, only this time the university made my refusal public. My reason is pretty simple. My wife is a doctor who spent years working incredibly hard to get her degree. My mother actually completed her doctorate in art when she was in her late fifties and I saw her work night and day to achieve her goal. I don't think then that I can just get a doctorate because I happen to be a famous cricketer, I need to have done something to earn it.'

In that well-reasoned response, you appreciate just how special Dravid really is. Cricketing great. Fine human being. Evolved mind. Conscience-keeper. A role model to be treasured and respected.

10

Mahendra Singh Dhoni

Small-Town Revolutionary

Indian cricket changed forever in 2007. On 13 September that year, at a glittering function in a five-star hotel, then BCCI vice president Lalit Modi unveiled his audacious new concept, the Indian Premier League. On stage were some of the biggest names in Indian cricket, including Sachin Tendulkar, Anil Kumble, Rahul Dravid and Sourav Ganguly, along with global stars like Glenn McGrath and Stephen Fleming. Just forty-eight hours earlier, Modi had been given a $25 million cheque by the BCCI president Sharad Pawar to prepare for India's inaugural Twenty20 franchise cricket tournament. 'I was confident of pulling it off, but no one in the BCCI really believed in me, except Pawar. Most of them thought it was a waste of money,' says Modi.

While the flamboyant Modi was playing impresario and promising big money for Indian cricket, a young team of Indian cricketers was flying that very morning to South Africa for the inaugural World Twenty20 tournament. Leading the team was a twenty-six-year-old who was making his debut as India captain. Mahendra Singh Dhoni's distinctive crop of long, wavy hair made him appear more like a rock band lead guitarist than someone with the onerous task of captaining a young, mostly untested Indian team.

Dhoni had become captain by fluke. None of the senior players seemed interested in playing 20-over cricket – it was dismissed by many as 'Mickey Mouse' cricket – and had voluntarily opted out. The selectors had to choose between Yuvraj Singh and Dhoni to lead the side and the then chairman of selectors Dilip Vengsarkar went with the latter on the back of strong recommendations from Dravid and Tendulkar. 'I liked his aggressive approach He looked like someone who understood the game well and importantly was seen as a calm presence in the dressing room,' says Vengsarkar.

The first match of the tournament was India versus Pakistan, a clash that always attracts eyeballs. The match, incredibly, ended in a tie, which resulted in international cricket's first-ever bowl-out, a unique concept where teams had to designate five bowlers to try and hit the stumps directly. No one had seen a bowl-out on live television, and the Pakistanis clearly had not prepared for it. The Indian team, by contrast, had practised for such a possibility. 'We had gone through the rules, made three teams and had fun practice sessions around who would hit the stumps and then chosen our first five bowlers in advance,' recalls Dhoni. When India won the bowl-out easily, the cricket world got its first glimpse of what Dhoni brought to the table. He was a street-smart cricketer, always ahead of the competition in a crunch situation.

The victory over Pakistan excited television audiences and made them curious for more. Meanwhile, an equally animated Modi had already flown to South Africa to sign up international players for the inaugural IPL. With typical swagger, he arrived in the Indian dressing room and made a rather extravagant promise to the team. 'Anyone who hits six sixes in an over will be given a gift of their choice!' While some team members suggested a Rolex watch, Modi was more profligate. 'I will give away a brand-new Porsche if any player achieves the feat,' he announced grandly.

Just two games later, India was in a must-win situation against England when Yuvraj Singh launched a savage assault against the English fast bowler Stuart Broad. The moment Yuvraj smashed a sixth straight six into the Durban skyline, he rushed in the direction of Modi, who was gleefully waving the keys of the car. 'I call it an answer to a prayer to God. Let someone do something that no one has done. And we got six sixes in an over! It simply lit up the screens in every home. Money can't buy that kind of thing, it just made Twenty20 cricket a must-watch,' enthuses Modi.

While Yuvraj was celebrating his new wheels, the captain was as calm as ever. 'The great thing about M.S. is that he takes life one day at a time, so he doesn't get carried away with victory or defeat,' says Lalchand Rajput, the 2007 team coach. Just days after the Durban excitement, India sneaked into the final, which was again a broadcaster's dream match – India versus Pakistan in Johannesburg before a sell-out crowd. Ahead of the marquee game, Dhoni had another big call to take; his most experienced batsman Virender Sehwag was carrying a slight injury, should he risk playing him or go with a younger player? 'We discussed it at night and I left the decision to M.S.,' says Rajput. The next morning Dhoni decided to leave out Sehwag and pick an unproven Yusuf Pathan instead. This was another Dhoni trait; he was unafraid of taking tough decisions.

The final played on 24 September was a nail-biting thriller. India, batting first, scored 157 runs, with Gautam Gambhir top-scoring with 75. Pakistan seemed down and out at 104 for 7 in 16 overs when suddenly Misbah-ul-Haq changed gears and began smashing the Indian bowling. Pakistan needed 13 in the last over with 1 wicket in hand. The experienced Harbhajan Singh had one over left when Dhoni turned to the little-known Joginder Sharma, also playing his first tournament for India.

'I chose Joginder over Harbhajan because Bhajji had gone for a fair number of runs in his last over. Besides, the opposition hadn't seen too much of Joginder, who had a good slower ball and change of pace which I felt was suited to the occasion,' says Dhoni. 'Mahi [Dhoni's pet name] just told me to keep it simple and have the confidence that I could do it,' recalls Sharma.

The first ball was a wide, the second went for six. Pakistan were now just five short of the Indian score. 'Even when I bowled a wide or was hit for a six, Mahi didn't say a word to me. He just told me to keep going,' says Sharma. The third ball was slower again; Misbah tried a scoop shot only to hit it straight to the fielder, S. Sreesanth. India had won by 5 runs. Sharma was an overnight star while the captain finally broke into a wide smile. Dhoni had shown another crucial match-winning attribute – the ability to stay calm under pressure.

'It was the perfect script for Twenty20 cricket. A bowl-out win over Pakistan, then the six sixes, now a victory in the inaugural World Twenty20 with a young team and without our best players. I was rubbing my hands with glee in the knowledge that there was no turning back. We had a winner in Twenty20 cricket; it was an unstoppable force,' says Modi exultantly. Adds Rajput, 'It was a young team being led by a new captain so there were no expectations. The best thing was that M.S. backed the players. He didn't want to chop and change the team but wanted every player to be given a fair chance.' This was to prove another Dhoni hallmark – he would be a captain who won the trust of his players.

As the team celebrated on the ground, Dhoni again did something unexpected. He suddenly took off his India shirt, gave it to a young fan and walked bare-chested around the field, his rippling muscles and long hair giving him the unique appeal of a newly assertive youthful Indian manhood. Five years earlier, when Ganguly did his shirt-stripping act at Lord's, he was criticized for going against the game's traditions. Dhoni was applauded for his generous gesture that would earn him the goodwill of the Indian cricket fan for years to come. 'It was purely spontaneous, I just felt like doing it at that moment,' he tells me.

Only one final act remained as Modi's astute event marketing instincts took over. The team was leaving the next morning for Mumbai and Modi telephoned Pawar suggesting a motorcade be organized to take the team from the airport to Wankhede stadium where a reception was being planned. 'Pawar warned me that it was raining in Mumbai and the celebration may fizzle out but I felt that it was worth taking the risk,' says Modi.

The IPL boss arrived in Mumbai at 4 a.m. to oversee the preparations. The team landed at 6 a.m. and was taken in an open-top BEST bus through the city. It was pouring rain. Yet thousands of Mumbaikars lined the streets as the team danced its way into the hearts of millions. The traditional Ganesh Chaturthi celebrations had just ended but for cricket fans, the Twenty20 victory was a chance to extend the festive season. The entire journey was telecast live across news channels and the surging crowds meant that a drive of just over an hour eventually stretched to eight. 'It was on that road journey that we realized what the win meant for Indian cricket. Till then we were just a group of young guys having a good time,' says Dhoni. 'If I had any doubts left over the appeal of the new brand of Twenty20 cricket, the Mumbai roadshow settled it,' affirms Modi.

The IPL dream was now slowly turning into reality and the timing couldn't have been better. India's economy was taking off – in 2007, growth rates had touched an unprecedented 9 per cent – and investors, domestic and foreign, were looking for fresh playgrounds. Indian cricket was poised to enter the multimillion-dollar global entertainment industry space.

The man with heavy-metal-star looks on top of the bus holding the trophy aloft would be the charismatic prime face of this latest cricket juggernaut. Mahendra Singh Dhoni's rustic, macho image was the ideal brand identity of the bright new Indian cricket universe. Nearly a quarter of a century earlier, Kapil Dev had given Indian cricket its first glimpse of the future by winning the World Cup at Lord's in 1983. Now another small-town boy had become an overnight superstar who had turned the cricket world upside down and threatened to spark off a twenty-first-century cricket revolution.

On still, echoing afternoons, the sun blazes down on the dilapidated emptiness of Ranchi. Its winding crowded lanes lead to a cluster of rough stalls hung with plastic baubles, a mournful conglomeration that passes for the city's main bazaar. The totems of 'modern' consumerist India – malls and multiplexes – have slowly reached the city, but it is still a city of limited means and restricted aspirations.

Despite the odds, a talent shot skywards from this dry earth, transforming a one-rickshaw town from dusty nothingness into a star's abode.

A few years ago, a stringer friend of mine in Ranchi invited me to his home in Jharkhand's capital city. In his prayer room, amidst pictures of different Gods, there was also a portrait of Dhoni. He explained, 'Sir, because of Mahi, the national news channels have some interest in Jharkhand. He is our rozi-roti, else the only other time our stories are carried is when people die in Naxal violence.' To much of the outside world, there is little else to the sleepy town of Ranchi other than Dhoni. If Ganguly is the Prince of Kolkata, then Dhoni is surely the Raja of Ranchi.

Dhoni's father Pan Singh, an Uttarakhandi, had moved to Ranchi in 1964 with the public sector firm MECON as a junior employee. When Dhoni was born in 1981, the youngest of three siblings, his father was a pump operator and the family lived in a one-bedroom house in the MECON housing colony. Father Pan Singh and mother Devki Devi are a dignified couple with serious careworn faces and upright postures. They speak to me of lives spent in hard work and difficult days. Their house was just 50 metres from the company's sports ground and 100 metres from the DAV Shyamali School. 'It was all very convenient for me, from school to sports, everything was walking distance. Besides, we always had many boys in the colony to play with,' says Dhoni.

From a very young age he would play tennis-ball matches in the colony with boys much older than him. 'I was very small and thin so they made me a wicketkeeper,' recalls Dhoni. At the age of twelve he was enticed into the world of hard-ball cricket. 'Until then I would play football, badminton and run a lot. I was actually flat-footed but I would run so much that it strengthened my legs at a very young age,' explains Dhoni. Even today the Indian team's fitness trainers will tell you that few can match Dhoni's speed over short distances.

Dhoni's display of skill as the junior school football goalkeeper led his sports master Keshav Banerjee to invite him to take a shot at cricket as a wicketkeeper. 'I saw him dive to catch a football and thought that he might make a good wicketkeeper. Besides, our senior keeper was in class twelve and we needed a backup. I asked Mahendra if he wanted to try his hand at cricket; his first reaction was, "Chance doge? [Will you give me a chance?]",' recalls Banerjee. Dhoni was then in class six. 'I played one match but hardly got a chance after that because the senior school keeper was soon back,' says Dhoni. 'It was only in my second year in cricket after my senior had left school that I finally got to play regularly.'

'The best thing about Mahendra was his sheer enthusiasm, he never missed a single practice session,' says Banerjee. 'And yes, he had this natural power and six-hitting ability from a young age.'

Dhoni's father was a keen sports watcher but had limited interest in cricket. For the lower-middle-class family, studies came first. 'My parents never stopped me from playing cricket but expected me to adhere to a strict discipline in school where sports had to coexist with my books,' says Dhoni. A typical school day would begin with assembly prayers at 7.40 a.m. and end at 3 p.m. after which he would rush to the ground to play for at least three hours every evening. 'In the school cricket nets, I barely got around fifteen minutes to bat. The rest of the time I was keeping, taking catches or just running,' he remembers.

Unlike Mumbai or any other big metro, opportunities to play regular cricket in Ranchi were limited. Jharkhand had a strong hockey tradition and was home to several Olympians but had no cricket hero to emulate. (In 1928, the first captain to lead India to an Olympic gold in hockey was a Jharkhandi, Jaipal Singh Munda, who would later become a strident advocate for tribal rights.) The city's main stadium had only one turf wicket so interschool matches were all played on matting, and often were just 25 overs a side.

'Even our school practice pitch was on a makeshift matting which we had to pull out from the school auditorium every day. The mat was uneven and the pitch was right next to the school building. Often when I hit the ball I would end up breaking a windowpane and when the guard asked what happened, we would joke that someone threw a stone,' says Dhoni with a chuckle.

It was during the interschool final in 1997 that sixteen-year-old Dhoni first announced himself as a big hitter by scoring a double century in an unbroken 378-run opening partnership with his schoolmate Shabbir Hussein. 'I allowed Dhoni to open in that match on the condition that he would bat the entire 40 overs. I jokingly warned him that if he got out there was no number three in the team to bat!' says Banerjee.

Dhoni responds, 'We had a strong school team and our coach wanted us to not just win, but also win in the fastest possible time. I guess that's how I became an attacking player who liked to loft the ball for sixes from the very beginning.' Banerjee, who admits to being more a physical education teacher than a cricket coach, says he never changed anything in Dhoni's batting. 'I worked on his wicket-keeping a bit since he used to catch the ball initially like a fish with its mouth open, but his batting style is his own. I think he developed it by playing so much tennis-ball cricket with the power coming from his strong forearms,' he says. According to Dhoni, the coaching mantra in Ranchi was far removed from classical batsmanship. 'No MCC- or Mumbai-style coaching for us. For us it wasn't so much about a straight bat technique but ensuring that the ball was hit hard and far.'

The double century in the school final meant that Dhoni became a star attraction for Ranchi's highly competitive A-division league. 'Both Shabbir and I first went to the MECON Cricket Club since our fathers worked there. They offered to take us on a staff quota but told us that we would have to share the kit and we wouldn't have a guaranteed place in the team. Then someone told us that the local SAIL

[Steel Authority of India Limited] team was offering a stipend of Rs 625 a month and a place in the team with Rs 25 cut if you missed practice. So we took it up and Rs 625 was my first wage,' he says.

A year later, Dhoni moved to the club of Central Coalfields Limited (CCL), a subsidiary of Coal India Limited, only because it had just laid out a turf wicket and was raising the stipend to Rs 2000 with a special Rs 200 bonus to Dhoni because he was a 'match-winner'. Adil Hussain, Dhoni's captain at CCL, remembers him as a shy teenager who came alive once he was on the cricket field. 'Two things stood out for me about the young Dhoni, his dedication and his confidence. We had a rule that practice would begin at 6 a.m., not a minute later. In the five years that Mahendra played with us, not once was he even a minute late. Off the field, he wouldn't say a word but once he was on the ground, he would just come to life and never hesitate in even telling a senior player if he was making a mistake. When I asked him where he wanted to bat, he immediately said he wanted to open,' says Hussain.

Hussain recalls a game in the Sheesh Mahal tournament in Lucknow where the CCL team was playing a side with two India fast bowlers, T. Kumaran and Debashish Mohanty. 'The fact that they were India bowlers made no difference to Mahendra, who was still a teenager; he hit them both for sixes! His self-confidence was always his biggest asset,' says Hussain. I ask him if he has seen any change in Dhoni's attitude over the years. 'No change at all, only now when I see him do his post-match interviews with such ease, I wonder what happened to the boy who would never open his mouth as a teenager!' says Hussain.

Dhoni's strong performance for CCL and in under-19 cricket for Bihar paved the way for his Ranji debut in 2000. That year he was also picked for the East Zone side but in a glaring example of bureaucratic ineptitude and Ranchi's status as a cricket backwater wasn't even informed of his selection. Enter Paramjit Singh, or Chhotu bhaiya as he is affectionately called, a soft-spoken sardar with a distinctly Jharkhandi accent who runs a sports shop on Ranchi's crowded Main Road (the shop is easily identified as 'Dhoni ke dost ki dukaan'.) Paramjit had played club cricket with Dhoni in 1995 and was convinced that his friend had a special skill. He was also the one who got Dhoni his first bat contract with Jalandhar-based company BAS. 'When I first went to Jalandhar and told them about this boy from Ranchi who I felt had the talent to play for India no one would believe me. I even told them, "Don't give me equipment for my shop but make sure my friend gets the best kit." It took dozens of phone calls and a lot of pleading before they finally agreed,' says Paramjit.

It was Paramjit who received a call from a Kolkata friend to inform him that Dhoni had been selected for the East Zone team by which time it was almost too late. The last train from Ranchi to Kolkata had left. But Paramjit hired a Tata Sumo and drove Dhoni along with two other friends (one of whom, Gautam Gupta, would later marry Dhoni's sister) overnight to Kolkata. 'It was crazy,' recalls Dhoni. 'Our car broke down in Jamshedpur; it took us two hours to fix but we had a lot of fun singing songs along the way.' By the time Dhoni reached Kolkata airport, the team had already left for Agartala and he ended up missing out his first game for East Zone. 'I don't think what happened to me that day will ever happen to a young cricketer today. Things are much more organized now,' says Dhoni.

A year later, in 2001, Dhoni was on the move again, this time to Kharagpur in neighbouring Bengal where he had been offered a job under the sports quota in South Eastern Railway. The divisional manager Animesh Kumar Ganguly was a cricket fanatic and had been looking out for young talent. He even had his own cricket pitch laid out in his bungalow and after bowling to Dhoni for forty-five minutes was satisfied enough to offer him a Class 3 job as a train ticket examiner so he could play for their team. 'The day I got the job in the railways, my father finally felt that my playing cricket was worth it. My salary was only around Rs 3000 but just the idea that his son had a secure job made my father happy,' says Dhoni.

Life in Kharagpur wasn't easy, though. It was the first time Dhoni was away from home and he had to live in a dormitory with five other railway employees. 'I won't forget the first few weeks. I was missing my mother's cooking and was staying with people mostly in their forties, much older than me. They had all been promoted to Class 3 and treated me like a son,' he says. Being ticket collector in one of the country's busiest railway junctions wasn't easy either. He had to often do the morning shift from 6 a.m. to 2 p.m. 'When the morning local would come from Kolkata, there would be a big crowd and it wasn't easy to check tickets and not get pushed around at the same time. But I learnt it all, including how to sort out tickets and arrange them in the right section,' says Dhoni. Fortunately, three months later, he was moved to the sports department where playing inter-railway cricket was the main focus during the winter. In the monsoon months he would play football and work on his fitness.

Years later, during the 2016–17 Ranji season, Dhoni would travel by train again – this time as part of the Jharkhand team. As a junior cricketer he had often travelled in unreserved compartments and even slept outside the toilet area – he had now graduated to an AC first-class bogie, with special security guarding him even as frenzied fans tried to catch a glimpse of their idol. 'It was fun being back on the train and chatting with the younger players till late into the night,' he says. Did he cross Kharagpur station, I ask. 'I think I was sleeping at the time.' He grins.

Rewinding the clock, I wondered whether the teenager working as a ticket collector at Kharagpur station had ever dreamt he would become India's most successful captain. 'I had no such dream. Where I came from, it was always about taking life one step at a time. So every little step mattered rather than the final destination. To be honest, I never thought of playing for India when I was sorting out tickets at the station, but just wanted to make the next grade in the railways,' he says poignantly. Kharagpur station may be only 150 kilometres from Eden Gardens but the psychological distance traversed by the young man from Ranchi was far greater.

A professional sportsperson's career rarely moves in a straight line. There are many forks in the road where tough calls have to be taken, where talent, luck and opportunity have to align for success. Dhoni's moment of truth came in the summer of 2003. He had been working in South Eastern Railway's Kharagpur division for two years but his cricket career was making little progress and he remained stuck in the Class 3 category. He had failed to make it to the Railways Ranji team, given just three balls to keep wickets and five minutes of batting in the trials before being summarily dismissed. 'I guess they had a strong team which was doing well; they didn't need me,' he says with a shrug. While he was happy playing for Bihar (later Jharkhand), his early first-class performances weren't particularly eye-catching. He could have wallowed in the mediocrity of being just another Ranji player for a state with limited cricket ambitions but he was keen to chart his own path. Dhoni made the difficult choice of leaving Kharagpur and going back to Ranchi with the quiet determination of doing 'his own thing'.

Abandoning the railways wasn't an easy call for a twenty-two-year-old. He was, after all, a breadwinner for his family. But as he would prove through his career, Dhoni wasn't averse to taking the road less travelled. 'You know it is often said that it is difficult to get a government job, but even more difficult to quit the government. So I didn't formally leave the railways right away but just decided to work at my cricket in Ranchi during the off season. Fortunately, no one even noticed that I had quit.' He laughs.

Through the monsoon of 2003, Dhoni worked even harder on his fitness, improved his wicketkeeping skills and kept up with his hard-hitting batting in local prize money tennis-ball tournaments across east India. 'It was all good fun, we used to initially be paid Rs 750 for the tournaments, later the amount was increased to Rs 5000 plus travel. I had a great time playing tennis-ball matches since I would get to bowl and bat in them.'

The 2003–04 season was make or break for Dhoni and in an early stroke of luck Prakash Poddar, a Bengal captain in the 1960s, came to watch him play in a match between Jharkhand and Assam. Poddar had been appointed the Talent Resource Development Officer for East Zone, part of a new national talent scheme unveiled by the cricket board to identify promising young players across the country. 'I was asked by our East Zone selector Russi Jeejeebhoy to travel to Jamshedpur to have a look at the game there. That is when I saw Dhoni for the first time and to be honest my initial impression was that he looked more like a Hindi film hero than a cricketer,' recalls Poddar. Dhoni scored 29 runs in the game but it was the manner in which he made them that struck Poddar immediately. 'There was a confidence to his stroke-making that stood out. His wicketkeeping was 50-50, but his batting was full of aggressive intent,' says Poddar.

On returning to Kolkata, Poddar filed a report to the chairperson of the national talent scheme, Dilip Vengsarkar, who forwarded it to Kiran More, the former India wicketkeeper and the then chairman of selectors. More, himself from Vadodara, had been pushing for the selectors to look beyond the major metros. 'Coming from a small town myself, I knew there was talent across the country waiting to be spotted. I would therefore often urge my fellow selectors to travel to centres outside their zones,' recalls More. A wicketkeeper himself, More decided to take the long journey to Jamshedpur to watch Dhoni play in a match between Jharkhand and Orissa. As it turned out, Dhoni scored a century in that game, kept wickets competently and created an instant impact on the selection committee head. 'You could see his natural ability to score quick runs from the very first ball. His technique may not have been classical, but his calculated aggression was unmistakable,' says More.

The runs and the recommendation couldn't have come at a better time. India had been desperately looking for a wicketkeeper-batsman ever since Nayan Mongia withdrew from the scene in 2000–01. For three years, India had tried nearly half a dozen wicketkeepers but with little success. The lack of options had even forced Rahul Dravid to turn wicketkeeper in one-day cricket, a move that had met with moderate success but one that was clearly a stopgap arrangement.

'Dhoni seemed to tick all the boxes for us, especially in one-day cricket, he was there at the right place, at the right time,' says More.

The clincher was the Duleep Trophy final in Mohali in March 2004 between North Zone and East Zone. With the entire selection panel present, More urged his East Zone counterpart Pranab Roy to allow Dhoni to keep wickets instead of the regular keeper Deep Dasgupta who was already playing for India. Under the guise of carrying a hand injury, Dasgupta played as a batsman to allow the boy from Jharkhand a chance to prove himself on the big stage.

Dhoni took five catches behind the stumps but the key moment came on the fourth day when East Zone, set 409 to win the game, sent him to open the innings. Against an attack that included three India bowlers, including pace spearhead Ashish Nehra, Dhoni hit a quickfire 60 off just 47 balls, with 8 fours and a six. The first ball he played off Nehra was hit one bounce over cover for four, the next ball was hooked for six. 'I think that was the moment when we realized that we may just have found an answer to our need for a hard-hitting wicketkeeper-batsman to play for India,' says More.

Dhoni was picked for the India-A team to tour Kenya and Zimbabwe in July 2004 as a reserve keeper, his first 'proper' foreign tour (he had gone earlier to play in an exhibition seven-a-side cricket tournament in Hong Kong). His rise from small-town local cricket to the Indian team had been gradual, each move being seen as another opportunity to take a step up in life. He had no godfather and no access to infinite resources but he was never short of grit. 'Nothing has come easy to me so I learnt to appreciate whatever little I got,' he says.

Indian cricket, like any other field, was getting very competitive and there was a fierce fight to get to the top. It was even tougher for a boy from Jharkhand – a state formed only in 2000 – to get noticed in the crowded talent pool. That he didn't get lost in the process is proof that cricket was now like any other open competitive exam in the country – if you had the talent and the marks to back your effort, no one could stop you.

If Dhoni's climb up had been slow and steady, his impact on
the India-A tour was immediate. When first-choice keeper Dinesh
Karthik was called into the national side touring England, Dhoni
took over in spectacular style. His run-making included a century
against Pakistan A in the tri-series tournament in Kenya, his first
international ton. He would hit another century against the Pakistanis
on the tour, his six-hitting exploits drawing crowds to the picturesque
Nairobi Gymkhana.

Aakash Chopra was Dhoni's roommate on the tour and has fond
memories of the future India star. 'He was just this very shy and
reserved guy who rarely said a word. I would order room service and
he would happily go and pick up a milkshake or a pastry. I asked him
what time he would like to sleep, and he said, "Don't worry, I will
sleep, Aakash bhai, whenever you decide to switch off the lights."
He just seemed very content with life, carefree but never careless
on and off the field. When he wasn't batting or keeping, he used
to happily bowl to us in the nets,' says Chopra. 'Look, my attitude
to life has always been to keep things simple,' responds Dhoni. 'I
was just happy to be travelling with the India-A team and getting
a chance to play. If you don't push for too much in life, you will
never feel disappointed.'

World Cup winner Sandeep Patil was then coach of the India-A
team and he quickly became a Dhoni fan. 'What I liked about him
is that he was an "impact" player who could change the course of
the match in just a few overs,' says Patil, himself a big striker of a
cricket ball. But it wasn't just cricket that drew the senior coach to
the debutant. 'Mahi was an enthusiastic singer too, he would always
hum Kishore Kumar tunes from *Muqaddar Ka Sikandar* and *Sharaabi*,
acting as if he was Amitabh Bachchan in those films,' remembers
Patil. Despite being the star 'discovery' on the tour, Dhoni wasn't
carried away by the initial success. 'What struck me is just how simple
and innocent he was. He is at heart a simpleton. I have known him
for over a decade now and the only thing that has changed is that

the long hair he had then has been replaced by a greying stubble,' says Patil.

Dhoni's African adventure was good enough for him to make his full international debut against Bangladesh in December 2004 in a one-day game. He didn't start on the right note, getting run out for a duck off the very first ball he faced. His highest score in his first four games for India was 12. The breakthrough came, as was often the case with Dhoni, in a rather dramatic fashion. Elevated to number three in the batting order, Dhoni scored a magnificent 148 against Pakistan in Visakhapatnam with 12 fours and 4 sixes to become the first regular Indian wicketkeeper to score a one-day century. 'It was a bit of a make-or-break innings for me,' says Dhoni. 'That was my fifth match and had I failed again the selectors would probably have dropped me, so getting a century ensured that I would at least play ten more games for India.' The decision to promote Dhoni was taken by coach John Wright and skipper Sourav Ganguly. 'I had watched his batting in one-day cricket for East Zone and felt that he had the attacking instincts that deserved a bigger platform. By putting him up the order, we not only gave Dhoni confidence but also surprised the Pakistanis,' says Ganguly.

It wasn't just the Pakistanis who were surprised. This was also the first real glimpse the entire country got of the Dhoni storm that would follow in the years ahead. Jharkhand was suddenly on the Indian cricket map. Interestingly, the very next game was in Jamshedpur's Keenan stadium where Dhoni had played much of his early first-class cricket. A packed house had come to watch their local hero even though Dhoni insisted that his family stay away because, he says, he didn't want them to feel any pressure. For his friends from Ranchi, this was the biggest moment of their lives – 'their' Mahi was now an India star. 'The pride that Dhoni has given us is unmatched. Even now when Mahi plays a game, we put on the television in my shop and all friends come in to watch,' says Paramjit, whose shop is an 'open house' during India matches for chai and shinghada, a local samosa.

Dhoni was now on the fast track to fame and success. Just months later, in August 2005, he equalled the record for the highest one-day score for India with an unbeaten 183 not out against Sri Lanka, an innings marked by 10 sixes. A Test debut followed against the same opponents in December that year and then a first Test century, against Pakistan, in early 2006. It wasn't just the runs he scored but the manner of scoring them that caught the eye.

'Normally in your first year in international cricket you are either a little tentative or a bit cocky, but with M.S. it was almost as if he was a veteran player even after a few matches for India. He wouldn't speak much initially but he had that quiet confidence which always stood out for me,' says V.V.S. Laxman, one of the many stalwarts sharing a dressing room with the boy from Jharkhand. 'Before my first match, the seniors made me stand on a stool and make a speech. I don't recall what I said but I didn't say too much. My attitude then and even now is never try and talk more than necessary, it's better to talk with runs than with words,' says Dhoni.

Indeed, in a team brimming with talent, M.S. etched out an instant identity for himself and became the crowd favourite. His brisk walk to the wicket signalled aggressive intent; his energetic running between the wickets gave further evidence of his assertive attitude; and his powerful sixes were the ultimate expression of batting machismo. And then there was the distinctive long hair.

It was attractive enough for then Pakistan president Pervez Musharraf to suggest at a prize distribution ceremony, 'I saw a placard saying you should cut your hair but if you ask my opinion, you shouldn't, you look good with it.' Not that Dhoni was too concerned. 'Actually, I was scoring runs with long hair, so there was a bit of superstition attached to it,' says Dhoni, while adding with a smile, 'By the way, I think soon after I cut my hair short, Musharraf was removed from office.'

If hairstyles reflect personality traits, then Dhoni's shoulder-length locks symbolized an unconventional persona who lived life on his own terms. When Chopra once suggested to Dhoni that the long hair may not fit in with the traditional Indian cricketer look, the reply was instructive. 'Aakash bhai, it's okay. I like my long hair, maybe one day all the other players will copy my style.' In a team of conformists, Dhoni was the non-conformist 'outsider' in batting and life choices. The other exception was Virender Sehwag, another cricketer with a distinctively belligerent attitude to batting and a relaxed attitude to life. As cricket itself became a more aggressive sport, complete with a premium on power-hitting in the one-day and Twenty20 formats, Dhoni was the ideal prototype for the evolving game. After his initial blazing innings in Visakhapatnam, the advertisers began to line up. 'I remember Pepsi ringing us up and saying, "Where was this guy all this while?,"' recalls Jeet Banerjee of Gameplan, the first agency to manage Dhoni's sponsor deals, adding, 'With his rugged looks and aggressive cricket, Dhoni had the X factor the advertisers were looking for.'

The World Twenty20 triumph in 2007 firmly established Dhoni as the rising star of Indian cricket. Just over a year later he was appointed one-day and Test captain. He was still only twenty-seven but captaining a team that included four former India captains, all senior to him. The seniormost was Tendulkar, who had made his international debut when Dhoni was just seven years old. As a child in Ranchi, Dhoni would ask his father to wake him whenever Sachin was batting in a late-night or early-morning game. 'He was my ultimate hero, I was a complete fan of his and never missed watching him play on TV as a teenager,' says Dhoni. In 2000–01, he first met Sachin on the field during a Duleep Trophy match between East Zone and West Zone. 'I was twelfth man in the game and carrying the drinks while Sachin and Vinod Kambli had a big partnership. I remember during one of the breaks Sachin asked me for a drink and I gave it to him and shook his hand for the first time. I don't think I washed my hands for the next few days!' he says.

Tendulkar, too, has great affection for his fan. 'From the very first time we met, Mahi has given me complete respect. Maybe he reminds me a bit of my father; be it in success or failure, Mahi is always calm like my father wanted all of us to be,' says Tendulkar. For Dhoni, captaining his childhood hero was like a fairy-tale come true but he wasn't getting carried away. 'You know J.P. Yadav [an MP and Railways cricketer who played 12 one-dayers for India] has a good joke. He would say that Sachin paaji destroyed a few young international careers because the youngsters would be so interested in knowing what Sachin paaji ate, drank and wore that they would forget they had to score runs themselves,' says Dhoni with a laugh.

Dhoni himself just felt blessed to be sharing the same space as his childhood hero. Less than seven years earlier, he was scrambling to catch ticket-avoiding passengers at Kharagpur railway station. Now he was a national superstar leading India on the cricket field. It was a dramatic turnaround of fortune, an incredible storybook fable being played out on the cricket field. Little did Dhoni know that the best was yet to come.

~

The 2011 World Cup in India, Bangladesh and Sri Lanka was more than just another tournament. It was the ultimate symbol of the power shift that had taken place in the sport – from Lord's to the subcontinent. In a sense, cricket was only a metaphor for the global transfer of power. The 'action' was shifting from West to East, from recession-hit Europe to the emerging markets of Asia. 'It wasn't enough for us to just host the tournament. We wanted to win it to show the world that India is the new superpower of world cricket,' says Sharad Pawar, the seasoned Maharashtra politician who was ICC president at the time.

There was another reason the masses craved victory. The tournament was played at a time when the Manmohan Singh–led United Progressive Alliance government at the Centre was hobbled with serious corruption charges. The prime minister was looking weak and ineffectual as the growing public anger against corruption (as mentioned in Chapter 7) ignited street protests led by ageing activist

Anna Hazare. The despairing nation was looking for a hero to lift the gloom and in Dhoni they would find the strong, decisive leader missing from the country's political class, a captain courageous who led from the front.

Preparations for the World Cup had begun in right earnest in early 2008 when Dhoni was appointed captain of the one-day side to play a tri-nation series in Australia as veterans like Dravid and Ganguly were dropped. It wasn't an easy call and Dhoni and the selectors were criticized. Vengsarkar, who was chairing the selection meeting, says that the decision was taken because the team needed to be injected with fresh talent after the 2007 World Cup debacle in the West Indies, where the Indians were knocked out in the first round after losing to Bangladesh. 'We had a new captain in Dhoni and felt this was the right time to blood youngsters who showed promise with an eye on the 2011 tournament,' says Vengsarkar. But the move also showed a decisive, even ruthless, streak, in Dhoni's persona. Ganguly, for example, learnt of his dropping from a journalist. As it turned out, the team defeated a powerful Australian side, setting the stage for the build-up to the World Cup. 'I think that victory was important for us,' says Dhoni. 'It gave us the confidence that we could take on the world.'

Joining Dhoni in his Mission 2011 was a new coach, the former South African opening batsman Gary Kirsten. Like Dhoni, Kirsten was a man of few words. But where Dhoni often relied on instinct, Kirsten was a 'process' person for whom diligent preparations mattered. After the team's turbulent phase under Greg Chappell, Kirsten provided a disciplined but more benign work environment. 'The great thing about Gary was that he was a good man manager who understood Indian work culture. We Indians work on what I call emotion, which is why we are probably the only country with 5000 patriotic songs. We are not professionals in a robotic sense; we like to have someone who will connect to us emotionally and give us a sense of comfort. And don't forget, each cricketer in a team has a different temperament, someone needs love and an arm around him, another person can live with a gaali [abuse],' contends Dhoni.

In 2013, I did a television show on leadership with Kirsten where he explained his success mantra for Indian cricket. 'Look, what can a coach tell Sachin or Dravid about batting? My task was to ensure that they were all in a happy space so that they could perform to the best of their abilities without any extra pressure. After all, there is no country where a cricketer is under greater pressure than in India, is there?'

This approach also suited Dhoni's temperament since he too was a great believer in leaving people to discover their needs. 'The best thing about M.S. that rubbed off on me and I think anyone who has played with him is just how calm he is under pressure. His life is highly compartmentalized so he would never fret too much if things didn't go to plan,' says Kirsten.

It was this Buddha-like calmness that would be tested in some of the most extreme theatres of the sport, playing in front of thousands of excitable Indian fans willing their team to win. No host team had won the World Cup since the inaugural edition in 1975.

When India won the World Cup in 1983, it was a shocker, the ultimate cricket heist pulled off from under the noses of the mighty West Indies. One-day cricket was still to find its feet in the country and the victory was akin to winning a once-in-a-lifetime lottery. Twenty-eight years later, India were firm favourites and anything less than triumph in the final would be seen as a failure. 'I would be lying if I say there was no pressure,' says Dhoni. 'Every hotel we went [to], every flight we took, we would be told about how much we needed to win the Cup as hosts. And I would try and lighten the mood by asking but why do we need to win because we are the hosts. Good hosts should let others win!'

In 1983 there were no mighty media machines or multimillion-dollar consumer goods markets to act as echo chambers for the sport. Colour television had just crept into India and Doordarshan was the monopoly player. (In fact, television sets went on the blink for a portion of the 1983 final because the signal to London was lost!)

Chhaya Geet, the weekly show of old Hindi film songs, and the Sunday Hindi film were the main sources of entertainment (the iconic soap 'Hum Log' started on Doordarshan only in 1984). There were no multiplex cinema theatres or fancy dance bars and restaurants. The mobile phone revolution was still two decades away, overseas 'trunk' calls had to be 'booked' and the lineman had to be bribed just to get your landline working. Air India and Indian Airlines ruled the skies while the Maruti 800 only made its debut in December 1983. Indira Gandhi was still the prime minister, the Indian economy was trapped in a slow 'Hindu rate of growth', the licence permit raj had limited the size of the market and the Sensex was just 212 points. The cricketers too were part of a socialistic ecosystem where money was scarce and luxury goods, be they designer jeans or glasses, were almost non-existent – a few members of the victorious 1983 team didn't even own a car or a house at the time!

By 2011, India was a member of the G20 high table of countries driving the global economy, Indians were making it to the list of Forbes billionaires, the Sensex was touching 20,000 points, every major MNC brand was now jostling for space in multistorey desi shopping malls, private airlines had transformed domestic travel, multiplex cinema halls, fast 'phoren' cars and international food chains were redefining aspirational urban lifestyles and the explosive growth in mobile phone customers symbolized a nation on the move. Cricket too was part of this expanding marketplace, competing with cinema for commercial advertising revenues, the staple diet for more than 500 round-the-clock news and entertainment channels. The players were all crorepatis endorsing dozens of products and the host broadcaster was demanding an India win, having poured crores of rupees into the telecast rights. The pressure to perform was enormous. 'We tried to keep away from all newspapers and television during the World Cup,' says Kirsten. 'We didn't want the players to be influenced by anything being said around them. It was like living in a bubble for two months.'

For a captain who stayed away from the media glare at most

times, the approach was typically Dhoni-like. 'I switched off my mobile phone [he often doesn't carry one even now], and just told the guys to take this one game at a time.' Dhoni says he doesn't read newspapers, avoids the sports pages in particular and only switches on television news for five minutes every morning and then late at night to catch the headlines. It was only when the team arrived for the semi-final in Mohali against Pakistan that they found it tough to ignore the pressure any longer. A World Cup semi-final against Pakistan at home, an entire subcontinent watching, every VVIP in the stands – it didn't get bigger than this in international cricket. Meanwhile, the man in the hot seat was busy playing video games in his room in the build-up to the big match. 'It's a good way to switch off from the external noise,' says Dhoni. 'Yes, India and Pakistan are traditional rivals and you want to win desperately but in the end it doesn't make a difference who is on the other side. You just have to win a game of cricket.'

But there was no way the captain could switch off at crunch time in the final. When Dhoni with his typical brisk walk came in to bat at Wankhede, the final with Sri Lanka was well and truly in the balance. India were 114 for 3 in 21 overs, needing 275 for victory. Dhoni had pushed himself ahead of the in-form Yuvraj Singh in the batting order. While the entire country may have wondered whether the skipper was taking an unnecessary gamble, for Dhoni it was the obvious thing to do. 'I had put my pads on when the second wicket fell and I was getting a bit restless. Then Virat gets out and my instinct tells me that I am the best person to go in at that moment. The Lankans had two off-spinners, Murali and Suraj Randiv, in their ranks, both of whom played with me at Chennai Super Kings. I could pick their doosra so I was confident of my game against them. There was also a bit of dew so I sensed that if I got on top of the spinners, I could control the game. Gary agreed with me,' he says. It was to prove the perfect strategy. More crucially, this was further evidence of a captain who was ever-willing to be in the trenches with his troops and lead from the front.

Fittingly, Dhoni would end the match with a six, a shot over long-on with a slight extension of the forearms and a perfect follow-through, his eyes intently watching the ball soar into the crowd before he twirled the bat in delight. He must have played the shot umpteen times, from the days when he would hit sixes in school matches in Ranchi for fun, but this stroke was special. With a full house screaming 'Indiaaaa' in an unprecedented patriotic frenzy, Dhoni had pulled off a special performance on the biggest stage of all.

Perhaps no single shot has been replayed more often on Indian television than Dhoni's winning hit. With that one shot, he had ensured an entire nation was in his embrace. For a country seeking comfort in a period of high inflation, slowing growth and political turbulence, the image provided hope and joy. Years later, Sunil Gavaskar would echo the sentiments of many cricket fans when he said, 'Before I die, the last thing that I want to see is the six that Dhoni hit to win the 2011 World Cup.' Dhoni says, 'Look, I didn't premeditate anything or plan to finish the match with a six, I was in the zone and it just happened.'

As he pulled out a stump in celebration and got a hug from the ecstatic Yuvraj and then the rest of his teammates, Dhoni couldn't but be overwhelmed by the moment. 'Yes, I cried, but the cameras didn't catch it. I was naturally excited but held back the emotions till a tearful Harbhajan hugged me. That's when I got teary-eyed but kept my head down so no one would see me crying,' reveals Dhoni. Yes, tough grown-up men are entitled to cry and get emotional. But even in Team India's moment of glory, there was a selfless streak – it wasn't Dhoni the team carried on their shoulders but Tendulkar. The captain wanted it that way. 'Don't forget I played this game as a teenager only by watching him bat,' he says.

With a World Cup victory on home soil, Dhoni had allowed an entire nation to live the ultimate cricket dream. Gautam Gambhir, Man of the Match in the final, recalls how as the team bus was returning from the stadium to the Taj Hotel in Mumbai, they saw a young family with three children on the pavement waving the tricolour. 'I don't think they knew where their next meal was coming from but they were celebrating as if they had won a lottery. I thought for once both the haves and have nots in India have a common reason to celebrate,' says Gambhir. Dhoni and his men in blue had united a country with the power of cricket nationalism, one that is inclusive and inspirational.

~

The 2011 triumph made Dhoni an eternal national folk hero. He was the first person to lead his team to victory in both the World Twenty20 and the World Cup. He was captain in 2009 when India rose to become the number one Test team in the world. In 2013 he added the Champions Trophy to his illustrious résumé. In between, he also led Chennai Super Kings to IPL triumph twice. Purely as a leader, in terms of what he has achieved, no India captain comes close to Dhoni.

So, is there a secret Dhoni formula, especially in the shorter format of the game? I turned to Stephen Fleming, the former New Zealand captain who was coach of the Chennai IPL franchise, for answers. 'The first thing that strikes you about Dhoni when you get to know him is how balanced he is in life. He is a man of a few words and I have never seen him stress too much, or get overexcited; he never lets his ego get in the way of what he needs to do on the ground. It is that inner calmness that is crucial to understanding the Dhoni persona and which I believe is the key to his success as captain, especially in the limited overs format where you need to hold your nerve in a tense situation,' says Fleming.

I ask Dhoni where he derives the extraordinary serenity in his behaviour. 'It's just the way I am. I don't like to complicate life too much and prefer to live in the moment. You may be up one day and down the next. You learn to accept what life has to offer so long as you do your best always. If you have a glass of water in front of you, you should be content with it, why seek a bottle of water when the glass will do for you?' For a moment, he sounds like a guru and not India's most successful captain.

While the on-field composure has led to the 'Captain Cool' label, there is another adjective often used to describe Dhoni's cricket – street-smart. A recognition of a person's capacity to use common sense resourcefulness to the maximum. Kiran More reveals that barely a few matches into his international career, Dhoni's street-smart skills were spotted by coach Greg Chappell, who told him that he would be a future India captain. 'His cricket brain is always ticking was Chappell's unqualified verdict to us,' says More.

Points out Fleming, 'He will do things on the field which will make you say to yourself, "Hey, what the hell is M.S. doing now? Why is he making a bowling change or a fielding shift?" And then suddenly you realize he's got it right again.' This ability to stay a step ahead of his rivals has been Dhoni's forte, especially in a limited overs game, which requires instant decision-making. 'I often go by my gut feeling which in turn is based on experience. I think it helped as a captain that I was also a wicketkeeper. As a keeper, you have to be focused on every single ball, plus you can see all the angles on the ground, know what the batsman is doing, how the pitch is behaving. Trust me, wicketkeepers make good captains,' he insists.

Suresh Raina, who has played a lot with Dhoni for India and the Chennai Super Kings franchise, recalls an incident from the Champions Trophy win in England in 2013 that typifies Dhoni's style of leadership. 'It was the last ball of the match, and England needed six runs to win with the tail-enders at the crease. The rest of us were already celebrating while Mahi calmly set the field and warned us, "Don't forget Javed Miandad once hit Chetan Sharma for a six off the last ball." That is how M.S. thinks on his feet, for him no game is won till the end,' says Raina.

Captaincy for Dhoni has always been more about instinct than method. His pre-match team meetings, he says, would be short and focused. 'When you are playing for India over a long period, you don't need too much planning, what you need is execution. You can make all the plans you want, in the end it's only the performance on the field that matters.' Perhaps the lack of diligent planning exposed him in Test cricket because the longer format demands a careful mix of patience and aggression. I ask Dhoni if he accepts the criticism that his Test captaincy, especially in overseas conditions, was found wanting (he won 6 Tests abroad and lost 15). 'Look, in the end you need 20 wickets to win a Test. When your bowlers perform, you will win. Maybe we didn't always have bowlers who could win you the games overseas on a regular basis,' he counters.

However, Dhoni accepts that the buck stops with him as captain. 'When I first captained India in Tests, we had all these seniors around me. On the field, I was conscious of doing the job I had been assigned. I would take advice from the seniors but in the end the decision was mine. I had to be convinced and they realized that. Off the field, I remained their fan, respected them and gave them the freedom to do what they wanted. It was a case of mutual respect. That is how a team ethic is built, especially in our Indian environment where people can get extra sensitive,' he says.

With peers and juniors, Dhoni was more friend and father figure. R. Ashwin, whose career took off under Dhoni's Chennai Super Kings captaincy, relates a story of how Dhoni backed him as a young emerging player. 'We were playing the Champions League in South Africa. The match went into a Super Over and I was hit for 23 runs and we lost the game. I was feeling down but Dhoni kept the faith. In the next game, he made me open the bowling once again. I picked up crucial wickets and won it for Chennai. If M.S. trusts you, then he backs you fully,' explains Ashwin.

Is it the unique Dhoni approach to the sport that combines natural ability with a rooted 'Indianness' that has made him so successful as a cricketer and leader? He has, after all, spent a large part of his early years playing tennis-ball cricket, which has a distinctive South Asian back street touch. In fact, while playing tennis-ball cricket Dhoni learnt a shot he quite uniquely made his own. Dhoni's trademark 'helicopter' shot is a perfect example of his core skill sets, combining hand–eye coordination, power, bat speed, innovation and, in the final analysis, sheer audacity. To a yorker-length ball, Dhoni will stay almost stationary in his stance but then with a last-minute lift-off from his powerful wrists and forearms send the ball soaring into the stands.

'It was actually a close friend of mine, Santosh Lal who invented the shot in tennis-ball cricket and I learnt it from him in exchange for samosas. We used to call it the "thappad" shot in tennis-ball cricket because it was like slapping the ball,' says Dhoni. 'It was a very effective way to hit sixes.' (Santosh passed away at the age of thirty-two because of pancreatitis. Dhoni got an air ambulance to bring him from Ranchi to Delhi for emergency treatment but the plane was stuck in Varanasi due to bad weather and Santosh couldn't be saved.)

The 'helicopter' shot is just one aspect of Dhoni's power game that has made him arguably the most dangerous one-day batsman of his generation, and certainly in his pomp the best finisher. 'Last over, 15 to 16 runs to get, and if M.S. is there, you almost feel that he's going to do it more often than not,' says Fleming, adding, 'He just has this confidence in his own ability, secure in the knowledge that he's done it so many times before that he can do it again.' So how does he manage to pull it off time and again in crunch situations? 'People only think that the batsman is under pressure to score the runs, don't forget the bowler is also under equal pressure to deny me the chance to open my arms and hit a six,' says Dhoni.

But why does he often choose to take the match into the last over instead of trying to finish it much earlier? 'Look, I don't want to take the match to the last over but sometimes that's just what happens. Remember, I used to mostly bat at number six, so I would often come in with only a few overs left and a mounting run rate. If you are batting at the top, you can take instant risks and get away because you know there are batsmen to follow. At number six you have to be a little careful and take it as deep as possible so that the opposition is also put under pressure. You just have to break down a target and know when to attack. Usually I like to target the 49th over in a 50-over game. Once you are in the zone, scoring 10–15 runs an over in the final overs is not difficult,' he says. The argument is made with the intense self-belief integral to his mental make-up. To understand Dhoni the 'finisher' is to respect a man of strong convictions. There is clearly a method to his last-over madness.

Which explains why Dhoni has succeeded as a wicketkeeper too, a skill for which he often doesn't get enough credit. Dhoni admits that in his early years he wasn't seen as a technically proficient keeper but he worked hard to become better. 'People initially used to think that I caught a ball like a football goalkeeper. I would only ask them one question. "Out kiya ki nahin? [Did I get them out or not?]"' he says. Kiran More, one of India's better keepers, says that Dhoni's keeping, like his batting abilities, benefits from his quick thinking. 'You won't see him drop too many chances but also just look at the number of chances he will create with a sharp run-out or an alert stumping. That's what makes him special,' he claims. Former all-rounder Ravi Shastri observes that the real skill of a wicketkeeper is tested when he keeps to spinners. 'I don't think I have ever seen a keeper effect a stumping with the speed of Dhoni,' he points out. It is again a tribute to his match awareness skills that Dhoni rarely misses the stumps when he has to throw them down with his gloves off. 'I wasn't very good at seven tiles and marbles in school but on a cricket field I know exactly what to do,' says Dhoni.

Maybe at least part of Dhoni's success is emblematic of the 'jugaad' culture that still lies at the heart of modern India's rise. Jugaad is the innovative 'quick-fix', now even an accepted management technique designed to maximize results with minimum resources. That the old-style quadricycle made of wooden planks and old jeep parts was the original vehicle of 'jugaad' is something that Dhoni, an obsessive auto freak, can probably identify with. He even has his own 'jugaad' story to share, one that epitomizes his ability to improvise. 'We were once travelling on the highway when our car's bumper almost fell off. I was wearing these mountain bike shoes with big laces. Within sixty seconds I had solved the problem by removing my shoelaces and tying the bumper with them.'

Would Dhoni be an automatic choice as wicketkeeper-batsman in an all-time India eleven? There will be those who prefer Syed Kirmani for his technical excellence or Farokh Engineer for his flashiness but the truth is Dhoni is easily the better all-round cricketer. Critics often point out his limited success in overseas conditions – all his 16 international hundreds have come in Asia – and there is evidence to suggest that Dhoni's limited footwork and tendency to push hard at the ball make him vulnerable to both the moving and the spinning ball. However, as his career is illuminated with so many match-winning innings it is difficult to look beyond Dhoni as India's finest wicketkeeper-batsman of all time (he has the highest average for any keeper in winning games). 'The best thing about Dhoni is that he copies no one, he has his own style. On his day, woh ek over mein raat ko din mein badal sakta hai [he can change night into day in one over],' gushes Sehwag.

Indeed, if Sehwag himself redefined the art of opening batting for India with his bold strokeplay, then Dhoni's intrepid heroism has given Indian cricket the competitive muscle it needs to take on the world. Forget Captain Cool, Dhoni has been Mr India, the superhero a nation trusts will come good in a crisis. He has achieved this stature without ever raising his voice in anger or forcing himself into the spotlight. His is the power of the silent warrior, a true leader on and off the field. When I ask him how he would like cricket fans to remember him and which of his major triumphs is most special, the answer defines the man: 'Cricket statistics and records really don't interest me. I just want to be remembered as a good human being.'

It is said in such an unpretentious manner that you believe him. Don't forget that in an age of ruthless combat, Dhoni has always walked when he is out without even waiting for the umpire's signal. 'It is one of the first lessons our coach taught us in school,' he says. The spirit of cricket nestles easily in one of the sport's shrewdest minds.

~

On 30 December 2014, Dhoni quietly announced his retirement from Test cricket after the third Test against Australia in Melbourne. He had just played a battling innings to help India draw the game and there was still one Test left in the series. Shastri, who was team coach, admits he was taken by surprise. 'I had no inkling of what was in his mind, but then that's typical of M.S. There are no half-measures in anything he does,' says Shastri.

A team meeting was hastily called soon after Dhoni, a veteran of 90 tests but still aged only thirty-three, rang up the cricket board secretary to inform him of the decision. Some players reportedly wept while others were stunned into silence. A terse press release was issued but there was no fanfare, no thought of a farewell Test for a great of the game. The no-frills drama was again typical of the man. 'I just felt it was the right time and the right thing to do. Virat was ready to lead and a young wicketkeeper was emerging in Wriddhiman Saha who I felt deserved more opportunities,' Dhoni tells me while disclosing that he consulted no one, not even family members, before taking the call.

But why retire midway through a series and why not complete a century of Tests before walking away, especially since no one retired any longer in their early thirties? 'Look, we had lost the series by then so there was no point hanging on. Virat was in great form and deserved a go. As for reaching 100 Tests, to be honest, milestones don't make a difference to me. Maybe if I had played 99 Tests, I might have thought otherwise, but I was happy with what I had achieved and was leaving with no regrets,' he says.

Two years after his Test retirement, in January 2017, Dhoni stepped aside as the Twenty20 and one-day captain as well, paving the way for Virat to captain in all three formats. 'I don't think split captaincy works in India, you need one leader to show the way.

Besides, I want to play till the 2019 World Cup, and I think the break from captaincy will give me the freedom to express myself better,' he says. Dhoni's candid confession that he intends to play the 2019 World Cup makes clear the man's desire to live on his terms. He will quit when he is ready and not when pundits tell him his time is up.

What Dhoni won't say is that after almost a decade on the road, the mind and body have begun to tire. Between 2007 and 2017, Dhoni played an astonishing 374 matches for India (Virat Kohli is the next highest in this period with 284). 'I don't recall when I spent more than a week at home at a stretch once I began playing international cricket. It was like being on a non-stop treadmill,' he says. That he never appeared tired on the field despite the triple role of captain, keeper and batsman is testimony to what he calls his 'natural fitness'. 'I think the only time I would feel tired was the first day of a new Test series when I had to keep for 90 overs. That one day it would take some time to get the body right, but once I was in the groove, I never had a problem with fitness,' he says and then reminds me, 'Don't forget, my family originally comes from Uttarakhand, we hill people are usually very fit.'

But what Dhoni won't concede is that the constant media criticism of his performance was slowly beginning to get to him. While he was still averaging more than 50 in one-dayers, from 2014 onwards his Test average dipped significantly. (Outside Asia, he averaged just 29.8 in this period.)

It wasn't just his on-field performance that was under the scanner; the IPL spot-fixing scandal that broke in 2013 brought Dhoni under scrutiny too. He was accused of protecting his Chennai team owner and then BCCI president N. Srinivasan's son-in-law Gurunath Meiyappan, who was arrested in a betting case. Dhoni was also vice president in Srinivasan's company India Cements, leading to accusations of 'conflict of interest'. Would it not be difficult for the India captain to testify against the BCCI president's son-in-law when he was also a vice president in the BCCI chief's company?

Meiyappan was routinely in the Chennai Super Kings dugout during matches. Dhoni was accused of not revealing the true extent of his involvement in the team before a Supreme Court–appointed panel that was investigating the betting and spot-fixing scandal. 'Let me tell you, it is an absolute lie that I told a probe panel that Meiyappan was only a cricket enthusiast, all I said is he had nothing to do with the team's on-field cricketing decisions. I can't even pronounce the word "enthusiast",' he says with a touch of sarcasm. A Supreme Court committee didn't buy the attempt to delink Meiyappan from Chennai Super Kings. In 2015, the team was suspended from the IPL for two years and Meiyappan banned for life from any involvement in cricket matches.

An unapologetic Dhoni defends his equation with Srinivasan, claiming that the former board chief was a true supporter of Indian cricket. 'I really don't care what people say, I found Srinivasan as someone who was always there to help cricketers,' he argues. Dhoni's loyalty to the former BCCI chief is revealing. It suggests a strong personality who is not swayed easily by criticism. But it also exposes Dhoni to the charge that under the outward image of rustic innocence lurks a sharp political mind. 'Make no mistake, Dhoni knows which way the wind is blowing, he knows how to manoeuvre his way through the BCCI's corridors of power when required,' says a board official.

The Dhoni–Srinivasan relationship had blossomed during the early IPL years when he was picked for Chennai Super Kings. It looked to be an unusual equation: an iconic player from a Hindi-speaking state was now Chennai's favourite son. The 'Whistle podu' team song had earned Dhoni a new legion of fans across the Vindhyas, a genuine connect that highlighted how India too was slowly shedding its linguistic parochialism. A Hindi-speaking hero was now a pin-up boy in a Tamil-dominated city.

'It was a bit like those Hindi films, boy from north meets girl from south and falls in love,' says Dhoni. Like the team song, Chennai's cricket too was a superhit; the IPL franchise won two titles and reached the finals on three occasions in the tournament's first six years. 'The people of Chennai are serious cricket followers. Dhoni embraced our cricket culture so readily; he really was the fulcrum of our team's success. We gifted him a bike when he joined Chennai Super Kings and he would take it for a spin, stop at traffic lights and just smile at passers-by,' recalls Srinivasan. The former board president tells me that when Dhoni once invited him to his house in Ranchi, he ensured masala dosa was on the menu. 'We appreciated his cricket, he gave us respect in turn, what is wrong with that?' asks Srinivasan.

But there are persistent accusations that Chennai players were given special privileges by the cricket board during the IPL. Lalit Modi claims that Srinivasan arm-twisted him into allowing Dhoni to be retained as Chennai's Icon Player in 2010 without being put through an auction. 'It was illegal since Icon Player status was meant to be only for the first three years of the IPL and yet Srinivasan was allowed to get away with it,' says Modi.

Veteran cricketer Mohinder Amarnath tells me that as national selector in 2012 he wanted to drop Dhoni as captain but Srinivasan shielded him. 'We were told that the board president and not the selectors will decide who the India captain is,' says Amarnath. 'Yes, it is true that I vetoed the decision to drop Dhoni as captain. How can you drop someone as captain within a year of his lifting the World Cup?' argues the former BCCI president.

Srinivasan's admission that he did veto the attempt to remove Dhoni as captain is significant. It only confirms that the India captain and the cricket board chief had a 'special' relationship that went well beyond the normal player–official equation. From an earlier era where players were subservient to the board, Indian cricket had entered an age where 'star' players called the shots and board officials were happy to pamper them. 'What you call favouritism I say is my respect for a top-class cricketer's achievements,' says Srinivasan sharply.

The Dhoni–Srinivasan 'friendship' extends to off-field financial benefits. In 2013, details emerged of how Rhiti Sports, a sports management company in which Dhoni had a large stake, was handling the contracts of both Chennai Super Kings and India players, leading to serious conflict of interest charges. That a captain who had an influence over team selection was also the owner of a management agency representing players is further evidence of how 'star' players in Indian cricket could now get away with tweaking the system for personal advantage. Rhiti Sports was also allowed a share in the endorsement deals signed by Chennai Super Kings as its marketing agents.

Rhiti had been set up by Dhoni in partnership with Arun Pandey, a close friend from his Bihar Ranji Trophy days. Pandey is a brawny, paan-chewing toughie from Varanasi who acts as Dhoni's personal gatekeeper and now handles all of his businesses. By 2014, the business empire was large enough for Dhoni to be listed as the fifth most valuable sports brand, with his annual earnings pegged at $30 million and endorsements valued at $26 million. 'Apart from managing more than two dozen cricketers, we now have our own sports shoe brand called 7; and lifestyle apparel, gymnasiums, football, hockey and super-bike franchise investments,' says Pandey.

The diversified portfolio suggests that Dhoni is an astute businessman but the cricketer insists that money doesn't drive him at all. 'I have more than I will ever need for one life. All these investments are handled by Arun and others, I don't have any role to play,' he claims. But Kolkata-based sports marketing consultant Jeet Banerjee, who once managed the cricketer's contracts and with whom Dhoni fought a messy court battle, argues that the former India captain is hard-nosed in contractual negotiations. 'Don't get taken in by his soft-spoken nature. When it comes to financial dealings, Dhoni can be ruthless. He even put the Ranchi police on to me and my family when we fell out,' he says.

The player-agent equation is a more recent trend in Indian cricket. When Farokh Engineer advertised for Brylcreem in the 1960s, he claims to have negotiated a decent 2000-pound contract on his own. Even Gavaskar and Kapil Dev, the two big stars of the seventies, didn't have agents to assist them in framing advertising contracts. The transformation came with the rise of the Tendulkar brand in the 1990s, Dhoni just took it to another level. 'Player agents are a new power centre in Indian cricket,' a board official tells me. 'They can sometimes dictate terms on behalf of their client.'

But perhaps the most troubling moment for Dhoni came in 2013–14 with the insinuation that he was involved in 'fixing' IPL matches. 'That is where I really have to draw the line. Please criticize me but how can you accuse me of something like fixing a cricket game after all that the game has given me. For mediapersons to say things like "there can be no smoke without fire" is crazy. That is why I don't want to even talk to the media,' he says.

The relationship between Dhoni and the media has been a peculiar one. No cricketer with the exception of Tendulkar has been so celebrated since the turn of the century, and yet no other player has so deliberately stayed away from the media whirl. No interviews, one-line staccato answers in press conferences, the odd witticism; Dhoni has managed to keep the prying media at bay. 'You can call it my "satyagraha" against the media. I don't want to speak when I do badly. I won't speak when I do well either, the media can write what they wish,' he says. After the World Twenty20 semi-final loss in 2016, when an Australian journalist asked him about retirement, Dhoni invited the journalist on to the podium and then cheekily told him, 'If you were an Indian, then maybe I would have asked you whether you have a son or a brother who is a wicketkeeper and can take my place.' As Dhoni smiled, the press lounge burst into laughter. 'Sometimes it is best to meet criticism with humour,' says Dhoni.

Is the irreverence simply a mask to hide the real Dhoni, or is this part of a well-considered strategy to keep the fans on his side? There is undoubtedly an air of mystery, an enigmatic edge due to his sheer inaccessibility. This is a cricket superstar who lives a shadow-like existence, who rarely keeps a mobile with him, or even if he does, won't respond to calls or SMSs. (When he became a father just ahead of the 2015 World Cup, he wasn't carrying a mobile so his wife sent

an SMS through his close cricket mate Suresh Raina to inform
him of the birth of his daughter!). Many Dhoni fans believe that an
incident in 2007 when India lost the World Cup and his house in
Ranchi was targeted was the turning point. 'Actually, it was a new
house that we were constructing so no one was living there. Some
people entered and just pushed a few bricks that we had laid out for
the construction, that's all. But yes, it deeply affected my family. Now,
you can visit my parents, they will give you chai, but won't speak to
the press any longer,' he says.

In 2016, the mask of extreme privacy almost fell off for the first
time when a biopic on Dhoni's life was released. The film took Dhoni's
remarkably inspirational journey to millions of homes and was an
instant hit. But the decision to bare his life on celluloid, he insists,
was not his. 'It's Arun and my team at Rhiti who did it all. Honestly,
I was not interested and actually a bit embarrassed. I thought the film
will take years to make so I didn't bother too much at first,' he says.
He didn't even get too involved in the film's promotion campaign
saying 'being on television and talking about my life is not my scene'.
The film depicts some aspects of Dhoni's life that were unknown till
then, including an early romantic relationship with a woman who
died in a car accident. 'It's all true, I wanted the film to be honest
and as close to reality as possible,' he says.

The film is perhaps the closest anyone has got to the otherwise
inscrutable Dhoni's private world. In 2010, when Dhoni married
Sakshi Rawat, a hotel management graduate, the cameras were kept
determinedly away from the wedding ceremony. Only a handful of
his cricket friends made the trek to Dehradun where the wedding was
held amidst great secrecy. 'If I had to have a big wedding, I would
have had to invite over a thousand people and wouldn't know who
to leave out. This way, those who I could contact at the last minute
managed to come and the rest understood my decision to keep the
wedding a small affair,' he explains.

The decision was quintessential Dhoni, a fierce individualist who
stays away from the page three celebrity circuit, avoids late-night

parties, doesn't touch alcohol – he didn't even have champagne after winning the World Cup – and whose rare indulgences include an occasional puff of scented hookah. He says he would rather sit around with close family and friends in Ranchi than be in the shimmering lights of the big city. Ranchi is his comfort zone which keeps him grounded, the place where it all began, and where he has just moved into a new farmhouse on the outskirts of the city. 'I prefer Ranchi to Mumbai or Delhi because here I can come in and out of home ten times in a day with no hassle. In the metros, where is the time and space to do your own thing? Once you leave home, you won't return for hours,' he says.

So how does Dhoni relax? 'Sitting around with my family [his first child, daughter Ziva, was born in 2015], meeting my friends where we talk everything but cricket, playing video games, listening to Kishore Kumar songs, especially the 'happy' songs, playing with my dogs [he has six of them], and then taking care of my old bikes [more than 50],' he says. Where did the bike fixation come from? 'You know in school one of our seniors used to come on a Yamaha bike and make us take hard catches in front of his bike. We were warned that if we missed the ball and it hit the bike, we would have to pay for the damage. From that day on, I guess I wanted to have my own wheels,' he confides. Even now, he will take his bike out for a spin in Ranchi when the mood grabs him. Doesn't anyone recognize him? 'Not with the helmet on, no,' he says. He even occasionally goes to his old school sports complex to play a game of badminton. 'He comes late in the evening when no one is around because otherwise there will be chaos,' says coach Banerjee, who is still the school sports master.

Raghu Iyer, the CEO of Rising Pune Supergiant, the franchise to which Dhoni moved after the Chennai team was banned for two years in the aftermath of the fixing scandal, aptly describes Dhoni as 'a unique person who marches to the beat of his own drum'. He relates a story of how Dhoni won Pune a match from a losing position against Sunrisers Hyderabad in 2017, a win which sparked off much celebration in the team. 'Everyone was excited with the victory but

M.S. was happy to sit quietly in his room and play video games with the awestruck young members of the team. He just kept an open door where anyone could walk in,' says Iyer. After a big IPL match day, Dhoni's schedule is to go to bed at 3 a.m. and then wake up the next day only at noon. 'Good sleep is the best form of relaxation,' he says.

While cricket has been Dhoni's driving force for much of his life, he has now discovered another abiding passion: the armed forces have almost become a parallel theme in his self-identity. In November 2011, months after the World Cup win, Dhoni was conferred the rank of honorary lieutenant colonel in the Territorial Army. 'When I wore the uniform for the first time, I was over the moon. I felt as happy as I had when we won the World Cup,' he claims. He reportedly slept in the uniform that first night. Even now, he will often wear army fatigues and military boots. He carries a licensed gun and is by all accounts a very good marksman who every 1 January likes to begin the New Year with a ritual visit to the nearest shooting range. 'I find shooting very calming. It's just you and the target and then silence all around you, it's an environment I feel comfortable in,' he says.

Dhoni has even done a course in para-jumping with the air force and has travelled to the Line of Control to spend time with jawans. 'That was an unforgettable experience. We went to over a dozen posts on the Line of Control and spent time with the forces and had "bada khaana" with them in the army mess. I loved every moment of it,' he tells me. He says that the army represents the best of India, a spirit of sacrifice and the idea of unity in diversity that he finds attractive. 'You will see a sardar being the commanding officer of the Madras Regiment and speaking in fluent Tamil. Where else do we find that?' he asks. On a cricket field, I gently suggest.

Would he have liked to join the forces if he were not a cricketer? 'I might have. After all, a soldier also has to wear a uniform like a cricketer, a uniform which stands for discipline, valour and sacrifice. I just feel that we as a nation should do more for our armed forces. We have a candlelight march when a civilian dies in India, so why not when a soldier is martyred? One of my favourite sayings now is that we all talk of Bhagat Singh's martyrdom but nobody wants their son to be Bhagat Singh,' he says with unusual loquaciousness.

It's the kind of punchline that is usually thrown by a general during a raucous television debate. The reserved Dhoni is unlikely to become a television talking head but I can visualize him with the troops on the border leading a commando operation. After all, right through his cricket career he has relished a challenge by leading from the front.

As my interview draws to a close (the first he's done with any journalist, he reminds me, since we last met in 2011) and I prepare to leave, his manager Arun Pandey has a suggestion. 'You should get Mahi to do a television programme with jawans. He will never say no to that.' I make a mental note for the future. The way to the heart of India's most enigmatic cricketer is to indulge his fascination for a career in the armed forces.

~

In 2008 management consultancy firm EY brought out a report titled 'The Dhoni Effect: Rise of Small Town India'. The report suggested that with the growth of the Indian economy, the rising rich and middle class were spreading beyond the metros to Tier II, Tier III and Tier IV cities. The phenomenon where the rapidly growing small towns of India were taking centre stage in the marketing strategies of the country's top brands was described as 'The Dhoni Effect'.

That a management company had titled a market trends report after Dhoni was a recognition that smaller cities and the middle and lower classes could easily identify with his rustic charm. Ad Guru Piyush Pandey was among the first to recognize the power of the Dhoni brand while doing a television commercial with him and Bollywood idol Shah Rukh Khan. 'Dhoni was an instant hit with the consumer, especially outside the metros. He was the underdog, the man who had come from nowhere to take on the world. Even Sachin was after all from Mumbai, the glamour city of cricket. Dhoni was the guy from the boondocks who no one thought had a chance of succeeding,' says Pandey.

With his meteoric rise, Dhoni came to represent the energies of small-town India that had felt marginalized for years and was only now beginning to assert itself. It's a theme that was well captured in the 2005 hit Bollywood film *Bunty Aur Babli*, tracking the rollicking escapades of a couple looking to strike gold in the big city. That the film was released just around the time Dhoni announced his arrival on the cricket stage may have been pure coincidence. But there was no doubting the rise of a 'new India' from the 'chhote shahar' (small town).

Competitive exams for IITs, medical colleges and civil services were the first to ride the wave of change, with remarkable success stories emerging from lesser-known places. Now, cricket had caught the surge. 'Since the turn of the century, small-town India is where the action is,' argues sociologist Dipankar Gupta. 'That is where the new white-collar middle class is growing, where the stock market cult is deepening, where there is a rapid expansion in ATMs, mobile stores, malls, multiplex cinemas and consumer durables.'

For this class, Dhoni was the poster boy of aspiration, the son of a humble public sector employee from Ranchi who had defied the odds to succeed at the highest level in India's most competitive mass sport. Small-town India, after all, has produced hockey and wrestling stars in the past but these sports lacked the nationwide popular appeal of cricket. Kabaddi is a rural sport but it is only in the last few years that its star players have been 'glamorized' for a wider audience by the telecast of the Pro Kabaddi League on satellite television. Before Dhoni, only Kapil Dev could claim to wear his rustic appeal on his sleeve. But Dev's rise was in the pre-liberalization India of the 1980s where the consumer market was still limited mainly to the metros. 'Like with Sachin, you could argue that Dhoni was also there at the right time and at the right place. If Sachin caught the first wave of liberalizing India in the early 1990s then Dhoni captured the ambitions of a consumer revolution that was spreading beyond the big cities,' suggests commentator Harsha Bhogle.

Cricket itself was reflecting the geographical shift that was taking place in a rapidly expanding market economy. When India won in 1971, the entire team comprised players only from the six major metros; half a dozen from Mumbai alone. Kapil Dev's 1983 team had only two players – Yashpal Sharma and Kapil himself – who didn't play for a big city Ranji team. When Dhoni lifted the World Cup in 2011, the team had six players from smaller Ranji Trophy teams, while a seventh, Zaheer Khan, had played his early cricket in the remote Maharashtra town of Shrirampur. An eighth, Virender Sehwag, was from Najafgarh, a rural township on the Delhi–Haryana border. 'Yuvraj, Zaheer and Harbhajan, all from small towns, preceded Dhoni into the Indian team but as captain of the team, it was Dhoni who really became an illustration and the catalyst of the change,' says Bhogle.

Many of the early small-town cricket heroes had to battle great odds, financial and sporting, to emerge stronger. Harbhajan Singh claims that his family in Jalandhar where he grew up had only one cycle at home for travel. 'I knew when I took the cycle to practice, my father, who had a small business of his own, would have to walk to work,' he says. When he first played cricket for the Punjab under-16 team, Harbhajan had only one pair of worn-out spiked shoes that had cost Rs 250 and a single pair of white shirt and trousers. 'I guess I had this junoon [obsession] to play the game so it didn't matter that I came from a small town with few facilities,' he says.

Zaheer Khan, who was also born in a semi-rural household with limited means, played only tennis-ball cricket in the taluka town of Shrirampur till he finally moved to Mumbai at the age of seventeen to chase his cricket dream. 'I was giving my twelfth standard exams when I watched the 1996 World Cup on television and was so carried away with the euphoria around it that I decided to give up my plans to join a rural engineering college and try and make it in cricket instead,' he says. Zaheer stayed with an aunt in a tiny studio apartment in Mumbai for three years, and admits that adjusting to life in the big city wasn't easy. 'Too many people, too few open spaces and yes, travelling on crowded local trains was never easy for a small-town person. I also knew that I was attempting something which only eleven in a billion will succeed at, an India cap!'

Today, the Indian team has more players from small-town India than from the big cities, the majority of them from humble backgrounds, an indication of the new 'class' and 'democratic' character of Indian cricket. Mohammed Shami grew up in a village in UP's Amroha district and then moved to a tiny rented accommodation in Kolkata to further his cricket. His fast bowling partner Umesh Yadav is the son of a coal mine loader who lived in a village near Nagpur and tried for a job as a police constable before his physical attributes helped him make the cut in cricket. Ravindra Jadeja's mother worked as a nurse in a government hospital in Jamnagar to help the family meet its financial needs. Ajinkya Rahane lived in Dombivili, a town in Thane district near Mumbai, and had to wake up at 5 a.m. every morning to take a train to go for early morning practice in the city. 'I guess those long train rides [it would take him almost two hours] into Mumbai to play on a turf wicket toughened me up,' he tells me.

Is there then a greater hunger to succeed that motivates the boys from low-income families and small towns, an ambition fuelled by hardship and adversity, I ask Dhoni. 'I don't think we can generalize, it isn't as if every small-town boy with talent will make it to the Indian team. Yes, maybe we now have more opportunities than before but I have also seen small-town boys lose their way easily. Look at Virat, he is from Delhi and is now a role model for the new generation. His passion and hunger to win are just as great as anyone else,' responds Dhoni.

Sociologist Gupta offers a more prosaic explanation for the rise of the small-town cricketer. 'I think it has to do with accessibility to playgrounds. Where are the open spaces in the big cities for kids to play? You have to travel miles through traffic to get to them which is why young kids in the city choose the vicarious entertainment of playing video games on their mobiles,' he points out. Dhoni concurs: 'I think it helped that there were no mobile phones when I was growing up. For me, the only source of entertainment then was playing sport on the field, sitting at home was simply not an option.'

Perhaps elite schools in the metros with their obsessive focus on exams and marks have left students with little time to play even as the lesser-known institutes are keen to showcase their sporting skills. 'When I was growing up, my parents would ask whether I have passed or not, now we first ask our children whether they have got 95 per cent or not,' says Sehwag, who has started an international school in Haryana's Jhajjar district where sports and academics go hand in hand.

Maybe the much-maligned BCCI deserves a bit of credit too. The more progressive state associations have set up turf wickets in almost every district and cricket academies have sprung up in remote corners as talent spotting centres. The biggest catalyst for this mini-revolution has been the IPL. 'I think it is the IPL which changed everything,' says former Mumbai captain Shishir Hattangadi. 'Cricket was always popular, but the IPL has now given parents in small towns the belief that it can provide a potentially lucrative career for their children.'

As a billionaire sports hero, Dhoni in a sense has become a symbol of hope for 'neo-middle-class' India, one that desperately wants to get on to the fast track to wealth and upward mobility. In 2017 when the Jharkhand government organized a 'Momentum Jharkhand' investors' summit to attract investment into the state, Dhoni was the automatic choice as brand ambassador. Dressed in jacket and tie and with a military-style short haircut, Dhoni made a powerful pitch to investors to look at Jharkhand beyond its chronic political instability and as an engine of growth instead. The speech even led to reports that Dhoni may be considering a post-retirement political career. 'To be in politics, you have to lie and I don't think I can do that,' is his firm response. And yet, as the most recognized face of Jharkhand, the prospect of Dhoni contesting for public office is alluring. In a state whose politics has been blighted by corruption and Naxal violence, Dhoni's calm presence might reassure Jharkhandis that there is a ray of sunshine creeping through an area of darkness. He is, after all, the small-town revolutionary who transformed Indian cricket. Could he one day alter Jharkhand's politics too?

~

Postscript: Tracking down Dhoni for an interview can be a real challenge. He is like a leopard in a jungle: a notoriously elusive animal who hides even as the world craves to spot him. In 2006, a prominent news editor tried to get Dhoni for his prime-time television show but the cricketer kept refusing his invite. The editor even rang up the then BCCI chief Sharad Pawar and the Jharkhand chief minister Arjun Munda but to no avail. The attempt to pressurize him to grant an interview backfired. 'Please tell your boss that now that he has tried to use VVIP influence on me, I will never speak to him,' Dhoni told the editor's assistant.

I was far more careful. Incessant mails to his manager finally resulted in me getting Dhoni's mobile number. But my texts to him went unanswered. My lucky break came when Sanjeev Goenka, the owner of the Pune IPL franchise, invited me to a dinner in May 2017 to meet his team. Raghu Iyer, the Pune team CEO, had already helpfully suggested that I should come early for the dinner and meet Dhoni. 'Are you sure he will be there?' I asked anxiously. 'Yes, he is coming,' assured Iyer. My concern was heightened because Dhoni had been removed as captain by Goenka at the start of the season, allegedly because the Pune franchise owner felt that Dhoni's 'heart' was still with Chennai. It was a decision that had drawn much flak. (Later, Dhoni would tell me that he had come to terms with his removal since the Pune team had failed to perform in its first year under his leadership. 'In franchise cricket, you must expect hire and fire,' he said with a touch of pragmatism.)

On the appointed evening, I pre-recorded my prime-time television show so I could make it to the dinner on time for once. When I arrived at around 9 p.m., Delhi's power elite were slowly trooping in. MPs, ministers and industrialists, these were the Lutyens movers and shakers in their familiar terrain. While the rest of the team had arrived on time, there was no sign of Dhoni. 'He is finishing a sponsor commitment, don't worry, he will come,' reassured Iyer. At around 9.30 p.m., there was a tizzy in the house. Dhoni, we were informed, was about to arrive. I nervously waited at the door to catch his eye. That's when he stepped out of his car in a loose T-shirt, looking very fit and sprightly, the slight strain of grey on his facial hair providing the only hint of ageing. He embraced Kapil Dev, the original small-town folk hero, and then turned to me with a smile. 'Yes, I know you have been trying to reach me,' he said. 'But what to do, I have been so caught up in the IPL.'

'But I have been trying for months to meet you and only need an hour of your time,' I promised. 'Don't worry, we will do it. Your father, after all, was a great cricketer and I respect you as a journalist,' he said affectionately. 'But when?' I asked anxiously. 'The day after the match come to the hotel at 12 noon. At the moment, I want to stay in the cricket zone,' he replied.

The interview did happen and he gave me much more than the hour I had bargained for, even pressing a do not disturb button on the hotel phone while we spoke. But in between, something else had happened at the Goenka dinner which stayed with me. Barely had he entered the house than Dhoni disappeared again for a brief while. Suddenly, we saw him in the garden with a small plastic bat and ball, playing with Goenka's grandson. The moment he had finished, the drivers and the staff of the house excitedly rushed towards him to take a selfie. While the VVIPs were clinking their wine glasses, a smiling Dhoni patiently obliged each of his fans with a photo. No one was refused. The staff was delighted. My driver Ramesh Mandal who hails from Darbhanga in Bihar, was excited to have his photo taken with the champion. 'Sir, apne Dhoni ji bahut achhe hain. Hamare Bihar ke bagal ke hi hain aur bilkul aam aadmi ki tarah hain [Sir, our Dhoni is very nice. He is from Bihar's neighbouring state and is just like an ordinary person],' he remarked. In his breathless elation, I could sense Dhoni's enduring appeal. His is the magnetism of the down-to-earth mass icon, the boy from small-town Ranchi whose astounding success fulfilled in a small way the covenant of 1947 when a nation's founders had dreamed of Indian citizens who would conquer the world through sheer talent and skill. Dhoni represents that founding dream of an India whose imagination would be captured not by slothful princes who reaped the benefits of dynasty and privilege but by someone with calloused feet and rough hands who could still spring into the air and catch and hit a cricket ball far beyond anyone's fantasies. That is the magic of Dhoni, looking at whom every Indian might say to himself: 'Yes, we can!'

11

Virat Kohli

Millennial Master

Adversity builds character. For an eighteen-year-old playing only his fourth first-class match for Delhi, 19 December 2006 should have been like any other day on the batting pitch. Brimming with the exuberance of youthful talent, Virat Kohli was returning home from the Feroz Shah Kotla ground, enthused about cricket and life. Karnataka had piled up a massive 446 runs and Delhi was struggling at 103 for 5 at the end of the second day's play but Virat was still batting on a well-made 40. He had struggled for form in his first few games but now appeared poised for a big score, which slightly stemmed the tide of the impending follow-on.

As he climbed the stairs to his first-floor home in the West Delhi colony of Vikaspuri, Virat had only one thought on his mind: rescue his team from a precarious position, score his first Ranji Trophy century and cement his place in a strong side.

Hours later, joy turned to sorrow. That night, Prem Kohli, Virat's doting father and the first to nurture his cricket dream, passed away after a sudden heart attack. The teenager faced a stark choice – stay at home and grieve with the family or leave for Kotla the next morning

329

and resume his innings. This is how the story unfolded in Virat's
own words.

'I had come home feeling good about my batting. I was 40 not out,
playing on a wicket I knew very well. I felt like I was in the zone and
wanted to capitalize on the opportunity, especially since I hadn't done
too well in my first few games. I knew my father had been unwell.
He had been under stress on the business side of things while looking
after the family [Virat's father had a criminal law practice and was
attempting to start his own business]. Because of the stress he was
under, he got a stroke and the left side of his body was paralysed.
He was a self-made man, so the physical disability and the fact that
he was now dependent on others got to him I think. He wasn't in
the best frame of mind when he got a cardiac arrest at around three
in the morning. My mother realized something was wrong but we
didn't have help or the resources needed to save him and he passed
away almost immediately. I was eighteen and my mind just blanked
out. I didn't know what was happening around me. All the relatives
were informed, and the house was in a state of shock.

'In the morning, around 6 a.m., I remembered that I was supposed
to go out and bat and I needed to take a call. So I called my coach
Rajkumar Sharma who was in Australia at the time and I told him
what had happened. He asked me what I wanted to do. I told him it
didn't feel right for me not to play, that's what my father would have
wanted me to do. So I went, I actually drove myself to the ground
which could only have happened because my mind had blanked out
completely. I remember telling my teammate Ishant Sharma, who
used to drive with me to the ground, that my father had passed
away, and he didn't believe it. When I reached, I didn't say a word
to anyone. I just wanted to be as normal as I could be. Ishant told
the team members about what had happened. I was fine till then but
when everyone came to console me, I broke down. That's when it
hit me as to what had actually happened – my father was gone. The
senior players told me I didn't have to go out and bat, but I said no,
I want to bat because I wanted to do what has to be done. I batted,

scored 90, and then got out to a bad decision – I was given out caught behind when I hadn't nicked the ball. I was disappointed but along with wicketkeeper Punit Bisht, we stitched together a partnership that helped us avoid the follow-on. Punit scored 150 but during the innings I hardly spoke to him. My mind was focused on scoring runs and saving the team. Nothing else mattered. From the ground, I went straight for the cremation ceremony.

'I didn't even tell my mother that I was going to the match. It was only my elder brother who informed her much later. I think everyone was in too much shock to even realize what was going on around them. Mentally we were all scarred. If you ask me today, I am not sure whether I would do the same thing all over again and play a match when you lose your father. But that day, it just seemed the right thing to do.' Virat narrates the agonizing story without getting overly emotional. His stoic nature is perhaps the mark of the man. Faced with tragedy, he sought strength from the field, the game his refuge and his armour.

His teammates remember the day well. 'He is my dear friend, I am sitting with him in the car, and I don't know what to say to him but he is ready to play the game,' says Ishant. Mithun Manhas, the Delhi captain for the match, recalls seeing Virat with bloodshot eyes sitting in a corner in the dressing room hours before the game. 'I remember going up to him and asking him what happened and he just mumbled, "My father has died". I didn't know what to say initially. Then I told him that he didn't have to bat and could go home. He insisted though that he would play. I was stunned.' Former India player Aakash Chopra, who was also playing the game, says the entire team was staggered by Virat's bravery. 'You've just lost your dad a few hours ago, you are only eighteen but you still haven't lost your focus on cricket. What can one say to such a person.'

Coach Rajkumar Sharma too has vivid memories. 'When Virat first rang me up to inform me and asked me what he should do, I didn't have an answer. I knew his father so I was naturally shocked. I called him back ten minutes later and told him that if he wanted to play, then it was a good decision,' says Sharma. The coach, a father figure for the young Virat, reveals that Virat called him again in the lunch break and this time cried over the phone. 'The first thing he said was "Sir, I was given out wrongly when I was just ten short of a century." Such was his obsession with cricket.'

In the plush multistorey house in Gurugram where he now lives there is a portrait of Virat's father as you enter through the main door. 'I just wish he had been around to see my success, but I know his presence is always there, that he is there to support me at all times, whenever I achieve something, I always thank him for being there for me in spirit,' says Virat. The loving father for whom his son's cricket dream had become his own personal mission, Prem Kohli often drove Virat to matches on his scooter. In a photo album there is a lovely picture of the child clinging to his father's shoulders at the dinner table, almost climbing on top of him with an impish smile. Prem Kohli, still wearing his blue helmet (probably just returned from work), smiles out of the photograph. 'Do you know my father was in hospital once and watching a cricket match on television when suddenly he turned to me and said, "Dekh lena, mera Virat one day will also play for India and be a big star," says elder brother Vikas. Prem Kohli's younger son is now a global cricket superstar and arguably the best batsman in the world.

This is a journey that began on a chilly December night soaked in tragedy, a night Virat can never forget. It strengthened his resolve to fulfil his father's dream to play successfully for India. Sometimes as he takes guard at the wicket, he knows he guards another dream. He hears a familiar whisper in his ear and feels a soft touch on his shoulder, his father's words echo: 'Mera beta India ke liye khel raha hai.'

~

West Delhi was once on the periphery of the national capital, an area populated by Punjabi refugee families who arrived in large numbers after Partition. The past tense is used advisedly here since the social geography and demographics of the capital city have rapidly changed in recent years. The spread of the Delhi Metro service and the wide expanse of flyovers have reduced distances and ushered in a mini-revolution. West Delhi's middle-class colonies remain congested but the small roadside businesses have given way to multistorey shopping malls.

'There is a hunger to succeed here that has sparked off an upwardly mobile ecosystem. We were once seen as the poor cousins of Delhi's urban elite, now we are showing the way, especially on the cricket field,' says Arun Jaitley, Union finance minister and cricket addict (he was president of the Delhi & District Cricket Association for thirteen years) who also grew up in the area.

Due to the emergence of role models and a strong work ethic West Delhi has slowly become the heartbeat of cricket in the capital. The majority of cricketers from Delhi who have represented the country over the last twenty-five years have come from West Delhi and surrounding areas: Virender Sehwag, Ashish Nehra, Ishant Sharma, Gautam Gambhir, Shikhar Dhawan, Aakash Chopra, and, of course, Virat, are all products of a cricket culture that could even rival Mumbai's Dadar Union–Shivaji Park dominance of the 1960s.

Chopra calls it a triumph of 'Punjabi aggression'. 'I guess as Indian cricket changed and became more competitive, it suited our Punjabi temperament,' he says. Gautam Gambhir, who belongs to an affluent family in the area and is an alumnus of the privileged Modern School, says he grew up listening to horror stories of Partition from his maternal grandfather which inspired him. 'My family had to flee from Pakistan and the tales I heard as a child gave me the stomach for combat which is important for a sportsperson,' he says.

Gambhir's opening partner Sehwag says that the environment in Najafgarh, a Jat-dominated rural township on the West Delhi–Haryana border where he grew up, toughened him up at an early age. 'Our area was known for its gang fights and crime. I have even seen two businessmen being murdered in front of my house. Once you've seen murders, then fast bowlers se darna kya!' he says. With little cricket infrastructure in the locality, Sehwag would travel almost two hours by bus to another West Delhi colony to play cricket. 'I would get up at 5 a.m., reach school at 7 a.m., then at 1 p.m. when school was done I would sleep for an hour in the school itself, then go to the cricket ground where I would help lay out the matting and water the pitch, practise from 3 p.m. to 6 p.m. and finally reach home by 8.30 p.m. and almost straight away go to sleep,' he recalls. Today Najafgarh has ten cricket academies as young children aspire to emulate their hero and become the next Nawab of Najafgarh. In the 1980s, however, there were no grounds and much of Sehwag's early cricket was played on an uneven road with a tennis ball.

At the heart of West Delhi's transformation was the Sonnet Cricket Club, begun in 1969 by 'Ustad' Tarak Sinha, Delhi's answer to Ramakant Achrekar who like his Mumbai counterpart can claim to have coached an India eleven. The purpose of the club was creating cricket opportunities for Delhi's youngsters beyond the scope of elite schools and colleges.

Atul Wassan, the fast bowler who played for India in the late 1980s, recalls how the boys from Sonnet with no club ground of their own had to fend for themselves, even laying out a matting wicket by carrying the mat on a cycle. 'We grew up in difficult conditions which made us more determined to succeed. We were battle-hardened Punjabi boys who always wanted to defeat the elite VIP kids of the NIS camp at National Stadium. We used to joke that they had the big cars, we had the bigger hearts,' he says.

By the mid 1980s, as many as nine members in Delhi's team were Sonnet products. They included Rajkumar Sharma, an off-spinner-batsman who played only a dozen games for Delhi over six years. This included a match against Imran Khan's formidable Pakistan team in 1987, about which he says, 'I was hit for four successive sixes by Manzoor Elahi.' The stocky Sharma started the West Delhi Cricket Academy in May 1998 with around 200 kids at the Saviour Convent School cricket ground. One of his first wards was Virat, still six months short of his tenth birthday. 'I remember his soft-spoken father bringing him on a scooter along with his elder brother Vikas, and just telling me, "He loves cricket, please just look after him."'

Until then, Virat's cricket had been limited to playing with the tennis ball in the middle-class self-financing colony in the Paschim Vihar area where he would play with children much older than him. 'I used to watch Sachin on television and try and copy some of his shots. My colony friends were so impressed that they told me I should go to a proper set-up because I had a skill, so I went up to my father and told him I wanted to take up the sport. That is when he took me to Sharma sir,' recalls Virat.

For a registration fee of Rs 200 a month, Virat became a member of the West Delhi Cricket Academy. 'From the very first day I saw him, I knew he had something special,' says Sharma. 'What struck me initially was his power and athleticism. I remember we were once playing a practice match and Virat was fielding at third man. He must have been ten or eleven years old and a slightly chubby little boy, but from 75 yards, he threw a hard parallel throw to the keeper and ran the batsman out.'

The other quality which caught Sharma's eye early enough was his fearlessness. 'He was only eleven years old and playing in the under-12 nets but he insisted on batting against the "big, fast boys" in the under-15 nets. He batted with ease against them but once got bruised on his arm. His worried mother came to me and said, "Please don't let him play just yet with the bigger boys",' remembers Sharma.

Not that a minor bruise was going to stop Virat from indulging his passion for the sport, and batting in particular. The academy would function from Thursday to Sunday and matches were played round the year. 'I would get Virat to play three to four matches every week, mostly 40-over games, after which we would come back to the nets to practice. What always struck me is how obsessed he was with the game. Even though I made him bat at number four, he would always be padded up. When he went to bat, he never wanted to get out. He would often take a single off the last ball because he wanted to retain strike just to stay in control of the innings. And when he wasn't batting, he wanted to bowl or take catches, he just wouldn't sit still, he had so much energy,' says Sharma.

'Ours was a relatively small club at the time so we didn't have the same number of good players as the bigger club sides in Delhi. Which is why I felt I must score as many runs as possible in every game so I could be recognized and the team could win,' explains Virat, adding, 'I think it helped to get so much match practice at such a young age and the fact that the team was relying on me even as a twelve-year-old helped shape my mindset to think clearly and absorb pressure.'

The similarities with Sachin are uncanny – the unbridled appetite for the sport from a young age, the presence of a caring coach who nurtured talent with fatherly benevolence, and the well-knit middle-class home environment. And if Achrekar didn't hesitate from occasionally slapping Sachin if he stepped out of line, neither did Sharma. 'Yes, I have hit him on a few occasions when I felt he deserved it, when he got out to a bad shot or scored 60 to 70 runs and the team lost because of him. But it never changed our relationship; for me, he is like a son,' says Sharma who, like Achrekar, works in the mornings for a few hours in a bank before heading to the ground to do what he loves most: coaching young children.

The special guru–shishya equation bore fruit soon enough. At fourteen, Virat was already playing in Delhi's highly competitive A-division league with men twice his age. He was still not picked though for the Delhi under-14 team, an omission that left him in tears. 'Yes, I cried because I knew I was good enough to make the team, but it also toughened me because I knew I would have to score more runs than anyone else to make a mark,' says Virat. Sadly, Delhi's cricket has for long mirrored the Machiavellian politics of the national capital. Sehwag, for example, was twice denied a place in the Delhi under-19 team after being given just four balls to bat in the trials. 'I think I hit two of the balls for sixes but since I had no godfather I wasn't selected,' he says. Chopra was removed as Delhi captain because he refused to accommodate an official's son in the team. 'When I played my first game for Delhi, an official warned me that this was going to be my last game even as I was preparing to bat. Delhi cricket has flourished despite the system not because of it,' he remarks.

But Virat's talent couldn't be hidden for long. In 2003, he scored a double century in the under-15 national tournament. A string of big scores in junior cricket meant that he was picked for a strong Delhi Ranji team in November 2006 just days after celebrating his eighteenth birthday. 'From day one, I was clear in my mind – I didn't want to just play one or two games for Delhi, I wanted to be a successful player for India and the best I could possibly be,' says Virat. Sharma echoes Virat's sentiment: 'The one thing about Virat which has always shone through is his self-belief. He is scared of nothing, he always wants to be aggressive on the field. Even today when he plays a game of football or volleyball with the other boys in my camp, he always wants to win.' Ishant, with whom he has grown up, says, 'As we say in our part of West Delhi, bande mein dum hai!'

~

In cricket, timing is often crucial in propelling a fledgling career forward. In April 2008, barely weeks after the Virat-led Indian team won the Under-19 World Cup, the IPL kicked off. The final of the tournament in Kuala Lumpur had been telecast live, suddenly placing the gen-next of Indian cricket in the arc lights. Never one to miss a marketing opportunity, the IPL chief commissioner Lalit Modi decided to hold a special draft auction for the junior World Cup winning players. All the eight IPL franchises would be allowed to pick two juniors through a draw of lots as 'catchment' area players. They would each get $30,000 (around Rs 15 lakh at that time). 'I wanted to send out the message that the IPL was not just about big-ticket Indian and international stars but also something talented youngsters could aspire for. Which nineteen-year-old could have dreamt till the IPL came along that he would be paid in lakhs for just seven weeks of cricket?' asks Modi.

The move would dramatically transform the lives of young cricketers like Virat. Under-19 and schools cricket had produced many Indian Test stars in the past but not before the players had gone through the hard grind of university and first-class cricket. Now the teenagers suddenly found themselves in a position where not going to college was actually an option because cricket was offering instant monetary rewards. Virat dropped out in class twelve because he was aware that cricket offered him a lucrative professional career. 'In our generation, the competition has become much more, you have to make an impact from an early age or else it is difficult to make the grade. The transition from under-19 to potential India star was much faster, not just with me, but several other under-19 players like Yuvraj, Kaif, Rohit Sharma and Piyush Chawla,' he points out.

Interestingly, the Delhi IPL franchise got the first pick among the junior players in the 2008 auction but it chose left-arm fast bowler Pradeep Sangwan and not Virat. The under-19 captain was picked instead by the Royal Challengers Bangalore (RCB) franchise, setting the stage for a relationship that would last the course. 'I liked him the moment I saw him,' says Vijay Mallya, the 'fugitive' liquor baron and original owner of RCB. 'He was perfect for the brand I wanted to build around the franchise – young, ambitious, aggressive and a real winner.'

The truth is, Virat flopped in his first season in the big league. In twelve innings, he scored just 165 runs with a highest score of just 38. Sharing a dressing room with the game's greats like Rahul Dravid, Anil Kumble and the South Africans Jacques Kallis and Dale Steyn, the teenager found it difficult to adjust to his new-found stardom. 'I must confess that when we first saw him, he seemed brash and arrogant; he walked and talked as if he thought he had already arrived in international sport,' says a senior RCB official.

Kohli apparently once insisted on being upgraded to a business class ticket 'like the seniors', and wanted a bigger room for himself in the team hotel. The IPL was pitched as an endless whirl of 'cricketainment' – from cheerleaders to all-night sponsor parties – and Virat seemed to struggle to make the transition from middle-class West Delhi to the psychedelic bright lights of the IPL circus. Stories began to circulate about the young man liking the high life, his fondness for alcohol and the few hours of sleep he would get in before a game. 'I guess I took things for granted in the first season and so lost my focus,' he admits.

Despite his poor IPL performance, Virat was picked for the India-A team participating in an emerging players tournament in Australia in July 2008. In the reserves for the first few games, he was eventually asked to open the batting because that was the only way to fit him in. Chasing a total of 280 against New Zealand, Kohli grabbed the opportunity and scored an unbeaten 120. 'I had never opened in my life till that day but was at a stage in my career when I couldn't really pick and choose,' he says.

Watching the game was the chief selector Dilip Vengsarkar who had just arrived from India. 'Dilip sir actually reached late that day, only when our innings was starting. Had we batted first, he may have missed watching me bat. I guess he was there at the right time and at the right place for me. That's life, you know, one door had shut on me during the IPL, and now suddenly another one opened,' recalls Virat.

Vengsarkar was impressed enough to select Virat for a one-day series against Sri Lanka in August 2008. 'The first thing that struck me was how well Virat handled the short ball on the Australian pitches, always a good sign for an international player,' says Vengsarkar. Selecting him wasn't easy, though – some of the other selectors preferred Subramanian Badrinath from Tamil Nadu but Vengsarkar was insistent. 'When N. Srinivasan, then board treasurer and controller of Tamil Nadu cricket, found out I had dropped Badrinath for Virat, he was livid and went and complained to the board president Sharad Pawar. The next day I was removed as chairman of selectors but fortunately they couldn't change my decision to pick Virat,' says Vengsarkar.

Less than six months after lifting the Under-19 World Cup trophy, Virat was an international cricketer. Just short of three years later, he was part of the senior World Cup–winning side. Nevertheless, Virat's early years as an India player were a roller-coaster ride, reflecting at times the inner struggles of an immature young man who suddenly found himself in the spotlight.

His first major one-day series at home against England was interrupted by the 26/11 Mumbai terror attack. 'I had been in the reserves for the first five games and had been told I would be picked for the last two matches. But then suddenly the terror attack took place and the series was aborted just before the last two games so I didn't get a chance. And then, for some reason, I was dropped from the team altogether and so for the next twelve months I was sitting on the sidelines wondering when I will play again for India,' he says.

A selector at the time tells me that Virat had become a victim of an 'image trap'. 'We were being fed stories of how Virat was binge-drinking in the 2009 IPL in South Africa and was more interested in his hairstyle and tattoos than his cricket,' claims the selector. In the fiercely competitive world of Indian cricket it seemed for a while that Virat was being 'punished' for his alleged off-field demeanour. Virat dismisses these reports as 'unfair rumours', saying he was judged by people who didn't even know him. In what he describes as a 'depressing' period in 2008–09, Virat did what many other determined young men before him had done – score so many runs in domestic cricket that the selectors just could not ignore him any longer. 'In sport, you can't crib and moan,' he says. 'You just have to go out and work as hard as possible to achieve something. Ultimately, only you can help yourself.'

Among those who gave Virat a pep talk in those tough times was Yuvraj Singh, an early role model for the young batsman. Yuvraj too had been typecast as a flamboyant cricketer and his Bollywood-like lifestyle was often used to target him when he failed with the bat. 'I think I once told Virat quite seriously that if you want to be a top-class player, don't copy me, make Sachin your inspiration. Be disciplined like him, not carefree like me,' he says with a laugh.

Ironically, Virat's next big break came after Yuvraj was injured in the Champions Trophy in South Africa in 2009. 'I had been told to keep my passport and bag ready while I was training in a camp in Bengaluru. From there, I flew straight to South Africa, landed and practised for a day before playing a game against Pakistan where I got just 16 and was out to a really bad shot. We lost the high-pressure game and I saw fans from the two countries fighting with each other in the stands. I got so depressed I blamed myself. I couldn't sleep till the next morning. I went to M.S. [Dhoni] and told him I was feeling under pressure because of not playing for a year and now failing against Pakistan also. He just told me not to worry and play my game. His support eased the pressure, I got 18 not out on a tough wicket against the West Indies in the next game and somehow felt a lot better. I think that period of early struggle in international cricket was a big learning. Until then in age-group cricket I had always dominated but it took me time to realize what it would take to succeed at a higher level.'

For the next fifteen months leading up to the 2011 World Cup, Virat established himself as India's key one-day batsman in the crucial number three position. Not only did he score centuries, but he also gained a reputation as a batsman who could take the team to victory when it mattered most, often during a tough chase. (He would end up holding the world record for the most centuries while chasing down a score successfully.) 'I guess a run-chase in a one-day game really gets my competitive juices going. You have a target in mind, you can plan for it, and build an innings that wins the team a game,' he says.

His first one-day century came in a run-chase against Sri Lanka in December 2009, where he shared a big partnership with his Delhi senior Gautam Gambhir. A few years later, the two would get involved in a nasty on-field confrontation in an IPL game, but that day Gambhir was so impressed with his partner's batting that he chose to hand over his Man of the Match prize to him. 'Look, I had gone through a lot of insecurities in my career so I didn't want Virat to go through the same,' explains Gambhir. 'This was my way of making him feel secure, important and a part of the Indian team, since he was just starting out. I am proud of what I did that day.'

That innings reflected the qualities that would become part of the Virat phenomenon in later years. A calmness under pressure while chasing a limited-overs target, the ability to run hard between wickets, play his shots with freedom and invariably find the gaps. This knack of absorbing the pressure made Virat an integral part of India's World Cup success in 2011. 'To be honest, I didn't really feel the pressure of the big stage because I was only twenty-one at the time. I knew I had nothing to lose, that I had time on my side, and it wasn't going to be my last World Cup. Yes, I wanted to do well but my situation was nothing compared to Sachin's, for whom this was the last shot at the title,' he says.

In a sign of things to come, Virat came in to bat in the final in Mumbai when Sachin was dismissed and India were 20 for 2 chasing Sri Lanka's total of 275. 'When I walked in at the Wankhede stadium, I felt like I was entering a graveyard, there was pin-drop silence. Sachin had been batting like a champion in the tournament and now he was gone. I was literally shaking when I took guard. But then the nerves settled and Gambhir and I put up a partnership that was the first step towards the win. That innings gave me a lot of self-belief, the confidence that I could handle any kind of situation.'

What followed was even more special and revealed a new-found maturity in the 'bad boy' of the early IPL years. Carrying Sachin on his shoulders along with Yusuf Pathan on a victory lap, Virat was asked about the spontaneous gesture. Pat came the reply, 'Sachin has carried the burden of the nation for twenty-one years, it's time we carried him.' The simple remark was uttered with such natural reverence that it came to define Virat's character, that of a young man who saw himself as the potential inheritor of a grand legacy, someone who was paying respect to a legend but without a trace of sycophantic hero-worship. If the image of Dhoni smashing a six to win the Cup will remain the defining one of the 2011 triumph, then Virat's sound bite is the best tribute any cricketer could have paid to a senior colleague in his moment of glory.

'I didn't plan or prepare to say anything. Through the tournament, all my focus was on the cricket and doing well. It's only when I saw the emotions in the dressing room after we had won the Cup that I realized what I was actually part of. When you see seniors like Sachin, Yuvraj, Viru crying, even M.S., who is always so balanced and cool in such situations, then you realize what this win meant to everyone. I mean Sachin had been playing for so many years for India and now his dream had been fulfilled. I felt like we were all part of something very special, a once-in-a-lifetime kind of moment.'

A year after the victory, Sachin would shower Virat with an equally effusive compliment. At a function in March 2012 to mark his 100 international centuries, Sachin was asked if he thought anyone could break his record. 'Yes, I think those who can are sitting in this room only . . . I can see those youngsters, Virat or Rohit [Sharma] are the ones. As long as an Indian betters it, I don't mind,' said Sachin.

Sachin's remark may have seemed premature at the time. Virat says he was pleasantly surprised but didn't get carried away. 'Look, he just didn't mention me, he mentioned Rohit too,' he points out. True, but as his cricket career has evolved, it has become increasingly clear that Virat is the new generation's Sachin equivalent, a cricketer with the aura and skill who is well on his way to becoming an all-time great. Perhaps the twenty-year-old who carried his cricket idol on his shoulders on that unforgettable Mumbai night will one day be lifted with similar awe and admiration by the next generation.

~

The art of Indian batsmanship has been traditionally defined by Test cricket. The original Indian greats were primarily masters of the

defensive technique. Vijay Merchant and Vijay Hazare in particular
set the template for future Indian batsmen with their ability to bat for
long hours, play straight in the traditional 'V', place a heavy price on
their wicket and studiously avoid lifting the ball. Sunil Gavaskar was
the ultimate exemplar of this skill, the kind of batsman whom you
would choose to bat if your life was at stake. Sachin Tendulkar was
more dominant than any of his predecessors but he too was tutored in
the Mumbai school of batting, where grinding the opposition to dust
was critical, where a five-day Test match remained the gold standard
and Gavaskar's record of 34 centuries the summit of the sport.

Virat, by contrast, is the product of a new age where Test cricket
has fierce competition from the one-day and Twenty20 game. Like
many others of his time, he first earned his spurs in limited-overs
cricket and played as many as 59 one-dayers and scored five centuries
before making his Test debut in the West Indies in July 2011. He was
already a World Cup winner by then but came to the realization that
he would eventually be judged by his performance in Test cricket.
'Look, my motto has been to compete and do well in any and every
form of the game but, yes, I knew that if I was to be seen as a truly
great Indian cricketer then I would have to perform in Tests,' he says.

That was easier said than done. The Indian middle order was
brimful with talent when Virat made his debut – Dravid, Tendulkar
and Laxman were the presiding trimurti while Rohit Sharma,
Cheteshwar Pujara and Suresh Raina were also banging on the door.
Virat's technique was also under scrutiny – with his strong bottom
hand, a tendency to play across the line and square of the wicket with
an angled bat, many pundits wondered if he would be good enough
to make the Test grade. 'I must confess that when I first saw Virat,
I thought he was more of a one-day than a Test player,' admits K.
Srikkanth, former chairman of selectors.

Aakash Chopra offers an interesting insight when he compares
Virat's career trajectory to that of Yuvraj Singh's. Like Virat, Yuvraj
too was initially pigeonholed as a one-day specialist. Unlike Virat,
though, Yuvraj was never able to quite make the transition to Tests.

'Yuvraj was such a natural striker of the ball and could hit sixes so effortlessly that he played one-day and Test cricket with an almost similar approach. Virat had to find more conventional ways to score runs, and that made it easier for him to adjust to Tests,' explains Chopra.

The England tour of 2014 was perhaps the turning point. Virat went into that series as the 'next big thing' in Indian cricket, the natural successor to Sachin. He ended it with a big question mark on his future as a Test player – in five Tests and ten innings, he scored just 134 runs at an average of 13.4. The moving ball in English seaming conditions seemed to have exposed an apparent basic weakness in Virat's technique, an inclination to go at the ball with hard hands outside the off stump. Jimmy Anderson in particular seemed to relish bowling at India's star batsman. 'I was filled with massive doubt during that series,' admits Virat. 'I think there was a mental block that left me feeling as if it was impossible to score runs.'

But as the dismal series ended, a 'switch flipped', as Virat puts it. In adversity, he again rediscovered an inner strength to emerge a much stronger player. Ravi Shastri, who had just taken over as team director, offered him some technical advice to stand outside the crease so he could negotiate any late swing. 'It was Ravi who suggested I widen my stance and stand outside the crease to cover the swing as long as I wasn't afraid of getting hit by a fast bowler in case they dropped short. I have never been scared of fast bowling so I told myself I would take up the challenge and make sure I become a better player.'

Back home, Virat went back to the basics with coach Sharma at the West Delhi academy nets, adjusting to a new middle-stump guard, working on his head and eye position, ensuring that the bat came down straighter. 'When we came back from England, I worked on my technique for about three hours a day in the nets for a fortnight till my hands and legs ached,' he says.

He even spent a few days in Mumbai with Sachin. 'I was struck by his desire to keep improving. For almost a week, we just talked cricket. I told him about how during my Sydney double century I had just willed myself not to play the cover drive because I was getting dismissed caught outside the off stump. At the highest level, cricket is played in the mind and Virat has a very strong mind and his focus is admirable,' says Sachin.

The hard work paid off. If Virat's tour to England in the summer of 2014 had been a disaster, the winter tour year to Australia the same year was a resounding triumph. In five Tests, Virat hit four centuries, including a century in each innings at Adelaide, when he captained India for the first time since skipper Dhoni was injured. Shastri describes Virat's second innings hundred as arguably the best innings he has seen by an Indian in overseas conditions. 'A last-day wearing pitch, a good attack, chasing a total of 400-plus, he batted like a champion and almost took us to an incredible win,' gushes Shastri.

What made Kohli's Adelaide 'double' even more special was the fact that he had been hit flush on the helmet off the very first ball he faced from pace spearhead Mitchell Johnson. It was a seminal moment in Virat's career; only days earlier, Australian batsman Phil Hughes had died after being hit by a bouncer, a dreadful incident that shook the cricket world. Now, struck by Johnson, Virat could have backed down like so many batsmen before him. Instead, he stood up to be counted.

'Johnson and I had had some kind of an argument in a one-day series in India before the Tests. He said something about me only being able to bat in Indian conditions. I told him, "Don't worry, I will take you on in Australia too, I am not scared of you." When I was hit first ball on the helmet, it rid me of all my fears and I became even more determined not to take a step back. I was captain of the team for the first time and wanted to set the tone for the series. I told myself that the next time he bowled short, I was going to pull or hook him, no matter what happened, or how many fielders he had on the boundary for a catch. So the hit on the helmet only fed my competitive streak.'

Virat was true to his word. He pulled the next ball that Johnson pitched short to the boundary, delivering a decisive blow to the opposition – the Indian batting line-up that would no longer be intimidated by pace. 'What Virat showed that day in Adelaide is that the days when Indian cricketers ran away from fast bowling were well and truly over. This is a new India, aggressive and courageous, one that will meet fire with fire,' says Shastri.

Indian batsmen of the past may have been cowed down by Australian on-field abuse but Virat seemed to relish the opportunity to swear back. He says that playing against Australia has helped him raise his game. 'I just love going to Australia. I have even thought of getting a holiday home there for an annual break. The sporting culture is just so positive and competitive and people appreciate what you do in a very genuine way. Even when the crowds target me there I enjoy it because it only motivates me to prove them wrong,' he says.

That series against Australia laid out a new marker for the future of Virat and Indian cricket. For almost two decades, Sachin had set the benchmark for Indian batting; he was the master batsman on the crease, a seemingly permanent presence who infused magic and muscle into the art of run-making. Supported by other stalwarts like Dravid, Laxman, Sehwag and Ganguly, Sachin had spearheaded the golden era of Indian batting. Virat's performance in Australia suggested that a new dawn was breaking in Indian cricket with Virat as its most shining symbol. In his first 29 Tests till the tour of Australia in 2014, Virat scored 1855 runs with 6 hundreds at a modest average of 39.46, while from Australia 2014 till the first quarter of 2017, he played a further 28 Tests and scored 2642 runs at an outstanding average of 60.04 with 10 hundreds. He averages almost 63 in away tests since December 2014. Those statistics suggest that Virat is the true heir to the Tendulkar legacy. 'I feel privileged,' says Shastri. 'I saw the birth of one superstar in Australia in 1992 and then of another in 2014.'

~

When Virat Kohli was formally anointed India captain in all three formats of the game at the start of the 2016–17 season, Team India was ranked second in Tests, six points behind Australia. A year earlier, when he had taken over as Test captain, the team was ranked fourth.

A come-from-behind victory in Sri Lanka was the first sign of revival. Then a long season of Test cricket with a series in the West Indies followed by 13 Tests at home was seen as a real opportunity to take a big leap forward and become the world number one Test team. 'When I took over as captain, I promised the team one thing: there is nothing I will ask you to do that I will not try and do myself,' he says.

However, there were still question marks over Virat's temperament as a leader – his critics saw him as a far too volatile presence on the field to handle the extra pressure of captaincy, especially as he was succeeding the remarkably calm M.S. Dhoni. His coach Sharma was less perturbed, saying, 'Virat has been a natural leader since he first joined me as a nine-year-old. The only thing I cautioned him about was to understand that not everyone in a cricket team is as skilful as him.'

Virat also had a new team coach by his side as the outspoken Shastri, in many ways a bit like Virat, was replaced by the low-key Anil Kumble. Virat and Kumble were a fire-and-ice combination and the latter knew he had to work very differently to win the trust of the team. 'This is a very different generation, very talented and professional but also exposed to a different lifestyle. So it was important to give Virat and his team the space to express themselves without imposing myself on them. In my time, team meetings were long, but now with the lower attention spans they are shorter. The net practice, especially fielding, is probably far more intense, though,' says Kumble who would eventually fall out with the captain.

With Kumble's oversight, the team even prepared a written 'charter' of dos and don'ts for the season. Ravichandran Ashwin, the match-winning off-spinner who played an important role in drafting it, describes it as a 'team Bible of sorts'. 'A key aspect was to focus on building good memories of a team that plays for each other, to make lasting friendships in a professional environment, which is not always easy. We wanted to create a sense of oneness at all times,' he says.

The other change that Kumble noticed was a more positive outlook to the sport, including a desire to win in any given situation. 'When I first played for India, the attitude was to first work on not losing a Test and then think about winning. The change started when the likes of Virender Sehwag began to play with a fearless approach and took the battle to the opposition. Now Virat has taken that never-say-die spirit a step forward by always looking for ways to win Test matches,' says Kumble.

I ask Virat about the 'fearless' mantra often cited as his USP. 'Look, I would never like any of the guys in my team to ever back down. Back down from whom and for what, I ask. We play the same sport as anyone else in the world so why should we be subdued and play like someone else wants us to play? So, yes, I want my players to be aggressive, to express themselves fully on the field. Maybe there is more fire in the belly now but what I will say for sure is that this is a team where everyone is willing to put his hand up in a challenging situation. If it is 50-50 position, I would rather look for ways in which to win from there than fear losing,' says Virat.

The conviction with which Virat explains his cricketing philosophy makes it clear that the self-doubt that shadowed Indian cricket in its early years is now a distant memory, perhaps a reflection of the changing contours of the nationhood. For the first thirty years after Independence, Indian cricket struggled to assert itself, much like the nation straining to find its place in the world – a 'third world' country still recovering from the yoke of colonial rule, trapped by a feeling of inferiority and a defeatist mindset.

The transformation began with economic liberalization in 1991. A country on the verge of sovereign default pulled itself out from the abyss to slowly expand the market and push towards becoming the fastest growing economy in the new millennium. Virat was just three years old in 1991 so he is a product, in a sense, of this rapidly changing India, a cricketer who has grown up with boundless ambition and an intense self-belief that tells him no mountain peak is insurmountable.

Which is why he never considered the goal of becoming the world number one Test side in the 2016–17 season a bridge too far. He led from the front in the first Test against the West Indies in Antigua by scoring a double century, his first in Test cricket, ticking off an important personal milestone. More importantly, India won the Test by an innings while playing with just five regular batsmen, a proactive move that showed the team had abandoned defensive strategies. 'We discussed this internally and Virat was keen on playing one less batsman because it gave us room for more attacking bowling options,' says Kumble. Adds Virat, 'Look, you need 20 wickets to win a Test and often you need this on good batting tracks, so having the additional bowler does help.'

It also meant more responsibility on the batsmen, a burden that the captain was happy to share by showing the way. The double century in Antigua was only an appetizer. Between July 2016 and February 2017, Virat would hit double centuries in four consecutive series against West Indies, New Zealand, England and Bangladesh, establishing a new world record. The young man who was in danger of being pigeonholed as a one-day specialist was now the world's top Test player. 'I just think Virat has taken his batting to another level, it's unbelievable what he has achieved in the last twelve months,' says Shastri admiringly.

So what has changed in his batting, I ask Virat. 'Actually, I started the 2016 Indian domestic season with a couple of low scores against New Zealand. I talked to Sanjay Bangar, our batting coach, and he said I was putting too much pressure on myself to always score big runs. So I just went out in the second innings of the Kolkata Test against the Kiwis and decided to play my shots. I got only 45 but suddenly felt much better. The next Test in Indore, I scored a double century and after that I guess there was no looking back. I just went out each time to enjoy my batting, focus on the process and not the end result. I now understand what I expect from myself and don't feel the urge to prove anything to anyone. This has liberated me from all external pressures and I know that if I can execute my plans on a regular basis and respect my opponents and the conditions the runs will come. Now if I get out on 120 I am not happy because I feel I should have scored a double century, if I score a double century I feel I should score 250,' he says.

Sharma insists that the hunger for big runs was always there, it's just that Virat has worked hard at removing all his weaknesses. 'When he started the game, he used to play with a strong bottom hand and mainly on the leg-side. He had this "flick" shot where he would hit across the line with a short stride forward and that would worry me since it could leave him a prime LBW candidate. Now he plays the same shot but with a much straighter bat, with a bigger stride forward and much less risk. His amazing bat speed and hand–eye coordination were always there when he played certain shots like his favourite cover drive but now he is more confident in executing every shot in the game,' says Sharma.

I watched the new Virat batting masterclass as he scored a double century against England at the Wankhede stadium in December 2016. Of his four double hundreds, this was arguably his best. The series was tight at that stage, and England had amassed a solid 400 runs first innings base. The Wankhede wicket had begun to show signs of wear and turn and 6 Indian wickets fell for 307. But not once did Virat falter, barring one tough caught-and-bowled chance to leg-spinner Adil Rashid. Batting for 515 minutes and 340 balls, he scored 235 runs with 25 fours and a six. Right through the innings in the energy-sapping Mumbai humidity, he ran the singles hard – a tribute to his remarkable fitness – and did not lift the ball till he had crossed 200. He focused on finding the gaps in the field and with the help of the lower-order batsmen took the team to an imposing and match-winning score of 635.

He didn't even do the usual effervescent celebration when he reached a hundred. 'I guess I was saving the energy for the next hundred runs, I was just so focused on batting,' he says. It was a marathon innings from a cricketer who was now building a reputation as an all-time great, a top-class batsman who never seemed to stop scoring.

Sitting in the Mumbai Cricket Association box with me were former Test players like Ajit Wadekar, Dilip Vengsarkar, Mohammed Azharuddin and Farokh Engineer. This was the first Test in Mumbai since Sachin Tendulkar had retired in 2013 and the first without a Mumbai player. Invariably, the conversation swung to comparisons of Virat with greats of the past. 'I think Sunny and Sachin would have been proud to play an innings like this,' remarked Engineer. 'He is certainly physically fitter than any Indian batsman of the past, but look also at the great big bats these boys now get to play with and all the support they get with computer analysts and fitness trainers,' interjected Vengsarkar. Azharuddin gently reminded me, 'Sachin had to face up to some of the world's finest pace attacks in the 1990s and Gavaskar batted without a helmet. By comparison, Virat is luckier.' Wadekar had the last word. 'We should just enjoy his batting without the comparisons, please.'

Later, I asked former Test player turned cricket analyst Sanjay Manjrekar to reflect on the transition in Indian batting between Sachin and Virat. 'Sachin's greatness is that he was the first Indian cricketer to dominate attacks in overseas conditions consistently; he batted in Australia, for example, like an Australian. But Sachin's batting style was shaped by Test cricket and also maybe by an element of self-doubt since Indian cricket was still not at the top spot. By contrast, Virat oozes a self-confidence I have never seen in an Indian cricketer before and that reflects in his ability to chase down any target, especially in short formats. He is more Viv Richards than Sachin in his fearless approach to the game,' says Manjrekar.

Virat himself stays clear of all comparisons, even when I suggest he could now be part of an all-time great Indian eleven. 'Look, when I started I had no such expectations, so why build such expectations now? Sachin played for twenty-four years, scored 100 hundreds, he inspired me to play the game. I don't see myself playing that long. I am just grateful for what God has given me. I have no statistical goals I want to measure myself by, I just want to give 120 per cent on the field and help the team win and take Indian cricket forward,' he insists.

I got a scent of this forward leap when I travelled to watch the final Test of the season against Australia in Dharamsala in March 2017, the first to be played in the lap of the Himalayas. With the series tied one-all, the images of the picturesque ground with the snow-capped mountains in the backdrop were extremely enticing. I checked into the same hotel as the two teams, a cosy mountain retreat guarded by special security for the players. The series had been hard fought until then and antagonisms from previous encounters had spilled over. Players from the opposing sides were consciously avoiding any interaction with each other, even having their breakfast and dinner in separate areas and at different times. 'There is a lot of bad blood on both sides,' an official warned me.

The Australians had come well prepared for the series and won the first Test on a nasty turning track in Pune. India won the second in Bengaluru in controversial circumstances with Virat accused of sledging the Aussies while he charged his rival captain Steve Smith of 'cheating'. 'I don't want to talk about it, it's over and done with,' says Virat, with a brief flicker of impatience. Coach Kumble was a little more forthcoming: 'Look, it was a high-pressure game and a few things may have been said on both sides. But I think Virat's aggressive intent lifted the team at a time when we were staring at a possible series defeat.' Ashwin, whose record-breaking wicket-taking feats played a major role in India's successes, concurs. 'With Virat as captain, the best thing is that you will never die wondering what next. He knows what he wants and will push you hard. The energy is infectious,' he says.

At the end of day two in Dharamsala, the teams were locked in an even combat. The Aussies had scored 300 in their first innings; the Indians were 245 for 6 with Ravinder Jadeja and Wriddhiman Saha at the crease. But when I saw the Indian team at dinner, Jadeja regaling his teammates with the latest viral jokes on his phone amidst much laughter, it didn't seem like the pressure of a series on the line had got to them. I asked him how he saw the game shaping up. Twirling his trademark moustache, he smiled. 'Kal ka kal dekhenge, for now bindaas, enjoy!' If there was any anxiety about what lay ahead of Team India the next morning, no one was mirroring it.

The next day Jadeja scored a brave 50 to take India to a small lead. Then, Umesh Yadav on a pitch tailor-made for Australian fast bowlers attacked the batsmen with a spell of sustained, aggressive fast bowling. 'I don't think I have seen an Indian pace bowler make overseas batsmen hop around like this in a long time,' said Manjrekar in the commentary box. Ashwin, who was bowling despite a sports hernia injury, then teamed up with Jadeja to slice through the Aussie line-up. 'I have often said bowlers adapt, batsmen complain,' says Ashwin with a laugh. That evening Ian Gould, the English umpire for the game, told us admiringly, 'The Indian bowlers today reminded me of the great West Indians of the 1980s, relentless in their attack, with both pace and spin.' There could have been no greater praise.

The final morning, with India on the verge of victory, I sat to have breakfast with Virat, who wasn't playing because of a shoulder injury. He was delighted with how the match had turned out. 'Cricket is a team game and I want every member of this team to be recognized as a future great so that ten years from now you will remember all the names and say "Wow, what a team that was." That is my vision for the future,' he said.

The Test and the series was wrapped up before lunch and a triumphant cricket season was complete. As Gavaskar handed over the Border–Gavaskar trophy to Virat and the number one Test team title was confirmed, the imagery could not have been more perfect. In the 1970s, Gavaskar had given Indian cricket self-esteem, in the 1980s, Kapil Dev gave it excitement, in the 1990s Sachin gave it stature; now the Kohli millennium generation has added a new word to the lexicon: dominance. When the team started the 2017-18 season with a perfect win record in Sri Lanka, it only endorsed the growing belief that Team India under Virat could stay at the summit of the sport for a long time.

~

I first met Virat Kohli at a Men of the Year award show in 2013 organized by a men's style magazine. He was the sportsperson of the year while I was chosen in the media category. Dressed in a chic custom-made jacket and tie, Virat made me look decidedly awkward in my rather plain suit when we appeared together on the cover. We didn't say much to each other at the award ceremony; he was surrounded by a large, mainly female, following. My daughter badgered me to get her a selfie with him. The hosts had organized an all-night party which I did not attend; Virat, I was told, was there till the wee hours.

The next time we met was during our interview for this book at his newly constructed Gurugram residence in June 2016. He had just come from his in-house state-of-the-art gym and looked totally fit in his loose T-shirt and trackpants, his rimmed glasses giving him a slightly serious look. It was around lunchtime and I could smell the staple Punjabi fragrance of chhole and aloo. But the table in front of Virat offered a rather non-Punjabi cuisine. Virat was drinking a large protein shake with a bowl of almonds and a banana on the side. It was all part of his gluten-free, no wheat, no rice, low-carb, high-protein diet. 'I guess I could now take on Novak Djokovic on a tennis court,' he said with a laugh.

The transformation of the chubby teenager into one of the fittest athletes on the planet best defines Virat's determination to excel at the highest level. His coach Sharma remembers how young Virat relished kebab rolls and biryani. 'Now, when he comes home and my wife offers him kheer, he refuses to have it. He will only eat sarson ka saag,' says Sharma.

The change first began in the latter half of 2012 when a relatively successful tour of Australia, including his first Test century, was followed by a tepid IPL performance. 'I took a hard look at myself and realized then that if I wanted to consistently compete at the top of the sport, I had to change my lifestyle, become more disciplined and, yes, become the fittest athlete I could be,' remarks Virat. He went to the RCB strength and conditioning trainer Shankar Basu for guidance. 'Virat had watched me train with India squash player Dipika Pallikal and seen what fitness drills an athlete goes through in an individual sport. "Why shouldn't a cricketer do the same?" he asked me. Today I can say with pride that Virat's fitness is equal to that of an Olympian athlete or a Grand Slam winner,' says Basu, who briefly trained the Indian side also.

Within six months in 2012, Virat's weight reduced from 84 kg to 73 kg as he gave up drinking and smoking, started sleeping early and stuck to a strict meal plan. This was followed in 2014 by a new weight training regimen. 'We started slowly, half an hour a day with a focus on technique, and then built it up. Soon Virat was training like a proper weightlifter, each exercise designed to complement the muscles he needed to become a fitter, better cricketer. Today, I liken him to a supple leopard on the field, powerful and swift,' says Basu.

Virat had been pulled out of his comfort zone and making the transition was not easy. 'Look, I am a typical Punjabi boy who likes his butter chicken and good food so the first few times were tough, the body ached and I struggled to adjust, but slowly it became easier and I began to relish it. Now I can't live without my gym training, it's a life choice,' he says, adding, 'If I am working hard in the gym and then go and eat a piece of cake, that's three gym sessions gone. So I might as well avoid the cake.'

Such is his commitment to fitness that once during the Twenty20 World Cup in 2016, Virat rang up Basu in the middle of the afternoon after a heavy morning workout to ask him which were the two exercises he had missed out in the first half of the day so he could come in for additional training. Virat's six-pack abs and well-toned muscles have become a benchmark for his peers and fans. Every teammate has now bought into Virat's fitness mantra and begun to emulate him. He even put up an Instagram video of his high speed running on a treadmill to connect with fans and inspire them to get fit. 'I think Virat's greatest impact is that he has changed the way any Indian aspiring to play professional cricket thinks. It's almost like a BC and AD era now, before Virat and after,' says Basu.

Virat's fitness obsession typifies the mindset of the young, upwardly mobile urban Indian professional. From vegan meals to intensive cardio workouts, staying fit is now the 'in' thing. There were hardly any recognized gyms in the country in the 1970s and 1980s; now every city has multiple gym chains. Most cities have their own marathons. More than 40,000 participated in the Mumbai marathon in 2017, making it the sixth largest such event in the world. Anil Singh, the managing director of Procam Sports, which organizes marathons across India, says, 'The craze to run and stay fit didn't start with Virat but with the growing health-conscious ethos since the turn of the century and he is now a role model for this new India.'

Cricket's old-timers might still scoff at the time modern players spend in the gym. Tendulkar tells me how Kapil Dev specifically told him as a youngster not to spend too much time in the gym and to avoid weight training. In an even earlier generation, Test cricketers, some with expanding midriffs, would come to the game only half an hour before a match, roll the arm a few times, have a light jog and be ready for a game. Now players go through intensive hour-long workouts before every match day. 'Cricket, like all sports, has changed. The Borg–Connors–McEnroe era in tennis has been replaced by the Djokovic–Murray–Nadal generation. Cricket today is a high-intensity professional sport and if you don't have the energy level to keep going you can't survive,' insists Basu.

In 2016, for example, Virat spent less than a month in his

Gurugram home as he travelled frenetically from one tournament to another. Cricket is now played round the year across three formats, making it necessary for the modern cricketer to constantly adapt. Gavaskar, for example, focused on Test cricket and only came to terms with the one-day game at the very end of his career. Tendulkar was a dominant figure in both Test and one-day cricket but never played a Twenty20 international. Virat, by contrast, has mastered all three formats – his CV now includes more match-winning one-day centuries than any player in the game's history (his 30 one-day centuries as of August 2017 have come in just 186 innings), the highest runs in an IPL season and a Test average of nearly 50. In an era where cricketers must be flexible while adjusting to all formats, Virat is a three-in-one genius. He can be both classical and brutal in his strokeplay, hitting a champagne cover drive and a powerful lofted shot with equal ease.

In 2012, he scored an incredible 133 not out off just 86 balls against Sri Lanka in India's chase of a must-win score. 'I broke down the 320-run Sri Lankan total into two Twenty20 games since we needed to score the runs in 40 overs to qualify for the final,' explains Virat. In 2016, he chased down more than 12 an over against Australia in a do-or-die World Twenty20 match, this time by wielding his bat like both sword and wand to generate power and precision. ('I was in the zone,' he says.) One extraordinary shot where he lifted a slower ball from James Faulkner for a six over mid-off typified the match-winning innings; he played it with a traditional straight bat but with enough bat speed for the ball to go soaring into the crowds. The same year, he pulled off the nine-hour Test match classic against England in Mumbai.

The transition from one form of the game to the other is now part of Virat's mental make-up. 'I guess at times we are playing three different sports even if the basics are the same. A Twenty20 match is like a 100 metre sprint with more focus on speed and risk-taking, a one-day game is like a middle-distance run which you need to time perfectly, and a Test match is like a marathon which is all about technique and endurance. You have to adjust your body and mind to all three,' explains Virat.

Just before a Twenty20 game, for example, Virat does a round of weights for fifteen minutes because it helps build 'explosive' body momentum needed to endure three hours of a high-pressure game. 'Just look at Virat in a Twenty20 game, whether he is in the field or he is batting, you will see him constantly on the move. He will captain a side but still be fielding in all the crucial positions on the boundary because he has so much energy,' points out Basu.

It is this dynamism on the field that has shaped Virat's brand image. Ad-film-makers turned to Sachin in the 1990s because he was seen as the ideal boy next door who represented the great Indian middle class dream; now they have moved to Virat because he is the representative of the aggression that fits in with a youthful India that doesn't want to hide its vaulting ambition in a cloak of political or social correctness. Where once crowds would chant 'Sachin, Sachin', they now have Virat's face and name painted on their cheeks and T-shirts. In the age of Snapchat, instant WhatsApp messaging, Twitter talk and 24x7 digital and social media, Virat is a symbol of an in-your-face vigour that reflects the youthful demographic every marketer is seeking to attract. 'This is the khullam-khulla generation, they want to let everything hang out,' says veteran ad-film-maker Prahlad Kakkar. 'Virat embodies the new India, unafraid and with a firm desire to excel,' says Piyush Pandey, award-winning advertising guru.

When Tendulkar's career was taking off in the early 1990s, the size of the Indian economy was $278.4 billion. By 2015, it had jumped to $2.1 trillion. If Brand Tendulkar rode the initial liberalization wave, then Brand Virat is being propelled forward by the mantra of globalization. Virat is the only Indian sportsperson to feature in the 2017 Forbes list of the world's top hundred highest paid athletes with annual earnings of $22 million (more than Rs 141 crore), while his overall brand value is pegged at around $120 million. His brand endorsements have made him the highest-earning contemporary cricketer. He reportedly charges Rs 5 crore per day in endorsement fees. (He now earns more than Rs 100 crore a year just from on-air advertising contracts.) In addition, his new bat sponsorship with MRF alone is worth a staggering Rs 100 crore over an eight-year period. 'Money is only the by-product of my cricket. Money can't buy you the happiness of going out on the field and winning a game for your country and people cheering you on. Money is not a motivator for me, only playing for India at the highest level is,' says Virat.

His agent Bunty Sajdeh endorses this, claiming that no sponsor contract is allowed to interfere with his client's cricket commitments. 'He will give us a maximum twenty-five to thirty days for any brand-related work, and never during a tour or a match,' says Sajdeh. Virat's diverse range of business interests now include a chain of gyms, a clothing line and an acoustics brand. 'Each of these resonate with the youthful image that Virat stands for. For example, he loves his catchy Punjabi music and he will often have headphones on and listen to it just before going to bat. So identifying Virat with a new-age acoustics brand makes sense to us,' says Sajdeh.

The mega celebrity tag in the age of endless media exposure is a double-edged sword, though, one that can deify and devour in equal measure. For example, Virat won't discuss his relationship with Bollywood actor Anushka Sharma, claiming it's his 'private matter' but won't hide it either. The couple now often post their pictures together on social media sites. Tiger Pataudi and Sharmila Tagore could go out for a movie in the 1960s when they were dating but Virat and Anushka can't risk any public appearance together without being tracked by dozens of camera teams. 'They were once holding hands in New Zealand in a quiet park and were shocked to find the pictures on social media in a matter of hours. If the media won't leave them in New Zealand, then what chance do they have in India,' says a friend.

When Anushka's presence at the 2015 World Cup in Australia led to Twitter trolls blaming her for Virat's low score and exit in the semi-finals, the cricketer was incensed. Holding her hand at the airport on their return from Australia was his first public statement of love and support. He later said the critics 'should be ashamed of themselves'. When I ask him about it, his response is firm. 'Look, I was standing up for her, like I would for any woman who is targeted for no fault of hers. If you want to criticize me for my cricket, be man enough to stand up and do so directly. Don't drag someone close to me who has nothing to do with my performance into it.'

Those firm remarks mark the maturity of Virat into a more caring, new-age man. 'People are very chauvinistic in this country,' he said in a 2017 interview to *Mint*. 'I would definitely want to think about life from the side of the woman.' Maybe that is the 'Anushka effect' or simply the realization that there's a world beyond the boys-only cricket dressing room. His social media posts now often call for compassion for animals – in April 2017 he adopted fifteen dogs from an animal rescue centre in Bengaluru – and he has set up a charity foundation; these are shades of the 'new' Virat, someone consciously trying to reinvent himself as a socially responsible, sensitive individual with more to offer than just runs on the field.

Like many contemporary celebrities in the public eye, though, Virat has found that adulation and controversy are uneasy bedfellows. Life in the bubble of high public expectations, of moving from ground to five-star hotel and back can be physically and mentally exhausting. It makes cricketers remote, inaccessible figures, surrounded by agents and sponsors and eulogized by fans and cheerleaders, which leads to charges of arrogance and egotism.

Virat's on-field spats, especially the one with Gambhir in the 2012 IPL, fuelled the image of him as 'spoilt brat'. In the high-profile match between the Kolkata and Bengaluru franchises, the two feisty India colleagues from West Delhi nearly came to blows and had to be separated by teammates after abusive words were exchanged on Virat's dismissal. 'Look, these things happen in the heat of the moment. It is just that I didn't do it smartly. There are a lot of cricketers who sledge between overs when the cameras aren't on but in this case, I did it during live action. Sport is about an emotional roller-coaster and we are not robots fitted with an all-smiles program,' says Gambhir in his defence. Virat too admits he could have handled the situation better and needs to control his periodic bouts of rage. 'Look, I have made mistakes, have crossed the line at times, but those mistakes have made me realize who I am now and feel more responsible for my actions. In pure competition, when someone says something to you, you feel like you have to hit back. But I now know where to stop. I said in one recent interview [to India Today TV] my aim is to be attached and yet detached from all I do, a bit like a monk in a civil world,' he says with Zen-like calm.

While Virat put the quarrel with Gambhir behind him, he found his attitude under question once again when an unseemly controversy broke out in June 2017 over his equation with coach Kumble. On 20 June, just a year into his job, Kumble resigned as coach, revealing in his resignation statement that the captain had expressed 'reservations' over his 'style' and the relationship had become 'untenable'. In hard-hitting remarks clearly directed at the India captain, Kumble said, 'Professionalism, commitment, honesty, complementary skills and diverse views are the key traits I bring to the table. These need to be valued for the partnership to be effective. I see the coach's role akin to "holding a mirror" to drive self-improvement in the team's interest.' Angry cricket fans blamed Virat for the bust-up. 'Arrogant Virat' was a Twitter trend as public sympathy was clearly with the coach. In his first public remarks Virat said he 'respected' Kumble and that the 'sanctity' of the dressing room meant that 'what happens in the dressing room stays there'.

What really happened in the row? Having spoken to people close to both, it is apparent that the relationship, despite success on the field, was perhaps never quite meant to be, a clash of two strong personalities with differing approaches to the game. Kumble is a strict disciplinarian, someone with an unshaken belief in 'system driven' methods and who wasn't averse to criticizing a player if he felt the need. For Kohli, a young captain used to having his way, what the experienced Kumble saw as well-meaning 'advice' to the team, especially the bowlers, was perceived as 'interference', bordering on 'intimidation'.

When Kumble pushed for playing left arm leg-spinner Kuldeep Yadav as a surprise weapon against Australia in the 2017 series and virtually overruled Kohli, the relations were further strained. 'Look, Virat belongs to a generation that doesn't like to be micro-managed and told what to do all the time. Kumble just didn't fit into this new generation ethos,' says a cricket board official. But another official argues that Virat staged a 'coup' against the senior cricketer because he was unhappy at the manner in which Shastri, who had been the team director till Kumble replaced him in 2016, was removed. 'Kohli felt comfortable with Shastri who gives the players greater freedom to do their own thing. He was just looking for an excuse to remove Kumble and get Shastri back,' claims the official.

Is Kohli then the most powerful man in Indian cricket, who by virtue of being captain and the team's most prolific batsman can virtually dictate terms to an enfeebled cricket board? From an era where most Indian players were meek and deferential to officials, are we now in a period where players are pampered superstars who call the shots? 'Make no mistake, at the end of the day, the buck always stops with the captain, he is the boss,' former India fast bowler and now match referee Javagal Srinath reminds me. A parallel can be drawn with the prevailing political culture in the country. This is the age of autocratic politics in India where be it Narendra Modi at the Centre or a regional party, power is often concentrated around an individual. The cult of the 'supremo' has now spread to cricket too where the captain is truly the supreme leader.

Maybe the fact that Virat's seemingly exhibitionist lifestyle doesn't fit in with traditional stereotypes of a self-effacing Indian sportsperson has made him more vulnerable to criticism. He likes to experiment with designer hairstyles – from a well-trimmed beard to a Mohawk look – and is partial to tattoos: he has four of them, including the names of his mother and father next to his India Test and one-day cap number. His favourite is that of a samurai warrior with a raised sword. 'I can identify with a warrior whose life is based on honour and discipline,' he says. He loves cars, an Audi S6 being a favourite among the several he possesses, and he has also bought luxury houses in both Delhi and Mumbai. 'People who don't know me talk about my lifestyle. I actually have very few friends, I don't go to parties much, and when I am in Delhi, you will find me more often than not relaxing at home playing FIFA on Playstation with friends and family,' he tells me

Virat's critics are possibly caught in the time warp of an older India, still coming to terms with the enormous riches that modern-day sport offers star athletes. Previously, cricketers were meant to be docile, salaried employees who often did day jobs in a nationalized bank, whose talent was expressed and recognized on the field but who remained mostly unrewarded off it.

Virat's generation is far better compensated and more celebrated but also more professional, putting in hours of effort to become fitter, stronger and better cricketers. In 2017, an Indian cricketer earns Rs 15 lakh a Test, Rs 7.5 lakh for a one-day match and Rs 4 lakh for a Twenty20 international, apart from a Rs 2 crore per annum central contract in the top bracket and multi-crore IPL deals. Financial security has only spurred a self-assurance that is often mistaken for conceit. The branded accessories worn by several team members can again be a source of misguided envy. As Jadeja puts it, 'I like to wear designer glasses; if I can afford them, why can't I flaunt them, what does my cricket have to do with my lifestyle?' (Jadeja, incidentally, owns a stable of horses in his Jamnagar farmhouse and drives the latest Audi car.)

Ashwin, like Virat, is well on his way to becoming an all-time India great. He describes the new-generation Indian cricketer as one who is not intimidated by any opposition and therefore plays with greater freedom. 'I remember as a kid watching cricket on television, and we would lose more games than we would win. Now there is a greater hunger to win which comes from the constant pursuit of excellence,' he says. In-depth video analyses, fitness trainers and a strong back room system have given Indian cricket a competitive edge. 'Sitting on the outside, it is easy to look at the money we earn and how we move from one plush five-star hotel to the next. But the fact is we barely get to spend any time at home, so every day on the field is like another day in the office where you have to perform to retain your India cap. It is professional pride that drives us,' says Ashwin.

The ever-observant Rahul Dravid puts the 'old' versus 'new' India cricket debate in some perspective when he reminds me, 'For the longest time I have heard people crib about Virat's flashy lifestyle. What people forget is that Virat is a hugely talented cricketer who works incredibly hard at his fitness and batting and is constantly looking to get better. You may like or envy his celebrity status but do recognize the hunger, the attitude, the intensity he brings to his cricket. You have to see both sides of the coin and learn to appreciate his skills.'

Virat is, in a sense, a prototype of the young millennial Indian. The impetuosity of this 'new' India is matched by its passionate desire to succeed, where a lack of respect for convention is complemented by a yearning to innovate. This is a start-up generation which is willing to take risks that their parents never would, an India of immense opportunities but also of cut-throat competition. Ambitious, determined, armed with a whatever-it-takes spirit, eyes fixed on national as well as international standards, Virat embodies an India of the smartphone and the sharp suit, of the tattooed urban Modi-era youth, the gadget-loaded new rich for whom New India means reinventing one's persona through talent and upward mobility.

This is an India where old value systems may collide with an unambiguous 'me-first' individualism, where aspiration and anxieties coexist, where for every first-generation Paytm-like success story, there are tales of hardship and failure, but where the sheer force of youthful energies and soaring ambitions is breaking barriers and toppling entrenched elites. Cricket is part of this unstoppable juggernaut.

As Kumble himself admits, 'I don't think I have seen a more talented group of cricketers than the Indian team today.' Virat as a leader may still need to mature further but as a cricketer he is already the master batsman and torchbearer of the millennial generation.

~

On 5 September 2014, Rajkumar Sharma's doorbell rang and he found Virat's brother Vikas at the door. Vikas dialled a mobile number and handed the phone to Sharma. 'Happy teacher's day, sir!' said the voice at the other end. Virat was on the line from the US where he was doing an advertising campaign. The next moment Vikas had thrust a pair of car keys into the coach's palm and taken him to the gate where a spanking new Skoda car was parked. It was Virat's teacher's day gift to his guru. 'I was speechless but Virat is like that, still the simple, respectful boy with this great passion for cricket,' he says.

Sharma tells me that when Virat was fourteen, he sent him to the BDM bat factory in Meerut to get his first bat contract. He recalls, 'They didn't know who he was and told me that he looks very chhota but I remember telling the bat manufacturer that this is a lambi [long-term] investment which you won't regret.' BDM gave Virat his first sponsored bat and cricket kit and the grateful cricketer used them even after he started playing for India.

Life may have changed dramatically for Virat but it hasn't for his coach. It is a blazing hot April afternoon in Delhi but Sharma seems unconcerned as he sits under a tree watching over a hundred young boys at the West Delhi Cricket Academy in Paschim Vihar. Each boy – aged eight to eighteen – comes and touches his feet before going out enthusiastically to practise. This is a routine that Sharma has been familiar with for almost two decades since he first set up the academy in May 1998. As mentioned earlier, that is when the young Virat had first come to him with his father. He still comes to the academy whenever he is in Delhi and before any major tour. 'Virat bats for around ninety minutes, encourages all the boys to bowl as fast as possible to him. He also brings lots of cricket equipment which he distributes among them,' Sharma tells me. And when he is finished with batting, he autographs bats, poses for photos and takes selfies with the youngsters. 'I don't have to advertise for my academy. The fact that Virat played here is enough for parents to send their kids here.'

The boys who are furiously practising in the six nets have come from far and wide. An under-19 hopeful from a village in Kangra district in Himachal Pradesh is staying with three friends in a rented apartment in Paschim Vihar. Another boy from Rohtak is living with an uncle in a neighbouring colony. In almost every age-group team in Delhi, at least one boy from the academy has been selected. As Sharma and I converse, a short, slightly plump young boy comes rushing to the coach and says, 'Sorry sir, I am late, my father was delayed from office in picking me up from school.' Sharma gently admonishes him and asks him to jog an extra round. He then turns to me and smiles, 'You know, Virat was just that height and also a little pudgy when he came to me first. Even now, sometimes he tells me, "Remember, sir, how I would come on a cycle with my kitbag placed on the handlebar?"

The modest cycle has given way to luxury supercars in a breathtaking journey that has ignited a billion dreams. When the little boy at the academy has finished jogging and is getting ready to bat, I ask him about his ambition. 'Sir, I also want to play like Virat.' I assure him that he will and he rushes away in glee. I watch as he races towards the field, snatches his bat and raises his face towards the incoming ball. The sun pierces the clouds and beams down at him. The boy dances down the pitch and hits the ball a fair distance. As it disappears into the skyline, I feel comforted that the great Indian cricket dream is truly alive and well.

Acknowledgements

A book, like any good cricket team, is only as successful as the many individuals behind it. I have many more than just eleven people to thank here though. Firstly, a big thank you to my publisher, the effervescent Chiki Sarkar at Juggernaut Books, to Nandini Mehta, and to Parth Mehrotra, my kind and brilliant editor who made an extra-special effort to keep the book on track and give it shape, to Shreya Chakravertty and Jaishree Ram Mohan, my copy editors, and Gavin Morris who designed the cover. It is always exciting to work with a young publishing team that is buzzing with ideas and enthusiasm.

To my friends in the cricket world, this book wouldn't be possible without all of you. So many of you opened your hearts and minds to me without inhibition. I guess my surname and goodwill for my father helped, even if they didn't work for me on the cricket field! Indeed, all the members of my democracy's eleven or, in the case of those who have passed on, their next of kin spoke to me on the record with rare candour that made my task easier. Each of you are legends so for you to spare the time for me meant a lot. To the many fine cricketers who are quoted in the book, your support was crucial. A particular mention of Shishir Hattangadi, a dear friend, who was always happy to read a chapter or two and offer his insights. This book has been a nostalgic journey of discovery with childhood heroes: I will never forget having vadas with Gundappa Viswanath at the Bangalore Golf

Club, filter coffee with Prasanna, and tea with Abbas Ali Baig, all members of the 1971 winning team. Many family members of my Democracy's XI were just as gracious: a special mention of Sharmila Tagore for giving me access to the Pataudi Palace.

I owe a debt to many of my journalist colleagues and cricket watchers. The ever-helpful Clayton Murzello, Gaurav Kalra, Vikrant Gupta, Jeet Banerjee, Harsha Bhogle, Raghu Iyer, Lokesh Sharma, Gautam Bhattacharya, Debasish Dutta, Boria Majumdar, Vijay Lokapally, Vedam Jaishankar, Kishore Bhimani, D.P. Satish, Bunty Sajdeh, Sunil Kumar, Vimal Kumar, Digvijay Singh Deo, Sunandan Lele, Nishant Arora, Sanjeeb Mukherjea, Ratnakar Shetty, Lokendra Pratap Sahi and Mudar Patherya were always on hand to share a memory or just a phone number. A special word for Gulu Ezekiel who has probably the best cricket library in the country and was happy to share his books on a strictly returnable basis. To the authors of the several cricket books I was delighted to read and occasionally quote from, your works have enhanced my knowledge. Collecting archival photographs was a challenge and many of you have generously shared rare pictures. A special thanks to N. Ram at *The Hindu* who gave me access to the newspaper's wonderful photo archive, Sharmila Tagore, Milind Rege, Romi Dev, Anju Bedi, Vikas Kohli, Sunil Kumar, Clayton Murzello and Prakash Parsekar for allowing me to dip into their personal collections. Thanks also to K.N. Shanth Kumar at the *Deccan Herald* and to *India Today* for allowing me to use their photographs.

I wish to especially thank Kalli Purie at *India Today* for never grudging me the time needed to write a cricket book amidst the rush of television news. Bandeep Singh's photo graces the back flap and Sayan Mukherjee's caricatures adorn the cover: thank you both. To my office staff, Surinder Nagar, Gagan and Ramesh Mandal, I am ever grateful. Surinder transcribed all the interviews.

This book would not have been possible without the statistical support given to me by the wonderful cricket analyst S. Rajesh: not one of the several queries I put to him went unanswered. He was always at hand to help me with his in-depth statistics and is easily amongst the best in the business. I owe a big debt to my friend and guide Ramachandra Guha for encouraging me to write this book. Cricket was our original meeting point many years ago and Ram and Keshava Guha were my accomplices in planning my eventual eleven!

To my family, which has dealt with my craziness for years, I can't but be grateful: Sagarika isn't a cricket fan but she has indulged my passion for years now, even allowing me to watch the game on our honeymoon in Kasauli! If there is the occasional literary flourish in this book, it is entirely to her credit. My children Ishan and Tarini are my life support system and best friends too. My sister Shonali and brother-in-law Taimur went through several chapters and offered critical suggestions on the book. Most of all, this book would not have been possible without my parents. To Nandini and Dilip Sardesai, cricket was their life and love for years. My mother's energy is infectious and she has read the book with the keen eye of an academic and cricket enthusiast. My father wanted me to play cricket but allowed me to find my own calling in the end. I could never play cricket quite like him, so this book is my way of saying thank you for giving me so much in life. He is the reason and inspiration for this book because he symbolizes the great Indian cricket story.

Juggernaut

THE APP
FOR INDIAN
READERS

Available for Android, coming soon on iOS.

www.juggernaut.in

THE APP
FOR INDIAN
READERS

Fresh, original books tailored for mobile and for India. Starting at ₹10.

www.juggernaut.in

CRAFTED
FOR MOBILE
READING

Thought you would never read a book on mobile? Let us prove you wrong.

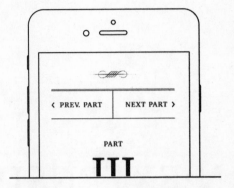

Beautiful Typography

The quality of print transferred
to your mobile. Forget ugly PDFs.

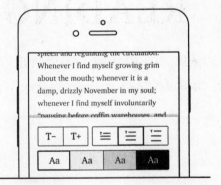

Customizable Reading

Read in the font size, spacing
and background of your liking.

AN EXTENSIVE LIBRARY

Fresh new original Juggernaut books from the likes of Sunny Leone, Twinkle Khanna, Rujuta Diwekar, William Dalrymple, Pankaj Mishra, Arundhati Roy and lots more. Plus, books from partner publishers and all the free classics you want.

www.juggernaut.in

DON'T JUST READ; INTERACT

We're changing the reading experience from passive to active.

www.juggernaut.in

Ask authors questions

Get all your answers from the horse's mouth.
Juggernaut authors actually reply to every
question they can.

Rate and review

Let everyone know of your favourite reads or
critique the finer points of a book – you will be
heard in a community of like-minded readers.

Gift books to friends

For a book-lover, there's no nicer gift than
a book personally picked. You can even
do it anonymously if you like.

Enjoy new book formats

Discover serials released in parts over
time, picture books including comics,
and story-bundles at discounted rates.

4

LOWEST PRICES & ONE-TAP BUYING

Books start at ₹10 with regular discounts and free previews.

www.juggernaut.in

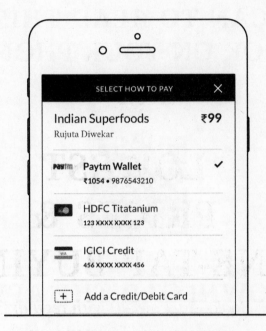

Paytm Wallet, Cards &
Apple Payments

On Android, just add a Paytm Wallet once and
buy any book with one tap. On iOS, pay with one
tap with your iTunes-linked debit/credit card.

Click the QR Code with a QR scanner app
or type the link into the Internet browser
on your phone to download the app.

SCAN TO READ THIS
BOOK ON YOUR PHONE

www.juggernaut.in

DOWNLOAD THE APP

www.juggernaut.in

For our complete catalogue, visit www.juggernaut.in
To submit your book, send a synopsis and two
sample chapters to books@juggernaut.in
For all other queries, write to contact@juggernaut.in

SCAN TO READ THIS
BOOK ON YOUR PHONE

DOWNLOAD THE APP